o E. COLETTA:

D0872217

The Unit
Navy and
Unific
1947-

The United States Navy and Defense Unification

1947-1953

Paolo E. Coletta

NEWARK
UNIVERSITY OF DELAWARE PRESS
London and Toronto: Associated University Presses

© 1981 by Associated University Presses, Inc.

Associated University Presses, Inc.
4 Cornwall Drive
East Brunswick, New Jersey 08816

Associated University Presses Ltd.
69 Fleet Street
London EC4Y 1EU, England

Associated University Presses
Toronto M5E 1A7, Canada

Library of Congress Cataloging in Publication Data
Coletta, Paolo Enrico, 1916-
    The United States Navy and defense unification, 1947-
1953.

    Bibliography: p.
    Includes index.
    1. United States. Navy--History--20th century.
2. United States--Military policy. 3. United States--
Politics and government--1945-1953. I. Title.
VA58.C75   359.6'0973   79-3111
ISBN 0-87413-126-X

PRINTED IN THE UNITED STATES OF AMERICA

To
those civil leaders and military men
who tried to fashion a workable, unified system
of national defense.

Contents

Acknowledgments

My thanks are due to many for aid in this study. Roy S. Basler, chief, Manuscript Division, Library of Congress, and Paul T. Heffron, assistant chief, steered me into the letter collections of important men in the unification process and controversy. Dr. Dean C. Allard, Head, Operational Archives, Naval History Division, Washington, D.C., Mrs. Katherine Lloyd, and Bernard Cavalcante provided the records of the General Board of the Navy. Extremely helpful also was the declassification officer, Lieutenant Commander Richard Mackay, USN. Professor Richard A. Evans, librarian, U.S. Naval Academy, proved indefatigable in making available or acquiring needed references, as did Miss Alice Creighton and Miss Pamela Evans in Special Collections. Dr. Thomas Belden, his successor as Chief, Office of Air Force History, Dr. Stanley Falk, and Mr. Herman S. Wolk, historian in the office, furnished advice and documents. Dr. James N. Eastman, Chief, Research Branch, The Albert F. Simpson Historical Research Center, Maxwell Air Force Base, Alabama, made available a number of Air Force records and studies. Commander John Poindexter, USN, Administrative Assistant to the Secretary of the Navy, obtained permission for me to use the papers of Secretaries of the Navy John L. Sullivan, Francis P. Matthews, Dan A. Kimball, and Robert B. Anderson, while Dr. Alfred Goldberg, Historian, Office of the Secretary of Defense, permitted use of the papers of the Secretary of Defense. Philip D. Lagerquist, Chief Archivist, Harry S. Truman Library, lent me the transcript of an oral interview of Admiral Robert L. Dennison, USN; Mrs. Elizabeth Mason, Associate Director, Oral History Research Office, Columbia University, furnished information leading to permission to use a number of transcripts of oral interviews. Dr. John T. Mason, Director of Oral History, U.S. Naval Institute, permitted the reading of a number of transcripts of oral interviews of naval officers. Dr. Benis Frank, Headquarters, U.S. Marine Corps, History and Museums Division, furnished transcripts of oral interviews of Marine Corps officers; Dr. Richard F. Haynes helped to steer me through the records of the Department of the Army. Particularly helpful at the National Archives, Washington, were Mr. Harry Schwartz, Dr. Robert

Krauskopf, Dr. Gibson Smith, Mr. William Cunliffe, and Mr. Edwin Allen Thompson. Similarly helpful at the Washington National Records Center, Suitland, Md., were Mrs. Ruby Beckett and Mr. James Duncan. Mrs. Patricia Maddocks of the U.S. Naval Institute cheerfully provided reference works and photographs.

I am further indebted to the following: to James N. Hewes, Jr., for a paper entitled "From Root to McNamara: Army Organization and Administration, 1900-1963"; to Dr. John R. Probert for a paper, "Executive Branch Organization for the Formulation and Execution of National Security Policy"' to Colonel William F. Schless, USA, for a paper, "The Service Secretaries—An Analysis," Student Research Report M-65-152, which he wrote while attending the Industrial College of the Armed Forces in 1965; and to Dr. J. Samuel Walker, University of Maryland, for a paper, "Henry A. Wallace and the Cold War." Professor Elmer B. Potter, U.S. Naval Academy, gave me a memorandum on the relations of Fleet Admiral Chester W. Nimitz with the secretaries of the Navy following his retirement, permitted the reading of Nimitz's diary, and also let me read parts of a biography of Nimitz. Dr. Robert Love, also my colleague at the Academy, provided a reference that Fleet Admiral William D. Leahy made with respect to the selection of a successor to Chief of Naval Operations Louis E. Denfeld.

Although they were directed to essays written by me on Secretaries of the Navy John L. Sullivan and Francis P. Matthews, critiques of these that proved most useful for this study were made by The Honorable John L. Sullivan, former Secretary of the Navy; Herbert R. Askins, former Assistant Secretary of the Navy; John H. Dillon, longtime former Administrative Assistant to the Secretary of the Navy; John F. Floberg, former Assistant Secretary of the Navy for Air; John T. Koehler, former Assistant Secretary of the Navy; Robert A. Lovett, former Secretary of Defense; Admiral Arleigh A. Burke, USN (Ret.), Captain William C. Chapman, USN (Ret.), Rear Admiral Paul Pihl, USN (Ret.), and the late Admiral Arthur W. Radford. Mr. Lovett also commented on the last two chapters of this work. Dr. K. Jack Bauer authorized the use of his essays on Dan A. Kimball and Robert B. Anderson, and Dr. Joseph Zikmund the use of his essay on James Forrestal, all written for *American Secretaries of the Navy*, published by the U.S. Naval Institute Press in 1980. Helpful comments were also received from Colonel Robert D. Heinl, Jr., USMC (Ret.), and Dr. Donald J. Mrozek, Kansas State University. Excellent constructive criticism and much-needed moral support came from my good friend Dr. Gerald E. Wheeler, State University of California, San Jose.

PAOLO E. COLETTA

U.S. Naval Academy
Annapolis, Maryland

Abbreviations Used in Notes

AF	*Air Force*
AHR	*American Historical Review*
AM	*American Mercury*
AN	*American Neptune*
ANAFJ	*Army, Navy, Air Force Journal*
ANJ	*Army-Navy Journal*
APSR	*American Political Science Review*
ARSN	*Annual Report of the Secretary of the Navy*
AUQR	*Air University Quarterly Review*
AW	*Aviation Weekly*
CH	*Current History*
FA	*Foreign Affairs*
JAH	*Journal of American History*
MA	*Military Affairs*
MCG	*Marine Corps Gazette*
MR	*Military Review*
NAN	*Naval Aviation News*
NDB	*Navy Department Bulletin*
NWCR	*Naval War College Review*
PHR	*Pacific Historical Review*
SA	*Scientific American*
SEP	*Saturday Evening Post*
USAS	*United States Air Services*
USNIP	U.S. Naval Institute *Proceedings*
USNWR	*United States News and World Report*

GB is used to indicate the General Board of the Navy; GPO to indicate Government Printing Office; ICAF, Industrial College of the Armed Forces; MDLC, Manuscript Division, Library of Congress; NARG, with number, National Archives, Washington; WNRC, Washington National Records Center, Suitland, Md.: NHD: OA, Naval History Division, Operational Archives; SECDEF, Secretary of Defense; SECNAV, Secretary of the Navy; ASECNAV, Assistant Secretary of the Navy; USECNAV, Undersecretary of the

Navy; JCS, Joint Chiefs of Staff; CNO, Chief of Naval Operations; DOD, Department of Defense; SECA, Secretary of the Army; SECAF, Secretary of the Air Force; JAG, Judge Advocate General; BUAER, Bureau of Aeronautics.

OFFICERS' TITLES

Army, Air Force, and Marines		*Navy*	
GEN	General	FADM	Fleet Admiral
MGEN	Major General	ADM	Admiral
LGEN	Lieutenant General	VADM	Vice Admiral
BGEN	Brigadier General	RADM	Rear Admiral
COL	Colonel	COMMO	Commodore
LCOL	Lieutenant Colonel	CAPT	Captain
MAJ	Major	CDR	Commander
CAPT	Captain	LCDR	Lieutenant Commander
LT	Lieutenant	LT	Lieutenant
2d LT	Second Lieutenant	LTJG	Lieutenant, junior grade
		ENS	Ensign

The United States Navy and Defense Unification 1947-1953

PART I

The Naval Administration
of John L. Sullivan

1
Implementing the
National
Security Act

Before leaving Washington to attend an Inter-American Defense Conference to be held in August in Rio de Janeiro, President Harry S. Truman nominated six of the twelve civilians who would administer the military departments and joint agencies provided in the National Security Act he had signed on 26 July 1947. It was ironic that he chose as Secretary of Defense the Secretary of the Navy, James V. Forrestal, who had opposed creating the position and who by accepting it took the first step in frustration that ultimately claimed his life. W. Stuart Symington, Assistant Secretary of War for Air, would be the Secretary of the Air Force; the last Under Secretary of War, Kenneth Claiborne Royall, would be the Secretary of the Army; and the Under Secretary of the Navy, John L. Sullivan, would be the Secretary of the Navy.

While a senator, from 1935 to 1945, Truman had served on the Appropriations and the Military Affairs committees. During the four wartime years he had been chairman of a Special Committee to Investigate the National Defense Program. In that capacity he had become well aware of inefficiency and mismanagement of government contracts, of waste, corruption, and favoritism in defense production, and of excessive costs resulting from having two military departments. During the war he said that the military services had "unquestionably squandered billions of dollars."[1] In his *Memoirs* he alleged that he "knew . . . that Army and Navy professionals seldom had any idea of the value of money. They did not seem to care what the cost was."[2] Although he had a lifelong love affair with things military and had a romantic view of soldiering, he would restrict generals and admirals to fighting battles and not let them interfere with economic or political matters.[3]

Having gained an unparalleled knowledge of military organization, Truman had criticized "the scrambled military setup" as an "open invitation to catastrophe." As a vice presidential candidate he had spoken of himself as "an ardent champion of a single authority over everything that pertains to

American safety" and written for *Collier's* an article entitled "Our Armed Forces Must Be Unified." As President, he sought three major military reforms: universal military training, desegregation, and a radical reorganization to achieve the unification of the armed forces. With respect to the last, he would reorganize the "antiquated" and "inadequate" military establishment so as to get the utmost in fighting capacity from each dollar. He alluded to the fact that "the Navy had its own little Army, that talks Navy, and is known as the Marine Corps," and that "it also has an Air Force of its own, and the Army, in turn, has its own little Navy, both freshwater and salt." He did not mention Admiral William D. Leahy, who had served President Franklin D. Roosevelt as military chief of staff, but he stated that he intended to get all admirals out of the White House.[4] On 19 December 1945 he had asked Congress for legislation that would combine the War and Navy Departments, as the Army wished, into "one single department of national defense." He had said, in part, "Air power has been developed to a point where its responsibilities are equal to those of land and sea power, and its contribution to our strategic planning is as great. Parity for air power can be achieved in one department or in three, but not in two. As between one department and three, the former is infinitely to be preferred."[5] Could he have had his way, there would be one civilian secretary, three assistant secretaries for the ground, sea, and air forces, and a general staff that would avoid political and economic issues and concentrate on directing the strategic and tactical operations of troops. Realizing that his plan would destroy military morale and contained explosive political ingredients, he had then conciliated the Navy, which opposed any merger in which it would lose control of naval air and the Marine Corps, by agreeing to three military departments, abandoning his proposal for a single chief of staff, and recommending that the Navy retain its carrier-and water-based aviation and the Marine Corps.[6]

The mere words of the unification law did not evoke the desired vital transformation in the hearts of military men, for most of them, although intensely patriotic, were steeped in long-cherished traditions of their services. Moreover, the simple act of reorganization federated rather than unified the services. A Republician critic of Truman called the "merger" a "sham that would contribute to the disintegration rather than the integration of our defense forces" and alleged that Truman was "evading" his responsibilities as commander in chief by unconstitutionally delegating them to a secretary of defense. As the military analyst for the *New York Times*, Hanson W. Baldwin, said, it created still another branch of the armed services and superimposed a directing agency over the three military departments. According to the *Minneapolis Tribune,* the act provided "expansion and confusion."[8] A case in point was the provision for an Air Force, Army aviation, Navy aviation, and Marine Corps aviation instead of a unified air force incorporating all strategic, tactical, and defensive air forces.

The service secretaries competed for funds, public prestige, and recognition for their respective services rather than organizing them to support foreign

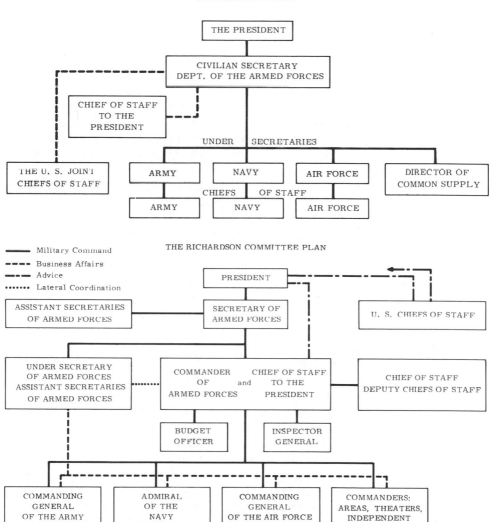

Various plans for the unification of the armed forces were made during World War II. *Shown above* is the plan suggested by General Joseph T. McNarney, U.S. Army Air Corps, which like a plan submitted by General J. Lawton Collins, USA, would have a chief of staff in the chain between the President and the Joint Chiefs of Staff. The Admiral James O. Richardson committee plan, *shown below*, would have the Chief of Staff to the President also command the Armed Forces. Much closer to the organization adopted in the National Security Act, 26 July 1947, was the plan suggested to Secretary of the Navy James V. Forrestal by Ferdinand Eberstadt, which included a National Security Council, National Security Resources Board, Research and Development Board, Central Intelligence Agency, Military Education and Training Board, and Munitions Board as agencies cooperating with the civilian secretaries of the armed services.

policies, the latter much enlarged since the end of World War II. These foreign commitments, furthermore, were to be affected over time, as by the $18 billion expended to rebuild war-torn Western Europe between 1945 and 1949, Russia's acquisition of the atomic bomb, the "loss" of China, and technological developments that for the first time made possible devastating attacks upon the United States and eradicated the "cushion of time" it had historically enjoyed to mobilize its manpower and industrial resources.[9]

A persistent problem remained, that of how to incorporate "the bomb," control over which Truman denied to the military, in the American defense organization along with a second, related problem: how that organization would operate when the President, instead of Congress or the leaders of the military establishment, set budgetary limits for the services and in reality determined the strategies they would follow. For by the end of World War II Truman had developed a "remainder method" of determining military budgets, that is, allocating to the armed services what "remained" after subtracting all anticipated expenditures of the civilian government from anticipated revenues.[10]

Although the Joint Board of the Army and Navy, established in 1903, had written *Joint Action, Army and Navy* (1926, 1935), it had been unable to adopt realistic joint doctrines prior to the attack on Pearl Harbor. Moreover, it had been unwilling to infringe upon the traditional doctrines of either service, so that the principles even as late as 1946 reflected the Navy's view on roles and missions. Most pertinent were the statements that neither service would attempt to restrict the methods or weapons the other service used in carrying out its functions; neither would attempt to restrict the other in the area of operations; and each would lend the other "the utmost assistance possible" in carrying out its functions. Under wartime pressure, however, better joint doctrine had finally been written, with the Army Air Corps nevertheless being most reluctant to provide tactical air support of ground troops. The independent Air Force created by the National Security Act would be a force searching for the principles that governed the employment of modern air power. Its leaders must decide on what internal organizations and policies to adopt. Because it took the Air Force six years, until 1953, to publish a basic doctrinal manual, and seven years to complete manuals dealing with such subjects as theater air operations, air defense operations, air operations in conjunction with amphibious operations, strategic air operations, and theater air reconnaissance, seven years passed before even tentative agreement on joint doctrines and procedures could be reached by the three services.

The National Security Act provided that only the Secretary of Defense, not the service secretaries, would be a cabinet member and that the Navy would be combined with the Army and the new Air Force into a National Military Establishment. The National Security Council created by the act would consider policies of common interest to all departments and agencies concerned with national security and assess and appraise the objectives, commitments, and risks of the United States in relation to actual and potential military power. To "insure a sound and adequate intelligence basis for formulation and execution of national security policies," a Central Intelligence Agency was to be organized under National Security Council direction. The National Security Resources Board, composed of the Secretary of Defense and secretaries of departments concerned with defense other than those of the military departments, would advise the President on the coordination of military, industrial, and civilian mobilization. The National Military Establishment itself consisted of the Secretary of Defense, who would have not three Assistant Secretaries of Defense but merely three special civilian assistants; the War Council, comprised of the civilian heads of the military departments and the Joint Chiefs of Staff; and the Munitions Board, which dealt with industrial matters related to defense procurement; the Joint Chiefs of Staff and their Joint Staff; the Research and Development Board; and the secretaries of the three military departments.[11]

To translate the principles enunciated in the National Security Act into actual practice promised to provoke innumerable questions, stimulate acrimonious debate, and call for many compromises. For example, how would the Air Force be organized? How would the defense budget be unified? What scope of budgetary control was contemplated at a level above that of the three departments? How would overlapping functions, roles, and missions be eliminated?[12] Should the War Council, as some of Sullivan's advisers suggested, be provided with a working staff of several senior officers from each service who would "bring the services into common action,"[13] or should it, as others advised, deal only with legal, legislative, and administrative matters while the Joint Chiefs of Staff worked on strategic problems, and thus "nip in the bud those who would merge the services instead of unifying them?"[14] How would naval aviation fit into Army and Air Force plans for the employment of strategic and tactical air and into the defense of the continental United States and of American bases overseas?

Answers to these and to other questions would take perhaps more than the two years provided by the National Security Act for completing the unification process, and as early as September 1947 Forrestal asked the service secretaries to hold to a minimum their public comments about the organization of their departments, at least until his own office was "set up."[15] Well aware of Air Force publicity, however, John Nicholas Brown, Assistant Secretary of the Navy for Air, suggested to Sullivan late in September that the Navy undertake a publicity campaign to educate the public on the position the Navy held in the new defense organization and to stress that its most important mission involved the use of naval aviation. Indeed, "The position of the Navy as a whole vis-a-vis Congressional appropriations will be immeasurably strengthened if the Navy succeeds in instructing the people in the essential role of Naval Aviation."[16]

Given the structure of the National Military Establishment, Sullivan had to compete for organizational position, strategic doctrine, and funds with the other service secretaries, the Bureau of the Budget, Congress, and the public, which meant that he had to use public relations as a command tool. However, he was greatly hindered in telling the Navy's story because very few of the small number of his public relations officers were adequately trained for the task.

Sullivan's attempt to square the Navy with the National Security Act was also made difficult because the act established the functions of the services in ambiguous terms. The Navy would include "such aviation as may be organic therein." "Naval aviation," said the act, "shall be integrated with the naval service as part thereof. . . ." The Marine Corps "shall include land combat. . .forces and such aviation as may be organic thereto." Last, "the Navy shall develop aircraft, weapons, tactics, technique, organization and equipment of naval combat and service elements; matters of joint concern as to these functions shall be coordinated between the Army, the Air Force, and the Navy." As for the Department of the Air Force, it would be "organized. . .primarily for prompt and sustained offensive and defensive air operations." There was no mention in the act of strategic air forces, let alone the grant of authority to the Air Force to acquire and operate them. When advocates of strategic bombing would put all military aviation in the Air Force—and rockets, space vehicles, and anything else that flew as well[17]—many Navy men felt as Rear Admiral Daniel V. Gallery did, that ". . .we might as well scuttle the fleet as give up control of our naval aircraft."[18]

Naval and Air Force functions were established by executive Order 9877, signed by Truman on 26 July. Early in August Forrestal in consequence appointed a committee headed by Vice Admiral Forrest Sherman "to recommend measures for implementation, within the National Military Establishment, of the National Security Act of 1947."[19] Furthermore, he kept the Navy fully informed of progress being made in unification. In addition, by early October 1947, a subcommittee of the Congressional Aviation Policy Board chaired by Representative Carl Hinshaw (R., Calif.) began hearings on such questions as the importance of aviation in national defense plans, the adequacy of aviation budgets, and the relation of the Air Force and naval aviation. Advising the group were General of the Army Henry H. Arnold (Ret.), and Admiral John H. Towers, USN, Chairman of the General Board of the Navy.

On 1 May 1947 the Navy had completed a statement of its basic doctrine in a series of U.S. Fleet publications, particularly in USF-1, *Principles and Instructions of Naval Warfare*. Written by a full-time panel of World War II officers who had had important command or staff experience, USF-1 represented "the best service opinion and best knowledge that obtains in 1946." Included were conclusions reached from use of the fleet as a huge laboratory for the testing of technological developments and tactics. Given the extremely broad scope of naval operations—surface, subsurface, air, amphibious—no single technology dominated naval thinking. Such new developments as atomic energy could be integrated easily in some part of the "balanced fleet," of which especially in the Pacific, World War II experience predicated that the carrier would be the heart. Particularly relevant were the efforts of such naval aviators as Gerald Bogan, Daniel V. Gallery, and Arthur W. Radford, and of such gunnery and ordnance experts as William H. P. Blandy and Arleigh Burke, in developing the carrier as a strategic weapon system. Notable also was the emphasis naval doctrine placed upon the fact that while naval officers were trained in at least one specialty, they owed their primary duty to the Navy as a whole and that they would some day obtain "command." While naval doctrine contrasted sharply with Army doctrine, which emphasized concentration on a military specialty, it perforce had to wait until the Air Force developed its doctrine before triservice comparisons could be made. When the Air Force developed its doctrine along lines followed by the Army Air Corps, little cooperation and coordination with the Navy could be expected. The Navy's ideal thus remained to integrate the various naval forces and train commanders to direct a unified Navy either while showing the flag or in actual war. In its task forces, which could be tailored to perform a specific mission, it found the solution to most operational problems.

Rather than pressing to define their doctrine, the prospective leaders of the Air Force entrusted the task to the Air University, in June 1946. With the unification law in the offing, Brigadier General Thomas S. Power, Deputy Assistant Chief of Air Staff for Operations, directed the Air University to provide a manual covering Air Force policies, procedures, roles, objectives, techniques, doctrines, strategies, and organization in such fields as operations, intelligence, logistics, communications, and administration. The results of the work, which began during the winter of 1947 and proceeded for about three years and included a study of Army and Navy publication activities, will be noted below. Enough for the moment to note that the basic document, *Air Power and the U.S. Air Force,* contained controversial statements unacceptable to the Air Staff. Its stating that "strategic bombing operations are normally conducted independently of ground and naval forces," for example, did not square with the Air Force position that Army and Navy forces were essential for the defense of overseas air bases required for a strategic air campaign. On the other hand, Army Air Force Chief of Staff General Carl Spaatz objected to a manual entitled *Joint Overseas Operations* that had been written by about fifty Army and Navy officers who had been convened at the Army and Navy Staff College (later National War College) and had forwarded their work to the Joint Chiefs of Staff on 15 August 1946. Spaatz would not accept the manual because it failed to provide an integrated triservice staff, dealt largely with amphibious operations overseas, and "did not consider the possibility that a hostile nation might be defeated by air attack."

The Army Air Force thereupon produced a paper entitled "Joint Procedures for Tactical Control of Aircraft in Joint Amphibious Operations." Army-Army Air Force doctrine already provided for a joint operations center to direct joint air operations. The new paper extended the procedure by placing naval air as well as the air-ground team under control of the joint task force commander. The Army was agreeable, but it was now the Navy's turn to object, for the new procedure contained "information which is contrary in many points to standard Navy doctrine and to experience gained in World War II, as spelled out in USF-6, *Amphibious Warfare Instructions,* which called for a fleet commander to command forces afloat and a landing force commander to assume command after the forces had landed. The Air University and Tactical Air Command retorted that the Air Force would not "compromise or appease." They demanded one unified commander for an amphibious operation and a joint Army-Navy-Air Force staff. While the Navy would be responsible for all naval activities and the Army for ground action, the Air Force would conduct all air action. The Air University thought that the Navy would "certainly be violently opposed." Perhaps its leaders were chagrined when the Army said the paper should be processed through the Joint Chiefs of Staff and would not accept it even as an interim statement of doctrine. The writing of joint doctrines and procedures was also undertaken by the Joint Chiefs of Staff—about which more anon.[20]

Forrestal was sworn in as Secretary of Defense at noon, 17 September; at midnight the unification act took effect. On the eighteenth Sullivan, whom Forrestal had suggested to Truman as his successor, was sworn in as the new Secretary of the Navy, W. John Kenney as Under Secretary of the Navy, and Symington as Secretary of the Air Force.

Would the organization provided by the National Security Act prove adequate? Could the services operate successfully with the functions assigned them?

NOTES

1 Richard F. Haynes, *The Awesome Power: Harry S. Truman as Commander in Chief* (Baton Rouge: Louisiana State University Press, 1973), p. 120.
2. Harry S. Truman, *Memoirs by Harry S. Truman*, 2 vols. (Garden City, N.Y.: Doubleday, 1955-56), 1:8; Roy S. Cline, and Maurice Matloff, "Development of War Department Views on Unification," MA 13(1949): 65-74.
3. Haynes, *The Awesome Power*, pp. 18-21, 93.
4. Truman, *Memoirs*, 2:46-48.
5. Cited in Harland B. Moulton, "American Strategic Power; Two Decades of Nuclear Strategy and Weapons Systems, 1945-1955," Ph.D. diss., University of Minnesota, 1969. Facsmile, Ann Arbor, Mich.: University Microfilms, 1973, p. 21.
6. Ibid., pp. 21-22; Haynes, *The Awesome Power*, pp. 93-105; Robert Frank Futrell, *Ideas, Concepts, Doctrine: A History of Basic Thinking in the United States Air Force, 1907-1964* (Maxwell Air Force Base, Ala.: Air University, 1971), Chap. 5.
7. *Chicago Tribune*, 29 Jan. 1947.
8. "Unification Becomes Reality," MR 27 (November 1947):47; Harry B. Yoshpe et al., *Defense Organization and Management* (Washington: ICAF, 1967), p. 18.
9. Bernard Brodie, "War Department Thinking on the Atomic Bomb," *Bulletin of the Atomic Scientists* 3 (June 1947): 151-52.
10. Truman, *Memoirs*, 2:61-102; Paul Y. Hammond, "NSC-68: Prologue to Rearmament," in Warner H. Schilling, Paul Y. Hammond, and Glen H. Snyder, *Strategy, Politics, and Defense Budgets* (New York: Columbia University Press, 1962), pp. 273-79.
11. Truman, *Memoirs*, 2:51-52, 155—60; "Unification Becomes Reality," MA 27 (November 1947):43-48; Ferdinand Eberstadt, "The Historical Evolution of our National Security Organization," NWCR 6 (January 1954):1-16; John R. Probert, "Staff Arrangements in the Organization for National Security," Ph.D. diss., University of Pennsylvania, 1956, pp. 194-234.
12. Secretary's Committee on Research and Reorganization (SCOROR) to M[ore] T[han] O[ne], 6 October 1947; Administrative Officer to SECNAV, 12 August 1947, WNRC, RG 80, Papers of the Secretary of the Navy, hereafter cited as SNP.
13. W. John Kenney, Acting SECNAV, Memorandum for the SECDEF, 1 June 1948, SNP.
14. CAPT L. A. Thackrey, Memorandum for the SECNAV, 20 May 1948: John Dillon,

Memorandum for the SECNAV, 14 April 1948, SNP. For the acrimonious interservice debate on roles and missions prior to passage of the National Security Act, see *Supporting Study: US Aircraft Carriers in the Strategic Role. Part I—Naval Strategy in a Period of Change; Interservice Rivalry. Strategic Interaction, and the Development of a Nuclear Attack Capability, 1945-1972,* part of *History of the Strategic Arms Competition 1945-1972* Falls Church, Va.: Lulejian and Associates, October 1975, *pp.64-68*. Hereafter cited as *Supporting Study*.

15. Forrestal to Kenneth C. Royall, 3 September 1947, SCOROR to MTO, 6 October 1947, SNP.

16. J. N. Brown, Memorandum for the SECNAV, 29 September 1947, SNP.

17. See for example Clark G. Reynolds, *The Fast Carriers: The Forging of an Air Navy* (New York: McGraw-Hill, 1968), pp. 213, 351-63, 394-97; W. W. Rostow, *The United States in the World Arena: An Essay in Recent History* (New York: Harper and Row, 1960), pp. 223-24; GEN Carl Spaatz, USAF, "The Evolution of Air Power," MA 11 (Spring 1947):3-16; Dale O. Smith, BGEN, USAF, "The Role of Air Power Since World War II," MA 19 (Summer 1955):71-76; LCOL James D. Hittle, USMC, "The Marine Corps and the National Security Act," MCG 31 (October 1947):57-59.

18. Daniel V. Gallery, RADM, USN (RET), *Eight Bells and All's Well* (New York: W.W. Norton and Co., 1965), p. 221.

19. Forrestal to Sherman, 8 August 1947, SNP. When Sherman was detached to assume command of U.S. Naval Forces Mediterranean, Sullivan wrote him that "Your title, Deputy Chief of Naval Operations for Operations, did not convey the full measure of the responsibilities entrusted to you. We in the Navy know that all the conferences, discussions and studies which brought into being our present National Security Act with success was largely because of the tact, energy, and good judgment which you contributed. . . ." (Sullivan to Sherman, 2 January 1948, SNP.)

20. Futrell, *Ideas, Concepts, Doctrine,* pp. 183-88.

2
Early Conflicts over Defense Organization and Roles and Missions

A short, round, and merry Irish Roman Catholic, John L. Sullivan was a hard worker with an ability to smooth troubled political waters. He was born in Manchester, New Hampshire, on 16 June 1899, to Patrick Henry and Ellen J. (Harrington) Sullivan. Since Patrick was trained as a lawyer, served as a county solicitor, and was also a personal counsel to Frank Knox, the newspaper publisher and Secretary of the Navy from 1940 to 1944, John L. grew up in an atmosphere of law, politics, and naval affairs.

Sullivan entered Dartmouth College but left in December 1918, when he met the physical and age qualifications to join the Naval Reserve as an apprentice seaman. His duty lasted but three months, however. After graduating from Dartmouth in 1921, and from Harvard Law School, he entered law practice, at first with his father's firm of Sullivan and White, then as his father's partner until the father died in 1931.

Sullivan was defeated in two bids as Democratic candidate for governor of New Hampshire, in 1934 and 1938. Then he went to Washington as Assistant Secretary of the Treasury, in which office he strove to repair strained relations between the Treasury and Congress and was brilliant in appearances before congressional committees.[1] President Franklin D. Roosevelt died before he transferred Sullivan to some post in the Navy Department. Sullivan thereupon resigned from the Treasury and resumed law practice, in Washington, for six months, when he was asked by President Harry S. Truman to serve as Assistant Secretary of the Navy for Air.[2] When Artemus Gates, the Assistant Secretary of the Navy for Air, was promoted to Under Secretary of the Navy on 1 July 1945, Sullivan succeeded him. While in this post, from July 1945 to

June 1946, he witnessed carrier operations in the Western Pacific and was much impressed by their power and versatility. As Under Secretary after 17 June 1946, following the resignation of Gates, his diplomatic talents smoothed the wrinkles out of the troublesome transition to the unified National Military Establishment, and it was often whispered that he would succeed Forrestal as Secretary of the Navy if Forrestal became the Secretary of Defense under the new unification plan.

Sullivan had no qualms about accepting high office, even though he knew (1) that Truman, an old Army and National Guard officer, preferred the views of the Army and the Air Force to those of the Navy, (2) that Truman disliked James V. Forrestal because he was almost the only cabinet member to disagree with many of his key policies, and (3) that funds for the military services would be meager.[3] He knew, too, that because the old European balance of power had collapsed, the U.S. Navy must be maintained in order to help support the foreign policy interests of the nation. So far, the United States had a monopoly on nuclear power. If a potential enemy obtained similar power, Sullivan would be the first Secretary of the Navy to serve in a total war environment.

John L. Sullivan being sworn in on 18 September 1947 as Secretary of the Navy by Chief Justice Fred M. Vinson. *From left to right:* Secretary of the Air Force W. Stuart Symington, Secretary of the Army Kenneth C. Royall, and Secretary of Defense James V. Forrestal.

On 17 September, even before he was sworn in as Secretary of the Navy, Sullivan discussed the role of the National Security Council in the National Military Establishment with Forrestal and its other members; on the twenty-second he joined the three other service secretaries and the Joint Chiefs of Staff in deciding what procedures the War Council would follow. On the twenty-third he allocated departmental duties and responsibilities to himself and to his civilian assistants. On 13 October he met with Forrestal, Secretary of the Army Kenneth C. Royall, and Secretary of the Air Force W. Stuart Symington to help establish the roles and missions of the armed services.[4] By 13 November, however, all members of the so-called Committee of Four Secretaries concluded that it was impossible to conduct all their business by meeting merely for ten minutes each day.[5] Henceforth they would correspond with each other and meet only occasionally. They met twenty-one times in 1947 and 1948, with some of their meetings enlivened by briefings by George F. Kennan and Charles T. "Chip" Bohlen, of the Department of State.

The first meeting of the three armed forces secretaries in the field occurrred on 17 February 1948 when they arrived at the U.S. Naval Station in San Juan, Puerto Rico, to observe the maneuvers of the Atlantic Fleet. *From left to right* are Admiral William H.P. Blandy, Commander in Chief of the Atlantic fleet; Secretary of the Army Kenneth C. Royall; Secretary of the Navy John L. Sullivan; Secretary of the Air Force Stuart W. Symington; Major General R.E. Porter, Commanding General USA, Antilles Department; and Captain Jack Lyon, USN, Acting Commandant of the Tenth Naval District.

OFFICIAL U.S. NAVY PHOTOGRAPH

"This thing is going to work," said Sullivan about unification. He would learn about the job of being Secretary, he added, by devoting two months to devouring the mass of paper that crossed his desk, paper generated in the administration of about 12,000 persons in the Navy Department, 283,000 in the continental United States, and 44,000 overseas. Thereafter he would delegate certain tasks to his civilian executive assistants and thus keep himself free to reach policy decisions in performing his primary task, policy control, or the administration and control of his department as whole, including the functions of public relations; legislative affairs; morale; the nomination, removal, and reassignment of the prinicipal civilian and military men in his department; and liaison with the other services and with the Department of State.[6] Meanwhile he asked the General Board of the Navy to study and report to him on the probable nature of warfare in the next ten-year period and also on how to bring the Navy to the highest point of effectiveness so that it could contribute to the warmaking capability of the nation within the framework of the National Security Act.[7]

While Sullivan assigned naval representatives to the numerous national security agencies, he also interested himself in revising the code of military justice; planning for the exploration, conservation, and development of the mineral resources of the subsoil and seabed of the continental shelf; in getting rid of racial discrimination in the Navy;[8] in supporting soil conservation methods on land owned by the Navy; and in establishing a Naval Arctic Research laboratory at Point Barrow, Alaska. Because he firmly believed that those who had a hand in deciding, influencing, or implementing naval matters should understand how the Navy operated, he invited Forrestal, Symington, and various congressmen to sea cruises on carriers or cruisers during wintertime exercises in the Caribbean; corresponded with many congressmen, businessmen, and labor leaders; invited various business and community leaders to attend a Navy Civilian Orientation Course to be held at Pensacola, Florida; and also asked the presidents, chief executive officers, and professors of Naval Science to attend an orientation course in the Naval Air Training Program, also given at Pensacola.

When Symington, however, asked him to furnish officers for the Air Force pending the construction of an Air Force Academy, Sullivan said he would not consent unless the Air Force sponsored legislation providing for the expansion of the Naval Academy, with such expansion estimated in January 1948 to cost $119 million. If the navy could obtain funds to expand the Academy and the new Postgraduate School at Monterey, California,[9] acquire an airfield near Annapolis, and be given $25 million besides, he would try to plan for one year even though he feared "that Academy midshipmen will stampede to the Air Force because of faster promotion and shore duty." Moreover, he stressed that he "could not accept any arrangement which would work to the great detriment of the Navy, if the arrangement would give the Air Force 25 to 50 officers a year, since the detriment would be out of all proportion to the benefit of the Air Force." Under pressure from Forrestal and Symington, in July 1948 he agreed that a maximum of 7 percent of the graduating class of 1949 could volunteer for service with the Air Force. In November, that figure was adopted by Forrestal, whereas 40 percent of West Point graduates could volunteer for Air Force duty. Subsequently, legislation authorized the membership of the brigade at the Naval Academy to expand from 3,468 in

Late in 1944, Admiral Marc Mitscher suggested building a large carrier able to handle large, long-range aircraft. The project was shelved for economy reasons but revived by Admiral Joseph J. Clark and others in 1947. The photograph is of an oil painting in the Naval Academy Museum, Annapolis, Md.

OFFICIAL U.S. NAVY PHOTOGRAPH

1949-50 to 3,686 in 1950-51, and to 3,812 in 1951-52. Meanwhile Forrestal established the Stearns-Eisenhower board "to study the general problem of service academies." When an airfield near Annapolis could not be acquired and the use of Andrews Air Force Base by midshipmen was ruled out, selected graduating midshipmen were sent to Pensacola for their air training.[10]

Another especially perplexing question Sullivan had to decide was whether the Navy should build a supercarrier that could handle heavy bombers and thus break the monopoly of the Air Force on atomic weapons. He was told that demands for such a carrier had been made by Admiral Marc Mitscher while he commanded Fast Carrier Task Force 38 off Leyte in the fall of 1944 and also late in 1945, when he was Deputy Chief of Naval Operations (Air). Forrestal had approved such a carrier while he was Secretary of the Navy, and it had been discussed in the War Council but shelved for economy reasons. However, Sullivan wanted proof of its merits, for the record, for the memory of some officers and his own recollections showed that Mitscher wanted merely a large carrier, one that could handle heavy, long-range aircraft that could carry up to an eight-thousand-pound bomb load over a radius of three hundred to two thousand miles with which to strike enemy naval forces. Such a carrier, endorsed by the Bureau of Aeronautics and the vice chief of Naval Operations, Admiral DeWitt Ramsay, Sullivan had approved as Assistant Secretary of the Navy for Air in February 1946. But the Bureau of Aeronautics had then suggested planes capable of carrying 1,200-pound bomb loads destined for particular targets "with some sacrifice of fuel and range." While it is easy to believe the rumor that naval advocates of atomic weapons said "An atomic bomb weighs 10,000 pounds. To carry such a bomb we need a plane of stated weight and and range. Therefore we will build a carrier or about 60,000 tons displacement which can service such planes," the record instead quite clearly reveals that the navy wanted merely a large carrier; any potentiality it might have for carrying planes that could deliver atomic bombs was an afterthought.[11]

Sullivan was told by the chief of the Bureau of Aeronautics, however, that Forrestal had asked Truman on 26 July 1946 to authorize facilities in carriers for delivering atomic bombs. After reviewing the capabilities of carriers for the president, he added that it was essential to modify both carrier aircraft and the servicing facilities carriers provided. As a result, on 19 November 1946, the Chief of Naval Operations, Fleet Admiral Chester W. Nimitz, directed the Deputy Chief of Naval Operations (Logistics) to modify the new forty-five-thousand-ton carriers CVS-41, 42, and 43 so that they could operate projected AJ aircraft with an atomic bomb load. By November 1947 the program was well under way. The *Coral Sea* (CVB-43) had been completely equipped to handle planes carrying the atomic bomb; the *Franklin D. Roosevelt* (CVB-42) would be completed about 1 January 1948; and the *Midway* (CVB-41) would be finished about September 1948. The first AJs would be flying by July 1948 and would be in group strength by 1949.[12]

Although this "CVB Improvement Program No. 1" made it possible to use the AJ, which weighed fifty-five thousand pounds, the AJ was the smallest plane that could carry a ten-thousand-pound bomb to a distance of nearly seven hundred miles and return to its base—with but one hour of fuel remaining. However, planes weighing one hundred thousand pounds should be able to operate from larger carriers. Unless such carriers were provided, a ceiling would be placed on the Navy's aircraft performance. In justification of building larger planes and carriers it was noted that in wartime land-based planes might not have overseas bases from which to operate. While such bases were being acquired and prepared by the Navy, carrier aircraft with a combat radius of two thousand miles would be in operation. In that critical period between the beginning of a war and the establishment of necessary strategic bomber bases, only carrier aircraft could be used offensively.[13] When Rear Admiral Joseph J. Clark, Deputy Assistant Chief of Naval Operations (Air), called attention to the plans for the original supercarrier, he was rewarded by a revival of interest in them, especially by the General Board of the Navy, which

Artist's sketch of the projected 65,000-ton superacarrier eventually named the *United States* (CVA-58).

COURTESY THE NATIONAL ARCHIVES

recommended to Sullivan that such a ship be built.[14] Convinced after sharp questioning of his top naval officers of the need of such a carrier, Sullivan told the Chief of the Bureau of Aeronautics: "I concur that the building of such a ship is essential to the maintenance of our sea-going air power," and he decided to seek funds for it in budget requests.[15]

The projected 65,000-ton carrier, which would displace 80,000 tons when fully loaded, would be the largest ship ever built. She would bristle with new radar-controlled guns, have an armored flight deck, speed of about 33 knots, and carry two catapults forward. She would be the seventh U.S. Navy ship too large to pass through the 110-foot locks on the Panama Canal. She would be flush-decked and carry a complement of four thousand men. An *Essex*-class carrier could operate aircraft weighing 30,000 pounds; a converted *Essex*, a plane weighing 52,500 pounds. Among her other aircraft, the new carrier would carry 54 to 80 fighters and 20 or more bombers as heavy as the B-29 or planes still under design that would weigh 100,000 pounds, have four turboprop engines or possibly pure jets, a top speed of 450 to 500 knots, operating radii of fiteen hundred to two thousand miles, and carry atomic bombs. Though faster than the Air Force's projected B-50, an improved B-29, the newest planes would have a shorter range, but the carrier could carry her planes within seventeen hundred miles of any point on earth. The ship was expected to cost $124 million and be built in forty-six months.[16] When completed, she would command the seas and the air as well. By February 1947 planes were far enough advanced to warrant including funding for design studies in the fiscal year 1948 building program. In December, although General Spaatz objected to some of her characteristics, she was approved by the Joint Chiefs of Staff in a report to the Thomas K. Finletter Commission that would investigate the future air power needs of the nation.

When the National Security Act, signed 26 July 1947, went into effect, the service chiefs were, *left to right*: Fleet Admiral Chester W. Nimitz, Chief of Naval Operations; General of the Army Dwight D. Eisenhower, Chief of Staff, U.S. Army; General Carl Spaatz, Commanding General U.S. Army Air Force; and General A.A. Vandegrift, Commandant of the U.S. Marine Corps.

The building of a supercarrier hindered the resolution of the question of where the authority of naval air ended and that of the Air Force began. When Truman signed the National Security Act on 26 July 1947, Lieutenant General James H. Doolittle, USAF, Retired, said: "This is the day Billy Mitchell dreamed of," for the Air Force became an independent entity. However, Navy and Air Force leaders disagreed violently on how military aviation should be integrated in the services.[17]

Sullivan avoided emphasizing costs when comparing Navy and Air Force programs. He estimated the cost of developing and providing twenty-four B-36 bombers and a field from which they could fly to be $155 million. A supercarrier would cost $124,460,000, a twenty-four-plane group of ADR-62 planes $105 million. Financial comparison, however, would lead to endless debate over the expense of a total strategic air bombardment effort versus carrier task forces, and would disappear once war came. "The answer is not the B-36 or any other strategic bomber which is now in sight. Such a plane will be much larger and more expensive than the B-36," Sullivan was advised. Hence his basic argument should be made on the military capability of the carrier and on what vehicles five years hence could be built in the United States that could deliver atomic weapons to the Russian heartland in the early stages of a total war.[18]

Yet Sullivan could not simply wave away the matter of costs or the reaction of the Air Force to the building of a supercarrier. In October 1947 the Board of Review of the Bureau of the Budget asked him if Project 6A had been approved by the Joint Chiefs of Staff. On 13 November, after discussing the characteristics of the supercarrier and of the aircraft she would carry with his staff, Sullivan telephoned James E. Webb, Director of the Bureau of the Budget since July 1946—to inquire whether the construction of the carrier needed to be cleared with the Air Force and the Secretary of Defense and whether everything the Navy wanted had to be so cleared. Webb answered that he did not so understand. Sullivan said that "he did not want to establish any precedent by which everyone would be running in circles and accomplishing nothing but a sense of frustration." Although he and Webb agreed that the Secretary of Defense could not coordinate the defense budget for the current year, Sullivan stressed the fact that Forrestal while Secretary of the Navy had approved construction of the carrier and closed the conversation by stating "that he was telephoning because any letter to the Bureau of the Budget would merely be asking for trouble. . .and that he did not feel that any other service had any right to question the construction of the new carrier."[19] Nor would Sullivan let the Air Force tell the Navy what it should or could do.

When Symington announced that agreement had been reached between the Army and Air Force on tactical air but that the agreement was being held up by the Navy, Sullivan retorted that he had never seen the paper on agreement. Because Symington was in St. Louis and the Chief of Staff of the Air Force, General Carl "Tooey" Spaatz was in a hospital, Sullivan telephoned Lieutenant General Hoyt S. Vandenberg, USAF, soon to succeed Spaatz, told him that he considered the matter to be one between the Air Force and the Army, that the Navy had done nothing to hold up the agreement, and that no one in the Navy had seen the paper on agreement. He would call Symington in St. Louis and tell him so, meanwhile telling the members of his secretariat that in so doing "he would protect the Navy in his conversation with Symington in case the proposed paper was broader than the title would indicate."[20]

Moreover, he would not comment on the matter until after a report was made by General Dwight David Eisenhower, USA, and Spaatz, whom Forrestal had asked to find out whether all elements in the services would be happy with this allocation.

In 1946 responsibility for continental air defense had rested with the Air Defense Command of the Army Air Forces, which relied heavily upon search radar stations and Army antiaircraft artillery but could call upon other military and civilian agencies for support. By November 1947 responsibility had been transferred to the Air Force's Air Defense Command, which employed six Air Forces for the purpose, one located in each of the Army's six areas. An Aircraft Control and Warning system for Alaska, Canada, and the United States, known by the code word SUPREMACY, was discussed by high-ranking Air Force officers and Symington during the winter of 1947 and again following the assignment of the mission of continental air defense to the Air Force in the Key West Agreement of March 1948, and in November 1948 the Air Force created a Continental Air Command. Because of the greater need for funds to go to the Strategic Air Command and Tactical Air Command, all that was accomplished by the Air Force during 1948 was to plan to establish seventy-five permanent radar sites for the air defense of the United States alone.[21]

Problems concerning unification rested even more heavily on Forrestal than on the service secretaries. On 20 September 1947, when he was piped over the side from "Main Navy" on Constitution Avenue and moved to the Pentagon, Forrestal approved in principle the various Army-Air Force agreements that would still have to be worked out in practice and said he did not expect immediate economy to result from unification. He would make no sweeping changes in the armed services, and he would deal with individuals instead of issuing numerous directives. Moreover, rather than centralizing press matters in his own office, he would let the service secretaries make their own public pronouncements.

For the three civilian assistants allowed him, Forrestal chose John Ohly, who would handle policy matters and act as liaison man with the Department of State; Marx Leva, who would handle congressional relations and legal questions; and a rear admiral in World War II, Wilfred McNeill, who would tackle fiscal matters. For his personal staff he wanted a senior naval aviator captain, a senior colonel aviator from the Air Force, and a senior Army colonel. The Army man would be his aide; the others would be known as his Air Force Assistant and Naval Assistant. Each was to give him his unbiased opinion on any subject instead of paralleling or duplicating the thinking of the chief of his service; none was to run to his service chief to learn the party line or ask for instructions. In this way Forrestal hoped to avoid the deadlock in the Joint Chiefs of Staff between the chiefs of staff of the Army and Air Force and the Chief of Naval Operations. The naval aide selected was Herbert D. Riley, Naval Academy class of 1927 and an aviator since 1930, who was working in the Long Range Plans Office, Strategic Plans Section, Office of the Chief of Naval Operations. Robert Wood was the Army man and Jerry Page the Air Force man. Because his civilian advisers lacked knowledge of military matters, Forrestal often asked his military assistants to help him decide split decisions forwarded by the Joint Chiefs.[22]

Forrestal knew that dividing missions among the services would be difficult; he also recognized that traditions and prestige were involved. Because many

Secretary of Defense James V. Forrestal chose an Army man to be his military aide and an Air Force Assistant and Naval Assistant. Each was to give him his unbiased opinion on any subject instead of paralleling or duplicating the thinking of the chief of his service. For his Naval Assistant, Forrestal chose Herbert D. Riley, Naval Academy class of 1927 and an aviator since 1930. At the time, Riley was working in the Long Range Plans Office, Strategic Plans Section, Office of the Chief of Naval Operations.

OFFICIAL U.S. NAVY PHOTOGRAPH

men were still inflamed by the long and sharp debate that preceded unification, he would seek to guide the military departments toward unity of purpose instead of structure, and to reconcile conflicting opinions about the new military establishment.

Forrestal's management concept, it should be noted early, was active rather than passive. Under a passive concept of leadership, which was favored by the Army and the Air Force, a civilian secretary would depend upon his chief of staff as a single responsible source of information and use that chief to carry out his decisions. Inside of dabbling in day-to-day administration, the secretary would be left free to work on any special problems confronting him. This method had worked well for the Army in World War II. Indeed, in his plan of defense reorganization offered in 1945, General J. Lawton Collins put a chief of staff at the top of the leadership pyramid, over civilians who would act as the Secretary, Under Secretary, and Assistant Secretaries of National Defense, and would use military men rather than civilians as heads of the military departments. If the civilian leaders provided in the National Security Act followed this passive concept, even if they took care to check the accuracy of the information and judgments offered by their chiefs of staff, control would really be exercised by their chiefs of staff. Forrestal preferred the active concept. He would control, and his decisions would be reached by relying not upon a single source of information but upon as many sources as were available. Military men would thus be among a number of top advisers and consultants who would develop for him the advantages and disadvantages of a particular course of action. Sullivan, like Forrestal, followed the active concept, while Royall and Symington preferred the passive.[23]

In his first address to the Navy, in mid-September, Sullivan stated that the Navy of World War II, the largest in the world, had shrunk. While he did not mention the Soviet Union, which was openly violating the Yalta Agreements, he noted that the challenge to American security remained great. The Navy must therefore offset reductions both afloat and ashore with increased efficiency and work with the Army and Air Force to insure the nation's position of leadership in world affairs.[24]

Particularly important in carrying out Sullivan's policies would be the members of the staff. Under Secretary of the Navy William John Kenney, a graduate of Stanford University and Harvard Law School, was responsible for policies dealing with procurement, active and Reserve personnel, and administration, the last of which he now must coordinate with the other two services. His serving for eight years, from 1941 to 1949, did much to provide continuity in the Office of the Secretary of the Navy. To succeed Kenney as Assistant Secretary of the Navy, in January 1948 Truman named Mark Edwin Andrews, a Texas oil man, who was quickly approved by the Senate.

John Nicholas Brown, the Assistant Secretary of the Navy for Air since 12 November 1946, had served as an enlisted man in World War II, then graduated from Harvard University. He was responsible for correlating naval air strength with the national air power to the end that the Navy would have control of the air under which its ships would operate. He said that the Navy had no quarrel with the Air Force "or anyone else." However, because the Air Force lacked an effective long-range bomber and carrier-based planes would be the first to strike an enemy, he believed that the Navy was the nation's first line of defense.[25] Such remarks and similar ones by other top-ranking civilian and military leaders led Forrestal early in February 1948 to direct that any proposed speech or article on a controversial subject must have his prior approval—a directive that provoked a cry of censorship from a number of newspapers.[26]

Sullivan's Navy was in transition to a new era of power and capabilities, even though no one could foresee the exact nature of a future war. Would traditional navies be outmoded by the atomic bomb, guided missiles, robot planes, and as-yet-unforeseen weapons? How could that Navy be used against the only potential enemy, the Soviet Union, with its landlocked mass situated in the heart of Eurasia? It was Sullivan's task to adopt new weapons and tactics capable not only of controlling sea communications but also of wreaking havoc upon an enemy wherever he was.

Following World War II the American public rejected any weapon that was not atomic or at least electronic, but lacked knowledge of the interplay of geography and technology upon which to base sound strategy.[27] Various naval officers warned against "Push-button Philia" and "Jules Verne Neurosis," pointed out that the development of military equipment was outrunning the ability of personnel to use it, and called for the training of men and officers in the techniques of an atomic-age Navy.[28] Although the Assistant Chief of Naval Operations for Guided Missiles, 1947 to 1949, Rear Admiral Daniel V. Gallery, would "orient the Navy's guided missile program [and] fit it in with those of the other services,"[29] John Nicholas Brown, Assistant Secretary of the Navy for Air, carefully guarded against Air Force attempts to obtain legislation that would give it a monopoly over "pilotless aircraft and missiles,"[30] and Nimitz well stated that Navy's case by noting that the Navy had accommodated itself to every technological advance that threatened to make navies obsolete and would continue to do so with respect to the atomic bomb and other weapons as well. "The American genius for the exercise of sea power will not be allowed to languish," he declared.[31]

The steps that led to the building of the first nuclear-powered submarine took place during Sullivan's tenure and with his blessing. In 1945 American scientists had released the power of the atom in a blinding flash at Alamogordo. Seven years later Captain Hyman George Rickover watched as the keel was laid for the ship he had designed, fought for, and pushed into existence, and heard Secretary of the Navy Dan A. Kimball assert that the work on the *Nautilus* was the "most important piece of development work. . . in the history of the Navy."

More so than anyone else, it was Rickover who convinced the Chief of the Bureau of Ships, Admiral Earle W. Mills, that such a weapon system should be added to the Navy's arsenal. From Washington, Rickover and a group of collaborators moved to Oak Ridge, Tennessee, and began working on a naval pile as an unofficial project to which the Atomic Energy Commission turned its face. To further the project, Rickover needed to have Sullivan declare an atomic-powered submarine a military necessity. He wrote the necessary letter, won over Admiral Mills, and with the help of then Lieutenant Commander Edward L. Beach and other submariners got the letter into the hands of another submariner, the Chief of Naval Operations, Nimitz, who won Sullivan's approval. Sullivan also helped by objecting both to changing the charter of the Armed Forces Special Weapons Project, a joint organization that used the special talents of officers regardless of service affiliation, and to the reallocation of research funds to the services, on the grounds that such allocation would violate the National Security Act and impede the legal obligations placed upon the Navy by the act to conduct research and development in "the fields of aircraft, weapons, ships, [and] tactics."[32] With his backing, moreover, Rickover was able to win the cooperation of the Atomic Energy Commission and, by May 1948, also of the General Electric and Westinghouse companies. By early August 1948 a new Nuclear Power Division in the Bureau of Ships headed by Rickover tackled the atomic reactor before going on with the building of the *Nautilus* herself; by 1950 preliminary work was complete and actual construction began on the *Nautilus*.[33]

Sullivan meanwhile countered charges, emanating largely from the Air Force, that surface ships and carrier-based planes had lost their value because ships were vulnerable to atomic bombs; that sea power would be unimportant in the next war because it would be an atomic war waged wholly by long-range aircraft or guided missiles or both, and would be over in a week or two, without the movement of major military forces; that the atomic bomb, because so destructive, was a quick key to certain victory; that long-range aircraft had eliminated the need for surface fleets and sea-going air power; and that the United States did not need a large fleet because no unfriendly power had a large one.[34] To a great degree the argument was fallacious. At a time when there was no defense against it, strategic bombing with atomic weapons could achieve great destruction at small cost in terms of men and resources. But the Air Force was deficient in intercontinental planes that could deliver the bombs, could not rely upon the use of foreign bases, and lacked the power to absorb or divert atomic attacks upon the United States. It had also to depend upon the other services for forces needed in any kind of war. Strategic atomic bombing could not show the flag, be tailored to the precise requirements needed for police actions, be useful in a conventional war, destroy enemy submarines or a widely dispersed fleet, or mount an amphibious invasion. Thus it could not undertake the invasion and occupation needed to consummate victory.[35]

Nevertheless, Sullivan had to counter literally tons of Air Force publicity that demanded that the Air Force be the predominant service because its strategic bombing capability would deter war or, if war came, could annihilate the attacker—early statements of the concepts of massive deterrence and of massive retaliation. To Secretary of the Air Force Symington; Air Force generals Henry H. Arnold, James H. Doolittle, George C. Kenney, George E. Stratemeyer, Vandenberg, and Spaatz; Army generals Elwood R. Quesada, Commanding General of the Tactical Air Command, and Major General James M. Gavin, of airborne operations fame; and the official *Air University Quarterly Review* and the unofficial publication *Air Force*—published by the Air Force Association—the Air Force had supplanted the Navy as the nation's first line of defense. Therefore, all conventional forces including aircraft carriers were made obsolete; the Navy need not develop any strategic air capability; the Navy should supinely give up its air arm—about 30 percent of the Navy—to the Air Force; and the Navy should be reduced to a minor auxiliary service dealing with antisubmarine warfare and sea transportation.[36] The attitude of the new magazine *Aviation Week*, which incorporated *Aviation* and *Aviation News*, was evident in its first editorial, in the issue of 7 July 1947, for it was "convinced that continuation of an air force in being—the largest in the world—backed by an efficient and expandable aircraft manufacturing industry, are [sic] the keys to peace." Among the members of the board of directors of *Air Force* were C. V. Whitney, Assistant Secretary of the Department of the Air Force, and Doolittle and Edward P. Curts, members of the Air Board of the Department, with the aim of the magazine being "a merger with the Air Force on top."[37] Most important was Symington himself. He was a self-made man who had succeeded brilliantly in business, in part by producing air weapons during World War II. He had then served as a troubleshooter for President Truman, beginning as Chairman of the Surplus Property Board and, after January 1946, as Assistant Secretary of War for Air. He was a man with a mission. Tall, handsome, courtly, athletic, and young (he was forty-six years of age in 1947), he had a truly combative spirit

Various Air Force leaders argued that the Air Force had supplanted the Navy as the nation's first line of defense and that the Navy should be reduced to an antisubmarine and transportation force. Among these were Secretary of the Air Force W. Stuart Symington *(above left)*; General George C. Kenney, who had commanded bomber forces in the Pacific in World War II *(right)*; General Carl Spaatz, who had commanded Army Air Corps forces in Europe during World War II and was the first chief of staff of the new Air Force *(below left)*; and Lieutenant General George E. Stratemeyer, a leader of the concept that air power was "indivisible" *(right)*.

OFFICIAL USAF PHOTOGRAPHS

and stuck tenaciously—some said fanatically—to his decisions. As Assistant Secretary of the War for Air he had been one of the architects of the Strategic Air Command, which began operating out of Washington in the spring of 1946 but as of 1 May 1949 had only one unit, located in New Mexico, capable of delivering atomic weapons.[38] Soon after entering his new office he determined that six hundred heavy bombers on widely scattered bases were needed to defend the nation. And that number was a mere beginning. Moreover, at least according to Hanson W. Baldwin, "Symington's methods were dirty pool, dirty politics." The "two-faced" Symington openly undercut Forrestal not only to obtain his own objectives for the Air Force but also to get rid of him and become Secretary of Defense. By calling Forrestal about every half hour to object to the building of a supercarrier he increased the pressure on Forrestal, who was already tense because of problems concerning unification and of Truman's dislike of him as a Roosevelt holdover and chief cabinet dissenter to his policies.[39]

Sullivan opposed a strategy that relied upon a single weapon and single delivery system because such reliance would cause stagnation in the development of other weapons and techniques. That he clearly preferred balanced and flexible forces was revealed in his approval of the reorganization of naval operating forces, effective 1 January 1947, into Atlantic and Pacific "task fleets" capable of dealing with "fast-moving situations." When the Sixth Fleet started operating in the Mediterranean, on 30 September 1946, the United States also picked up the burden the British laid down of policing the world's sea lanes "to insure unvexed travel at sea."

Sullivan enjoyed the counsel of Fleet Admiral Nimitz, the Chief of Naval Operations, only until 17 December 1947, when he ended his active duty. Asked who should succeed him, Nimitz named five eligible admirals: William H. P. Blandy, Commander in Chief Atlantic Fleet; Louis E. Denfeld, Commander in Chief Pacific Fleet; DeWitt C. Ramsey, Vice Chief of Naval Operations; Richard L. Conolly, Commander of U.S. Naval Forces East Atlantic and Mediterranean; and Charles M. Cooke, Commander Naval Forces Far East. Fleet Admiral William D. Leahy recommended to Truman the names of Harold Stark and Denfeld.[40] When the President asked Forrestal who could succeed Nimitz, Forrestal replied "Ramsey, Blandy, and Denfeld," Later he said: "I was somewhat concerned about Denfeld's political activity . . . . However, it's obvious that the President would find Denfeld the easiest of the lot to work with,"[41] "Spike" Blandy, the incisive senior member of the "gun club," was preferred by battleship admirals. Aviators preferred Ramsey, the senior naval aviator. On 12 November Truman approved Denfeld as a compromise candidate, but for a two-year term.[42] On 15 December 1947, the day he became Chief of Naval Operations, Denfeld recognized the importance of naval aviation by choosing an aviator, Arthur W. Radford, as Vice Chief of Naval Operations, a selection Sullivan heartily applauded.

Born in 1891, Denfeld graduated from the Naval Academy and was commissioned an ensign in 1912. After seeing duty in destroyers during World War I, he served in various capacities until June 1937, when he became an aide to Leahy, then Chief of Naval Operations. Throughout most of World War II he served as Assistant to the Chief of the Bureau of Navigation, known after 21 May 1942 as the Bureau of Personnel. After serving as the commander of a

Three contenders as successor to Fleet Admiral Chester W. Nimitz as Chief of Naval Operations were Louis F. Denfeld (*above left*), a battleship admiral; DeWitt Ramsay, the senior naval aviator shown *(right)* with Admiral William F. Halsey while attending a performance of "Brother Rat" in a theater at a South Pacific base during World War II; and Admiral William H.P. Blandy, shown *(below left)* with Admiral Joseph J. Clark to his right. On 15 December 1947, Secretary of the Navy John L. Sullivan congratulated Denfeld as the new Chief of Naval Operations *(right)*.

OFFICIAL U.S. NAVY PHOTOGRAPHS

battleship division that supported the Okinawa landings and as Chief of the Bureau of Naval Personnel, he took over command of the Pacific Fleet on 28 February 1947. The *New York Times* believed he had "one of the most inquiring minds and the most engaging personalities in the Navy," while the *Worcester* (Mass.) *Telegram, Washington Star,* and *Washington Post* thought he would well serve the Navy because of his wide experience in personnel and manpower work. On the other hand, he was not intellectually brilliant and lacked experience in the kind of infighting that characterized the proceedings in the Joint Chiefs of Staff.[43] A personnel man rather than a member of the "Gun Club," he was nevertheless favored by the latter. To prove his friendliness to naval aviation, he wisely chose as his deputy the Navy's senior aviator, Arthur W. Radford.

Sullivan's major tasks were to square his administration with directives Forrestal issued as he sought to unify the services, to operate the Navy efficiently under the extremely tight budgets provided the services by the Truman administration, and to defend what he considered the Navy's proper strategy and roles and missions until these could be redefined to the satisfaction of all three services. If future strategy were to be nuclear strategy, the roles and missions of the services must be modified to fit the new military art. Each service wanted nuclear power; each demanded what it considered to be its rightful share of the defense budget in order to provide it. The result was that the three services simultaneously followed six strategies, one conventional and one nuclear for each. In any event, by late 1947 the Joint Chiefs of Staff, groping toward a procedure for defining and funding a national strategy, decided to reach agreement on a strategic concept and on an outline strategic war plan before attempting to fit their budget within limits established by Forrestal's comptroller.[44]

Forrestal and the service secretaries worked under certain other great difficulties. Truman kept the National Security Council at arm's length because it was unable to prescribe national policy with precision and decisiveness. In part because they lacked a precept for national policy, the Joint Chiefs of Staff failed to provide sound answers to the questions of how much of the nation's resources should be allocated to the services, which service should get what weapons, and which of alternative strategies should be followed. Lacking this information and unwilling to cut deeply into the domestic sector, the President set a military budget ceiling and the Bureau of the Budget and the Secretary of Defense had to cut the recommendations of the Joint Chiefs of Staff to fit it.[45] Small success was enjoyed by the boards and agencies provided in the National Security Act to "coordinate" with the rest of the system. Indeed, to coordinate with their sister services and domestic and foreign defense agencies, by April 1949 the headquarters of the services had representatives on about one hundred and twenty boards and committees.[46] Nor did Congress define for itself the foreign policy objectives of the nation or show clearly how its military budgets related to national policy objectives. The result was that power, although diffused among the three co-equal military services, slowly gathered into the hands of the Secretary of Defense and of his staff, the latter of which ubiquitously intruded into what the service secretaries believed to be their vested rights, thereby making them the men in the middle—required to support Department of Defense policies even if these were ill-considered or unpopular with the services.[47]

Moreover, as members of the National Security Council, the service secretaries had to deal with foreign policy as well as military matters. In 1947 and 1948, for example, they sought solutions to problems connected with such occupied or liberated areas as Italy, Korea, Iran, Trieste, Yugoslavia, Germany, Berlin, China, Japan, and even the Trust Territory of the Pacific Ocean. Service differences over solving American problems in Mediterranean lands must suffice. Overflights of B-29s and of carrier aircraft were made over Italy in mid-December 1947. However, Navy public relations officers on duty in the Mediterranean failed to alert the Italians to the significance of the overflights and of the presence of American carriers in the Mediterranean, whereas the Air Force obtained sensational coverage when it sent a flight of thirty B-29s in mid-April 1948 from Smoky Hill, Kansas, to Germany and when, on 18 September, it had fifty B-29s fly nonstop from Europe, Hawaii, and Japan and two by two fly over twenty-five American cities.[48] When the commander of U.S. Naval Forces Mediterranean asked Sullivan if *Midway* planes could overfly Greece in a show of force, Sullivan talked first with the Under Secretary of State, Robert A. Lovett, then with the Secretary of State, George Marshall. Marshall advised that it would be better not to make it appear that the United States was promising further support to Greece. In consequence, no American naval vessels came closer than five miles from the Greek coast and no overflights were made.[49] Sullivan also had Turkey on his agenda, for he asked the Chief of Naval Operations to prepare a paper on the strategic importance of that country and prepare recommendations on "what we can do to strengthen Turkey and your evaluation of our ability to keep open supply lines to that country in the event of war."[50]

By mid-November 1947 Forrestal had ordered the transfer of functions, personnel, and property to the new Air Force, established policies and procedures concerning defense public relations, directed that no military department make a report or recommendation on proposed or pending legislation to Congress or to the Bureau of the Budget except through interdepartmental coordination, and established a coordinated procurement program for the three services. In this program, one service would acquire a number of major items for all three services. Last, he brought the Munitions Board, the Research and Development Board, and the Joint Chiefs of Staff, formerly outside of it, into his own office.

Representatives of Sullivan, Royall, and Symington met often between early October and mid-november 1947 to aid Forrestal reach decisions on matters involving budget, finance, legislation, personnel, organization, and administration. Of prime importance would be an increase in military pay, improvement in service housing, and augmentation of manpower. With respect to the last, the administration, and about 75 percent of the people polled on the question, favored universal military training and a reorganization of the reserve forces.[51] While Major General Harry Vaughan, Truman's military aide, and various congressmen spoke emphatically for a merger of the Army and Air Force Reserves with the National Guard,

Forrestal directed a Committee on Civilian Components to undertake a "brutally realistic" consideration of all reserve organizations and to report to him as quickly as possible.

During 1947, while the Navy continued long-range research and development programs, it also stored $2 billion worth of weapons found to have been most useful in World War II. Wartime lessons had been built into new ship designs. Many naval bases around the world had been rolled up, however, and the number of operating combatant and auxiliary ships had been reduced drastically, as had the officer corps and enlisted ranks. Provision had been made for an atomic proving ground at Eniwetok. Additional Marines had been sent to join the *Midway* and her escorts in the Mediterranean to support the Truman Doctrine, announced 12 March 1947. Sullivan's directing Nimitz to send a task force to operate in the Gulf of Oman and the Arabian Sea during the summer of 1948 for the stated purpose "of acquiring the knowledge and limitations imposed by the climate and methods of alleviating those conditions" also showed his determination to put pressure on the Russians by a show of force in the Middle East.[52]

While he was still Under Secretary of the Navy, at Forrestal's request Sullivan asked Nimitz how many carriers would be available in the first month of a war to hold the Western Mediterranean, how many would be needed to hold the entire area, and the importance of holding the area in the event of war. Nimitz replied that to prevent the Soviets from building up their strength in the Mediterranean the minimum number of carriers needed to hold a part of the area would be one task group of four carriers; to hold the whole Mediterranean, two task groups of eight carriers; that to put eight carriers in the Mediterranean on D-day twelve carriers would be needed; and that to rotate carrier air groups would require sixteen of these. "If we throw away [our aircraft capability]," Nimitz added, "we shall be restricted to an air campaign of strategic bombing only from one main base. . . .I am of the opinion that to permit our strategic thinking to evolve about a single concept in which air conducts. . .strategic bombing from the United Kingdom will be very unsound." It was Nimitz's judgment that "maintenance of the Mediterranean will be the keystone to any successful war against Russia." If we did not use carriers, the Soviets would take over the entire Mediterranean. "We have the capability; it can be valuable; we should not give it away."[53]

The first session of the Eightieth Congress, which met in January 1947, had been called to consider problems of interim relief for Europe and inflation at home rather than service legislation. As Forrestal put it, the less spent on American military forces, the more could be given to European friends.[54] However, at a time when the Russians were busily subverting Iran, Greece, and Turkey, Spaatz, first Chief of Staff of the Air Force, shocked the American people by saying that he lacked a single squadron that could fight with wartime efficiency.[55] Forrestal therefore assumed a great risk, for although the United States had a monopoly on atomic weapons, its very small stockpile of atomic bombs, unassembled because of the shortage of skilled personnel, was stored in New Mexico instead of being in place in aircraft.[56] Moreover, delivery systems were yet modest: the B-29 had a three-thousand-(later four-thousand-) mile range, but Moscow was six thousand miles distant via the North Pole and the B-36 would not fly until mid-1948. Even after bases were acquired for the B-36 in England in 1948 and four jet engines had been added to its six piston engines, it was not truly an intercontinental bomber. In any event, Forrestal did not involve himself in the preparation of the individual service budgets for fiscal year 1948 even though he was well aware that Air Force enthusiasts were unhappy with what they said were "disproportionate" funds going to the Navy, which in fiscal year 1948 would sustain a strength of 5,793 aircraft.

It might have been better if Forrestal had looked into the service budgets, for Sullivan considered the Navy's budget critical. He told Forrestal that "in that Navy appropriations would be in line with the national economy, it must be assumed that a 'calculated risk' must be taken." Such curtailment would "(a) make it necessary to curtail maintenance and logistic support for the fleet, (b) provide only one group of planes for each carrier, and (c) curtail amounts which could be allocated to material improvement and war reserves." He added: "When I used the expression 'one-shot Navy' before the President's Air Policy Commission, the implication was that, in the event of action, our carrier task forces in the Mediterranean, for example, would have no replacements, trained, ready, immediately available to provide for attrition."[57] To save money, moreover, he had already closed the Navy's West Coast lighter-than-air stations, put them in caretaker status, and shifted all lighter-than-air activity to the Atlantic Fleet and East Coast.[58]

Sullivan had already decided on which ships, planes, and weapons to retain. But how much funding should go to new weapons such as improved submarines, jet aircraft, and a giant carrier that could carry heavy jets? The fiscal year 1946 defense budget was $45 billion; that of 1947 only $14.5 billion; and the $11.25 billion recommended by the Bureau of the Budget for 1948 favored the Army and Air Force with $6.7 billion compared with $4.4 billion for the Navy. Truman spent twice as much time on budget preparation as any preceding president had done. Having built the budget on a "tripod" consisting of himself, the Secretary of the Treasury, and the Director of the Bureau of the Budget, he refused to let the military departments "unbalance" it and so deny the civil sector its due. He believed that each military department would demand a third of the military budget no matter what its actual needs were, and he held the Navy to be the worse offender in this respect.[59]

In the first week in December 1947 Symington and Spaatz's deputy—the tactical air expert General Vandenberg, in his quiet, easy, yet convincing way —told the President's [Thomas K. Finletter] Air Policy Committee that the Air Force needed 131 air groups, or 12,441 planes—70 groups comprised of first-line combat planes and a reserve of 5,295 craft—and an annual production rate of 3,200 aircraft.[60] Neither they nor Air Force officials who succeeded them ever publicized how the magic figure of seventy groups would provide security for the nation or support its interests abroad beyond saying that this was the minimum number needed and that it had taken 243 groups to win World War II. "The size and composition of the 70-group Air Force," it has been said, was "largely pulled out of the blue. It had, in fact, been first advanced early in 1945, before the disappearance of the Alamogordo tower had even so much as demonstrated the feasibility of the fission bomb."[61]

Sullivan told the same committee that naval aviation progressed by "evolution" rather than by "revolution." He wanted only that naval air strength consonant with the Navy's needs. He could point to high efficiency and morale in the Navy's air arm and to the fact that the promotion of currently young aviators meant that in time they would be able to exercise a determining influence upon the Navy's outlook. Although the statements by Symington and Vandenberg had caught Sullivan off guard, he had in rebutting them served notice that the Navy reserved the right to fight for a slow, evolutionary change.[62] As example of this he cited that while the Air Force in 1948 planned to shift almost completely to jet aircraft, the Navy ordered only sixty jets. Of the 1,632 new planes ordered by the Navy in 1948, 95 percent were conventional, propeller-driven types of late-wartime vintage already well integrated into carrier groups. By introducing jets slowly, the Navy compromised between combat efficiency and economy but kept its training, maintenance, and operating expenses for naval aviation at a minimum.[63] However, proof was ample that jets could operate from carriers. They had first operated on a carrier on 21 July 1946. In March 1948 the FJ-1 *Fury* was tested on the *Boxer*, and on 5 May the first all-jet fighter squadron, comprised of sixteen FH-1 *Phantoms*, qualified for carrier duty.

Much was accomplished between the passage of the National Security Act on 26 July and the investiture of Forrestal as the first Secretary of Defense on 17 September, and the end of 1947. The new policy-making machinery provided by the act was in operation, the Air Force was established as a separate entity, functions were assigned the several services, and the leaders of the National Military Establishment began to take hold of their responsibilities. Several shortcomings in organization and administration were nevertheless apparent. The National Security Council was unable to provide specific prescriptions for foreign policies the services were to support, and membership on it by the service secretaries consumed time and effort better spent in administering their own services. Short of assistants, Forrestal was terribly overburdened, and his attempts to lead the services toward unification butted up against the stone walls of service traditions and of mutual jealousies to the point where he had to restrict to a degree the public utterances of their leaders. While the National Security Act gave him "general control" over the military departments, he lacked the power to appoint civilian personnel within them. The act also stated that the military departments would be separately administered, that the service secretaries would have all powers and duties not specifically given to the Secretary of Defense, and that they could appeal directly to the President and to the Bureau of the Budget. In consequence, Forrestal's power was so diluted that he could not follow the active concept of management. Nor could he follow the passive concept, because there was no single top military commander. While he had won his battle in the years 1945 to 1947 against a military merger under a single chief of staff, he had also kept the authority of the Secretary of Defense limited to supervising the military departments and coordinating their procedures. The irony of the situation, as has been said, "is that [he] had unwittingly performed an act of self-emasculation."[64] The top military commanders, the Joint Chiefs of Staff, were similarly divided: they were the primary military planners for the President and for the Secretary of Defense, but because they could not free themselves of individual service particularism they could not plan in the corporate sense and were therefore rendered incapable of movement or of stability.[65]

This is not to say that some happy arrangements were not made. Sullivan and Symington had reached agreement whereby the Naval Academy would provide input to the Air Force until an Air Force Academy provided its own graduates, and the Navy would furnish assistance for continental air defense. Yet bitter argument still continued over which service would have priority in strategic atomic air warfare, in the form both of aircraft and of guided missiles. Sullivan's hackles were raised by a fabulously effective Air Force propaganda campaign that promised more than it could deliver—for the Air Force as yet lacked a truly intercontinental bomber but strenuously opposed the Navy's building of a supercarrier whose improved planes could drop atomic bombs on any spot on earth. Only tentative steps had been taken by the Joint Chiefs of Staff to provide a correlated service budget and to decide on alternative military strategies and the roles the services would play in them. Not until the autumn of 1948 would they establish a committee to devise joint policies and procedures for the three services. Although the Navy was slowly adopting jet aircraft, Symington and his major military advisers demanded a seventy-group Air Force that was extremely expensive to provide and operate. The bedrock solution to the problem was money. Would the President's budget finance the strategies suggested by the Joint Chiefs of Staff? Or would that budget, by favoring the Air Force, cause dollars to determine strategy?

NOTES

1. Robert Greenhalgh Albion and Robert Howe Connery, *Forrestal and the Navy* (New York and London: Columbia University Press, 1962), p. 211.
2. Ibid., pp. 211-13, 214-16; transcript of oral interview by Jerry N. Hess of ADM Robert Lee Dennison, USN (RET), Harry S. Truman Library, 1972, pp. 60-63; Merle Miller, *Plain Speaking: An Oral Biography of Harry S. Truman* (Published by Berkley Publishing Corporation, Distributed by G. P. Putnam's Sons, New York, 1973, 1974), p. 210.
3. Albion and Connery, *Forrestal and the Navy*, pp. 208-16.
4. Walter Millis, ed., with the collaboration of E. S. Duffield, *The Forrestal Diaries* (New York: The Viking Press, 1951), pp. 317-18, 320, 329, 342.
5. Top Secret. H. C. Beauregard, Memorandum for the SECNAV, 13 October 1947, SNP.
6. "John L. Sullivan: The Secretary of the Navy," ANJ 85 (25 October 1947):195.
7. VADM C. H. McMorris, USN, Chairman, The General Board, "General Board of the Navy," ANJ 85 (25 October 1947):195. On 1 January 1948, Sullivan also directed the General Board to "make a study of the composition of the reserve fleets for the purpose of assisting the evaluation of the contribution of the reserve fleets to national security in comparison with the cost of maintenance." (Sullivan to Chairman, GB, 1 January 1948, SNP.) Late in 1949 the boundaries of the ten continental naval districts were made to coincide with those of the six Army and Air Force areas.
8. On 17 April 1948, "items in disagreement" between the services included standards for voluntary enlistment, allocation of inductees, and the race question. The Navy's position on these points was that each service would set its own recruiting standards, which need not be the same for all services; the larger proportion of inductees with high mental caliber should go to the Army and Air Force; and allocations should be made by a mechanical method without regard to race or color, with Negroes to be accepted on the basis of individual qualifications. SECNAV to SECDEF, 17 April 1948, SNP.
9. Seattle, Los Angeles, Monterey, and several other West Coast cities vied to obtain the postgraduate school. The Navy wanted Monterey but could not say so in public. Knowing that Sullivan was an avid golfer, his naval aide, CAPT Fitzhugh Lee, suggested that Sullivan visit the proposed sites. Knowing of the beautiful golf course near the old Hotel Del Monte in Monterey, Sullivan flew to the West Coast with a golfer friend. A senator from Washington was pushing him hard to select Seattle, but it was obvious to Sullivan, golf course or not, that Monterey was the best site. "The Reminiscences of VADM Fitzhugh Lee, USN (RET)," transcript of oral interviews by CDR Etta-Bell Kitchen, USN (RET) (Annapolis, Md.: U.S. Naval Institute, 1970), pp. 199-200.
10. Top Secret. W. John Kenney, Memorandum for the Secretary, 16 December 1947, and Secret. Fitzhugh Lee to John L. Sullivan, 15 January 1948, including ideas dictated by ADM James L. Hollway, Superintendent, USNA, in Minutes of the War Council; H. C. Beauregard, Memorandum to SECNAV, 19 January 1948; Restricted. H. C. Beauregard, Memorandum for the SECNAV, 4 February 1948; Restricted. H. C. Beauregard, Memorandum for the SECNAV, 10 February 1948, Record of Meeting of Four Secretaries on 10 February 1948; John L. Sullivan, Memorandum to the SECDEF, 9 July 1948; Air Force Department, Memorandum to Mr. Forrestal, 27 November 1948; John L. Sullivan, Memorandum for Mr. Symington, 30 December 1948; John L. Sullivan, Memorandum for the SECDEF, 31 January 1949, SNP; USNA Archives, Record Group 12. Dean of Admissions. Subgroup: Registrar's Office. Series: Registrar's Records, Box No. 10.
11. Chief, BUAER, Memorandum to CNO, "Development of Large Bombers for Carrier Based Operations, Discussion Of," 11 December 1945; CAPT A.A. Burke (OP—23), Memorandum for the JAG, "History of the 6A Carrier Project," 11 May 1949, NHD: OA, OP-23 Files; interview with RADM Arthur M. Morgan, USN (RET), Andrews Air Force Base, 6 July 1972.
12. Secret. Chief, BUAER to SECNAV, 1 November 1947, SNP: Scott MacDonald, "CVB's: The Battle Cruisers," NAN, January 1963, pp. 26-28, and "Evolution of Aircraft Carriers: The Turbulent Post-War Years," NAN, October 1963, pp. 22-26.
13. Thomas A. Combs, RADM, USN, Acting Chief of BUAER, to the SECNAV, 7 November 1947, SNP.
14. Although Denfeld and Radford strongly approved the promotion of Clark to Vice Admiral,

in May 1948 Sullivan disapproved because Clark had opposed triservice unification. Denfeld and Radford told Clark to stand by. If, as expected, Dewey should defeat Truman in November and Sullivan should leave office, Clark would relieve VADM Gerald F. Bogan as Commander Air Force Atlantic Fleet and obtain his promotion. Clark served as an inspector for ADM John D. Price, Deputy Chief of Naval Operations (Air) until he was given command of a carrier division in the Atlantic Fleet. On the day after the elections of 1948, Sullivan called Denfeld and said, "You get me another man than Clark for [Bogan's] job!" Denfeld chose VADM Felix Stump to relieve Bogan while Clark hoisted his flag as Commander Division 4 and in January 1949 reported for duty to VADM Forrest Sherman, Commander Sixth Fleet. ADM Joseph J. Clark, USN (RET), with Clark G. Reynolds, *Carrier Admiral* (New York: David McKay Co., 1967), pp. 356-61.

15. Sullivan, endorsement on letter by RADM Thomas A. Combs, 7 November 1947, SNP. See also Millis, ed., *Forrestal Diaries*, p. 333; Paul Y. Hammond, "Super Carriers and B-36 Bombers: Appropriations, Strategy, and Politics," in Harold Stein, ed., *American Civil Military Decisions: A Book of Case Studies* (University: University of Alabama Press, 1963), p. 470.

16. Memorandum for VADM Radford from J. D. Price, OP55R-5, Washington: NHD, OA: Papers of the Chiefs of Naval Operations (hereafter cited as CNO Papers); "Truce in Navy-Air Rivalry," USNWR 25 (3 September 1948):16-17.

17. Futrell, *Ideas, Concepts, Doctrine*, p. 98; "Life Begins at Forty," AF 30 (September 1947):12-13.

18. Secret. Fitzhugh Lee, Memorandum for the SECNAV, 30 January 1948, SNP.

19. Top Secret. H. C. Beauregard, Memorandum for the SECNAV, 13 November 1947, SNP.

20. Conf. H. C. Beauregard. Minutes of the Secretary's Meeting of 7 November with the Secretariat, CNO, and VCNO, 7 November 1947, SNP.

21. James N. Eastman, Jr., Chief, Research Branch, The Albert F. Simpson Historical Research Center, Maxwell Air Force Base, Ala., to the writer, 14 January 1974; Conf. Air Defense Command. AC/S. A-5. Project No. 14. Responsibilities for Air Defense, 19 July 1946; Secret. HQ, Air Defense Command, Mitchell Field, New York. Project 14 A. Responsibilities for Air Defense. 20 November 1946 (courtesy Dr. Eastman); Clement L. Grant, "Air Defense of North America," in Alfred Goldberg, ed., *A History of the United States Air Force, 1907-1957* (Princeton, N.J.: Van Nostrand Reinhold, 1957), pp. 129-38.

22. "The Reminiscences of VADM Herbert D. Riley, USN (RET)," transcript of oral interview by John T. Mason (Annapolis, Md.: U.S. Naval Institute, 1972), pp. 299-303; "The Reminiscences of Hanson W. Baldwin," transcript of oral interview by John T. Mason (Annapolis, Md.: U.S. Naval Institute, 1976), p. 465.

23. H. Struve Hensel, "Changes Inside the Pentagon," *Harvard Business Review* 32 (January-February, 1954):99-101.

24. ANJ 85 (27 September 1947):82.

25. John Nicholas Brown, "Amphibious Warfare and the Atom Bomb," MCG 31 (September 1947):56-58.

26. MAJ Guy Richards, USMC, "Target Eurasia and the Next War," MCG 31 (December 1947):10-18; ANJ 85 (November 15, 1947):11; "Naval Air Power," ANJ 85 (7 February 1948):582, "Inter-Service Controversies," ANJ 85 (February 14, 1948):610; "Sees Strength and Air Power," ANJ 85 (March 20, 1948):749, 755.

27. Dr. Vannevar Bush in *New York Times*, 1 January 1947.

28. See for example CDR John S. McCain, Jr., USN, "Where Do We Go From Here?" USNIP 75 (January 1949):47-52; CDR Edward J. Fahy, USN, "Pushbuttons Need Men," USNIP 75 (February 1949):149-53; Walmer Elton Strope, "The Naval Officer and To-morrow's Navy," USNIP 75 (March 1949):279-87; and MAJ Guy Richards, USMCR, "The Riddle of Combined Arms," USNIP 75 (August 1949):881-89.

29. RADM Daniel V. Gallery, USN (RET), *Eight Bells and All's Well* (New York: W. W. Norton and Co., 1965), pp. 217-19.

30. John Nicholas Brown to Legislative Council, Office of JAG, 12 March 1948, SNP.

31. FADM Chester W. Nimitz, cited in MR 26 (February 1947):23.

32. John L. Sullivan to Forrestal, 19 February 1948, John L. Sullivan, Memorandum for the SECDEF, 26 May 1948, SNP.

33. See Clay Blair, Jr., *The Atomic Submarine and Admiral Rickover* (New York: Henry Holt and Co., 1954), pp. 1-5, 96-115; Heather M. David, *Admiral Rickover and the Nuclear Navy* (New York: G. P. Putnam's Sons, 1970); Richard G. Hewlett and Francis Duncan, *Nuclear Navy, 1949-1962* (Chicago: University of Chicago Press, 1974), pp. 1-257; Ronald Schiller, "Submarine in the Desert," *Collier's* 133 (5 February 1954): 88-91; CAPT Sherman Naymark, USN (RET), "Underway on Nuclear Power: The Development of the *Nautilus*," USNIP 96 (April 1970):56-63.

34. Defense of the Navy during 1947 and 1948 is well illustrated in LT William H. Hessler, USNR, "Geography, Technology, and Military Policy," USNIP 73 (April 1947): 379-90, COMMO Ernest M. Eller, USN, "Sea Power and Peace," USNIP 73 (October 1947):1161-73; Walmer Elton Strope, "The Navy and the Atomic Bomb," USNIP (October 1947):1221-27; MAJ Guy Richards, USMCR, "The Navy's Stake in the Future," USNIP. 74 (Feburary 1948):183-95; LCOL Robert E. Cushman, Jr., USMC, "Amphibious Warfare: Naval Weapon of the Future," USNIP. 74 (March 1948):301-07; and LCDR Malcolm W. Cagle, USN, "The Jets Are Coming," USNIP 74 (November 1948):1343-49. See also Kenneth L. Moll, "Nuclear Strategy, 1945-1949: America's First Four Years," M.A. thesis, University of Omaha, 1965, pp. 69-70.

35. Bernard Brodie, "War Department Thinking of the Atomic Bomb," *Bulletin of the Atomic Scientists* 3 (June 1947):150-55, 168, "Navy Department Thinking on the Atomic Bomb," ibid. 3 (July 1947):177-80, 198-99, and "a Critique of Army and Navy Thinking on the Atomic Bomb," ibid. 3 (August 1947):207-10.

36. See the editorials in AUQR for 1947 and 1948, and such articles as LCOL Frank R. Pancake, USAF, "The Strategic Striking Force," AUQR 2 (Fall 1948):48-56; COL Dale O. Smith, USAF, "Air Power as Peace Power," AUQR 3 (Summer 1949):3-14; MAJ John D. Reid, USAF, "Sentinels of United States Foreign Policy," AUQR 3 (Fall 1949): 25-45; MAJ Robert J. Seabolt, USAF, [Prize Editorial] "Why Emphasize Air Power?" AUQR 3 (Winter 1949):203; GEN Carl Spaatz, USAF, "Evolution of Air Power," MR 27 (June 1947):3-13; MGEN E. R. Quesada, USA, "The Tactical Air Command," MR 27 (September 1947):3-8; LGEN G. E. Stratemeyer, USAF, "Air Defense of the United States," MR 27 (November 1947):307; MGEN J. M. Gavin, USA, "The Future of Airborne Operations," MR 27 (December 1947):3-8; Clark and Reynolds, *Carrier Admiral,* pp. 250-52; Stefan T. Possony, *Strategic Air Power; The Pattern of Dynamic Security* (Washington: Infantry Journal Press, 1949), esp. pp. 1-13, 296-307.

37. Secret. Unsigned memorandum to the SECNAV, 16 March 1948, SNP; Editorial, "Aviation Week Takes a Stand," AW 47 (7 July 1949):82. See also "Budget Wrangle," AW 47 (20 October 1947):7, and in addition Marshall Andrews, *Disaster Through Air Power* (New York: Rinehart and Co., 1950), Louis A. Sigaud, *Air Power and Unification: Douhet's Principles of Warfare and Their Application to the United States* (Harrisburg, Pa.: The Military Service Publishing Co., 1949); Gordon B. Turner, "Air and Sea Power in Relation to National Power," in Gordon B. Turner and Richard D. Challener, eds., *National Security in the Nuclear Age: Basic Facts and Theories* (New York: Frederick A. Praeger, 1960), pp. 227-52.

38. GEN G. C. Kenney, USA, "Strategic Air Command," MR 27 (August 1947):3-7.

39. "Reminiscences of Hanson Weightman Baldwin," transcript of oral interview by John T. Mason (Annapolis, Md.: U.S. Naval Institute, 1976), pp. 459-61.

40. RADM William D. Leahy, USN (RET), to Robert Love, 11 August 1973, courtesy Dr. Love.

41. Millis, ed., *Forrestal Diaries,* p. 325 (entry of 6 October 1947).

42. "The Reminiscences of ADM Charles Donald Griffin, USN (RET)," transcript of oral interview by John T. Mason (Annapolis, Md.: U.S. Naval Institute, 1973), p. 183.

43. Ibid., pp. 192-93; Baldwin, "Reminiscences," p. 465.

44. "Moll, Nuclear Strategy," pp. 132-33; John C. Ries, "Congressman Vinson and the 'Deputy' to the JCS Chairman," MA 30 (Spring 1966):16-24; Paul Richard Schratz, "The U.S. Defense Establishment: Trends in Organizational Structures, Functions, and Interrelationships, 1958-1970," Ph.D. diss., The Ohio State University, 1972), pp. 145-46, 216-17.

45. Memorandum by the Director, Joint Staff to the JCS, on Correlating of Budgets of Army, Navy, and Air Force, with Strategic Planning, 23 October 1947, JCS File 1800/1, CNO Papers.

46. Air Adjutant General, Department of the Air Force, Boards and Committees on which

HQ USAF has Representation, April 1949, copy in SNP.

47. Walter Millis, with Harvey D. Mansfield and Harold Stein, *Arms and the State: Civil-Military Elements in National Policy* (New York: The Twentieth Century Fund, 1958), pp. 181-85; Paul Y. Hammond, *Organizing for Defense: The American Military Establishment in the Twentieth Century* (Princeton, N.J.: Princeton University Press, 1961), pp. 232-47, and "The National Security Council as a Device for Interdepartmental Coordination," APSR 54 (December 1960):899-910; John C. Ries, *The Management of Defense: Organization and Control of the U.S. Armed Forces* (Baltimore, Md.: Johns Hopkins Press, 1964), p. xvii; Edward Kolodziej, *The Uncommon Defense and Congress, 1945-1963* (Columbus: Ohio State University Press, 1966), pp. 36-37; Russell F. Weigley, *History of the United States Army* (New York: Macmillan, 1967), pp. 494-95; Eugene M. Zuckert, "The Service Secretary: Has He a Useful Role?" FA 44 (April 1966):458-49; Alfred D. Sander, "Truman and the National Security Council," JAH 59 (September 1972):369-88.

48. Top Secret. H. C. Beauregard, Memorandum for the SECNAV, 1 December 1947; Conf. Fitzhugh Lee, Memorandum for the SECNAV, 16 December 1947, 19 April 1948, SNP.

49. Top Secret. H. C. Beauregard, Memorandum for Secretary's Diary, 6 January 1948, SNP.

50. Chairman GB to SECNAV, May 4, 1948, H. G. Beauregard to the SECNAV, 11 May 1948, John L. Sullivan, Memorandum for SECDEF, 11 May 1948, SNP.

51. Popular thinking on universal military training may be followed in George H. Gallup, *The Gallup Poll: Public Opinion, 1935-1971*, 3 vols. (New York: Random House, 1972), entries for 17 February and 13 June 1947; 19 January and 9 April 1948; 4 March 1949; 16 and 26 August 1950; 16 March 1951; and 11 January and 14 March 1952.

52. John L. Sullivan, Memorandum to ADM Nimitz, 30 September 1947, SNP.

53. Sullivan, Memorandum for CNO, 7 February 1947; Nimitz, Memorandum for the SECNAV, 9 February 1947, CNO Papers.

54. Millis, ed., *Forrestal Diaries*, pp. 350-51.

55. Zuckert, "The Service Secretary," 459.

56. Harry S. Truman, *Memoirs by Harry S. Truman*, 2 vols. (Garden City, N.Y.: Doubleday, 1955-56), 2:245-46.

57. John L. Sullivan to Forrestal, 10 February 1948, SNP. On VJ-day, the Navy had operated about 1,500 combatant ships; in 1947, about 270. Serious reductions had also been made in the numbers of mine, patrol, amphibious, and auxiliary ships. On VJ-day, the Navy had operated 99 carriers: 20 large, 8 light, and 61 escort. Soon after VJ-day, 2 large, 2 light, 2 heavy escort, and 16 regular escort carriers partially built were scrapped, leaving, however, 3 *Midway* CBVs, 7 *Essex* CVs, 2 *Wright* CVLs, and 9 CVE's on the building ways. Among the ships blasted at the Bikini atomic experiments were the *Saratoga* and the *Independence*. Norman Polmar, *Aircraft Carriers: A Graphic History of Carrier Aviation and Its Influence on World Events* (Garden City, N.Y.: Doubleday & Co., 1949), pp. 478-79.

58. John Nicholas Brown, Acting SECNAV to Hon. Jack Z. Anderson, House of Representatives, 31 July 1947, SNP.

59. Truman, *Memoirs*, 2:33-34.

60. "Air Force Seeks 12,441 Planes for Adequate U.S. Defense Force," AW 47 (8 December 1947):11-12; Editorial, "A Sound Program," ibid., 66.

61. Warner R. Schilling, Paul Y. Hammond, and Glenn H. Snyder, *Strategy, Politics, and Defense Budgets* (New York and London: Columbia University Press, 1962), p. 37. Walter Millis suggested that the number was probably based "more on a deduction as to what the taxpayer would stand for and the air industry could reasonably supply than on a calculation of the probable military requirements." (*Arms and Men*, p. 277.) More to the point is Perry McCoy Smith, *The Air Force Plans for Peace, 1943-1945* (Baltimore and London: Johns Hopkins Press, 1970), pp. 54, 71-74. Smith states that the 70-group figure was reached after two years of discussion by the Post War Division, Air Staff, Plans, and other agencies within and without the Air Staff of the Army and then of the independent Air Force. Five plans were written, starting with 105 groups in July 1943, and ending with 70 groups in August 1945. A 78-group plan included 638,286 men and 32 squadrons; a 75-group plan, 485,000 men. The number of groups in the end depended on the number of men available. It was believed that 400,000 volunteers could be obtained, enough for 70 groups. Since 70 rather than 68 or 69, and the round figure of 400,000

were easy to grasp and remember, the Air Force was set at 70 groups. Two restrictions imposed by General Marshall helped reach this conclusion: the regular postwar military establishment had to be an all-voluntary force, and set budget figures could not be exceeded.

62.   "The Aviation Week," AW 47 (15 December 1947):7.
63.   "Navy Orders 1,632 Planes," AW 48 (12 January 1948):13.
64.   Haynes, *The Awesome Power*, p. 110.
65.   Hensel, "Changes Inside the pentagon." 103.

3
Strategies, Missions, and Defense Budgets: Fiscal Years 1948 and 1949

The second session of the Eightieth Congress, which met on 6 January 1948, would consider revision of the military pay schedules; the military budget for fiscal year 1949, which would go into effect on 1 July 1948; the reports of the President's Commission on Air Policy and of the Congressional Aviation Policy Board; the Marshall Plan; universal military training; selective service; and how unification of the services was progressing. Also to be considered would be legislation involving various Navy public works, to make the Waves permanent, to establish a single system of military justice, and to revise *Navy Regulations 1920* in consequence of World War II experience.

Secretary of the Navy John L. Sullivan said little for two months while he familiarized himself with departmental problems. Well timed to influence Congress was his release during the first week in January 1948 of a paper the Chief of Naval Operations, Fleet Admiral Chester W. Nimitz, wrote before leaving office the previous December. In this paper, entitled "The Future Employment of Naval Forces," Nimitz asserted that the United States would use its command of the sea only to assure its national security and in support of the United Nations. Naval air-sea forces had contributed mightily to the destruction of Germany and of Japan in World War II; these must be maintained in balanced fashion. As he saw it, the Navy would be used defensively against any attacker and offensively by delivering bombing attacks from land- and carrier-bases, occupying selected advanced bases, and destroying enemy lines of communication. These functions, both defensive and offensive, could be undertaken best by the Air Force and Navy, with the Navy carrying the war to the enemy so that it would not be fought on United States soil.[1]

At the moment Nimitz wrote, the Secretary of the Air Force, W. Stuart Symington, demanded a seventy-group Air Force program to include 6,869 aircraft, among them 436 medium and light bombers, some 1,800 trainers, 936 transports, 2,188 fighters, and miscellaneous craft. "But the headline item," it has been said, "was a request for 988 heavy bombers. The glamour girl in that category was to be the B-36."[2] However, the budget makers for fiscal year 1949 would provide only two thousand airplanes for both the Air Force and the Navy.[3] As expected, Congress balked at providing the $6 billion Symington wanted—a sum almost five times greater than Air Force appropriations for fiscal year 1948—but Symington was bolstered by the report of the President's Air Policy Commission, which was chaired by Thomas K. Finletter. The report, entitled *Survival in the Air Age* and made public on 13 January 1948, stated that the "military establishment must be built around the air arm." It made the front page of almost every newspaper and provided *Time* with its story of the week. The voice of the Air Force Association, *Air Force*, devoted an entire issue to it, an issue it distributed not only to members of the association but to national, state, and local leaders.

Thomas K. Finletter was chairman of the President's [Truman's] Air Policy Commission, which on 13 January 1948 reported that the "military establishment must be built around the air arm." From May 1950 to January 1953, Finletter was the Secretary of the Air Force.

OFFICIAL USAF PHOTOGRAPH

While a Navy and Ground Force would be maintained, said the report, "it is the Air Force and Naval Aviation on which we must mainly rely. Our military security must be based on air power." In fiscal year 1948, ground and sea forces received $7.25 billion and the Air Force $2.85 billion. For fiscal year 1949, the report suggested $7.75 billion for the ground and sea forces and $5.45 billion for the Air Force. It called for a first-line force of 12,400 new planes organized into 70 regular, 27 National Guard, and 34 Air Reserve groups and in addition 8,100 modern replacement aircraft and 401,000 men in Air Force uniform. Among other items, it called for the Navy immediately to increase its annual aircraft procurement in order to equip the fleet with modern planes after those of World War 11 vintage were exhausted, and for the Air Transport Service and the Naval Air Transport Service to be consolidated. The last was accomplished on 4 February, effective 1 June, with a Military Air Transport Service directed by an Air Force general with a Navy rear admiral as his deputy. During the spring of 1949 the Navy was assigned responsibility for operating all military sea transportation.

The Finletter report concentrated on air policy, not military policy as whole, for the two years or so that the United States was expected to enjoy its atomic monopoly.[4] It did not recommend the augmentation of ground and naval forces for a war of limited scale such as might have to be fought in Italy, Greece, Korea, or Palestine. To the public, oversold by Air Force propaganda—Air Force writers always capitalized Air Power—air power meant the Air Force. Navy men saw the report as an Air Force document, which it largely was, that provided for only a temporary policy and grossly overlooked both the usefulness of the naval air arm and the fact that there was no defense against the atomic bomb.

Rear Admiral Edwin A. "Batt" Cruise, who headed the Air Warfare Division in the Office of Deputy Chief of Naval Operations (Air), spoke for naval aviators when he said that the number of naval aircraft and of both fleet and escort carriers called for by the report was too low. The report recommended 5,793 aircraft and 11 fleet and 3 escort carriers; the Joint Chiefs of Staff instead approved 16 large and medium carriers and 16 light and escort carriers. Moreover, the commission cut the Joint Chiefs' recommendation of 23,199 aircraft for the Air Force to 12,400. Cruise also bridled at the statement in the report that a counteroffensive air force, alone, could not only deliver retaliatory strikes but would also have the ability "to seize and hold the advanced positions from which we can divert the destruction from our homeland to [the enemy's]."[5] How could the Air Force "seize and hold" advance bases without the Army and Navy? Could not a number of mobile carriers do the job better, especially if overseas bases were unavailable to the Air Force? By inference, at least, naval aviators challenged the capability of the Air Force to perform its offensive air mission. And this at a time when the Navy had few officers really knowledgeable about atomic weapons and their delivery systems.

Nimitz's concept of bombing the heartland of Russia with naval aircraft and the Navy's demand for supercarriers sat badly with Symington, even though Sullivan stated that the Navy had no intention of assuming Air Force responsibilities for strategic bombing and the Secretary of Defense, James V. Forrestal, wondered if the Air Force "had really faced up to the urgent strategic and tactical problem of whether or not the bomber could survive against modern radar defenses and the new jet fighters armed with Rockets."[6]

In late 1941 when the B-17, with a radius of six hundred miles, was the most advanced strategic air weapon available, the Army Air Corps contracted for two experimental B-36's with the Consolidated Aircraft Corporation. The B-36 was to be an intercontinental bomber that could fly ten thousand miles at 250 to 350 miles per hour and carry a ten-thousand-pound bomb load. In 1943 the War Department authorized the Army Air Forces to contract for one hundred of these planes. When the war ended, Hoyt S. Vandenberg, Deputy Chief of Operations, Army Air Forces, nevertheless continued the contract. In the summer of 1946, after an experimental XB-36 actually flew, General George C. Kenney, Commander of the newly established Strategic Air Command, suggested canceling the contract because the plane was too slow, had a sixty-five hundred rather than ten-thousand-mile range, lacked self-sealing gasoline tanks, and was inferior to the advanced B-29 known as the B-50. General Nathan F. Twining, Commander of the Air Material Command, said that improvements in the B-36 could be expected, as did the Chief of Staff of the Army Air Forces, General Carl Spaatz. Since other bombers like the B-47 and the B-49 "Flying Wing" were on the way, a special Air Force Aircraft and Weapons Board was convened in the summer of 1947 to decide whether to keep or cancel the contract for one hundred B-36s. Given the urgency of the international situation, the board decided to keep the B-36 as an "interim" heavy bomber.[7] Even though perhaps half of the top officers in the new Air Force would cancel the B-36, Symington, it has been said, "cast the deciding vote to push on with the best of a bad deal."[8]

Forrestal let each service secretary air his views, even though he might disagree with what was said. Symington took advantage of this permissiveness and in an article in the *Saturday Evening Post* challenged Nimitz's views on naval aviation. In rebuttal someone leaked to the press, and Drew Pearson made capital of it, a memorandum written to Nimitz by a strong advocate of naval aviation, Rear Admiral Daniel V. Gallery, who held that the Navy was the service "destined to deliver the atom bomb" and concluded that "it is time right now for the Navy to start an aggressive campaign aimed at proving that the Navy can deliver the atom bomb more effectively than the Air Forces [sic] can."[9] After getting Nimitz to sign a statement that the Gallery memorandum did not represent his views, Sullivan reprimanded Gallery and disavowed the memorandum.[10] As yet, Sullivan well knew, the Navy had done little to prepare itself for atomic operations.[11] But he must have known, for Gallery pointed it out, that the Air Force wanted production of atomic bombs restricted to the ten thousand-pound "Fat Man," which Air Force bombers alone could deliver, and to stop development of lighter but even more powerful bombs that naval aircraft could carry.[12]

On 12 January 1948, President Harry S. Truman asked Congress for an $11 billion defense appropriation for fiscal year 1949, only $121 million less than the year before, with about half to go to aviation activities and half to ground and surface forces. Of the total the Air Force would receive $4.7 billion, enough for fifty-five but not seventy groups; the Army also $4.7 billion; and the Navy $3.5 billion. Sullivan accordingly suggested reductions in shipbuilding but increases in naval air power. His shipbuilding program, which would cost a modest $230 million over a five-year period, called for an expenditure of only $16 million in 1949, with $6 million to go toward construction of a supercarrier. Moreover, because of "revolutionary" postwar developments in undersea warfare he preferred to emphasize antisubmarine training instead of operating battleships.

Late in December 1947 the Director of the Budget, James E. Webb, had notified Sullivan that following the item "Procurement of Ships" in the fiscal year 1949 budget there was the statement "No 1949 Program." Sullivan urgently appealed for reconsideration, saying that Webb was striking a serious multiple blow at national defense. He concluded that "all of the types recommended for the 1949 naval shipbuilding program are considered to be mandatory and especially to the national security. Only by the continuance of the building program can we avail ourselves of our technological advances, maintain our striking capabilities, and guard against attack," and he recommended that $30.4 million be restored to his budget.[13] However, Webb would agree to the building of the supercarrier only on condition that Sullivan sponsor legislation to stop construction on thirteen ships and transfer the funds thus saved to her.

Contracts for all wartime naval ship construction not more than 20 percent completed were cancelled by 1 March 1946, leaving thirteen ships on the stocks. Sullivan agreed that the $337 million allocated to them be transferred to the supercarrier. He would also stop the conversion of a battleship and of a cruiser to guided missile ships and use the $308 million thus saved for building four fast-submergence types among fourteen new submarines, building a new antisubmarine "killer" ship larger than a destroyer, modernizing one carrier and one submarine, and building various new "prototype" ships that would give the Navy invaluable experience in building larger numbers if they were needed.[14]

After nine months of study, in the first week in March 1948 the Joint Congressional Air Policy Board, chaired jointly by Senator Ralph Owen Brewster (R., Me.) and Representative Carl Hinshaw, reported, with Brewster asking Sullivan to propose legislation to place the report in effect.[15] The board had asked Sullivan to provide by 1 December 1947: "(1) number of operating aircraft presently required; (2) the requirements for aircraft in storage; (3) operating requirements at the time American cities are open to mass destruction; and (4) procurement in the event of hostilities.'' In conference with the Army and Air Force, the Navy had agreed that the target date for planning purposes would be 1955. Admiral Forrest Sherman had stressed that the decisions to be reached by the Navy and presented to the Joint Chiefs of Staff were the most serious decisions since V-J Day, and Admiral Nimitz had required input from both the operations and material bureaus ''since aircraft and ships cannot reasonably be separated from the integrated whole.''[16]

On 12 March 1948, Hinshaw stated that delay and diversion had created a ''shocking, deplorable situation'' in the National Military Establishment and that instead of ''unification'' the American people were getting ''triplification.''[17] The Brewster-Hinshaw report reflected this conclusion. Overlooking the great difficulties the Joint Chiefs of Staff faced in trying to define military roles and missions, it severely criticized them for remaining loyal to single service traditions and failing to furnish a unified strategic air defense plan. In consequence the committee had had to proceed merely on statements of requirements prepared separately by the service secretaries. It also criticized the naval policy of rotation of duty for naval aviators, noting that in many cases these had to do ''deck duty'' before qualifying for promotion in certain ranks—a criticism Sullivan rejected because aviators must know how to command as well as how to fly. Whereas the board recommended a seventy-group Air Force program, or 20,541 planes, the Air Policy Commission had recommended 8,000 first-line planes for the Navy until the Joint Chiefs prepared strategic plans and integrated requirements, and a total of 14,500 naval aircraft. After again noting that loyalty to traditions prevented the services from integrating their air programs, the board set 30 June for the presentation of such plans to the President and Congress. While the report dealt with various matters, it included a favorable statement on naval air: ''Existence of opposing weapons in quantity, and carriers to deliver them is a restraint upon any nation contemplating attack. Possession of weapons in quantity, and carriers to deliver them in overwhelming force, if attack comes, is judged the best and surest protection against defeat and slavery.'' Last, the report held the Bureau of the Budget in grave error in underestimating the costs of the air program. If the programs suggested were adopted, Congress must either raise taxes or engage in deficit financing. Better, then, to reduce other than military governmental expenditures.[18]

Bolstered by a draft statement on ''Balanced Defense Forces'' prepared by Sullivan,[19] Forrestal pointed out that an increase from fifty-five to seventy air groups would cost from $15 billion to $18 billion and necessitate a complete realignment of the balanced-power concept of the armed forces. If the Air Force expanded, carrier, cruiser, submarine, tanker, and other fleet elements must also increase in order to supply and sustain overseas Air Force bases. Then, even though the Joint Chiefs were still considering the seventy-group program, the House Committee on Armed Services unanimously approved it, on the ground that it should be accomplished before Russia acquired the atomic bomb. The committee then endorsed an additional appropriation of

$725 million, of which $450 million would go to the Air Force and the rest to the Navy's air arm, and the House approved.[20] Truman, Sullivan, and the Chief of Naval Operations, Louis E. Denfeld, as well, had supported Forrestal's call for a fifty-five-group Air Force. However, Symington had availed himself of the privilege granted service secretaries in the National Security Act to go over the head of the Secretary of Defense, pressed the seventy-group plan on the House, and won his point even though Sullivan noted that the Navy would have to increase from 460,000 to 550,000 men if the Senate and the President approved.[21]

On 12 February, Sullivan met with the National Security Council, which discussed America's position and policy in Greece, Turkey, Italy, Palestine, and China. While the Joint Chiefs would send additional arms to Italy, they agreed that to send enough American soldiers to be of consequence in Greece would involve a partial mobilization of the nation. However, Forrest Sherman, commanding the Sixth Fleet, immediately showed the flag by deploying his ships to Greek ports. Upon learning that the Royal Hellenic Air Force lacked planes to fight communist guerrillas, Symington suggested sending various SB2Cs Sullivan had as a surplus. Sullivan reacted instantly: he had two planes put in a Greek merchantman ready to sail from New York and forty-nine others in the escort carrier USS *Sicily*.[22] Rear Admiral Joseph J. Clark, whose TF-87 visited Greece, observed loyal Greeks using the SB2Cs effectively.[23] With respect to China, the National Security Council decided to furnish Chiang Kai-shek $550 million and then try to solve the problem of upholding his "corrupt, inefficient, and impotent government without at the same time withdrawing entirely from its support." In a briefing he gave at the White House, General Alfred Gruenther, Director of the Joint Staff, stated that American commitments in the field of foreign relations exceeded the nation's military capabilities. Secretary of State George Marshall put the dilemma extremely well when he spoke about the Greek situation and the need for universal military training, saying that "the trouble [is] that we are playing with fire while we have nothing with which to put it out." Unfortunately, the defense establishment was not yet "unified"; there was as yet no really unified military policy or strategic plan to follow; and the demand for a seventy-group Air Force undercut the proposal for universal military training that Truman had laid before Congress and that was avidly supported by the Army.[24]

After hearings, from 14 February to 8 March, were held on Sullivan's budget request by the House Committee on Appropriations, Sullivan, Secretary of the Army Kenneth C. Royall, and Symington, without consulting the Joint Chiefs of Staff, concurred on a budget report to Forrestal that recommended adding 240,000 men to the Army, 63,000 to the Navy, 11,000 to the Marine Corps, and 35,000 to the Air Force. Cross purpose was evident when Royall asked for "undisputed air supremacy" and the retention of "our present sea superiority."[25]

When Sullivan was busy with budget and building problems, Congress approved an organization for his department that centralized power more than ever in the Office of the Secretary of the Navy and in the Office of the Chief of Naval Operations. Effective 5 March 1948, the organization of the Navy found effective during the war was made permanent. Under its civilian leaders the Navy Department would have a Chief of Naval Operations appointed by the President for a four-year term. He would be the principal adviser to the Secretary of the Navy and be responsible to him for the use of the operating forces. A Vice Chief of Naval Operations, also to be nominated by the President, would have those duties determined by the Chief of Naval Operations. Six Deputy Chiefs of Naval Operations detailed by the Secretary of the Navy would head the various bureaus, while an undesignated number of Assistant Chiefs of Naval Operations could be named by the Chief of Naval Operations. A new office, that of Naval Inspector General, would inquire into matters relating to the efficiency of the Navy; and the Secretary of the Navy could appoint a Chief and a Vice Chief of Naval Material. Except for the Chief of Naval Operations and Vice Chief of Naval Operations, the Secretary of the Navy was thus authorized to name all the bureau chiefs and the chiefs of the two material posts. The bureau chiefs therefore lost much of the autonomy they had previously enjoyed. The Navy's bilinear organization was retained, with the transfer of the Hydrographic Office, Naval Observatory, and Communications Annex to field activities, effective 1 July 1948, being made only in order to clarify their status as operational activities instead of administrative offices of the Navy Department.[26] With the organization of his office now stabilized, on 31 March 1948 Sullivan allocated duties and responsibilities to himself and to his civilian executive assistants. He himself would be responsible for "policy control," public relations, and morale and welfare of the Navy, and would provide naval representation on the Military Liaison Committee to the Atomic Energy Commission.[27]

At Forrestal's request the military departments had submitted their views on how Executive Order 9877, which assigned roles and missions, should be revised. Upon reviewing them Forrestal wrote the service secretaries that he realized that reaching unanimous agreement on roles and missions would be extremely difficult. Moreover, such agreement could not be reached until the Joint Chiefs of Staff completed their joint strategic plans. However, he preferred to have the Joint Chiefs finish their strategic plans to issuing new orders and then having to rescind them.[28]

As already inidicated, the Joint Chiefs, limited to a staff of one hundred officers from all the services, had worked hard and long on reaching accord on service roles and missions. Forrestal had asked for a final report on the matter by 8 March, "with a split paper if necessary." On the third the chiefs had tried for most of the day to agree on a paper. However, a report to Sullivan by his counsel stated that

the Army and Air Force are lined up against the Navy on the roles and missions of Navy aviation and the Marine Corps. Army and Air Force are still adhering to their fundamental philosophy, favored by Dr. [Vannevar] Bush, that there should be really only one military department and one military service. Admiral

Arthur Radford pointed out that the major difficulty in having the JCS draft a single overall plan was that such a plan is impossible until the United States plans to initiate an offensive. A dictator's staff can come up with a single plan because they know when the dictator plans to move.[29]

Two days later, after the Joint Chiefs met again, Sullivan was told by Admiral Denfeld that "the JCS deliberations on assignments of roles and missions were still deadlocked with the Army and Air Force lining up against the Navy. The

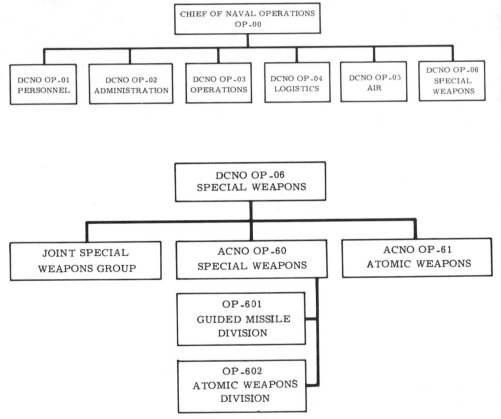

After a life of thirteen months, DCNO, OP-06 was disestablished in favor of OP-57, an ACNO for Guided Missiles in the Office of DCNO (Air), OP-05, and the atomic energy and atomic weapons development functions were placed in OP-36, in the Office of DCNO (Operations), OP-03, and renamed the Atomic Defense Division. OP-55 was the Air Warfare Division and, until Secretary Matthews disbanded it, OP-23 was under DCNO, Administration, OP-02. This organizational pattern was retained until 1954.

Army-Air Force party line is that the Unification Act is wrong and needed to be amended. The attack is on the Marine Corps and the role of naval air . . . .''[30]

In October 1947 Lieutenant General Lauris Norstad, the Army Director of Plans and Operations—soon to become the first Deputy Chief of Staff, Operations, USAF—wrote Royall that there were great differences between Army and Army Air Corps and the Navy "that cannot be resolved by the exercise of patience, tolerance, and mutual confidence on both sides." These concerned organization and operations, planning concepts, and personnel. The first item grew out of the National Security Act, the third out of recruiting and other practices of much less importance. The second, however, the planning concepts, involved differences over budget allocations, which in turn controlled plans and forces. Whereas the Navy would be happy with a general statement in a joint outline strategic war plan that allowed commanders flexibility to meet novel conditions, the Army would add detailed statements to such a plan. Norstad thus locked plans and budget into a straightjacket that countered naval wartime experience and froze future service roles and missions.[31] While Nimitz told Sullivan that he interpreted Norstad to mean that "there is an Army view to the effect that as a preliminiary to future planning the naval establishment should be reduced starting with naval aviation and the Marine Corps,"[32] on 28 February Royall fanned the flames by writing Forrestal, sending copies to Sullivan and Symington, that

> it seems to me that the fundamental difficulty is the different approach of the Navy on the one hand and the Army and the Air Force on the other hand. The Navy seems to me to want a completely integrated striking force which includes land, sea and air and which enables the Navy to perform its functions without any reliance on the other departments. The Army and Air Force each seem to favor the maximum of reliance on the other departments for activity within the normal fields of these other departments.

The differences of approach were so fundamental that they must be resolved before "we can hope to move much further forward toward unification," Royall concluded.[33]

On 4 February Sullivan had been given a report that reviewed the long and acrimonious Marshall-Arnold-King correspondence on the employment of aircraft for antisubmarine warfare during World War 11 for any light it might provide on what had formed the basis for restricting the employment of naval land-based aircraft. The review revealed the basic differences in organizational concepts. While it did not provide a basis for agreement for restricting the employment of naval land-based aircraft, it well described the Navy and Air Force concepts of the employment of air power:

> The *Navy concept* maintains that the *function* should be the basis of organization, i.e., the Army, Navy, and Air Force should be assigned basic functions and given the weapons and equipment to fulfill the functions regardless of whether the weapons operate on land, sea or in the air. The Navy concept maintains further that the fundamental objective of all military services is

essentially the same: that no service should be artifically restricted in the employment of its weapons as opportunity offers, provided of course that the basic function is also fulfilled.

> The *Army-Air Force concept* maintains that the *weapon* should be the basis of organization, i.e., that the Air Force, for instance, should control and operate all aircraft and perform all functions of which the aircraft is capable, the Navy should have control and operate all ships, etc. . . .
>
> The Army-Air Force concept has no counterpart in business and government but is a purely military concept devised by military authorities in Germany and England, i.e., the German Army and the Royal Air Force.[34]

Thus forearmed, on 10 March Sullivan prepared a fairly heated response to Forrestal about Royall's memorandum. Forrestal knew, he began, that "the Navy *has* had an integrated striking force for many years. It desires to retain this force in the interest of national security and in accordance with the National Security Act of 1947. This does not lessen in any way the Navy's strong desire for complete cooperation and joint utilization of facilities and services where such can be done without prejudice to the interest of national security and where economies can be effected." He agreed with Royall that the differences of approach were fundamental and must be resolved before more unification could be achieved. However, Congress had considered all phases of the problem of unification before adopting the National Security Act, and "The Navy accepted this resolution as final." The arguments now being propounded within the Joint Chiefs of Staff had also been fully aired and digested. Therefore, Sullivan concluded, the differences of approach were due to the degree with which the services supported the National Security Act, with the Army and Air Force attacking the act itself by countering the integrated functions it gave to the Navy and its aviation and to the Marine Corps.[35]

Starting in February 1948 two officers of the Air Force, two of the Army, one of the Navy, and Lieutenant General Merwin H. Silverthorn, USMC, had talked roles and missions. As Silverthorn recalled, " . . . the great disagreement was between Naval aviation and the Air Force. The Air Force, of course, wanted to run everything that flew. . . . Second to that was the Army versus Marine Corps in amphibious operations. There was not good feeling on that committee." He added:

> The Air Force was a brand-new outfit, and they just wanted anything they could get ahold of. . . . It was absolutely heresy that anybody could operate an airplane if he didn't have an Air Force uniform on. Everything had to be theirs. . . . Of course the Air Force were Army officers . . . until a few months before, . . . so there was still a good bond between those two. And so the Army certainly gave the Air Force psychological backing if not verbal backing. They remained silent if they didn't actually side in with the Air Force on certain things.[36]

After arguing all day, "discuss, discuss, discuss *ad infinitum, ad nauseum,*" Silverthorn in the late afternoon would brief Admiral Radford and plan the Navy replies for the next day. He would then brief the Commandant of the

Marine Corps, General Clifton B. Cates. Last, he would talk with General Ray "Torch" Robinson, USMC, Director of Plans and Policies, who would break out some of his people to assemble data needed for the next day. In this way, finally, definitions were provided for service roles and missions. When Forrestal could not get the Joint Chiefs to agree to them, the committee was set to work again. Their conclusions were taken by Forrestal to Key West. [37]

Forrestal excluded the service secretaries and the Commandant of the Marine Corps—the last of whom felt as though he had been slapped in the face[38]—from the secret meeting that, with Truman's permission, he called with the Joint Chiefs of Staff and various others for three days starting 11 March at Key West, Florida, to determine upon military roles and missions as a vital step toward reaching agreement upon a defense budget. One of the notes he prepared for the meeting read: "The Navy . . . would keep its own air power, but would have to realize that budget limitations might compel it to 'make do' with help from others; that it would, for example, have to give the Air Force crews training in antisubmarine work and the close support of amphibious landings." Moreover, "function of strategic bombing is the Air Force's," and "the Navy is to have the Air necessary for its mission, but its mission does not include the creation of a strategic air force."[39] To those who wanted him to shut the Navy out of the strategic air bombing mission and build the world's greatest air force, he replied that the nation could not rely solely upon a single agent or weapon as an assurance for peace. That assurance could be obtained only through the coordinated efforts of the entire military establishment.[40]

The debate at Key West was heated at times, as when Admiral Radford charged the Air University with teaching the doctrine of "ONE Air Force" and that the aircraft carrier was obsolete, a charge that Hanson Baldwin repeated in the *New York Times* after he had visited the Air University.[41] Sullivan promptly called the charge to the attention of Forrestal, Symington, and Royall. On the fifteenth of March he directed that the memorandum he had written to Forrestal on the tenth not be sent,[42] a decision he rued when Silverthorn, who was on duty in the Strategic Planning Section, Office of the Chief of Naval Operations, sent his Committee on Research and Reorganization nine pages of documentation of Army and Air Force attacks on the Marine Corps alone subsequent to the passage of the National Security Act.[43] In consequence of the latter, on 10 May Sullivan sent to Symington with a copy to Forrestal, a rebuttal to Symington's having taken umbrage at the Navy's criticism of the teaching of the Air University, which included lectures by such extreme devotees of air power as Alexander P. de Seversky and the use of texts critical of the effectiveness of carriers in World War II.[44]

The paper entitled "Functions of the Armed Forces and the Joint Chiefs of Staff," it was reported early in April, assigned certain hitherto disputed duties as the "primary" responsibility of one of the services and at the same time made them "collateral" or supporting functions of certain other services. Strategic bombing, for example, was a primary Air Force function but a collateral function for the Navy and Marine Corps. Moreover, Forrestal stated that the Navy would not be prohibited from attacking any targets, inland or otherwise, necessary for the accomplishment of its mission.

As was revealed later, Section I of the paper dealt with such principles as integration of the armed forces, prevention of unnecessary duplication, and the coordination of operations. Section II defined the "common functions" of the services and authorized the Secretary of Defense to designate one of the military departments to serve as the executive agency for unified commands. The chain of command ran from the Secretary of Defense to the service secretary. Since the latter was to designate his military chief as executive agent in providing the strategic and operational direction of forces at war, and since the military chief would act in such circumstances in the name of the Secretary of Defense, in effect the service secretary was bypassed. Section III authorized the Joint Chiefs of Staff to permit unified commanders to establish subordinate unified commands and, more important, charged the Joint Chiefs with preparing "a statement of military requirements based upon agreed strategic considerations, joint outline war plans, and current national security commitments" to be used by the Secretary of Defense and the Departments in preparing the budget. Sections IV, V, and VI set forth the primary and collateral functions of the services, and Section VII contained a glossary of terms and definitions.

In addition to the normal ground forces function, the Army was given the function of organizing, training, and equipping antiaircraft artillery units and primary interest in developing airborne doctrines, procedures, and equipment of common interest to the Army and Marine Corps. The Navy would prepare primarily for prompt and sustained combat operations at sea "and for air and land operations incident thereto." Another Navy primary responsibility was for the "amphibious training of all forces as assigned for joint amphibious operations." Further primary functions included naval reconnaissance; antisubmarine warfare; protection of shipping; minelaying, including its air aspects; and naval, including naval air, forces for the defense of the United States against air attack. While the Marines could operate with the fleet and seize or defend naval bases, they could also conduct "such land operations as may be essential to the prosecution of a naval campaign." However, it was specifically provided that "these functions do not contemplate the creation of a second land Army." Primary missions of the Air Force included strategic air warfare and the air defense of the United States. Collateral functions included the conduct of antisubmarine warfare, protection of shipping, and aerial minelaying.

The Joint Chiefs of Staff were to act as single service members who would present to the Joint Chiefs as a corporate entity the budget authorization and the weapons systems needed to perform both primary and collateral functions. Any chief who disagreed with another in a field of primary responsibility could go directly to the Secretary of Defense for a decision.[45] Forrestal approved the Key West Agreement on 21 April. If Truman also approved, he would issue a new executive order placing it into effect and repeal Executive Order No. 9877, dated 26 July 1947, which he issued after signing the National Security Act. Truman asked Clark Clifford to study the agreement. Clifford consulted with Admiral William Leahy, General Harry Vaughan, leaders of the Bureau of the Budget, and others and recommended approval of the first revisions in the military reorganization provided for in the National Security Act.

Truman's Executive Order No. 9950, of 21 April 1948, unlike the revoked No. 9877, stated that the roles and missions of the armed services could not be amended merely at the will of a president.[46] Instead of being an operational or command document, however, the Key West Agreement served merely as guidance for planners in determining force requirements and budget estimates for strategic plans. It reflected the Joint Chiefs' agreement, on the least-common-denominator level, on how the services would fight a war with the most likely enemy, the Soviet Union, with doctrine and weapons largely derived from World War II. It did not address itself to service functions and cooperation needed for limited war, coalition strategy, or nuclear war, even though a paragraph most probably written by Forrestal stated that the Secretary of Defense would be responsible for modifying service roles and missions in keeping with technological advances and changes in the international situation. And it failed to mention national interests and objectives and the strategic concepts that would be employed to support them.[47] In a Memorandum for the Record dated 26 March 1948, Forrestal disseminated to all concerned a paper entitled "Functions of the Armed Forces and the Joint Chiefs of Staff." In a memorandum for the Joint Chiefs of Staff on the Functions Paper, however, under date of 1 July 1948, he modified paragraph 5 so as to read:

> Nothing in the foregoing shall, in itself, be construed as placing arbitrary restrictions on those material development programs and projects of an individual service which are considered essential by that service . . . . It is intended that an individual service is to be permitted to carry through the development stage any material improvement or new weapon development program considered by that service to be essential in the interest of increased effectiveness of its weapons, material, or equipment. The ultimate application and utilization of the product of such a development program shall, of course, be subject to the examination and recommendation of the Joint Chiefs of Staff on the basis of its contribution to the over-all war effort.[48]

Fundamental disagreements between the services over basic strategy still remained, and some definitions of roles and missions were broad enough to permit differences of interpretation. Professional military men devoted to the objective of national security could thus disagree on how the objective could best be achieved and therefore on how the defense budget should be allocated. As before, the mission of the Army was still to defeat enemy ground forces, that of the Navy to control the sea, of the Air Force to control the air. As before, by implication at least, the balanced-forces concept would be followed by equal budgeting for the services. The heart of interservice differences, fear of the cannibalizing of one service by the other with a resulting one-or two-service structure, had not been obviated. Nor was the apparently insoluble problem solved in which the technological annihilation of time and space made impossible neat distinctions between ground, naval, and air power and caused each service to seek weapons systems of the other services denied it by constricted defense budgets.[49]

In any event, Sullivan was greatly pleased to learn that the Key West Agreement approved a supercarrier. "Navy not to be denied use of A-bomb" and "Navy to proceed with development of 80,000-ton carrier and development of HA [high altitude] aircraft to carry heavy missiles therefrom," Forrestal reported to Truman on 15 March. The question whether the supercarrier must be approved by the Joint Chiefs of Staff remained moot, however. When Spaatz asked him whether there were to be two air forces, Forrestal said that he had to administer the National Security Act as written, and Spaatz agreed that changes in the Act could be made only by Congress.[50] In contrast to Spaatz, Sullivan told the Navy on 14 July 1948 that he would use the principles enunciated in the Key West Agreement and the resulting Functions Paper to support the National Security Act.

The Soviet rape of Czechoslovakia on 24 February 1948—to which American public opinion reacted violently—revealed that defense against the Soviets must include psychological as well as economic and military measures. After the communist coup, tension was also reported with respect to Berlin. The tension soon led to the Berlin Blockade, to which Western Powers responded by supplying Berlin by air alone for almost a year in the greatest air transport operation undertaken up to that time.[51] While before Congress on 17 March, Truman labeled Russia the "one nation" blocking efforts toward world peace. But he did not ask for defense funds beyond the $10 billion in new obligational authority provided in his original budget for fiscal year 1949. Nor did he ask for the lifting of personnel ceilings for the services, which were 350,000 short of authorized strength and stood at 1.3 million men. Instead he asked for prompt enactment of the Marshall Plan of economic aid for Europe and the provision of some military aid as well, the adoption of universal military training, and the "temporary" reenactment of Selective Service.

In briefing major congressional leaders Forrestal stuck to his philosophy of splitting the defense dollar three ways lest the nation have "an unbalanced military organization and an illusory sense of security."[52] Sterling Cole (R., Ill.) and George Bates (R., Mass.), formerly rock-ribbed Navy supporters, lined up behind the Air Force, as did Carl Vinson (D., Ga.), the latter despite a personal plea from Forrestal not to do so. At a meeting held in Forrestal's office on 22 March, Symington devoted himself "almost entirely to a justification of the 70-group program" while "Mr. Royall's thesis was overwhelmingly that of an air advocate who justified every other service as a hewer of wood and carrier of water for the Air Force."[53] Those Americans questioned on whether the Air Force, Navy, or Army should be increased also disagreed with Forrestal, as revealed by the results of a Gallup poll released on 19 March. On the question, 61 percent favored the Army, 63 percent the Navy, and 74 percent the Air Force. On the question of which service would play the most important part in winning another war, 74 percent said the Air Force, 6 percent the Navy, and 4 percent the Army.[54] In any event, on 24 March Forrestal requested a $9 billion supplemental appropriation. When Truman agreed to $3 billion, Forrestal submitted his requisition for that sum to Congress on the next day.[55]

Sullivan testified late in March at congressional hearings held on Forrestal's defense program. Like Royall, Symington, and the Joint Chiefs of Staff, he supported the legislation Forrestal considered necessary, especially to augment military manpower and to undertake a limited rearmament program as insurance for what could be a long cold war. As he knew, the Navy's postwar demobilization was essentially complete, and very low retention levels were set for his department. The result was the depletion of material inventories, particularly those of war reserves. In consequence he was told: "Against the requirement of $11.25 billion which have been set as necessary to support mobilization until procurement could become effective, the amount on hand approximates $3.3 billion (30 percent) . . . . "[56] Forrestal had suggested raising the personnel limit from 1,385,500 to 1,734,000, with most of the men to go to the Army and Marine Corps, and the appropriation of an additional $3 billion. For fiscal year 1948, about $775 million would be spent by the Air Force and Navy on new aircraft and air research, but the Air Force would remain at fifty-five groups, not the seventy Symington wanted. Forrestal sought a "balanced" military force; for the Air Force to go to seventy groups, he said, would cost not the $800 million Symington estimated but approximately $15 billion in addition to bringing the Army and Navy into proper proportion, which the Joint Chiefs estimated would cost $9 billion.

In an executive session of the Senate Armed Services Committee, on 7 April Symington asserted that both Forrestal and the Army erred and concluded that "there should be no additions at all to the Army and Navy just to balance the 70-group program." Moreover, he wanted an improved version of the B-29 that could fly ten thousand miles with a ten-thousand-pound bomb load, meaning that it could bomb Russia from the continental United States and return home. Symington's basic concept was "that Russia has the all powerful Army, the United States the all-powerful Navy, and that the Air Force will tip the balance." Spaatz added that plans called for bombing Russia from the United Kingdom by night and the making of day raids with fighter escort. He admitted, however, that the day raids, "would be short of Moscow," and Symington confessed that appropriations necessary to achieve a seventy-group Air Force would approximate $5.44 billion in 1949 and $6.51 billion in 1950.

While Senator Wayne Morse interjected that the Air Force "ignored fuel needs and the necessity for the Navy to convoy and the Army to defend air base areas" and Forrestal pointed out that the fuel consumption of a jet Air Force was approximately forty-five times that of a traditional air force and that he had asked the Joint Chiefs to evaluate the seventy-group program and decide what should be done, Army spokesmen insisted that they needed 15,000 additional men in any event and that to service a seventy-group Air Force the Army must grow from 782,000 to 836,000 men. They questioned, however, Forrestal's estimate of an extra $15 billion to bring the Army and Navy into "balance" with a seventy-group Air Force.

Senator Richard Russell noted that aircraft carriers were extremely useful, for 'they can run in and out." Forrestal added that carriers "could be torpedoed, but that an air base could be bombed," and Forrestal, Russell, and General Dwight D. Eisenhower agreed that "an Air Force is not mobile at all until it has its bases established and defended."[57]

Royall and General Omar Bradley supported Forrestal's balanced program. Since the Air Force requested $1.8 billion more than the President allotted it in his budget, however, the Army would ask for an additional $2 billion "in order to obtain all it needed." Said Royall, "If one service is going to present an independent, uncoordinated budget, then the other two need to also. There is no need for a Secretary of Defense, and the position should be abolished." After Royall heatedly questioned whether the Air Force should determine the number of additional men needed by the Army, Senator Leverett Saltonstall suggested that Royall was angry "because the unified plan had been thrown out of line." Royall agreed. Last, Bradley enumerated the widely scattered bases the Army must protect in order to make them useful to the Air Force. The Army, he added, had "a unilateral requirement . . . whether we have 55 groups, 70 groups, or any other number of groups."[58] Soon thereafter Admiral Robert B. Carney, Deputy Chief of Naval Operations (Logistics) estimated the cost of very heavy bomber airfield construction at various locations. Two are of particular interest. A "Bradleyville" in Saudi Arabia would need 586,716 men, use 1,069 merchant ships, and cost $1,985,370,000, while a "Symingtown" on the north coast of the Indian Ocean would take the same number of men and ships but cost $2,165,000,000.[59] Moreover, a comparison of moving 100,000 tons of cargo a month over a 6,600-mile route by air and by sea showed the need of 2,044 planes, 245,310 men, 195,335,792 gallons of fuel a month for 6,222 flights a month, and the use of 37 tankers, whereas the task could be performed by 37 ships, 4,886 crewmen, the use of 9,831,730 gallons of fuel per month, and the making of 20.6 trips a month—with no tanker requirements.[60]

On 15 April Hanson Baldwin had written in the New York Times that unification was a "joke." On the twenty-fifth he noted that nine months after passage of the National Security Act "most of the ranking officers of the Air Force are convinced . . . that there should be only one Air Force in the nation instead of the Air Force and Naval Aviation." Leading Air Force officers supported Spaatz's contention that there was no need for a Navy because there was no other navy for it to fight and objected to seeing the phrase Naval Aviation in print, in legislation or executive orders, or motion picture films, even though the term Naval Air Force had been used officially by the Navy as early as World War I. "While not of great importance," Sullivan's naval aide, Captain Fitzhugh Lee, told Sullivan, "it indicates the degree to which the Air Force directly and indirectly is influencing our freedom to speak freely on facts concerning Naval Aviation." The result of the Air Force's restriction on what the Navy could say while it continued its anti-Navy propaganda campaign would reduce the Navy's budget and, Lee added, "Naval Aviation will in fact be merged with the Air Force into one Air Force—an eventuality which will not be in the best interests of National Defense." Lee concluded with great prescience that "an important element contributing to this will be the gradually lowering morale with resultant loss of efficiency in Naval Aviation.[61]

On 15 April the House had agreed to Forrestal's aircraft procurement bill. Overriding both his and Truman's recommendations, it then added $822 million to it for starting a seventy-group Air Force and sent it to the Senate. Fortified by a unanimous conclusion of 19 April that the Joint Chiefs would support a $3.25 billion supplemental appropriations bill but tell Congress they really needed an extra $9 billion, on 21 April Forrestal offered a compromise plan in which the Air Force would have sixty-six groups, many of them augmented by demothballed B-29s rather than by new planes. That corresponding increases would be made in the Army and Navy is a fact that cannot be overstressed, and Denfeld was quick to provide a plan whereby the naval air arm would reach 14,500 planes—and parity with a seventy-group Air Force—by adding 1,200 planes off production lines to 2,400 taken out of storage.[62] Sullivan added that he would expand naval aviation training and told Symington that he used different methods from the Air Force in calculating the aircraft requirements of the Navy and Air Force.[63]

The Denfeld-Sullivan plan would cost $481 million in addition to the Navy's share in the initial $11.25 billion defense budget and $3.5 billion supplemental appropriation for fiscal year 1948. It would also make the Navy the dominant service, financially speaking, and the Air Force the weakest of the three services in manpower. In the end, after the Senate voted for a seventy-group Air Force by a vote of seventy-four to two, Truman on 21 May approved granting the Air Force $822 million more than he had recommended. On 3 June, the House approved the Navy Department's appropriation. When the Senate increased the amount by about $125 million, the measure went to conference, which provided a total of $3,749,059,250.[64]

For fiscal year 1949, Forrestal suggested $14.5 billion. Truman gave only qualified approval to the supplemental appropriation for fiscal year 1948 and directed that it go via the Bureau of the Budget to Congress. The budget director, James Webb, who told a friend that 'Forrestal has lost control completely,'[65] advised Truman to cut the $3.5 billion supplement for fiscal year 1948 to $2.5 billion. He started by cutting the $3.5 billion to $3.1 billion, then suggested that the Air Force be cut to fifty-five groups and that the Navy's air and antisubmarine components and the Army's reequipping be deferred. He also made it clear that the defense establishment must be so reduced that it could live for the foreseeable future on a $15 billion annual budget—thus freezing military spending and strength. When Forrestal had gone to see Truman, on 9 December 1948, the President had said that his budget represented "preparing for peace and not for war," the armed forces must not cut too deeply into the civilian economy, and he agreed with Webb on the figure of $14.4 billion for fiscal year 1949. Forrestal ran into a similar stone wall on the twentieth, even though he stressed the use of the atomic bomb as the chief weapon in retaliating against Russia. The budget that Truman approved greatly strengthened the Air Force, which on 11 January 1949 said it would shift emphasis from fighters to B-36s and B-50s, but did not correspondingly strengthen the Army and Navy. On 3 February Sullivan stated that he must reshape his forces to concentrate on antisubmarine warfare and cut 29,500 men from the Navy. At a meeting held at the White House on 13 May, moreover, Truman set a limit of $15 billion for fiscal year 1950, "about all the economy could stand," with that figure to remain fixed "unless world conditions deteriorate much further." He would support the supplemental appropriation for fiscal year 1948, now cut to $3.19 billion, only on condition that the services not spend it! Truman made his budget program "administration policy" and expected "every member of the administration to support it fully both in public and in private." Not only did he and Webb eviscerate the $16.9 billion compromise budget Forrestal had offered on 21 April; Truman ordered reductions of military personnel and directed that the Air Force not spend the $822 million Congress had granted it for the seventy-group program until he approved.[66]

Truman said that he would review the military budget for fiscal year 1950 in September and again in December and warned Congress that defense spending must proceed with an eye on its impact upon the civilian economy. He renewed an earlier warning to Forrestal that any acceleration of the defense program must be undertaken at a steady rate of increase instead of by an immediate, very large increase. Forrestal should either take equipment out of use or discharge enlisted men. Forrestal sent Truman's dictum to the service secretaries and arranged to talk about it with them.[67] Taking the hint, Sullivan directed the General Board "to study prospective requirements for naval forces during the next ten years, and to recommend a shipbuilding program covering that period. . . ."[68]

Forrestal finally realized that the budget must allocate funds not only to the services but to nonmilitary functions and foreign aid programs as well. By 23 June 1949 he had drafted a memorandum for the service secretaries on the subject. During the next ninety days, he said, the preparation of the fiscal year 1950 budget would be the most important business facing the military establishment. The Joint Chiefs had acceded to his request to advise him on the division of funds within the budget ceiling imposed. If they could not agree on the division, he would detail three high-ranking officers, one from each service, to perform this duty between 15 July and 15 September. Although the men he mentioned were never detailed, the Joint Chiefs created a board of three budget deputies—General Joseph T. McNarney, USAF, Vice Admiral

Robert B. Carney, USN, and Major General George J. Richards, USA—who as the McNarney Board would work to rationalize the operations of the military establishment.[69]

On 26 August 1947 Forrestal had requested the preparation of joint integrated plans for the deployment of armed forces based on a joint strategic concept. He would then seek funds to support the concept. The Joint Chiefs had thereupon agreed to provide the Secretary of Defense with an annual statement on the world situation, a discussion of strategic considerations, and a statement on military requirements. To insure the proper coordination of strategy and funding, recommendations of the budget advisers would be passed upon by two Joint Staff agencies, the Joint Strategic Plans Committee and the Joint Logistics Plans Committee, before being sent by the Joint Chiefs of Staff to the Secretary of Defense.[70]

The appropriations committees in both houses had looked kindly upon Sullivan's request to stop construction work on thirteen ships and to concentrate on others considered more important, especially on the proposed supercarrier, which he denied was particularly vulnerable. In support of his contention he cited statistics provided by the Vice Chief of Naval Operations, Vice

In 1948 General Joseph T. McNarney, USAF chaired a committee that assessed the Air Force's needs with respect to the strategic bombing of Russia. In 1949 he headed an interservice committee charged with rationalizing the operations of the military establishment. With the advent of Louis A. Johnson as Secretary of Defense, he became Johnson's major adviser on fiscal and organizational matters.

OFFICIAL USAF PHOTOGRAPH

Admiral Radford, who had written him that only four large carriers and one light carrier were sunk during 350 ship-months of World War 11 operations, only 40.5 months were spent in repairing damage to carriers, and that "Not a single CV or CVL was sunk during the entire war by land-based aircraft."[71] Before the Senate Armed Services Committee on 1 June Sullivan repeated his willingness to support legislation canceling the completion of thirteen ships. Although he carefully avoided implying that his building program would conflict in any way with the functions of the Air Force, he noted that budget estimates called for the conversion of two *Essex*-class carriers so that they could handle heavier planes and that "the President's program also calls for the construction of a prototype flush deck carrier, the size of which is dictated by the size, weight, and importance of the carrier aircraft of the future"—a comment certain to make the Air Force see red. He concluded that 'the wartime statistics concerning our carriers in itself, without reference to new defensive weapons, constitute ample refutation of uninformed statements that carriers are excessively vulnerable. . . ."[72]

Denfeld, who followed, related how the supercarrier had been approved all along the line, adding that "one is all we want at this time in order to work out the capabilities of a ship of this type." He could have stopped there; instead he added that the prototype carrier was needed to support the primary functions of the Navy assigned to it at Key West and particularly to "exploit fully the revolutionary advance in [jet] aircraft."[73]

That Carl Vinson was somewhat hurt was clear, for he had worked very hard to obtain the thirteen ships that Sullivan, in agreement with Webb, abandoned in favor of the supercarrier. That he was not too unhappy, however, was revealed by his announced intention to ask the Chief of the Bureau of Ships, Admiral Earle Mills, why the Navy did not ask for two supercarriers, for these could not transit the Panama Canal. In reporting on "Mr. Vinson's thoughts," Sullivan's counsel, Henry C. Beauregard, told Sullivan that "It is believed by Admiral Radford and Admiral Mills that this may be Mr. Vinson's very canny way of saying that we should have two flush-deck carriers immediately instead of only one, which will be consistent with our ultimate plan for having four."[74] Representative Hinshaw, however, noted that the expense of supporting ships must be added to the cost of the supercarrier, questioned the military value of a ship that could handle only a small number of aircraft, and suggested that its value be established by a board of "relatively disinterested persons" before Congress adopted it.[75]

In his report to Symington for 1948, Spaatz had emphasized the seventy-group plan as the sine qua non of security. He also revealed that the Air Force had concentrated upon strategic bombing and neglected tactical and reconnaissance operations,[76] no doubt because the first regular production models of the B-36, even if slow, had carried ten-thousand-pound loads for a distance of more than eight thousand miles in tests carried out in April and May, and the B-36 appeared particularly important if war with Russia grew out of the Berlin Blockade. Even after he retired he fired another shot against the carrier program by saying that he and Denfeld varied in their interpretations of certain actions taken by the Joint Chiefs of Staff before Denfeld became a member, in forwarding the report of the President's Air Policy Commission. It had been said that the Joint Chiefs approved a seventy-group Air Force and "the four oversized carriers of which Admiral Denfeld has spoken." The Joint Chiefs did provide the Finletter Commission figures on national military air requirements but " did not approve in detail the supporting information contained in the report. Specifically, and I wish to make this perfectly clear, the Air Force action did not include approval of new and larger type aircraft carriers." However, the President had approved building a prototype supercarrier. When Truman had asked the Joint Chiefs if they also approved, as one of his subordinates Spaatz had replied that the President's decision was acceptable to him. Spaatz nevertheless asserted that a demand for such a carrier must be presented to the military branch having primary responsibility for strategic air operations, namely, the Air Force, or to the Joint Chiefs. Denfeld thereupon asked the Joint Chiefs to formally approve the carrier. The vote was three to one in its favor, with the Chief of Staff of the Air Force, Vandenberg, opposed. Bradley later stated that he too had voted for the carrier only because it had been his understanding that 'it had been approved by those in authority and I accepted it as a fait accompli.'"[77]

Thus the matter of the supercarrier stood as Congress approved the fiscal 1949 budget, which allotted $4.7 billion to the Air Force, $4.9 billion to the Navy, and $4.2 billion to the Army, with Truman holding out $600 million for the stockpiling program and impounding the extra $822 million Congress had provided to build the Air Force up to seventy groups.

Sullivan's recommendation that $156 million from the Navy's supplemental appropriation for fiscal year 1948 he devoted to modernizing forty-two ships was reduced by the Bureau of the Budget, with Forrestal's concurrence, to $50 million with which to convert fourteen ships. He was then denied $322.3 million with which to build fourteen ships and $83.2 million to modernize eight ships in fiscal year 1949. In addition he lost the $337 million in the Treasury account. With the $230 million left for his building program, he could build six new ships at a cost of $117 million and convert three others at a cost of $32 million, leaving $81 million for the supercarrier. Most new construction would be of prototype ships acutely needed for air warfare and antisubmarine warfare and included a hunter-killer ship of five thousand tons, two antisubmarie submarines, and two submarines.

In his first annual report to the President, for the fiscal year ending 30 June 1948, Sullivan noted particularly how the Navy had worked to implement the National Security Act and paid special attention to research and planning. In cooperation with the other services, a number of unified commands had been established. The number of overseas bases had been reduced to the minimum needed to support current operations. While the number of naval aircraft had dropped considerably during the year, the Navy had agreed with the other services on which service would undertake the development of specific guided missiles. The Navy's personnel strength of 951,930 on 1 July 1946 had been cut to 502,747 on 1 January 1947, and to 477,384 on 30 June 1947, meaning that some shortages existed, especially in specialist ratings, and that a great imbalance marked the various ratings. Although no new ships had been laid down during the year, twenty of thirty-three ships building had been completed. Work had been suspended on the cruiser *Hawaii* and battleship *Kentucky*, which were to have been converted to guided missile ships, and on the *Oriskany* (CVS-34) in order to permit inclusion of extensive design changes. On the other hand, a research program designed to increase the scientific and technical potential of the Naval Establishment included more than six hundred projects and engaged more than two thousand investigators.

While Sullivan did not say so in his report, a conference held in May 1948 at the suggestion of the Military Liaison Committee between representatives of the Bureau of Ships and of the Argonne National Laboratory reported the desirability of having the General Electric Company provide a design for a liquid-cooled atomic power plant for a submarine.[78] In mid-July 1948 Captain Hyman G. Rickover was designated as the liaison officer in the Washington headquarters of the Atomic Energy Commission for nuclear ship propulsion. Thereafter, David E. Lilienthal, chairman of the Atomic Energy Commission, kept Sullivan informed of progress being made in atomic energy developments via Rear Admiral T.B. Hill, Sullivan's appointee to the Military Liaison Committee, and Sullivan kept Forrestal informed of advancements being made in the production of the nuclear-powered submarine plant.[79]

As Sullivan noted in his report, agreement had been reached upon which missiles would be developed by each service. What he naturally did not divulge was an internal battle, between the Bureau of Ordnance and Bureau of Aeronautics, over which would develop what missiles, with the chief of the former having alerted the Chief of Naval Operations, Nimitz, to the struggle. After referring to the problems involved in obtaining defense unification and noting the need to avoid airing internal Navy Department dissention, Nimitz had wisely suggested deferring decisions in the matter to a later date.[80] When the question was raised again, as indicated below, it involved an interservice rather than simply an intraservice squabble.

The first session of the Eightieth Congress passed the National Security Act, peacetime selective service, and a new Military Personnel Act. The second session provided for a draft law that would bring the armed services the men they needed, took a step forward toward a unified system of military justice, provided for a supercarrier, secured permanent status for Navy Department organization in keeping with the provisions of the National Security Act, and in consequence of an agreement between Sullivan and Webb supplanted the Navy's 1948 building program by that of 1949. Between the end of the second session and the special session Truman called for 26 July 1948, Forrestal named Major General Wilton B. Persons, USA, to coordinate all legislative proposals reported to him by the three budget deputies of the armed services; and Admiral William D. Leahy, of the Joint Chiefs of Staff, the service secretaries, and agency leaders in the National Military Establishment forwarded to Forrestal at his request initial statements of their requirements for the first truly unified budget, for fiscal year 1950, which, as already indicated, Truman had limited to $15 billion. By way of explanation—none of the budget requests of the military services was presented to the Joint Chiefs of Staff or cleared with the other services for the simple reason that the requests were due on 15 September 1947, Forrestal did not take office until the seventeenth, and the National Military Establishment did not begin operating until the eighteenth. It was too late to go over the figures without running into the budget process for fiscal year 1950. In any event, by the summer of 1948 Truman's niggardly treatment of the services provoked Forrestal to a divergence from presidential policies that eventually would lead to a request for his resignation.

By the fall of 1948, moreover, debate between the Navy and the Air Force reached new heights. The Air Force alleged that Forrestal and Sullivan refused to let it tell the public that Air Force planes had reached supersonic speed, and Vandenberg told Forrestal that moneys should not be provided for "two duplicating programs, particularly when one involved the use of obsolescing weapons." He meant Navy participation in strategic bombing with atomic bombs and its use of carriers.[81] In *Life*, Spaatz asserted that instead of working to provide a truly balanced defense structure around one air force, the Navy sought to build a second strategic air force about supercarriers.[82] When all leading Air Force generals declined the Navy's repeated invitation to make cruises on carriers, at a National Aviation Clinic held in Detroit in October, Rear Admiral Edwin A. Cruise, Chief, Air Warfare Division, Office of the Chief of Naval Operations, blasted the Air Force for conducting publicity campaigns that tried to convince Americans that it had magic devices for safeguarding the nation, as in plans for a thirty-day "air blitz" or "flash" war that with atomic bombs would accomplish more in one mission than air power had accomplished in two years in World War II.[83] Whereas the Navy was willing to extend a planned "radar fence" across the northern border of the United States by operating radar picket ships up to two thousand miles offshore from Seattle to Los Angeles and from northern Maine to Charleston, the Army and Air Force had serious reservations about them.[84] Arguing that separate annual armed forces celebrations provided more public relations and better served to maintain service traditions, Sullivan opposed Forrestal's proposal to have a single Armed Forces Week.[85] He also objected to granting additional duties to the Director of the Joint Staff, as the Army and Air Force wished to do. He admitted that Forrestal needed all the military and civilian help he could get to coordinate the activities of the numerous agencies created by the National Security Act. However, increasing the duties of the Director of the Joint Staff would cause a direct conflict with the responsibilities resting upon the staffs of the service secretaries and bypass the legal chain of responsibility, with consequent reduction in "responsible leadership" and the creation of "a state of unhealthy confusion within the ranks." More important, the position of the director would evolve into one of chief of staff of the armed forces who, with a general staff, would either place the Joint Chiefs of Staff in a subordinate position or force them out of existence. He countered with a proposal that Forrestal be furnished a secretariat manned by Army, Navy, and Air Force general and flag officers who would function as "technical and administrative servants to you and to the Departments which the members represent." The secretariat, responsible to Forrestal alone, would serve as a coordinating and advisory agency without detracting from the authority and responsibility of the service secretaries.[86] Unable to agree with Royall and Symington on which foreign military bases should be retained, Sullivan won agreement from his colleagues that they would collate their respective priority lists and submit the result to Forrestal, who would then discuss it with the Secretary of State, George C. Marshall.[87]

On a lower administrative level. Under Secretary of the Navy W. John Kenney bristled when the Under Secretary of the Air Force indicated that he should clear with the other services contracts made with aircraft manufacturers. While he would agree to the establishment of certain common interservice policies and standards and was trying to get information from and closer contact with the Army and with the Air Force in the matter, he pointed out that he considered it "impractical and unwise to require clearance with the other two departments regarding the particular terms upon which contracts for our respective requirements are to be negotiated."[88] On the other hand, about nine months of discussion ended when the Air Force finally agreed with the Navy's proposed contributions to the air defense of the continental United States and of American overseas bases.[89] Early that month too, the Air Force made much of the fact that a B-50 Superfort named *Lucky Lady II* girdled the globe in ninety-four hours with four inflight refuelings.[90]

On 10 June, 1949, a "Plan for the Air Defense of the United States" was promulgated by the Air Force. According to this plan, radar picket ships off coastal areas, the aircraft of all military, civil, and private agencies, antiaircraft artillery, and whatever ground-to-air guided missiles were developed would be used. But operational control of units allocated to air defense would remain with their parent organizations until given to the Air Defense Command by the Joint Chiefs of Staff or by mutual agreement between the services. The plan, although prepared by the Commanding General, Air Defense Command, included advice and assistance from the Army, Navy, and certain civil agencies; provided for joint training and liaison by the Army and Navy with the Air Force; and enjoined the Navy, including the Marine Corps, to provide fighter and antiaircraft forces not necessary to the accomplishment of primary naval missions.[91]

On 31 March 1948 Sullivan, Symington, Royall, and the Joint Chiefs of Staff had met with Forrestal and various Department of State representatives to consider alternative courses of action if the Soviets tried to deny the Western powers access to Berlin. On 24 June the Soviets halted land traffic to the city. A commentary on the effectiveness of the National Security Act is that the Central Intelligence Agency failed to foresee and report the approach of the crisis, the National Security Council did not quickly advise the President on what policy to follow, and the War Council had no policy to transmit to the services. On 27 June Sullivan again joined Forrestal and various high-ranking military officers and representatives of the Department of State to help decide whether the United States would fight, leave Berlin, or seek an accommodation with the Soviets. With his demands for universal military training obviously getting nowhere, Secretary of State Marshall avidly sought to rearm the five nations of the Western European Union formed in March 1948—the United Kingdom, France, Belgium, The Netherlands, and Luxembourg. Not until 15 July did the National Security Council advise the sending of additional B-29 bombers to Britain and Germany, within striking distance of Moscow. Even if the sixty planes dramatically transferred to England did not carry atomic bombs, there was no way for Moscow to know that.[92] More important, as Walter Millis said, the appearance of the atomic weapons in Europe made it plain "that the atomic arsenal had entered American thought as an appropriate instrument of the policy for the future."[93]

Truman's decision that the United States would remain in Berlin while seeking an accommodation with the Soviets that would avoid war highlighted the fact that the only quickly usable military power the United States possessed was the A-bomb. In May, Bradley had suggested up to a 40 percent cut in naval appropriations; in July, as already noted, Vandenberg suggested denying the Navy the use of strategic air and of carriers. In July also, Truman denied Forrestal's repeated importunate requests to set policy on the use of atomic weapons and to transfer their custody from the Atomic Energy Commission to the Air Force.[94] Symington then exacerbated the rivalry between the services by stating publicly that air power should be put in balance not with the Army or the Navy but with that of potential enemies, by assailing those "dedicated to obsolete methods of warfare," and by referring to the "disjointed" defense budget. Forrestal thereupon asked for his explanation of "an act of official disobedience and personal disloyalty." He told Truman he would ask for Symington's resignation if Symington could not satisfactorily explain his remarks. Then, as has been said, he "thought twice and lost a golden opportunity."[95] At a dinner meeting of 19 July with Sullivan, Symington, and Royall, Forrestal tried to get at the root causes of Symington's motivation and generously glossed over his misconduct. Nevertheless, disagreement between Symington and Sullivan was deep if not wide. Walter Lippmann said that with respect to fighting for a seventy-group Air Force, Symington was "clear, forceful, and untroubled by doubt."[96] Another said,

The Secretary of Defense had to deal with a group of men led by a fighting Secretary who believed air power the key to the military future of the world—who had failed both to understand the difficulties of wartime strategic bombing, especially without fighter cover, and the horrendous new problem of atomic bombing: all they knew was that the Air Force had carried the bombs in each case and could do so again.[97]

Sullivan conceded primary responsibility to Symington for strategic warfare but denied that the Navy should be limited to the use of atomic bombs upon particular targets. Royall, however, told Sullivan that the Navy should be "subservient" to the Air Force in the matter of strategic warfare in the same way that the Air Force was "subservient" to the Navy in the matter of antisubmarine warfare. Forrestal thought the matter could be settled by giving the Air Force primary responsibility for strategic warfare, limiting naval use of atomic bombs to targets indicated by the Air Force or upon "purely naval targets," and giving the Navy the right to appeal this settlement to the Joint Chiefs of Staff and then to the Secretary of Defense. In a subsequent talk with Vandenberg, Forrestal mentioned "(1) the Navy belief, very firmly held and deeply rooted, that the Air Force wants to get control of *all* aviation; (2) the corresponding psychosis of the Air Force that the Navy is trying to encroach upon the strategic air prerogatives of the Air Force." The Air Force must have primary responsibility for strategic warfare, he went on, but he would not deny another service the right to develop a weapon it thought it needed. While he opposed building a fleet of supercarriers, one such supercarrier capable of carrying the weight of a long-ranging plane should go forward, even it it served only as an interim weapon system until guided missile ships could be built. He concluded that if the Joint Chiefs could not decide the issue, he would. Vandenberg had suggested that the key was "money," that if funds were limited they should go to the strategic air force—which would then control the atomic bomb. Forrestal recalled to active duty the two leading elder statesmen of the Air Force and of naval aviation, General Spaatz and Admiral John Towers, to define the issues for him. In their report, in which they "interpreted" the Key West Agreement, Spaatz and Towers recommended that the Navy be equipped to bomb strategic targets within the area of naval operations, including atomic bombs. The Air Force thus inferentially approved the Navy's proposed new carrier capable of launching atomic bombs.[98]

Meanwhile, because of "Soviet aggression, increased international tension, the general deterioration of world relations, and the necessity for National security," early in August Representative Chester E. Merrow (R., N.H.) recommended that the 14,500-plane Navy planned for 1954 be realized by 1 July 1949. It was debatable whether Congress would provide the $2 billion needed for telescoping a five-year program into one. However, a thorough appraisal of the capabilities of present and future weapons in the light of their cost and capabilities of delivery and various problems in connection with strategic warfare would be made when Forrestal, the Joint Chiefs of Staff, and their respective aides met at the Naval War College, Newport, Rhode Island, on 20-22 August.

As a result of the Newport Conference, Forrestal reported, the services had agreed to consider the forces of other services in planning their own functions. As his diary notes, operational control of the atomic bomb was vested temporarily in the Air Force pending a decision on the organization for the control and direction of atomic operations to be reached by the services and their link with the Atomic Energy Commission, the Military Liaison Committee. The establishment of a weapons evaluation group was "desirable and necessary." In the field of its primary mission, each service "must have exclusive responsibility for planning and programming," but, "in the execution of any mission . . . all available resources must be used . . . . For this reason, the exclusive responsibility and authority in a given field do not imply preclusive participation." The Air Force, thus, must use whatever strategic bombing capabilities the Navy might develop.[99]

The compromise reached at Newport stilled the Air Force-Navy dispute only momentarily. Whether the projected supercarrier was included in the decision was moot, but Forrestal was quick to point out that "the decisions themselves reflect neither a victory for the Air Force nor a defeat for the Navy. Neither do they indicate a victory for the Navy nor a defeat for the Air Force."[100] Admiral Denfeld had defended naval air and Marine Corps aviation from the Air Force, and the Marine Corps from possible absorption by the Army. He had tried to maintain interservice harmony but admitted that each Joint Chief had had to withdraw from "an extreme position" he had held with respect to his service and that they had adjourned with the feeling that "the Newport Conference spelled out a reasonable basis for making . . . agreements." However, the synicated columnist Marquis Childs thought that all the Newport Conference accomplished was to transfer the heated interservice squabble to a cooler climate,[101] and the *Washington News* suggested that better interservice cooperation could be obtained if Forrestal would "lop off a few official heads."[102] Distressed by the continued interservice bickering, particularly with the public demand for one air force by Generals Doolittle and Spaatz, Forrestal on 8 November sent a memorandum on the subject to the service secretaries. He believed that it was "entirely appropriate in . . . a presentation [to Congress or to the public] for a service to use the most persuasive arguments in defense of its competence to perform its missions." However, he added, "I think it is most inappropriate . . . and certainly not conducive to the spirit of cooperation between the services, to permit such an exposition to develop into an attack upon, or criticism of, the competence, equipment, or weapons of another service." Therefore the service secretaries would forward to him any presentations violating this directive prior to their delivery. What he sought was "the development of an attitude which will find reflection in a disciplined restraint and moderation whenever other services are concerned."[103]

On the anniversary of the passage of the National Security Act, in speaking to the Baltimore Squadron of the Air Force Association, Sullivan paid public tribute to the "superlative job" the Air Force was doing. He was pleased with progress made in the first year of unification, adding that "most of the inter-service projects during the past twelve months have worked smoothly and successfully. Most of these were the unpublished, rather dreary, run-of-the-mill operations—the kind . . . that win wars."[104] A week later, in addressing seventeen hundred members of the Navy Industrial Association at

New York, he asserted that American naval ships in European and Mediterranean waters were "a constant stabilizing force in areas where explosive incidents might occur," and bluntly warned communists that the United States would take every step deemed necessary to preserve peace. He then noted that the achievements of aircraft carriers in World War II refuted criticism that they were at the mercy of land-based aviation. Last, he said that the importance of the supercarrier, on which construction would soon begin, "cannot be exaggerated,"[105] an idea he stressed in an article honoring the Navy on Navy Day. In this article he emphasized the speed and power with which the Navy could respond to challenges to American security. It also served as a deterrent to aggression. The Navy was a member of a defense team. The functions and responsibilities of all members of this team were now clearly defined in the unified organization that replaced the shambles created by postwar demobilization.

Sullivan then concerned himself with an unprecedented executive order in which President Truman demanded the strengthening of the reserve forces and a simultaneous pronouncement in which he noted that the armed services had asked for $23 billion for fiscal year 1950 but must conform to the $15 billion limit he had set. Whether Truman would remain as President or give way to his Republican challenger, Thomas E. Dewey, would soon be known. If he were reelected, Truman stated, the $15 billion limit on the military budget would be lifted only if world conditions so indicated. He prohibited public discussion by officials of the National Military Establishment of the defense budget. There would be no cabinet changes if he remained in office, he indicated, but Fleet Admiral William D. Leahy, who had acted as his Chief of Staff and as chairman of the Joint Chiefs of Staff, would not be replaced when he retired.

Two years of interservice squabbling had greatly impeded the unification of the military services hoped for by the authors of the National Security Act of 1947. Guided by Nimitz, his successor, Denfeld, and his own staff, Sullivan had staunchly defended the Navy as the first line of national defense and particularly demanded that naval aviation be given a prominent position in national strategy. In 1948 two congressional studies approved air power as the primary war weapon, one of them suggesting naval air parity with the Air Force, the other calling for an increase of the Air Force from fifty-five to seventy groups. When Congress overrode his budget limits and granted the Air Force an additional $822 million with which to expand toward seventy groups, Truman impounded the extra funds. The Navy's answer to Air Force strategic bombing by planes not yet truly intercontinental and lacking bases abroad remained fixed upon a supercarrier capable of handling new large and fast planes that could bomb any spot on earth. By cutting down his shipbuilding program and giving up other funds, Sullivan managed to obtain enough money to begin construction on a supercarrier while yet emphasizing vitally needed antisubmarine forces.

Following his philosophy of balanced forces, Forrestal would divide the military budget fairly equally between the services. When Symington obstreperously demanded the balancing of the Air Force with the military forces of potential enemies, Forrestal and Sullivan replied that both the Army and the Navy must be increased substantially if they were to serve an expanded Air Force. Moreover, backed by Denfeld, Radford, and others, Sullivan insisted that air power was the sum of the air power of the nation, not just that in the Air Force, and won approval for the building of a supercarrier in both the Key West and Newport conferences, even if strategic bombing would remain a collateral rather than primary naval air function.

Still very firm in stating that funds granted the military services must not cut too deeply into the civilian sector of the economy, Truman nevertheless approved huge expenditures for economic and military aid for the rebuilding of Western Europe. Their funds limited to roughly $14 billion for fiscal year 1948 and again for 1949 instead of the $23 billion they determined they needed, at least for fiscal year 1949, the Joint Chiefs could not agree on how much each service should get. Forrestal finally realized that the budget must be constructed with the government's nonmilitary functions and foreign aid programs taken into account, and he planned to detail three high-ranking officers, one from each service, to act as budget advisers and determine upon the division of the budget. When he failed to act, three budget deputies were assigned the work by the Joint Chiefs of Staff, with their conclusions to be reviewed by several committees within the Joint Chiefs of Staff organization before being presented to the Secretary of Defense by the Joint Chiefs. The budget for fiscal year 1950 would be the first written under this system. When Symington, backed by Royall, suggested amendments to the National Security Act that would strengthen the authority of the Secretary of Defense over the military services, presumably so that the Air Force particularly would benefit, Sullivan stood pat on the original National Security Act.

NOTES

1. "Ad. Nimitz Sees Navy With Air as First Line," ANJ 85 (January 10, 1948): 472, 295. Nimitz signed the report on the day of his retirement, and Sullivan released it to the press. Chester W. Nimitz Diary, 15 December 1947, to 5 March 1948, entry of 7 January 1948 (courtesy Professor Elmer B. Potter.)
2. Carl W. Borklund, *Men of the Pentagon:From Forrestal to McNamara* (New York:Praeger, 1966), p. 74.
3. W. Barton Leach, "Obstacles to the Development of American Air Power," *The Annals of the American Academy* 299 (May 1955): 70.
4. U.S. President's Air Policy Commission. *Survival in the Air Age: A Report by the President's Air Policy Commission* (Washington: GPO, 1948).
5. RADM E. A. Cruise, Memorandum for OP-50, "Comments on the Finletter Report," 8

March, 1948, NHD: OA, OP-23 Files. See the extended discussion in *Support Study,* pp. 73-78.
6. Borklund, *Men of the Pentagon,* p. 76. Richard G. Hubler, SAC: *The Strategic Air Command* (New York: Duell, Sloan and Pearce, 1958), pp. 68-72.
7 Kenneth L. Moll, "Nuclear Strategy, 1945-1949; American's First Four Years," Master's thesis, University of Omaha, 1965, pp. 146-50.
8. Borklund, *Men of the Pentagon,* p. 76.
9. Drew Pearson in *Philadelphia Bulletin,* 10 April 1948.
10. Borklund, *Men of the Pentagon,* pp. 75-76; Paul Y. Hammond, "Super Carriers and B-36 Bombers: Appropriations, Strategy and Politics," in Harold Stein, ed., *American Civil-Military Decisions: A Book of Case Studies* (University: University of Alabama Press, 1963), pp. 472, 480.
11. Moll, "Nuclear Strategy," p. 156.
12. Daniel V. Gallery, RADM, USN (Ret), *Eight Bells and All's Well* (New York: W.W. Norton and Co., 1965), pp. 221-22.
13. Secret, John L. Sullivan to James E. Webb, via SECDEF, 27 December 1947, SNP.
14. *New York Times,* 24 June 1948; *New York Herald Tribune,* 25 August, 12 October 1948; ANAFR, 1 January 1949. For details, see U.S. Congress. House Subcommittee on Appropriations, *National Military Establishment.* Hearings before Subcommittee, 80th Cong., 2d Sess., March 16-May 22, (Washingon: GPO, 1948).
15. Sullivan to Brewster, 27 February, 19 March 1948, SNP.
16. Top Secret. H.C. Beauregard, Memorandum for the SECNAV. Minutes of Meeting of the Secretary's Council, 19 November 1947, SNP. See also Conf. Nimitz to Sullivan, 4 December 1947 [U.S. Naval Policy for Fleet Air Defense], SNP.
17. *New York Times,* 12 March 1948.
18. Report of the Congressional Aviation Policy Board, *National Aviation Policy.* Senate Report 949, 80th Cong., 2d Sess. (Washington: GPO, 1948).
19. John L. Sullivan, Memorandum for the SECDEF, 22 March 1948, SNP.
20. Calvin William Enders, "The Vinson Navy," Ph.D. diss., Michigan State University, 1970; Ann Arbor, Mich.: University Microfilms, pp. 176-78.
21. "Balanced Arms Urged by Defense Secretary," ANJ 85 (10 April 1948): 833, 841; "House Approves 70-Group AF and Naval Air Funds," ANJ 85 (17 April 1948): 857, 859.
22. CAPT Walter Karig, USNR, CDR Malcolm Cagle, USN, and LCDR Frank A. Manson, USN, *Battle Report: The War in Korea* (New York: Rinehart and Co., 1952), pp. 1-11; Moll, "Nuclear Strategy," pp. 111-13.
23. Joseph J. Clark, ADM, USN (Ret), with Clark Reynolds, *Carrier Admiral* (New York: David McKay Co., 1967), p. 261.
24. Walter Millis, ed, with the collaboration of E.S. Duffield, *The Forrestal Diaries* (New York: Viking Press, 1951), pp. 370-73.
25. U.S. House. Committee on Appropriations. *Hearings on Department of the Navy Appropriations Bill for 1949.* 80th Cong., 2d Sess. (Washington: GPO, 1949); Editorial, ANJ 86 (27 March 1949): 785.
26. John L. Sullivan to James E. Webb, 30 September 1847; SECNAV to All Ships and Stations, 28 November 1948; JAG to M[ore] T[han] O[ne], 22 April 1948, SNP; *Federal Register* No. 135, of 13 July 1948; John R. Probert, "Staff Arrangements in the Organization of National Security," Ph.D. diss. University of Pennsylvania, 1956, pp. 6-34.
27. Navy Department Bulletin, 48-200, 31 March 1948, in NDB.12 (31 March 1948): 9-11.
28. Forrestal, Memorandum for Secretaries of Army, Navy, Air Force, 3 February 1948, SNP.
29. Restricted. H.C. Beauregard, Memorandum for the SECNAV. Minutes of Secretary's Meeting of Friday, 27 February 1948, SNP.
31. LGEN Lauris Norstad, Memorandum for the SECA, "Differences Between the Department of the Army and the Department of the Navy," 2 October 1947, cited in *Support Study,* pp. 69-70.
32. FADM C. W. Nimitz, Memorandum for the SECNAV, cited in *Support Study,* p. 70.
33. Kenneth C. Royall, SECA, Memorandum to the SECDEF, 28 February 1948, copies to SECNAV and SECAF, cited in *Support Study,* p. 70.
34. CAPT L. A. Thackrey, Memorandum for the SECNAV, 4 February 1948, cited in *Support Study,* p. 70.
35. John L. Sullivan, Memorandum for the SECDEF, 10 March 1949, cited in *Support Study,,* p. 70
36. Transcript of oral interview by Benis M. Frank of LGEN Merwin H. Silverthorn, USMC (RET) (Washington: HQ, USMC, History Division, 1969), p. 439 (hereafter cited as Silverthorn, "Reminiscences"). See also "The Reminiscences of VADM Wellborn, Jr., USN (RET)" transcript of oral interview by John T. Mason (Annapolis, Md.: U.S. Naval Institute, 1972), pp. 22-29.
37. Silverthorn, "Reminiscences," pp. 432-37.
38. Transcript of oral interview by Benis M. Frank of GEN Clifton B. Cates, USMC (RET) (Washington: HQ, USMC, History Division, 1967), pp. 22-29.
39. Millis, ed., *Forrestal Diaries,* pp. 390-91.
40. "Defense Sec. Presses for War Role Clarity," ANJ 85 (13 March 1948): 722.

41. *New York Times,* 27 May 1947.
42. John L. Sullivan, Memorandum to the SECDEF, 9 April 1948, John L. Sullivan to Air Force Department, SECDEF, Army Department, 10 May 1948; Secretary's Committee on Reorganization and Research, Memorandum to the SECDEF, 10 May 1948, SNP.
43. Secret. M. H. Silverthorn, Memorandum for SCOROR, 16 March 1948, SNP.
44. John L. Sullivan, Memorandum for Mr. Symington, 10 May 1948; idem, Memorandum for the SECDEF, 10 May 1948, SNP. See Seversky, *Victory Through Air Power* (New York: Simon and Schuster, 1942), and James C. Shelburne, "Factors Leading to the Establishment of the Air University," Ph.D. diss., University of Chicago, 1953.
45. DOD, Memorandum to the Service Secretaries and Joint Chiefs of Staff, "Functions of the Armed Services and the Joint Chiefs of Staff," 21 April 1948, SNP; text of "Functions Papers" printed in ANJ 85 (20 March 1948): 807, 809, 822, 823. See also R. Earl McClendon, "Unification of the Armed Forces: Administrative and Legislative Developments, 1945-1949" (Maxell Air Force Base, Ala.: Documentary Research Division, Research Studies Institute, 1952), App. A., H., I.
46. *Fed. Reg.* No. 80, 23 April 1948.
47. Arthur O. Sulzberger, *The Joint Chiefs of Staff, 1941-1954* (Washington: USMC Institute, 1954), p. 54; CAPT Robert P. Beebe, USN, "The Vital Key West Agreement," USNIP 87 (September 1961): 35-41.
48. JCS 1478/24, of 7 July 1948, in NDB 13 (31 July 1948): 19-21.
49. General Nathan F. Twining, USAF (RET), *Neither Liberty nor Safety: A Hard Look at U.S. Military Policy and Strategy* (New York: Holt, Rinehart and Winston, 1966), pp. 30-31; *Supporting Study,* pp. 78-82.
50. Millis, ed., *Forrestal Diaries,* pp. 393, 395-96.
51. Restricted. H.C. Beauregard, Memorandum for the SECNAV. Comments on Meeting at 1930 in Conference Room in OSD, Monday, 22 March 1948, SNP.
54. George. H. Gallup, *The Gallup Poll: Public Opinion, 1935-1971,* 3 vols. (New York: Random House, 1972), 1:719-20, 2: 791-92, 858-59; "Forrestal Fails to Stop Air," AW-48 (26 April 1948): 7.
55. "Letter [of President Truman] to the Speaker Regarding Additional Appropriations for the National Security Program, April 1, 1948," in U.S. President. *Public Papers of the Presidents of the United States: Harry S. Truman, Containing the Public Messages, Speeches, and Statements of the President,* 8 vols. (Washington: GPO, 1961-1966), 5: 198-99.
56. Secret. VADM A.C. Miles, Chief, Material Division, Memorandum for the SECNAV. Current Navy Demobilization Activities, 9 April 1948, SNP.
57. Conf. H.C. Beauregard, Memorandum for the SECNAV. Synopsis of Air Force and Army Presentation in Executive Session Yesterday, Wednesday, 7 April 1948, SNP.
58. Conf. H.C. Beauregard to the SECNAV. Subj: Testimony of Secretary Royall and General Bradley in Executive Session before the Senate Armed Services Committee on Monday, 12 April 1948, 13 April 1948, SNP.
59. Restricted. Robert B. Carney, DCNO (Logistics). Secret. Memorandum for the SECNAV, 3 June 1948, SNP.
60. "What Cargo Planes Can Do," USNWR 25 (6 August 1948): 21-23.
61. Fitzhugh Lee, Memorandum for Mr. Sullivan, 14 May 1948, SNP. Moreover, Lee told Sullivan that the Air Force followed the doctrine of "pure" air power based largely upon the writings of Italian general Giulio Douhet, "whose book *The Command of the Air* first appeared in 1921. . . . Its theme has been the bible for the extreme air power enthusiasts from Billy Mitchell to Jimmy Doolittle" (Lee, Memorandum for Mr. Sullivan, 22 April 1948, SNP.)
62. Though he did not say so, naval aviation would thus reach parity with a seventy-group Air Force. He estimated that the adoption of his plan would cause plane production for fiscal year 1950 and thereafter to go to 33,000 units in order to maintain a 14,500-plane program.
63. John L. Sullivan to Symington, 7 April 1948, SNP; "Navy Expanding Plane Strength to 14,500," AW 48 (10 May 1948): 11; "Navy Now Expanding Aviation Program," AW 49 (6 September 1948): 19-20.
64. U.S. House. Military Functions, *National Military Establishment Appropriations Bill for 1949.* Hearings before the Committee on Appropriations House of Representatives, 80th Cong., 2d Sess. 4 Parts (Washington: GPO, 1948), Part 4; "Fight for 70-Group Air Force Flares Again on Capitol Hill," AW 48 (5 April 1948): 11-12; "Navy Reveals New Air Program," AW 48 (April 5, 1948): 13; "New Air Force Test: The Senate," AW 48 (26 April 1948): 13; "Congress Scorns 'Mothball' Plan," AW 48 (May 3 1948): 11.
65. Robert H. Ferrell, *George C. Marshall* (New York: Cooper Square Publishers, 1966), p. 243.
66. Millis, ed., *Forrestal Diaries,* p. 439; Borklund, *Men of the Pentagon,* pp. 43-44; Edward Kolodziej, *The Uncommon Defense and Congress, 1945-1963* (Columbus: Ohio State University Press, 1966), pp. 78-81; *Papers of Harry S. Truman,* 5: 255, 272.
67. Truman to Forrestal, 3 June 1948; Forrestal, Memorandum to Secretaries of the Army, Navy, Air Force, Joint Chiefs of Staff, Mr. McNeil, Mr. John A. McCrone, 4 June 1948; Forrestal,

Memorandum for the SECNAV, 5 June 1948, Miscellaneous File, SNP.
68. SECNAV to Chairman, GB, 16 July 1948, SNP.
69. Forrestal, Memorandum for the JCS, 26 August 1947; Memorandum by the Director of the Joint Staff to the JCS, 23 October 1947; Memorandum of the CNO to the JCS, 17 November 1947; Memorandum for Admiral [Nimitz], 21 July 1947, Washington: NHD: OA, JCS File 1800 Series, in Papers of the Chiefs of Naval Operations (hereafter cited as CNO Papers).
70. C. W. Nimitz, Memorandum for JCS, 26 August 1947, JCS File 1800/1, CNO Papers.
71. Conf. Radford, Memorandum for SECNAV. Vulnerability of Carriers to Attack by Land Based Planes, with enclosure, 30 April 1948, SNP.
72. "Secretary's Statement before the Senate Armed Services Committee on Tuesday, 1 June 1948, SNP. Sullivan had routed his statement to various advisors, including CAPT Walter Karig and ADM Radford prior to delivering it. H.C. Beauregard, Memorandum for the VCNO, 25 May 1948; CAPT Walter Karig, USNR, to CAPT Hollingsworth, 26 May 1948, SNP.
73. Statement by ADM Louis E. Denfeld, CNO, before the Senate Armed Services Committee, 1 June 1948, SNP.
74. H.C. Beauregard, Memorandum for the SECDEF, 15 May 1948, SNP.
75. CR, 80th Cong., 1st Sess. 94, Part 6, pp. 70-82.
76. Report of the Chief of Staff, United States Air Forces, to the Secretary of the Air Force (Washington: GPO, 1948).
77. Carl Spaatz to Senator Chan Gurney, 24 May 1948, copy in SNP; Hammond, "Super Carriers and B-36 Bombers," p. 481; "Super Carrier," AW 48 (May 24, 1948): 12, and "Carrier War," AW 48 (May 31, 1948): 9.
78. BUSHIPS to AEC, 12 May 1948, copy in SNP.
79. Lilienthal to Sullivan, 23 February 1948, Military Liaison Committee to SECNAV, 27 May 1949, BUSHIPS to AEC, 16 July 1948, John L. Sullivan to SECDEF, 4 August 1948, SNP.
80. Chief, BUORD to CNO, referencing CNO Memorandum of 12 August 1948; CNO to SECNAV, 25 September 1947, CNO Papers.
81. Millis, ed., Forrestal Diaries, p. 467.
82. GEN Carl Spaatz, "Atomic Warfare," Life, August 16, 1948, p. 94.
83. "Blueprint for a 30-day War," USNWR 25 (15 October 1948): 15-16; "Navy Air Arm Debate Flares at Clinic," AW 49 (October 25, 1948): 12, and "The Aviation Week," AW 49 (November 8, 1948): 7.
84. Top Secret. LCDR E. M. Volberg, USNR, Memorandum for the SECNAV, 13 December 1948. SNP.
85. John L. Sullivan, Memorandum for the SECDEF, 7 October 1948. SNP.
86. Ibid., 16 October 1948.
87. John L. Sullivan to Symington, 18 September 1948, ibid.
88. W. John Kenney, Memorandum for the Under Secretary of the Air Force, 16 November 1948, ibid.
89. Conf. John L. Sullivan, Memorandum for SECA and SECAF, 15 June 1948, rewritten 10 September 1948; C.V. Whitney, Memorandum for Mr. Sullivan, 1 December 1948; CAPT R.W. Ruble, Aide to the SECNAV, Memorandum for the Secretary of the Air Force, 22 March 1949, SNP.
90. See James N. Eastman, Jr., "Flight of the Lucky Lady II," Aerospace Historian 16 (Winter 1969): 9-11, 33-35.
91. Secret. United States Air Force Policy on Doctrine and Procedures for the Air Defense of the United States (Washington: Department of the Air Force, HQ, USAF, Office of the Deputy Chief of Staff, Operations, 1949); Secret. MGEN John B. Carey, USAF, Deputy Director of Plans, DCS/O, to Joseph W. Angell, Jr., 31 October 1956; Secret. Directorate of Historical Services. Office of Information Services. Continental Air Defense Command. Historical Studies No. 9, 1 December 1955, courtesy Dr. James N. Eastman, Jr., Archives Branch Research Studies Institute, Maxwell AFB; Clement L. Grant, "Air Defense of North America," in Alfred Goldberg, ed., A History of the United States Air Force, 1907-1957 (Princeton, N.J.: Van Nostrand Reinhold, 1957), pp. 129-38.
92. Harry S. Truman, Memoirs of Harry S. Truman, 2 vols. (Garden City, N.Y.: Doubleday, 1955-1956), 2: 120-31; "Britain: Base for Air Showdown," USNWR 25 (30 July 1948): 13-15; Robert A. Divine, "The Cold War and the Election of 1948," JAH 59 (June 1972): 91.
93. Millis, ed., Forrestal Diaries, p. 458.
94. Richard F. Haynes, The Awesome Power: Harry S. Truman as Commander in Chief (Baton Rouge: Louisiana State University Press, 1973), pp. 142-43.
95. Ferrell, Marshall, p. 239.
96. Editorial, "The Air Force Secretary," AW 50 (March 14, 1949): 50.
97. Ferrell, Marshall, pp. 239-40.
98. Frank Robert Futrell, Ideas, Concepts, Doctrine: A History of Basic Thinking in the United

States Air Force 1907-1964 (Maxwell Air Force Base, Ala: Air University, 1971), pp. 99-100; Millis, ed., *Forrestal Diaries,* pp. 462-68, 476; Arnold A. Rogow, *James Forrestal: A Study of Personality, Politics, and Policy* (New York: Macmillan, 1963), pp. 296-99; Hammond, "Super Carriers and B-36 Bombers," pp. 451-54.

99. Hanson Baldwin in *New York Times,* 23 September 1948; Millis, ed., *Forrestal Diaries,* pp. 476-77; Robert L. Smith, "The Influence of U.S.A.F. Chief of Staff General Hoyt S. Vandenberg on United States National Security Policy," Ph.D. diss., American University, 1965. Xerox. Ann Arbor, Mich.: University Microfilms, 1973, pp. 70-72.
100. Millis, ed., *Forrestal Diaries,* p. 477.
101. Marquis Childs, "The Battle of the Pentagon," *Harper's* 199 (August 1949): 50.
102. "Closer Accord Seen as Result of Conferences," ANJ 85 (28 August 1948): 1433, 1435, 1459.
103. SECDEF, Memorandum for Secretary Army, Navy, Air Force, 8 November 1948, Navy Department Bulletin 48-854, NDB 13 (15 November 1948): 17-18.
104. "Secnav Praises Air Force," ANJ 86 (18 September 1949): 70.
105. *New York Times,* 30 September 1948.

4
The Defense Budget for Fiscal Year 1950:
First Steps

In the spring of 1948, when it began working on its budget for fiscal year 1950, the Air Force had assumed that it would be granted funds for seventy groups and asked the Secretary of Defense, James V. Forrestal, for $8 billion. "Word got around," said the Secretary of the Air Force, W. Stuart Symington, "that again the three services were going to ask for everything they could get on a unilateral basis and then we were all going to be cut proportionately because there was no agreement on strategic plans against which to buy." Symington raised his demand to $11 billion, with the result that the total defense budget approximated $30 billion. As already noted, President Harry S. Truman allotted only $14.4 billion to defense, and Forrestal had to make a decision between the demands of the military services and the limit set by the president. When the National Security Council failed to answer his request for advice, Forrestal had turned to the General Joseph T. McNarney budget review board, which reduced the defense figure to $23.6 billion but could go no lower. With $14.4 billion, said the Joint Chiefs of Staff, all the United States could do was to launch atomic air strikes at the Soviet Union, whereas $16.9 billion would permit such strikes and in addition guarantee control of the Mediterranean. Forrestal talked with Truman on 5 October 1949. Truman stuck to $14.4 billion and suggested that a supplemental appropriation could be made if one was needed to hold the Mediterranean.[1]

On 6 October, the Joint Chiefs of Staff formally submitted to Forrestal a report on the military budget for fiscal year 1950. They had "come up with a plan," and suggested $4.483 billion for the Army, $4.624 billion for the Navy, and $5.025 billion for the Air Force. Although the similarity of the figures made it appear that the Joint Chiefs had again attempted to keep the services "balanced," Forrestal noted that "there was only really one major split decision which was on the question of the plan of construction of additional new, big carriers. That question I had to resolve myself."[2] In the first week in August, a contract to build a supercarrier had been given to the Newport News Shipbuilding and Drydock Company. Forrestal decided that no more such ships would be built.

While the board of budget deputies had suggested a budget of $23 billion for fiscal year 1950, the Chief of Staff of the Army, General Omar N. Bradley, and the Chief of Staff of the Air Force, General Hoyt S. Vandenberg, had submitted identical figures to Forrestal, with Bradley taking umbrage at the fact that the Sixth Fleet was designed to fight air battles and ground forces, functions that had been given to the Air Force and Army, respectively. Vandenberg also noted that the Air Force must be reduced to forty-eight groups and change its aircraft purchasing program. The Secretary of the Army, Kenneth C. Royall, objected not only to the $14.4 billion limit set on the military budget by the president but insisted on lopping off almost $1 billion from the $5.9 billion the Navy hoped to get if the budget was raised to $16.9 billion.[3] Truman and Forrestal had asked General Dwight D. Eisenhower, who had resigned from the Army to become the president of Columbia University, to come to Washington and "talk fundamentals: policy, budget and our whole military-diplomatic position." Eisenhower had held the Joint Chiefs in day-long sessions until he suffered a case of gastroenteritis. On 15 October, Forrestal also had a long meeting with the Joint Chiefs of Staff and others. He admitted that under the president's budget ceiling "You cannot have a satisfactory and usable military power. . . . You can do a patchwork job. You cannot do a thorough one." But a second figure, an intermediate figure of $17.5 billion or $18 billion, with which to support American policy vis a vis Russia could be supported before Congress and the public.[4] Pressed by the Bureau of the Budget for his requirements, on 29 October he asked the Joint Chiefs for a definite schedule for the resolution of the problem by 9 November and offered two budgets, one of $14.4 billion, the second of $17.5 billion. "If no agreed recommendation can be reached," he added, "I request individual recommendations."[5] Unable to agree, the Joint Chiefs dumped their revised requests—of $4.8 billion for the Army, $4.6 billion for the Navy, and $5 billion for the Air Force—into his lap.[6] The Chief of Naval Operations, Admiral Louis E. Denfeld, also reported disagreements on how many carriers should be used, for the Army suggested one group of six, the Navy two groups of six each, and the Air Force one group of only four.[7]

After reading the memorandum of disagreement on budget from the Joint Chiefs, Forrestal wrote in his diary what he considered a sound answer to most of the interservice arguments:

> I do not believe that air power alone can win a war any more than an Army or naval power can win a war, and I do not believe in the theory that an atomic offensive will extinguish in a week the will to fight. I believe air power will have to be applied massively in order to really destroy the industrial complex of any nation and, in terms of present capabilities, that means air power within fifteen hundred miles of the targets—that means an Army has to be transported to the areas where the airfields exist—that means, in turn, there has to be security of the sea lanes provided by the naval forces to get the Army there. Then, and only then, can the tremen-

dous striking power of air be applied in a decisive—and I repeat decisive—manner.[8]

On the next day, 9 November, he told the Joint Chiefs that "My decision is to authorize the Navy to maintain 2 carrier task groups (8 carriers) including appropriate support, provided that the forces shown as the Navy program . . . can be maintained within the $4.6 billion budget allocated by me on recommendation of the Joint Chiefs of Staff."[9] He also quickly sought to admonish Admiral Arthur W. Radford, vice chief of Naval Operations, who had criticized the B-36 before the Ferdinand Eberstadt Committee, which was looking into the matter of Defense Department reorganization, in a letter to the Secretary of the Navy, John L. Sullivan. The letter stated that one could defend the competence of his service to perform its missions but must not attack the competence of another.[10] He never sent the letter.

On 31 October, Rear Admiral Daniel V. Gallery had said confidentially what Radford had said in secret. Upon reading a report by General J. Lawton Collins, USA, that urged adoption of the German general staff system and cutting the Navy down to an escort of convoy force, Gallery had written a ten-page confidential memorandum to Denfeld to the effect that the Navy was better suited for strategic bombing than the Air Force and that unless the Navy kept its foot in the door for that mission it would soon be out of business and the country would be the loser. Bombers flying from overseas bases could not depend upon those bases, whereas no one's consent was needed to sail carrier task forces or missile-carrying submarines in international waters. If the Navy were cut down to an escort force, "we might as well scrap it." If considered heresy by Forestal and those who agreed that the strategic bombing mission belonged to the Air Force, Gallery's paper found favor with most of the Navy's very important people. Gallery later claimed that he did not know how Drew Pearson obtained a copy of his memorandum, which Pearson published verbatim. He did recall, however, that "The published memo hit the Pentagon like an earthquake. The Secretary of Defense and the Air Force raised hell. Secretary of the Navy Sullivan blew his gasket, and . . . wanted to hang me from the top of the Washington Monument." While friends sent Gallery on an inspection trip to isolated places and told him to take his time getting back, all copies of the memorandum were recalled to Denfeld's office and the Office of Naval Intelligence was directed to find out how Pearson had obtained his copy. Years later, after he had retired, Gallery could not find a copy of the memorandum in his own files. Nor could he find a copy in the files of the chief of Naval Operations, leading him to conclude that all copies had been burned. However, a call to Pearson produced a copy.[11]

While Gallery's demand for the development of a naval air atomic capability, which was matched by that of Herbert Riley and others, may not have been the causative factor, the Navy did dig more deeply into a comparison of the "military suitability of aircraft carriers and land bases." Undertaken by the Navy's Operations Evaluation Group, the study, in brief, concluded that the delivery of weapons by air became extremely expensive at ranges beyond 500-1,000 miles and that carrier-based aircraft were less expensive than land-based aircraft at extended ranges. Should not the effectiveness of strategic atomic bombing by carrier-based aircraft be explored? For the moment, while the services angrily debated roles and missions, the Navy Department suppressed the report and vetoed further action.[12]

Matching Gallery's blast against the Air Force was the attack upon the operations of the Army's 27th Division in World War II by General Holland M. "Mad" Smith, USMC. Smith had submitted manuscripts for a book and magazine articles to Sullivan based upon it. Sullivan knew that General Clifton B. Cates, commandant of the Marine Corps, his predecessor, General A. A. Vandegrift, and other friends had begged Smith to tone down his critique of Ralph Smith, the commanding general of the 27th he had summarily relieved during the battle for Saipan.[13] He also received from Cates a summary of the facts in the Army-Marine controversy. Cates personally discussed the book with H. M. Smith and urged him not to publish it. When Smith demurred, Cates said, "General, [General Roy S.] Geiger was a good friend of yours, wasn't he? One of your best?"

Smith replied, "Yes, he was."

Cates said, "Well if he was alive today he wouldn't want you to publish that book."

With tears starting to come down his cheeks, Smith looked at Cates and then jumped at him so suddenly that Cates thought he would hit him. He then said, "Goddam it, don't hit me below the belt."

Cates replied, "All right, go ahead and publish it."[14]

Late in September 1947, after "suffering in silence" for three years in order, it said, not to impede national security, the 27th Division Association, meeting in convention, let loose a strong attack on published criticism of the division's battle conduct on Saipan. Because its historian published a vindication of the 27th that was being given wide publicity, Cates asked for and Sullivan approved immediate declassification of Marine Corps records on the subject. Hoping to preserve harmony between the Marine Corps and the Army, and perhaps to mollify various admirals "Mad" Smith had criticized,[15] Sullivan told Smith that he had no intention of restricting him in any way but that he should check his facts. Unmoved, Smith told Cates that "in my opinion the Army is determined to abolish us or reduce us to an ineffective strength and this was determined long ago." Although Smith furnished him a brief on the controversy, Sullivan shunted the problem to Forrestal. One of Smith's articles was already in press. At Sullivan's suggestion he made several minor changes in it. To insure that they would not be made in print, he sent them to the publisher by mail rather than using the telephone. Despite Sullivan and his Marine Corps friends, moreover, he published his book, *Coral and Brass*, which makes good reading. To Cates, at least, it stated the facts, cleared the air, and did not exacerbate interservice rivalry.[16]

Sullivan had also been embarrassed by the publication by the Naval War

College of a pamphlet entitled *Concept of World War III*, dated 7 October 1948, that disparaged the Air Force. When Secretary Symington learned about it and asked for a copy, Sullivan replied that the pamphlet had been prepared without the knowledge of the chief of Naval Operations, who upon reviewing it had ordered all copies destroyed. Therefore no copy could be furnished.[17] When Symington then asked for a statistical study of naval aviation in World War II, Sullivan replied that publication of the study, completed on 17 June 1946, had been disapproved and all proof copies had been recalled.[18] According to Roscoe Drummond, writing in the *Christian Science Monitor*, the Navy had been "throwing the biggest rocks it can lay its hands on against the Air Force concepts of strategic warfare." It had been doing so for months, "not very subtly, and certainly not very surreptitiously," as revealed in the War College pamphlet he stated was being circulated by the chief of Naval Operations. Drummond then asked "how much longer will James Forrestal continue to tear his hair over leaks disclosing armed services disunity instead of dealing with the disunity itself?"[19] As though in response to Drummond, on 23 January 1949, Marshall Andrews, a reporter for the *Washington Post*, charged that the Air Force planned to use its funds to build up a strategic force at the expense of other elements of air power, indeed, to "double the number of B-36s at the expense of everything else." He offered two reasons for the Air Force action: "(1) to win the sympathy of Congress and of the public so as to obtain additional funds for other aircraft without sacrificing the 'strategic bombers' it is determined to have, and (2) a stubborn insistence on going ahead with its own private concepts of warfare and be damned to everything else." Were the Air Force to carry out its plan, Andrews concluded, it would "reveal a degree of irresponsibility to the other services which renders its motives suspect."[20]

Continued within and without the services, the argument over which service would get how much for which weapons was not always bereft of petty self-interest or of human and institutional jealousy. On 16 December 1948, Symington had sent Sullivan a collection of comments on the Air Force made by Sullivan, former Assistant Secretary for Air John Nicholas Brown, Admirals Nimitz, Gallery, Radford, Denfeld, E. A. Cruise, Robert Carney, and others in the Navy. It was entitled *The Silent Service* and, Symington said, was disparaging in nature. "Some of these [comments] look a bit far fetched but others really do hurt," he told Sullivan.[21] On 4 January 1949, Sullivan reciprocated by sending Symington a forty-five page collection of quotations from Symington himself, Assistant Secretary C. V. Whitney, Generals Carl Spaatz, E. R. "Pete" Quesada, George C. Kenney, James Doolittle, Vandenberg, and various official and unofficial Air Force publications critical of the Navy. Entitled *The Modest Service*, it had been prepared by a think tank and special public relations group in the Office of the Chief of Naval Operations known by the code number OP-23. Sullivan admitted that "two or three" of the quotations in the *Silent Service* were improper, adding that their authors had been admonished. However, the inclusion of secret material in the unclassified Air Force brochure showed that there was a leak in Symington's department. More important, "some of the comments indicate a degree of sensitiveness that seems to verge upon the pathological." For example, "A good word about the Navy spoken by an admiral was not a slap in the face to the Air Force." Moreover,

> The comments in your brochure illuminate an immature attitude that has persisted far too long. The consequences of this attitude are serious, since it tends to impose upon the people of the United States a distorted view of their defenses and may induce them to reach calamitous decisions. I cannot divest myself of the view that matters related to national security deserve more cool and profound consideration.[22]

An excellent example of Sullivan's comment was furnished by Air Force opposition to an article written by Gallery for *Science Illustrated*. Denfeld and Sullivan had directed Gallery to recall an earlier article submitted to the *Readers Digest* and denied him permission to publish a second. The Air Force objected not to the text but to the illustrations in the *Science Illustrated* article. Captain Walter Karig, USNR, in Navy Public Relations, checked with Steve Leo, in charge of Air Force public relations, who said the protest was "strictly on security grounds." However, Gallery's illustrations had been taken from articles previously published by Generals Spaatz and Kenney, among others, and his text, considered to be noncontroversial, had been cleared by Denfeld and Sullivan as well. The Air Force was thus left in the ridiculous position of objecting to illustrations it had itself published.[23] Similarly, the Navy looked askance at the pressure the Air Force put on Jack Warner not to show the film *Task Force*, which the Navy wanted to show first on 4 July 1949, until 1950.[24]

Public relations efforts were going on in several Navy offices, for Captain Herbert D. Riley wrote Admiral Radford about a letter being prepared by Cedric Worth, the former Hollywood script writer and journalist who was working in the office of Dan A. Kimball, assistant secretary of the Navy for Air, and another by H. A. Lotta Lawrence. Retaliation to the Air Force in kind, as in the *Modest Service*, was not the answer, Riley added. The Worth letter was much better and could prove useful if its exposition were improved and supporting data was provided for some of the points it made.[25] Asked to comment on the issue, Lawrence suggested that "(1) if interservice cooperation is desired, disregard the whole matter and have the Joint Chiefs of Staff acknowledge receipt; (2) if no interservice cooperation can be gained, suggest a reply similar to the 'Worth Letter'." He preferred the former course, for "it would be impossible to formulate any reply or replies to the Air Force . . . which would convince them they are wrong and the Navy right."[26]

At one point, Denfeld got involved with Drew Pearson. On 6 August 1946,

Forrestal, then secretary of the Navy, had written to Senator David J. Walsh, chairman of the Senate Naval Affairs Committee, and enclosed a copy of the report of the Joint Chiefs of Staff Evaluation Board on atomic test "A" held at Bikini on 1 July and a preliminary report on test "B." The tests had been suggested among others by Senator Brian McMahon and Lieutenant General Barney Giles, commanding the Army's Strategic Air Forces in the Pacific. They had been approved by General H. H. Arnold, commanding general of the Army Air Forces, who broached the issue in the Joint Chiefs of Staff on 18 September 1945. Busy with "bringing the boys home" and other matters concerning the postwar demobilization, Admiral Ernest J. King had endorsed the proposal and offered various suggestions on how the tests should be conducted. If the Navy was unenthusiastic about the tests because they might provide unfavorable results, the Air Force ardently wished to prove its capability of delivering the atomic weapon and thus enhance its drive for organizational autonomy. With dour forbodings that the tests would reveal weakness in ships and equipment that would cause the public and Congress to restrict the size of the Navy and heighten the influence of the Army Air Force, the Navy nevertheless provided most of the ships, equipment, and personnel for them. A spark of hope was generated when the Army Air Force B-29 that dropped the 20 KT bomb on 1 July missed its designated target by 1,500 to 2,000 feet, thus questioning the capability of that service. The second test, held on 25 July, was an underwater blast that went according to schedule.

"In general," Forrestal wrote, "it may be said that these tests are indicating changes in naval construction and in naval tactics in order to combat any future enemy using atomic weapons, but properly designed naval vessels and properly controlled naval forces are by no means considered obsolescent. Naval vessels and naval forces are considered to remain highly essential to our naval defense."[27] After reading a column Pearson had written about the Bikini tests, Denfeld wrote:

Dear Drew:

I start each day with orange juice and Drew Pearson and this morning I thought somebody had slipped a lemon into my eye-opener. . . . What you had to say . . . was based on a combination of inadequate fact and erroneous information.

Denfeld explained that the ships had been placed much closer together than they would be in normal operations, and had been anchored at that, in order to expose them to maximum damage. The Navy had given out all "permissible facts," those that did not reveal military secrets to a potential enemy. Pearson should have checked his data with Denfeld or Sullivan's public information people. Denfeld added, significantly, "Apparently you also seem to be supplied with most of your material about the new big carrier from sources richer in prejudice than information."[28] According to Captain Fitzhugh Lee, Sullivan's naval aide, Pearson had developed a sour taste for the Navy since he

124-25; Robert L. Smith, "The Influence of U.S.A.F. Chief of Staff General Hoyt S. Vandenberg on United States National Security Policy" (Ph.D. diss., American University, 1965. Xerox. Ann Arbor, Mich.: University Microfilms, 1973), pp. 82-83.

3. Conf. Kenneth C. Royall, Memorandum for SECDEF, 25 October 1948, SNP.

4. Millis, ed., Forrestal Diaries, p. 514 (entry of 27 October 1948).

5. Secret. Office of Budget to Office of SECDEF, 29 October 1948; Secret. Forrestal to the JCS, 29 October 1948, Washington, NHD, OA, JCS File 1800/48, in Papers of the Chief of Naval Operations (hereafter cited as CNO Papers).

6. Secret. W. G. Lawlor and J. H. Ives, Joint Secretariat, "Note by the Secretaries to the JCS on Allocation of Forces and Funds for FY [1950] Budget," 8 November 1948, JCS 1800/48, copy in CNO Papers; Millis, ed., Forrestal Diaries, pp. 493, 499-500, 502-11.

7. According to Robert L. Smith, "The Influence of U.S.A.F. General Hoyt S. Vandenberg," Vandenberg wrote Forrestal on 13 December 1948 that the carriers used money better given to the Army and Air Force and that the JCS were unable to agree on how many carriers the Navy should operate. Vandenberg recommended four large carriers, the Army six, and the Navy nine.

8. Millis, ed., Forrestal Diaries, p. 514 (entry of 27 October 1948).

9. Forrestal, Memorandum for SECA, SECNAV, SECAF, 8 November 1948, ibid., pp. 515-17.

10. Draft letter, 29 October 1948, ibid., p. 514 n. 13.

11. Daniel V. Gallery RADM, USN (RET), Eight Bells and All's Well (New York: W. W. Norton, 1965), pp. 228-30. Gallery had written two memoranda on the subject, dated 31 October and 17 November 1947. On 31 December, he had then summarized the two in a third memorandum for Nimitz, who used it to prepare his valedictory address, "The Future Employment of Naval Forces," which he sent to Sullivan on his last day of active Duty, 17 December (Daniel V. Gallery, Memorandum for RADM Clark, "The Navy's Role in a Future War," 14 November 1947, NHD. OA.) The Gallery letter to VADM Donald B. Duncan is revealed in an interview with Gallery on 9 April 1975 at Oakton, Va., cited in Supporting Study: US Aircraft Carriers in the Strategic Role. Part I—Naval Strategy in a Period of Change: Interservice Rivalry, Strategic Interaction, and the Development of a Nuclear Attack Capability, 1945-1951, itself part of History of the Strategic Arms Competition 1945-1972 (Falls Church, Va.: Lulejian and Associates, October 1975), p. 58 n. 33 (hereafter cited as Supporting Study). See also "The Reminiscences of Daniel V. Gallery, RADM, USN (RET), transcript of oral interviews by John T. Mason (Annapolis, Md.: U. S. Naval Institute).

12. Operations Evaluation Group. Study No. 27. "Preliminary Study of the Comparative Military Suitability of Aircraft Carriers and Land Bases," 26 February 1948, copy in NHD, OA, OP-23 Files.

13. Holland M. Smith, Coral and Brass (New York: Charles Scribner's Sons, 1949), pp. 159-80; Cates, Memorandum for SECNAV, 1 August 1947, SNP.

14. Transcript of oral interview by Benis M. Frank with Gen Clifton B. Cates, USMC (RET) (Washington; HQ, USMC, History Division, 1967), pp. 222-23, (hereafter cited as Cates, "Reminiscences").

15. See LGEN Holland M. Smith, USMC, "Tarrawa Was a Mistake," SEP 231 6 November 1948; 15-17, 91, 94, 96-98, 101, 102; "My Troubles with the Army on Saipan," SEP 13 November 1948): 32-33, 65-66, 73, 74, 76-78, 80, 82; "Iwo Jima Cost Too Much," SEP 20 November 1948): 32-33, 48, 53, 55, 58, 61-62, 64-65.

16. Cates to Smith 16 April, 10 July 1948; Smith to Cates, 19 July 1948; Smith, Memorandum for the SECNAV, 2 August 1948; Forrestal to Sullivan, 4 October 1948; Ben Jibbs, ed. SEP, forwarded to Forrestal to Sullivan, 6 October 1948; John L. Sullivan, Memorandum for Secretary Forrestal, 18 November 1948, SNP; Cates, "Reminiscences," pp. 223-24.

17. Secret. Symington, Memorandum for John L. Sullivan, 18 November 1948; John L. Sullivan to Symington, 23 November 1948, SNP.

18. John L. Sullivan, Memorandum for SECAF, 29 November 1948; H. C. Beauregard to USECNAV, 3 February 1949, SNP.

19. Christian Science Monitor, 19 November 1948.

20. Washington Post, 23 January 1949.

21. Secret. W. Stuart Symington to John L. Sullivan, 16 December 1948, SNP.

22. Secret. John L. Sullivan to Symington, 4 January 1949, SNP.

23. Walter Karig, Memorandum for Adm Denfeld, 28 January 1949; Louis E. Denfeld, Memorandum for Secretary Sullivan, 28 January 1949, SNP.

and Robert S. Allen, who had collaborated in writing the book, *Washington Merry Go Round (1932)*, had applied for military service when World War II began. Allen was taken into the Army as a major, but the Navy would offer Pearson nothing more than the grade of junior lieutenant, which Pearson rejected. Lee met several times with one of Pearson's star workers, Jack Anderson, in the hope of "bringing facts into print" in Pearson's columns, which quoted the works of William B. Huie occasionally—but to no avail.[29]

More important than the effect of Huie and his ilk was the fact that the Joint Chiefs of Staff Evaluation Board report on tests A and B recommended that research be continued on nuclear weapons and also on defenses against any produced by an enemy nation. Although it did not mention the Army Air Force, that service was the only conceivable agency capable at the time of providing such defense. Even before the submission of the report, however, various officers in OP-602, Atomic Weapons Divisions, wrote a letter requesting that the president "authorize the Navy to make preparations for possible delivery of atomic bombs in an emergency in order that the capabilities of the Carrier Task Force may be utilized to the maximum advantage for national defense." Because Forrestal was witnessing the Bikini tests, the letter went to the Acting Secretary, Sullivan. Upon his return, Forrestal replied to the Navy's first formal request for the development of a nuclear attack capability by saying that presidential authority was not necessary and that the Navy should continue converting the AJ-1 aircraft so that it could carry an atomic weapon.[30]

On 6 November 1948 Truman had asked Forrestal to submit by the twenty-ninth the subjects he wanted included in the State of the Union message and the Economic Report of the President to be presented to Congress in January 1949 and also a report on the proposed legislative program of the National Military Establishment.[31] Forrestal in turn had asked the service secretaries to forward similar data to him by the twenty-second.[32] Sullivan had nothing to offer for the Economic Report and agreed with Forrestal's draft of items to be included in the State of the Union message except on two points, both bearing on the Eberstadt Committee report that had been completed on 1 November: (1) because he already had the power to exercise "general direction, authority, and control" over the departments and agencies of the National Military Establishment, a statutory increase in the authority of the secretary of defense would make it appear that he had not been able to administer those departments and agencies well; (2) because he had power of decision over the Joint Chiefs of Staff, "It would be a grave mistake to create by statute a military Chairman for this body and thus to delegate to an agent this most important function and power of the Secretary of Defense.[33]

Meanwhile Sullivan had directed all naval agency heads to report by 1 December on a review of their five major problems, to indicate "whether they be organizational, functional, or otherwise," list them in order of priority, and append recommendations for solving them.[34] On 12 January 1949 his counsel, Henry C. Beauregard, sent Sullivan a twenty-page summary and a four-page brief of the replies. In order of priority, the reporting activities listed their problems as: (1) unification; (2) operations; (3) Naval Reserve; (4) budget; (5) pay, housing, and morale; (6) personnel; (7) material; (8) transportation; (9) management; and (10) public relations. For our purpose, the first is the most important and deserves quoting from Beauregard in full:

> The philosophy of merger . . . is unsettling the whole Navy. The progress of unification to date has resulted in an uncoordinated and excessive use of personnel . . . and . . . in exorbitant demands on the Navy for personnel, time and effort. Unification is showing an imbalance between the philosophy of unification as such and the needs of the individual services, exemplified by a zeal for consolidation which is not balanced against the necessity for a framework for rapid expansion in the event of an emergency. . . . The Army has a continuing and apparently coordinated effort to abolish the Marines, and the Army must realize that the Marines should continue to exist as an effective amphibious force.

As for operations: "Vital decisions on national policy must be made before top planning can become firm. Our national intelligence is very weak." On budget: "Mostly a matter of shortage of funds, which means that a Navy of the present size and missions cannot be maintained on the present budget and that the equipment of a modern offensive task force of moderate size does not appear probable within the next five years." Beauregard went on to state that "the dollar determines strategy" and that too many agencies were involved in the preparation of the budget. On management, one bureau chief felt that "there is so much management control over a bureau because of directives from the Secretary of Defense, all the unification agencies, the Navy Secretariat, the Chief of Naval Operations, Office of Budget and Review, the Fiscal Director, and others, that no bureau chief could hope to understand and execute all such directives."[35]

By 17 November Forrestal had been provided with details on budgets amounting to $14.4, $16.9, and $21.4 billion, but the director of the budget would hear of nothing beyond $14.4 billion.[36] On the twenty-second, Forrestal talked with the Secretary of State, George C. Marshall, who impressed upon him the need to provide arms for Western European nations, particularly for France. On the twenty-third, Sullivan sent Forrestal a Navy budget fitting a total of $4.6 billion and also one of $5.375 billon that might prove useful for determining whether the administration would have to place controls over the national economy.[37] On the same day, at Forrestal's request, the service secretaries, the Joint Chiefs of Staff, and representatives from the departments of State and Treasury met to discuss the capabilities of the military forces under budgets of $14.4, $16.9, and $21.4 billion and the availability of military equipment for Europe during the next six to eight months, thus taking into account Marshall's desire to rearm Western Europe.[38] On 1 December Forrestal submitted his budget and told Truman and then wrote him that the Join Chiefs of Staff

do not believe that our national security can be adequately safeguarded with the forces which can be maintained under this 14.4 billion budget. It is their recommendation that forces are needed which could require an amount approximating 23 billion dollars be appropriated for the maintenance of our national security during FY 1950. I therefore recommened the figure in between, or 16.9.[39]

Various top naval officers objected to Truman's budget figures, with one of them saying that the total "By no means provides the balanced forces considered necessary by the JCS. . . . and entails a reduction of naval readiness below that now existing."[40] The director of the Navy's Office of Budget and Reports, Rear Admiral Herbert G. Hopwood, pointed out to Forrestal's comptroller, Wilfred McNeil, that the Navy's force levels could be maintained in fiscal years 1950, 1951, and 1952 only if there were no increase in the cost of labor and material and no increase in the funds allotted for aircraft procurement. Moreover, the freezing of naval aircraft procurement would result in smaller operating forces, or of less effective forces consisting of second-line aircraft, because neither a 14.6 billion nor a 15.375 billion budget provided for attrition losses or for the replacement of about one-hundred obsolescent aircraft.[41]

On 9 December Sullivan, the other service secretaries, the Joint Chiefs, and various civilian budget experts had presented to Truman a defense program they believed to be adequate from the military point of view and reasonable from the budgetary standpoint. During the last five months, Forrestal had spent about six-hundred hours with the McNarney board. In consequence, the $30 billion originally suggested by the Joint Chiefs had been cut to $16.9 billion. Truman listened politely, found the presentations "very interesting," but remained unmoved.[42] Indeed, on the fourteenth he directed Forrestal to cut his $14.497 billion budget to $14.197 billion. Subsequent attempts by Forrestal to get Truman to lift the ceiling proved unavailing, and on the seventeenth Sullivan bowed to the inevitable and notified the Bureau of the Budget that he would declare a one-year shipbuilding holiday and devote savings thus accrued toward a supercarrier.[43]

Arriving on Truman's desk at about the same time as Forrestal's budget was the report of the Eberstadt Committee, to which we will turn before returning to the budget problem.

NOTES

1. Samuel P. Huntington, *The Soldier and the State: The Theory and Politics of Civil-Military Relations* (Cambridge, Mass.: The Belknap Press of Harvard University Press, 1967), pp. 445-46; Walter Millis, ed., with the collaboration of E. S. Duffield, *The Forrestal Diaries* (New York: The Viking Press, 1951), p. 493; *New York Herald Tribune*, 8 August 1948.
2. Robert Frank Futrell, *Ideas, Concepts, Doctrine: A History of Basic Thinking in the United States Air Force 1907-1964* (Maxwell Air Force Base, Ala.: Air University, 1971), pp.

24. Alan Brown, Memorandum for Mr. Sullivan, 9 May 1949, SNP.
25. Riley, Memorandum for ADM Arthur Radford, 12 January 1949, SNP.
26. H. A. Latta Lawrence, Memorandum to ADM Radford, 10 January, 1949, SNP.
27. Letter, SNP. for the results of the atomic tests, see especially William A. Shurcliff, *Bombs at Bikini: The Official Report of Operation Crossroads* (New York: William A. Wise, 1947), and VADM William H. P. Blandy, "Operation Crossroads: the Story of the Air and Underwater Tests of the Atomic Bomb at Bikini," *Army Ordnance* 31 (January-February 1947): 341-43.
28. Denfeld to Pearson, 19 February 1949, CNO Papers.
29. "The Reminiscences of VADM Fitzhugh Lee, U. S. Navy (RET)," transcript of oral interview by CDR Etta Belle Kitchen, USN (RET), (Annapolis, Md.: U. S. Naval Institute, 1970), pp. 185-87.
30. John L. Sullivan, Acting SECNAV, draft of a letter to the President, NHD, OA, A, A. Burke, Personal File.
31. Truman to Forrestal, 6 November 1948, SNP.
32. Forrestal, Memorandum for the SECA, SECNAV, SECAF, 8 November 1948, SNP.
33. John L. Sullivan, Memorandum for the SECDEF, 29 November 1948, SNP. Sullivan also charged the Secretary's Committee on Unification, headed by the USECNAV, to prepare recommendations for changes in the National Military Establishment that would be needed in case of an emergency. (Secret. H. C. Beauregard to USECNAV, 8 December 1948, SNP).
34. John L. Sullivan to Distribution List, 12 November 1948, SNP.
35. Top Secret. H. C. Beauregard, Memorandum for the Secretary, 12 January 1949; Top Secret. Beauregard to Assistant Secretary of the Navy for Air, 16 January 1949, SNP.
36. Secret. SECDEF, Memorandum to the JCS, 17 November 1948, CNO Papers; James E. Webb to SECDEF, 1 December 1948, SNP.
37. John L. Sullivan to SECDEF, 9 November, 1 December 1948, SNP.
38. Forrestal to Bradley, 19 November 1948; Forrestal, Memorandum for All Service Secretaries and the JCS, Snyder, Lovett, Draper, 22 November 1948, JCS File 1800/18, CNO Papers.
39. Director, BOB, to SECDEF, with enclosures, 1 December 1948, JCS File 1800/18; Note by The Secretaries to the JCS of Allocation of Funds for FY 1950 Budget, 18 November 1948, JCS File 1800/19; SECDEF to the President, 1 December 1948, SNP.
40. RADM R. N. Libby, Op-001, and VADM A. P. "Rip" Struble, Deputy CNO (Operations), were two of Denfeld's staff who objected to the Truman figure. (Top Secret letters of November and 22 November 1948, respectively, in JCS 1800/18, SNP).
41. Hopwood, Memorandum for the SECDEF. Attn: McNeil, 8 December 1948, SNP.
42. Millis, ed., *Forrestal Diaries*, p. 536.
43. Secret. John L. Sullivan to James E. Webb, 17 December 1948, SNP.

5

Defense Reorganization Plans, the Defense Budget for Fiscal Year 1950, and the Resignation of James V. Forrestal

In May 1948 Ferdinand Eberstadt was selected to head a task force to study the National Security Organization under the Commission on Organization of the Executive Branch of the Government, or Hoover Commission, and explore how the nation could be provided with maximum security at minimum cost. Among the twenty-three men were business leaders, presidents of higher institutions of learning, a journalist, a newspaper publisher, and various retired Army, Navy, and Air Force officers. Herbert Hoover himself opened the initial session on 8 June; the report would go directly to the President "on or about 1 November."

The military reporter Hanson W. Baldwin, a member of the Eberstadt committee, told an interviewer in 1976 that Eberstadt knew his way around Washington, where all the bodies were buried, and what was going on behind the scenes. Moreover, he realized that "everybody then was riding the economy band wagon" and that many were worried that the Russians would cause the United States to spend itself into bankruptcy. Therefore "we were going to have to be careful about . . . not having a garrison state in the atomic age, and, at the same time, not having a bankrupt state."[1]

After spending five days on the organization for national security, the committee would hear among others, from representatives from the Joint Chiefs of Staff (12-14 July), Office of the Secretary of Defense (27-28 July), and from the services (10-11 August) on organizational problems. The military budget would be the subject for 5-7 October. "The Air Force and the Navy Air Arm" would be discussed on 18-20 October and again on 5 November.[2]

On 22 June the Secretary of the Navy, John L. Sullivan, directed all naval bureaus, boards, and agencies to suggest by 28 July the areas the Eberstadt Committee should investigate, and his Committee on Unification began formulating recommendations and seeking the personnel to make the presentations.[3] On the twenty-fifth he received a covering letter and an eighty-three page report from the General Board on "National Security and Navy Contributions Thereto for the Next 10 Years" that dealt with political, economic, and military matters and "Concepts of War and Navy Contributions."[4] Above all, said the report, the "United States . . . urgently needs a national plan of action. . . ." The most important contribution of the study was "THAT A COORDINATED OVERALL PLAN OF ACTION FOR NATIONAL SECURITY SHOULD BE PREPARED AT THE LEVEL OF THE NATIONAL SECURITY COUNCIL, KEPT UP TO DATE, AND MADE AVAILABLE TO ALL WORKING PLANNERS OF DEPARTMENTS AND AGENCIES." The Report noted the need to aid the free nations of Western Europe and Asia and for the United States to retain its economic, social, and governmental stability; to become and remain militarily strong; and to maintain a sound, strong, and consistent foreign policy the nation could support both economically and militarily. Moreover, "correct balance in strength of naval, land, and air must be achieved."

The naval air input into this 'balance" included four fast carrier task forces each comprised of one flush-deck carrier, one *Midway*-class carrier, two modernized *Essex*-class carriers, one guided missile ship, eight major support ships, and twenty-four destroyers in the screen. One air group embarked, one in reserve, would serve each carrier, with the heaviest and longest-ranging planes on the largest carriers, those of medium range on the *Midways*, and those of short range on the *Essexes*. Although 2,818 aircraft would be involved, only 45 of these would be AJ-1s or ADR-42s, each capable of delivering atomic weapons. This mix was the best available at the time, with the decision of how many of what type of plane to be embarked involving resolution of the perennial question of high-low mix—the more of one type of carrier the less of the others, so that a carrier with many heavy bombers might lack sufficient fighters and other types.

Particularly illustrative of the board's outlook upon unification and attitude toward the Air Force are the following comments:

> (1) Tactics and methods must be quickly modified to take full advantage of the potentialities of advanced weapons and techniques of war. . . . Nonetheless, we must be wary of our national predilection of panaceas, which tempts us to act as though future possibilities were today's facts. Concentration of available resources upon a single concept of war, method, or tool is an almost irretrievable act. . . .

> (e) There is no cheap or easy way to win a major war. . . .

> (g) The destruction of enemy industry and military support can be effected most quickly through airpower utilizing weapons of mass destruction, if they can be brought to bear in sufficient quantities. . . . At the present, the greatest single threat to the United States' military effectiveness overseas is

the possibility of an efficient enemy submarine force using submarines equal to or better than the German type 21. . . .

(j) In the foreseeable future, all the manifold requirements of naval operations for conduct of sea warfare will be encountered. . . . There will be greater emphasis than ever before on naval air, amphibious, and antisubmarine operations.[5]

Sullivan most likely expected that naval testimony given the Eberstadt Committee would follow the points in the General Board's report and be equally moderate. That the report itself was moderate in tone has been ascribed to the fact that the Air Force monopoly on atomic weapons precluded the Navy's estimating its own atomic warfare potential: it as yet lacked a specific nuclear military policy to follow, suitable aircraft given the size and weight of extant atomic bombs, knowledge of how many weapons it could obtain, and information on whether the Air Force would have overseas bases to use in time of war. The Navy thus offered its carriers as supplements rather than alternatives to land-based bombers.[6] Sullivan nevertheless directed that statements to be offered Eberstadt's committee be forwarded to his own Committee on Unification, with which he kept in close personal touch, and be approved by him prior to delivery.[7] Early in August, however, he was so irritated by the Secretary of the Air Force, W. Stuart Symington, that he gave him a terrific blast.

In reply to a request from Forrestal for suggested amendments to the National Security Act, Symington indicated that he would strengthen and centralize the authority of the Secretary of Defense, grant him an Under Secretary, and provide for a single chief of staff responsible to him alone. Moreover, by deleting the service secretaries from membership therein, he would let the Secretary of Defense be the only military representative on the National Security Council. Forrestal leaned towards Symington's suggestions except for the single chief of staff. The Secretary of the Army, Kenneth Royall, as noted below, parroted Symington,[8] and Truman was pleased.

In Los Angeles, on 16 July Symington criticized "axgrinders dedicated to obsolete methods," asserted that the "unbalancing" of the appropriations for the military services was unimportant, and demanded that American air power be put in balance with the military power of potential enemies.[9] He was echoed by a large number of high-ranking Air Force officers, who spoke about the applicability of Douhet's theories and strongly advocated a strategic bombardment strategy.[10] Symington then particularly aroused Sullivan's anger by a paper he sent him on 21 July entitled "The Position of the Air Force with Respect to the Question of the Navy Dropping the Atomic Bomb," with copies to the Secretary of Defense, James V. Forrestal and Royall. The major question was: "Should the Navy be authorized or required to drop the atomic bomb in the event of war if a decision has been made to use the atomic bomb?" Sullivan began by stating that " . . . I express to you my strong conviction that a unilateral development program directed toward achieving atomic weapon delivery systems would be unsound and fraught with gravest consequences." While he admitted that the Air Force had primary responsibility for strategic air operations, he disagreed with Symington's contention that any naval atomic air operations should be under the direction of the Air Force, that the Navy should develop neither special equipment nor organization for dropping such weapons unless there were ample resources available to all the services, and that since the Air Force could provide large bombs there was no need for the Navy to develop small ones. To support his own objections, Sullivan added that atomic bombs should be dropped only against targets of greatest strategic significance. The Navy would drop atomic bombs only on those targets included in strategic plans of the Joint Chiefs of Staff and in coordination with the Air Force. It would, however, drop such bombs upon naval targets in keeping with its primary mission. Were he to heed Symington and not develop equipment and organization to drop atomic bombs, the result "would guarentee against readiness of the Navy to deliver atomic weapons in a war emergeney." In consequence, the Navy would "survive only as a luxury item in the budget." Navy men helped to develop the atomic bomb, Sullivan reminded Symington, and the Navy intended to develop its organization and equipment, particularly in fast carrier task forces, for atomic bomb delivery.

Sullivan then offered the "Navy Position." The Navy's development program would produce more powerful atomic bombs for the future. Delivery systems could be expected to change radically in the next five years, with "the advent of jet fighters and antiaircraft guided missiles accelerating the obsolescence of the conventional VLR [Very Long Range] bomber." At war, the United States might lose land bases from which long-range bombers could be lauched. Sullivan then noted that, in view of the considerations he had mentioned, "it is mandatory that the United States avoid narrowness and rigidity, and maintain flexibility in development of atomic weapons and delivery systems including organizations." The Key West Conference, he added, stipulated "full utilization of . . . each service." Moreover, the Joint Chiefs of Staff on 21 June 1948 had approved naval task forces carrying aircraft capable of delivering atomic weapons necessary to accomplish the Navy's mission. His acceptance of the Air Force's position would "paralyze and stultify development of atomic weapon delivery systems by the Navy [and] provide an apt example and warning of the hazard of monopoly when applied to development." Sullivan therefore would: "(a) cooperate and support the development by the Air Force of reliable and effective long range delivery and atomic bombs from land bases; (b) [foster the] ability to deliver atomic bombs as a *normal* mission of the Navy, in performing both its primary and collateral functions; (c) as an item of high urgency and importance [develop] . . . seagoing atomic weapon delivery systems, including organizations."[11]

On 4 August 1948 Forrestal had asked Sullivan to provide recommendations for amending the National Security Act. Sullivan thought that the first year of experience under the Act had been quite good. Although some of the agencies it authorized were still being shaped and staffed, "experience to date has shown . . . that the Act . . . provides the basis for a smooth-running, balanced . . . organization. . . . Consquently, I feel that the Act should be given at least another year of trial before expanding the time and effort which any attempt to amend it would draw from another more vital matters demanding the attention of the Congress and the Military Establishment." However, certain improvements could be made by executive action, without amending legislation. Among these changes, as he had told the Eberstadt Committee, was the provision of a joint secretariat for the War Council, such a secretariat to serve the Secretary of Defense. Second, he would change the National Security Resources Board from a planning agency to a "central advisory and coordinating agency." Except for those changes, he would leave the Act alone "at this time."[12] As for the suggestion of "establishing a special group of officers permanently separated from their individual services to serve the National Military Establishment," he offered a peremptory negative. On the other hand, he supported universal military training.[13]

Sullivan thus stood pat on the agencies and service roles and missions provided by the National Security Act, the latter as "interpreted" by the Key West and Newport Conferences. Within a week of his telling Forrestal so, Royall told Forrestal that

> my observations of the disputes between the Navy and Air Force convinces me that it is going to be difficult to reach any satisfactory solution as to military air power unless all such air power is placed under one department. This could be done in two ways: (a) by the abolition of the Air Force and the transfer to the Navy of all the present functions of the Air Force, and (b) by combining naval air and the Air Force into a single department, leaving to the Navy the maintenance and protection of carriers on somewhat the same basis that the Army services and protects the land airfields.

Royall also suggested that the matter be "presented squarely to Congress at the next session."[14]

While Sullivan provided answers to questions posed by Forrestal with respect to naval aviation,[15] Henry C. Beauregard furnished Captain Paul Pihl a very long and detailed outline of the presentation the Navy would make to the Eberstadt Committee. Since 1945 Pihl had been Special Assistant to the Chief of the Bureau of Aeronautics and Assistant Chief of Plans, Office of the Chief of Naval Operations; in 1948 he was the first head of the Office of the Assistant Chief of Naval Operations (Air Logistics). He headed a team of nineteen men who were preparing the presentation. Among them were Beauregard himself; a civilian aide to the Assistant Secretary of the Navy for Air, Cedric Worth; Rear Admirals Daniel V. Gallery and E.A. "Batt" Cruise; and Captain L. A. Thackrey.[16] "Any discussion of the organization of naval aviation, if any," Beauregard began, "requires answer[s] to the following basic questions:

> (a) Can strategic bombing alone win a war or must there be a balance of naval, Army, and Air Force forces?

(b) Can all necessary air operations be successfully executed from CONUS?
(c) If not, can all necessary air operations be successfully executed from CONUS: plus actual and potential foreign shore bases, or is sea-based air necessary?
(d) If sea-based air is necessary, should it be under Air Force or naval control?
(e) Should the Navy have no other air than sea-based air?

Beauregard countered the proposition that strategic bombing alone could win a war on historical, economic, moral, and diplomatic grounds and supported the need of sea-based air in extenso. The latter being the case, "air should be an integral part of the Navy, (this is the 'guts' of the case)." He closed by saying that "when it is necessary to puncture the [Air Force's] extravagant claims, the tone should be almost paternal toward boyish overenthusiasm."[17]

When Pihl forwarded the "master outline" for the presentation, Beauregard criticized its belligerent tone. Indeed, one item came close to "giving the lie" to the Air Force. He may have referred to such statements as that "the long-range bomber was a weapon of very little value—not worth developing," or that "the heavy bomber is the Maginot Line weapon that lulls us into defense lethargy." Better, he advised, to rephrase the whole in polite terms yet without losing the desired effect.[18]

The Navy's case was presented to the Eberstadt Committee in mid-October—three weeks after Truman had announced that Russia had exploded an atomic bomb—by the Assistant Secretary of the Navy for Air, John Nicholas Brown, and Vice Admiral Arthur Radford, Deputy Chief of Naval Operations (Air).

Stating that Eberstadt had asked for a discussion of whether the Air Force should absorb naval aviation, Brown replied that "naval air is so interlaced with the whole Navy that another agency cannot take responsibility for it with comparable efficiency. . . ." The Joint Chiefs of Staff, he added, had no plans that indicated that victory over the Soviets, the only possible enemies, would be "either quick or easy. The desire for some cheap and rapid way to bring an enemy to submission is old, but always fresh because so appealing." Brown doubted that Air Force bombers had the range to bomb targets in Russia, particularly if bases in Britain, Europe, the Middle East, or Africa were denied to it.

Backed by the advice of Fleet Admiral Ernest J. King and others, Radford launched his first thunderbolt against the Air Force by denying its assertion that it could "quickly and completely [win a Russian war] by the application of a single military force—long range bombers with atomic weapons." Was the Air Force assured of bases on the perimeters of Europe and Asia? "Push button warfare" had not arrived, and "there can be no shortcut to victory." To rely upon a single weapon and single delivery system was "extremely dangerous." Good planning required the meeting of all contingencies of war. On the theme that "naval Air power is vital to the security of this country," Radford enumerated the various missions the Navy could perform and then asserted that nothing could match the superiority of American carrier forces. Because Russia had no naval air power, we need fear only her submarines. Naval planes could get much closer to Russian targets and could put many more bombs on targets than could Air Force long-range bombers.

Radford's second bolt was to assert that "the United States Navy can best operate its own naval air weapon." The Air Force had long tried to submerge naval aviation within its own organization. The history of World War II proved that nations that put naval air in their air forces, as had Germany, Italy, and Britain (the last until 1939), did not perform as well as nations such as the United States and Japan, which did not. While Air Force officers *in time* could learn how to operate carrier aircraft and even carriers, naval officers performed these functions and in addition commanded ships and task groups, task forces, and fleets of which aircraft were important components. "Aviators who are not sailors are out of their element at sea. Absorption by the Air Force of naval aviation would be an act of division and not one of integration. . . . Until all Air Force aviators were qualified for carrier and other naval duties, the Air Force would be divided also." By taking naval aviation from the Navy, the Air Force would "extract from the Navy the heart of its power." National air power was the sum of the air power in the Navy and Air Force." Last, "The balance between the elements of national air power should not be fixed by law—it should continue to be decided by the Congress on the basis of military requirements."[19]

Much upset by the Navy's presentation, on 25 October Symington obtained Forrestal's permission and wrote to Eberstadt that a year of unification proved the need of increasing the authority of the Secretary of Defense and that he disagreed that "(1) the Air Force was incapable of performing the functions assigned to it by the plans of the Joint Chiefs of Staff; and (2) the Navy is capable of performing and, in fact, is required to perform, the Air Force function." Since, added Symington, Eberstadt had not raised the question whether the Air Force should absorb naval aviation and the Navy presumed to challenge the ability of the Air Force to accomplish its primary mission, "I wish to record the fact that the Air Force denies categorically the validity of the challenge and questions the propriety of such a presentation before your body." He would not engage at the moment in a "public brawl" before the committee. However, "if . . . the Navy's presentation will have any material influence on the findings and recommendations of your body, we would be compelled to reconsider this position."[20]

As Secretary of the Navy during the negotiations that produced the National Security Act of 1947, Forrestal in December 1946 had assured Symington, then Assistant Secretary of War for Air, that "no sensible person in the Navy ever entertained any idea about the creation of a strategic air force in the Navy."[21] How then, could one explain that the Navy was designing both a supercarrier and aircraft capable of delivering atomic bombs? At any rate, Forrestal, who would be among the last to testify, had been reading the transcripts of the hearings. He asked his Naval Assistant, Herbert D. Riley, and his Air Force

Assistant, Jerry Page, to work up a presentation on strategic bombing. After Forrestal had testified, he told Riley and Page that they would testify on the morrow but that they were not to tell their service chiefs that they would do so. Because he would be giving his personal opinion on the subject, Page feared an adverse reaction from his primary contact, General Lauris Norstad, USAF, Deputy Chief of Staff for Operations and Plans, but stuck by the paper, which at request was read to the full committee. The committee then adopted its conclusion: "That . . . strategic bombing covered such a broad area that it required the operation of carriers as well as the Air Force, that the two elements should be coordinated, not duplicated." Riley and Page reported to Forrestal after he had already talked on the phone with Eberstadt, who said that the committee would send the two men letters of appreciation. But Page's forebodings were well grounded, for the following morning a telephone call from Norstad's office indicated that a colonel more knowledgeable in strategic warfare was being sent to Forrestal's office to relieve Page. Army Colonel Robert Wood, Forrestal's Aide and Army Assistant, went directly to Forrestal, who directed that Norstad be informed that Page would remain with him for his normal tour of duty. On the next morning Norstad tackled Wood in person. Wood politely told him to see Forrestal if he wished—and there the matter rested.[22]

The committee report, completed early in November but not forwarded to Truman until January 1949, indicated that the National Military Establishment was not soundly structured and was expensive. Including the interest on the public debt, veterans affairs, atomic energy, and foreign aid, the total ran to 25 percent of the federal budget for fiscal year 1949 and imposed strains upon the civilian economy. In some areas the "integrating process" was not working well, as in accounting, inventory control, and the functioning of some of the most important security agencies. The Central Intelligence Agency, for example, could not yet be depended upon to furnish proficient estimates.[23] Inadequate liaison existed between foreign policy and military power, with the result that the lact of clear policy directives left the Joint Chiefs of Staff working in a vacuum with respect to drafting plans. The military budget needed "a major overhaul," scientific research and development work was poor, mobilization plans were faulty, and adequate provision had not been made "for—and against—new and unconventional means of warfare" (pp. 2-7, 26, 71-73, 87, 93, 96). On the other hand, the committee had found encouraging evidence of substantial progress and improvement in the functioning of the national security machinery after only nine months of operation, even though many of its leaders were the same ones who had bickered over unification before 1947 and still gave "certain conspicuous instances of disunity at the top levels of the military establishment" (p. 39). It noted, for example, that the final stages of the hearings had been marked "by a recurrence of the old argument between the Air Force and the Navy concerning the role of strategic bombing" (p. 40). Yet the Air Force had been separated successfully from the Army, military air transportation had been merged, and joint education and joint training were proceeding well, particularly between the Air Force and Navy Air. Some Air Force officers had been "checked out" in carrier landings and flown naval planes in war games while naval planes had participated in a demonstration put on by the Air Force's Tactical Air Command. Although the services must be taught to operate together as a team, "there are very real advantages in the maintenance of a reasonable degree of service autonomy, not only from the point of view of training, morale, and administration but from the point of view of strategic planning and of the development of new weapons and tactics. . . . But service rivalries must be kept within reasonable bounds if effective teamwork is to be achieved . . . ." (p. 41). In sum, "the instances of a surviving disunity are outweighed by the substantial . . . progress that has been achieved . . . toward a generally unified system" (pp. 42, 79-80).

Although it had been pressed by former Secretary of War Robert P. Patterson to merge the military departments into a single department under a single chief of staff and by others to merge the naval air arm with the Air Force, the committee had declined to do so (pp. 9, 53-54, 95, 103).

The committee recommended that the authority of the Secretary of Defense over the military departments and the national security budget be clarified and strengthened by deleting the word *general* from the original National Security Act and by giving him power to exercise "direction, authority, and control" over all security departments and agencies. Conversely, the proviso that gave the service secretaries the right of appeal to the President and to the Director of the Budget should be repealed (p.11), as should the provision granting "reserved" powers to the service secretaries. To relieve the Secretary of Defense of the burden of routine administration, he should have an Under Secretary. His office should remain small and simple, however; he should not be given assistant secretaries or build up his office "to a huge operating establishment" (pp. 13, 52-55). While the service secretaries should be denied Under Secretaries, they themselves should not be demoted to Under Secretaries of the Secretary of Defense (pp. 60-61).

A nonvoting chairman should be added to the Joint Chiefs of Staff; while he would exercise no command or military authority over the other members, he would expedite their business as a planning body and keep their work current (pp. 13, 66-70, 78). Moreover, the Secretary of Defense should have a chief staff officer, or principal military assistant, to represent him but not have membership on the Joint Chiefs of Staff, and bring "split decisions" to his attention for resolution (p.13). The Secretary of Defense should also have additional civilian assistants in the form of a comptroller and aides for personnel, legislation, and public relations matters. "Public displays of interservice friction have often gone beyond the bounds of healthy rivalry. To the average citizen most of them seem childish. The Secretary of Defense's instructions in these matters do not appear to have been scrupulously observed," noted the committee, which called for improved top-policy control in the matter of public relations (pp. 84-85). While the statutory limit of one hundred officers on the Joint Staff should be lifted "moderately" (pp. 14-15), the committee

opposed the creation of a special segregated command corps intensively trained for joint-service command and staff work (pp. 85-86).

The Secretary of Defense alone, not the service secretaries, should have
membership on the National Security Council, although the latter should be
invited to attend its meetings (pp. 16, 62-63). The Joint Chiefs of Staff or Joint
Staff should advise the Secretary of Defense on how to formulate policies not
only for the joint training of the military forces but also for coordinating the
education of military men. To advise both the Secretary and the Joint Chiefs,
there should be created a Civilian Advisory Board of experts in the field of
education and training. More joint education should be given service
undergraduates; more officers should attend the schools of other services;
more officers should be transferred between the services (pp. 17-18, 82-84).
And a weapons evaluation board was sorely needed (p. 19). Forrestal
established such a board in December 1948.

The committee noted that "instead of policy determining strategy, and
strategy in turn determining its military implementation in terms of the size
and nature of the military establishment, the tendency is in the reverse direction. To far too great an extent, the unilaterial aims and policies of the military
services are combining to make the strategy they are supposed to serve, and the
strategy is tending to make the national policy." On the other hand, Truman's
placing of a ceiling of $15 billion on defense for fiscal year 1950 had apparent-
ly been issued without the formal advice either of the Joint Chiefs of Staff or of
the National Security Council. "There is thus a disconnection at the top as well
as at the bottom of the system." The committee used the history of the
seventy-group Air Force program as an example of these tendencies. The program, adopted in the late spring of 1948, had been accepted by the Joint Chiefs
of Staff "instead of imposing their own estimate on the Air Force." At the
prodding of the President and the Secretary of Defense, the Joint Chiefs accepted a reduction of the seventy-group program but Congress cancelled the
reduction. "The result was . . . a case of a service program making national
policy rather than national policy being implemented by a service program"
(pp. 38, 42).

The greatest expenditures of the defense budget, $8 billion in fiscal year
1949, were being made for the air power of the Air Force and Navy and the Army's servicing and support of the Air Force (p. 46). However, suggestions to
merge the naval air arm with the Air Force or the Air Force with the Navy had
been rejected. What new technology the future would bring could not be
assessed, but the committee believed it unwise to "put all our eggs in one
basket" and that "for the present, at least some duplication of effort between
Air Force and naval air power seems reasonable . . . " (pp. 46-47). Some day,
perhaps, truly intercontinental bombers would be provided, hence eliminating
the need for carrier-based planes, or guided missiles would make manned
bombers absolete. At the moment, however, the nation was in "a rather painfully expensive transitional period, in which the safest course is not the
cheapest." The cost of air power must be kept within reasonable limits; Air

Force and naval air power must be "so coordinated in plan and program that each dollar spent will bring a maximum return in military efficiency"; and the Air Force-naval air argument must cease (p. 47). The Key West and Newport conferences on roles and missions were steps in the right direction, but much more remained to be done (p. 48).

The committee hoped that Congress would act promptly upon its recommendations and not make major changes in the national security organization until several years had passed and it had been "given a breathing spell during which to strengthen its structure and perfect its operation."[24]

As noted above, on 9 November Forrestal had drafted but not sent a letter of admonition to Sullivan prompted by Radford's testimony before the Eberstadt Committee. Instead, he used the draft as the basis for a memorandum to the service secretaries that stated that "any report or presentation by a responsible official of your Service to an agency outside of the Military Establishment, which involves any criticism of another Service, be submitted to me prior to delivery." When Beauregard called John Ohly, one of Forrestal's assistants, to ask whether the Navy's presentation before the Eberstadt Committee had prompted the memorandum, he was told that the Navy had been too pointed and brusque in referring to the Air Force. Beauregard replied that the Navy had not asked to testify, that it had been invited to speak "fully, freely, and frankly," and that it should include the issue of naval aviation. "How could one discuss whether the Navy should transfer its aircraft carriers and aircraft to the Air Force without comparing the efficiency of Air Force bombers with that of carrier aircraft?" he asked. Despite Forrestal's memorandum, moreover, Symington forcefully asserted to Eberstadt that the testimony given his committee by Brown and Radford had been "an unwarranted attack upon the Air Force" and added that "action must be taken to resolve the present conflict resulting from the Navy's continuous attacks, even if the solution means consolidation." The Navy's case remained unpublished, while Symington's letter gave the Air Force a publicity advantage.[25]

On 3 December Forrestal issued his first annual report. After two years of working almost inhuman hours, he had decided that the Secretary of Defense must be something more than a coordinator of a loosely knit federation. In his report and in legislation he offered to the President, he agreed with most of the recommendations made by the Eberstadt Committee. He was not sure, however, that all command functions should be taken from the Joint Chiefs of Staff or that the service secretaries should be demoted. In his report Forrestal wrote kindly about the Navy, which had always been "a tightly organized, self-contained service." While strategic air was a part of modern warfare, tactical air must be made capable of close cooperation with ground troops. He added: "I likewise hold the view that carriers and naval air will have a part to play in any war of the foreseeable future. The time may come when both the carrier and the long-range bomber are obsolete weapons, but that time has not yet arrived." Furthermore, new developments in submarine warfare, like the snorkel, made the solution of antisubmarine problems "one of the first importance to the Nation's security, and [I] have urged upon the Department of the Navy all possible acceleration in the research and tactical experiments necessary to solve the problem.

"Costs," said Forrestal, "are becoming a matter of concern. The Navy's operating requirements are being met, but only by extensive use of war-reserve stocks and operating inventories, and these are being depleted to an unwise degree." In part because of inflation, the Navy had had to defer maintenance work ashore. The Navy had continued developments in weapons and equipment, especially in jet aircraft, which now flew faster than the speed of sound, and in submarines, whose speed on the surface had been doubled by use of the snorkel, even though its personnel inventory had shrunk. In his conclusion Forrestal stressed two points: "The atomic bomb does not give us automatic immunity from attack, as some people would like to believe, nor does its mere possession guarantee victory if war should come," and "true unification of the armed might of the United States cannot spring from legislation alone. The spark generated by the Unification Act must be fanned into flame by the thoughts and actions of generals and admirals, ensigns and lieutenants, soldiers, sailors, and airmen, and civilians."[26]

Most press comment on the Eberstadt Committee report and on Forrestal's legislative proposals agreed that unification had proceeded much too slowly and wastefully. When Mark S. Watson, military commentator for the *Baltimore Sun*, suggested that the service secretaries be replaced with candidates "less 'tainted' with long service affiliation and more immediately responsive to the Secretary of Defense,"[27] Forrestal would not go that far. Instead he said that the National Military Establishment was divided by "barriers of doubt and suspicion" and that "mutual understanding" and "mutual education" by the services was needed. He trusted that the gradual evolution of a joint staff would weaken "the strong attachments to individual services."[28]

For a week beginning 29 December 1948, an Air Force Senior Board consisting of General McNarney, Acting Chairman in place of General Muir S. Fairchild, who was ill, and members Lieutenant General Lauris Norstad and Lieutenant General H.A. Craig, used the concept of the strategic bombing of Russia to access the Air Force's needs. Among other witnesses they heard Lieutenant General Curtis LeMay, commander of the Strategic Air Command since mid-October. LeMay thought that "the fundamental goal of the Air Force should be the creation of a strategic atomic striking force capable of attacking any target in Eurasia from bases in the United States and returning to the points of take-off." For it to do so would require four groups of bombers, one group of strategic reconnaissance aircraft, and an atomic stockpile. The best plane with which to bomb Russia was the improved B-36 (B-36B) which, with four jets added to its piston engines, he said could fly in at 45,000 feet at a maximum speed of 378 knots. The board concluded that B-36s could reach 97 percent of Soviet targets from North American bases and that the Strategic Air Command should have four groups of B-36Bs and one group of RB-36Bs.

Meanwhile ten groups of medium bombers such as the B-47 or B-50 could carry either atomic or conventional bombs against the Soviet Union. Other types of aircraft—weather-reconnaissance, light bombers, tactical reconnaissance, and transports—must suffer even if fighter groups did not. Although the cutback from seventy to forty-eight groups seriously reduced both the offensive and defensive capabilities of the Air Force, Vandenberg approved the report, as did Symington, the latter on 13 January 1949. When the Joint Chiefs of Staff also approved, on 5 February, the Air Force sought permission from Forrestal to divert some $270 million in excess of the needs of forty-eight groups to purchase 32 B-36s and 7 RB-36s and to modify extant B-36s by the addition of jet pods. Shortly before he resigned on 28 March, Forrestal approved the purchase of additional B-36s, and on 4 May Truman released the funds for their purchase and for the modification program.[29]

The best hope for the Air Force lay in Forrestal's replacement by an air-minded Secretary of Defense who would reallocate the defense budget in its favor. None of those most often mentioned as successors to Forrestal, who said he would retire long before the end of Truman's second term—Army Secretary Royall, financier Eberstadt, and Sullivan—was likely to do so.[30] However, a fourth contender, Louis A. Johnson, was a protagonist of air power. Moreover, the elections of 1948 caused various Republicans formerly in key congressional positions and favorable to aviation to give way to Democrats. Both Millard E. Tydings (Md.), who would be the new chairman of the Senate Armed Services Committee, and the aggressive Carl Vinson, who would chair the House Armed Services Committee, had formerly sponsored the Navy. Since they both supported the seventy-group Air Force, they could now be considered air-minded. Air Force leaders gagged by Forrestal on budget matters simply let Shell Oil's James Doolittle and C.R. Smith, president of the Air Force Association, lead the campaign for the merger of the Air Force and naval air into a single air force.[31]

In his State of the Union message of 10 January 1949, President Harry S. Truman exaggerated somewhat when he stated that "great progress" had been made toward unification during the past year. He demanded universal military training as essential to American security and alloted $14.4 billion for defense, with the sum almost equally divided between the services but with the fifty-group Air Force to be reduced to forty-eight instead of being expanded to seventy groups, as Symington and Vandenberg still insisted it should be.[32] The Air Force was rapidly aging its transport planes in the Berlin Airlift—of which approximately 25 percent of the load was carried by the Navy—yet Symington realized that the budget favored the Air Force. Forrestal saw the point also, for he told Truman that "with reference to the budget . . . the 14.4 billion ceiling limitation, we would probably have the capability only of reprisal against any possible enemy, in the form of air warfare, using England as a base."[33] By this time the United States had a stockpile of atomic bombs and an improved B-36 to drop them and the production of B-36s was being given a priority second only to atomic weapons. The Joint Chiefs of Staff therefore naturally concentrated on strategic air power, even though various American and British political and military figures stated that strategic air bombing in World War II had been "an extravagant failure." Retired Fleet Admiral Chester W. Nimitz, for example, did not believe it economical to use bombers possessed of only a six-thousand-mile range. The nation should be prepared to conduct amphibious operations, he added, and each service should be permitted to design the weapons it needed to carry out its traditional functions.[34] Displeased with the "enthusiasm of single-weapon experts" and with the reduction from eleven to eight attack carriers and a substantial reduction in other operating ships, Sullivan nevertheless supported the budget. In contrast, top-ranking Army spokesmen did not question Air Force strategy and applauded what they called the first "correlated" defense budget.[35]

On 20 April the Chief of Staff of the Air Force, Hoyt S. Vandenberg, briefed Truman on the war plans of the Strategic Air Command. On the twenty-first, Truman asked the Joint Chiefs to evaluate the success of the plans, including the dropping of atomic bombs on Russia. The reply was that they were already working on such an evaluation.[36]

Forrestal forwarded his suggestions for amending the National Security Act to Truman early in December 1948. At Truman's request he revised them with the aid of the Director of the Bureau of the Budget, Frank Pace, Jr., and the White House counsel, Clark Clifford. Truman was pleased, for the result approximated his original request for unification made to Congress on 19 December 1945. He was further strengthened by the report of the Hoover Commission, dated 28 February 1949, for it concluded that "the authority of the Secretary of Defense, and hence the control of the President, is weak and heavily qualified by the provisions of the act of 1947 which set up a rigid structure of federation rather than unification. . . . The National Military Establishment . . . is perilously close to the weakest type of department."[37]

On 5 March Truman asked Congress to create a Department of Defense possessing full and unquestioned control over the military services. When he also promised changes in the National Security Act that would speed unification, he was promptly challenged by Vinson, who spoke for many congressmen when he said that Truman's budget was not "holy" and that representatives were not sent to Congress to become "stooges of the budget." Moreover, he asserted that Congress rather than the President had the authority to reorganize the military establishment. Although Vinson would add $800 million to the Budget of the Army and Navy, he would also give an additional $800 million to the Air Force.[38] He then shocked the Navy by introducing a bill authorizing a seventy-group Air Force and prohibiting the Navy from building additional supercarriers unless Congress gave its express authorization—a challenge that did not go unanswered by Sullivan and the Navy.

In 1942 William Bradford Huie, a wartime consultant to Secretary of War Henry L. Stimson and a popular writer on military affairs, had written a book, *The Fight for Air Power*, that denigrated the Navy. In 1946 a second book, *The Case Against the Admirals: Why We Must Have a Unified Command*, contained a highly distorted attack on the Navy that asserted that surface fleets had been obsolete since World War I and that strategic air power had won World War II. It also used scurrilous tones to demean the Navy for its alleged reluctance to amalgamate, unify, and integrate with the other services. Using the letterhead that he had provided at its request, the Army had sent a copy to each congressman and congressman-elect to make it appear that it came directly from him.[39]

Naval aviator Captain Fitzhugh Lee had been Nimitz's public information officer when Nimitz was at advanced headquarters in Guam late in the war. He had met Huie among the hundreds of press correspondents in the Pacific, and said of him that he "did not have the respect of most of his contemporaries in his own profession."[40] Lee became Sullivan's naval aide while Sullivan was the Assistant Secretary of the Navy and stayed with him when he became Under Secretary and finally Secretary. While in this billet he interviewed Huie and learned, as he put it, "that he didn't believe a thing he wrote in the book, but that he was paid to write it, and that he was a professional writer and a professional writer took on any assignment that he was given." Huie would not divulge who paid him to write *The Case Against the Admirals*, but it was crystal clear to Lee that "the motivation was to undercut the Navy's case in the struggles which were going on."[41] To make matters worse, in the December 1948 issue of *Readers Digest*, which enjoyed a circulation of six million copies in the United States alone, Huie published the first of a series of articles (the others appeared in January, March and April 1949), written probably with the help of high-ranking Air Force officers, that were extremely critical of naval aviation. The conjunction of Huie's attack and that of the Air Force, and the need to prepare the Navy's counterproposals to additional unification, stirred the Navy to action.

In the name of loyal duty to the public good, the Navy offered battle to other interest groups laying claim to scarce resources.[42] Sullivan had his own public relations outlets. He contacted congressmen, appeared before congressional committees, and delivered public addresses. In his own office were the Office of Information, Office of Civil Relations, and Office of Public Relations, the last of which had to work under a Forrestal directive of 15 March 1948 that "service stories and claims" must be brought into "a proper perspective—the perspective of national security, not the perspective of single service advantage."[43] "Backstopping" Sullivan were retired naval personnel, reserve officer organizations, the U.S. Naval Institute, and the Navy League, the last of which, with Sullivan's blessings, early in 1949 began to counter the Air Force with a five-year $500,000 publicity program.[44] Such representatives as Sterling Cole, a Captain in the Naval Reserve, could be depended upon to support the Navy against the Air Force. Newspapers like the *Boston Globe* and the *Buffalo Evening News*, journals such as *U.S. News and World Report,* and commentators such as Hanson Baldwin of the *New York Times* were critical of Air Force strategy, with Baldwin stating on 15 April 1949 that talk about the strategic bombing of Russia was nothing but "Brave, slightly sickening, talk." In the *Baltimore*

Sun Mark Watson added that the reputedly "invulnerable" B-36 would soon need escorts against interceptors and eventually would succumb to guided missiles.[45]

Naval officers generally avoided politics, yet in emergencies they used covert operations and ad hoc agencies to improve the Navy's public image. In October 1945, Forrestal had appointed a group to lead the Navy's countercampaign against unification. This Secretary's Committee on Research and Reorganization lasted until the passage of the National Security Act.[46] When the threat of further reorganization appeared late in 1948, the task of preparing the Navy's defense was given to the Organizational Research and Policy Section, better known by its CNO office code number OP-23, and headed in January 1949 by Captain Arleigh "Thirty-one Knot" Burke.[47] Meanwhile legislation based on the Hoover Commission Report authorized the President to submit to Congress proposals for the reorganization of agencies within the executive branch that went into effect in sixty days unless both houses of Congress disapproved them. But the military establishment and six regulatory agencies were excluded from presidential purview. Deeming the exclusion "disastrous," Truman asked his special counsel, Clark Clifford, among others, to prepare new legislation embodying the suggestions of Forrestal and of the Eberstadt Committee. The result was known as Reorganization Plan No. 8.[48]

Despite the cold war, Truman would keep the armed forces practically at their current strength, thus provoking the "great debate" over the fiscal year 1950 budget. Although willing to spend $2 billion annually on universal military training, he would not expand the Air Force. Sullivan asked for a naval air arm of 14,500 planes. Truman's budget would cut naval air strength from 8,550 to 7,450 planes, enable the Navy to operate only 281 combat vessels among its 731 ships, and provide only limited funds to proceed with the construction of the supercarrier, to which the Air Force was still violently and vociferously opposed.[49] Sullivan nevertheless offered Truman the names *Pearl Harbor, George Washington,* and *United States* for the supercarrier. He himself preferred the last, to which Truman agreed.[50]

The equal division of the defense budget, said Air Force spokesmen, provided political, not military, balance. The Navy, 60 percent "Air," was hiding a second air force under the label "Sea Power." The claims for accomplishments by carriers as strategic weapons were a myth, for carriers could not escape detection, were vulnerable to submarines and land-based planes, could not be used profitably against such self-sufficient enemies as Russia, were expensive, and used money better spent on strategic air forces. Moreover, revolutionary improvements in its performance enabled the B-36 to "deliver an A-Bomb to any conceivable target on earth from available bases and return without refueling. Not only that, tests under combat conditions prove conclusively that at forty to forty-five thousand feet it is all but impervious to any existing weapon of interception."[51] The supercarrier, therefore, was "keel deep in waste and is a deliberate effort to duplicate unnecessarily a proved and experienced land-based organization."[52] Instead of seeking to answer the question whether strategic bombing or balanced forces were better overall strategy, and disdaining the logistic support role to which both the Air Force and the Army would relegate the Navy, Sullivan, Louis E. Denfeld, the Chief of Naval Operations, Radford, and others answered in favor of strategic bombing performed from carriers instead of by Air Force bombers. Sullivan also countered attempts by Symington, backed by the Army, to amend legislation prescribing the composition of the armed services so that the Air Force alone would have exclusive domain in the realm of strategic air warfare; to add statements of policy, roles, and missions in defining force strengths; to allege that promotion opportunities in the Air Force and Army were better than those in the Navy; to seek to increase the number of civilian employees of the Air Force and Army but not those of the Navy; to augment the guided missile programs of the Air Force and Army but not those of the Navy; and to authorize the Air Force and Army but not the Navy to spend funds for four years in addition to the year in which they were appropriated.[53]

With respect to his budget, Sullivan told Forrestal that he would lose thirty thousand men, must inactivate various ships, air squadrons, and naval air stations, and greatly reduce his shipbuilding, modernization, and research programs. In sum, the Navy budget provided only "the minimum active naval power consistent with our national needs."[54]

On 2 February Sullivan wrote the chairmen of the Armed Services and Appropriations committees that he completely supported the fiscal year 1950 budget even though it was $600 million less than that for fiscal year 1949. Moreover, he was reducing personnel, ships, planes, and the supporting establishment so as to end the fiscal year 1949 at the level of operations planned for fiscal year 1950.[55] When before a subcommittee of the Senate Committee on Appropriations on the sixteenth, he noted that the budget cut was acceptable only "because of the overriding necessity for a military budget consistent with the needs of our national economy. . . . "[56] He knew that about $21 billion was going toward the European recovery program and that peace had not been restored to the world. Yet by showing the flag, particularly in the Mediterranean, the Navy was helping to further peace and stability. Until international agreements were obtained that guaranteed peace, "we cannot discard our weapons, desert our responsibility, and leave in jeopardy our farflung occupation forces overseas" (pp. 2-3). Nor must we forget that, rich as we were, we were a "have-not nation" with respect to various strategic materials that came to us by sealanes that must be protected in time of peace as well as in time of war. "We intend that within the screen of naval power if need be, and under the umbrella of air protection, those cargoes will always be able to move, In short, these considerations explain in part why we cannot abandon our naval strength, and why we cannot predicate our naval needs on a mere relative comparison with the navies of other powers" (p.3).

Among questions asked of Sullivan was one by the chairman, George H. Mahon, of Texas: "It has been said, and there is a popular belief, that the Navy to some considerable extent has served its usefulness as a fighting weapon. I say 'a popular belief.' There is a popular belief that the atom bomb and the long-range airplane have sort of made the Navy obsolete. . . . In the fiscal year 1950 . . . how effective and useful and necessary would the Navy . . . be to the United States?''

Sullivan pointed to a world globe nearby, noted that 70 percent of it was represented by water, and retorted: ''I would say the Navy would be more important, and would be more useful, and more ready than it has ever been at the outbreak of any war in our history,'' adding that because of the curtailment of the British Navy the American Navy was more important than ever before (pp. 15-17).

Were not aircraft carriers ''sitting ducks'' for land-based aircraft? asked Senator Harry R. Sheppard. Sullivan replied that in World War II, one third of the forty-two carriers sunk by land-based aircraft, the others succumbing to carrier planes, submarines, or naval surface gunfire (p.17). When Sheppard wondered whether carriers could be defended against high-flying aircraft, Admiral Radford, who had accompanied Sullivan, replied affirmatively, adding, '' We feel no hesitancy in stating that our fighters today can take care of any high altitude attacks that will come at us with the planes in existence and the planes that we have projected in the future can take care of anything that comes at us that is planned for that type of operation'' (p.18). When Sheppard persisted in his questioning, Sullivan asserted: ''I think a good deal of our difficulty comes from the enthusiasm of single-weapons experts. I do not mean to address this against the Air Force, because we have in the Navy people who are so enthusiastic about their own particular specialty that they always have to be kept in bounds.'' ''What about the vulnerability of carriers to guided missiles?'' asked Robert F. Sikes. Sullivan turned to Radford, whose reply was off the record (p. 19).

Sullivan's general statement of the weaknesses that would result from the prospective 1950 budget was supported in detail by Denfeld, Radford, and Rear Admiral Herbert G. Hopwood, Director of Budget and Reports (p.28), with Denfeld and Radford in addition expressing their pleasure with the definition of roles and missions in the Key West and Newport conferences (pp. 58-59), and Radford making it clear to the committee that ''the air power of the United States consists of the total of the air power of the Air Force and the air power of the Navy. . . . ''[57]

Forrestal had planned to retire gracefully from public life if Truman were defeated for reelection. With Truman and a Democratic Congress elected, he faced new congressional leaders. Furthermore, the resignation in December 1948 of Secretary of State George C. Marshall because of ill health, and of his Under Secretary, Robert A. Lovett, with whom he had worked in unison, greatly affected Forrestal because Dean Acheson would become Secretary of State and James E. Webb, his nemesis as Director of the Bureau of the Budget, would succeed Lovett. Webb's successor, Frank Pace, influenced by the antimilitary posture of Edwin C. Nourse, Chairman of the Council of Economic Advisers, would soon cut the President's announced military budget of $15 billion to $13.5 billion.[58]

On 8 January 1949 Symington's first annual report renewed his demand for a full seventy air groups and reopened the Air Force-Navy controversy, thus further undercutting Forrestal and leading such hostile critics as Walter Winchell and Drew Pearson to predict Truman's acceptance of his resignation within a week, which the White House denied.[59]

Late in 1948, Hanson Baldwin recalled, Forrestal invited him to have breakfast at his home on Prospect Street in Georgetown at 0700. Baldwin saw that the man "never had any peace." Even before breakfast he spoke about problems in Washington, in the Navy Department, in unification, about his feeling that he lacked the President's support while the Russians were increasing their military power. On another occasion Baldwin accepted an invitation to cocktails. When he wished to leave, Forrestal said, "Oh, no, don't go. Stay for dinner. We'll go up and have dinner with Josie." Josie, Mrs. Forrestal, was an alcoholic. "We went up and had dinner on our knees, sitting alongside the bed, and she talked. She made a little sense, not too much." Baldwin was also conscious that Forrestal was "nervous and tense. He would skip from one subject to another." Truly, then, Forrestal had no peace.[60]

When Forrestal on 11 January handed Truman his pro forma resignation, he was asked to stay on. According to Attorney General Tom Clark, Forrestal was "as nervous as a whore in church."[61] Drew Pearson is the authority for the comment of 25 February that "Forrestal is definitely out but is demanding that there be a face-saving arrangement whereby it won't look as if he were fired. He wanted Secretary Royall to act in his place for six months in order to ease the situation. Truman is quite aware that Royall is a nitwit but still tolerates him."[62]

Despite his evident nervousness, weariness, and frequent inability to make decisions, symptoms of overwork and overstrain, Forrestal remained on duty because of the important military legislation pending in Congress and because, at his request, on 21 January General Dwight D. Eisenhower would begin temporary duty as chief military adviser to the President and to himself as presiding officer of the Joint Chiefs of Staff. It had been rumored that Sullivan and Symington might resign after Royall said he intended to, on about 1 April, in order to leave Truman free to remold the National Military Establishment. Neither resigned, but both Assistant Secretary of the Navy Mark E. Andrews and Assistant Secretary of the Navy for Air, John Nicholas Brown, did. On 9 February the Assistant Counsel General of the Navy, John T. Koehler, was named to succeed Andrews. On 9 March Dan A. Kimball, a pilot of the Army Air Force during World War I, currently executive vice president of the Aero Jet Corporation and vice president and director of the General Tire and Rubber Company, succeeded Brown. He had been suggested to Truman by Sullivan as a friend he could depend upon.

In his first annual report to the Secretary of Defense, Sullivan pointed out that spiraling prices precluded the adequate financing of naval programs. On the one hand, he wanted more pay for Navy enlisted men than that Forrestal recommended; on the other, budget limitations for fiscal year 1950 forced him to reduce personnel, operations, and support functions all down the line.[63] It was also quite evident to him from testimony Symington gave to the Appropriations and Armed Services committees early in January that Symington supported Truman's defense budget ceiling if funds could be cut from the other services. He was nevertheless shocked when on the fifteenth Wilfred McNeil, Comptroller of the Defense Department, asked him to reduce carrier strength from eight to six and to accept a $100 million reduction in obligating authority.[64] On the twenty-sixth he wrote a secret six-page letter in vigorous opposition. A memorandum by Denfeld of 18 December 1948, fully endorsed by Sullivan, and subsequent action by the Director of the Bureau of the Budget and by the President, had led Sullivan to believe that it was no longer necessary to so reduce the Navy. The three budget deputies in the Office of the Joint Chiefs of Staff, the General Joseph McNarney Board, had provided for twelve large carriers and sixteen carrier air groups, Sullivan continued, but the Joint Chiefs could not agree on the alloacation of service funds under the $14.4 billion defense budget ceiling until Denfeld agreed to $4.6 billion for the Navy—much less than Sullivan thought it required. The Army and Air Force then made a concerted attack upon carrier strength, with the Army recommending one task group of six ships and the Air Force only one group of four. Denfeld had thus been put into the untenable position of keeping the Navy in readiness to meet its commitments without the means to do so. Forrestal had decided upon eight carriers and so informed the President, who had confirmed the decision in his budget message. Mobile carriers, Sullivan believed, were vital for delivering swift and powerful counteroffensives against any enemy: "Carrier air operations in reasonable strength are the only means which the National Military Establishment now possesses to accomplish this task whose ability to do so has been proved by past performance." Denfeld thought that twelve attack carriers was the minimum number needed. The $4.4 billion Navy budget would reduce the number to nine lest the operating forces become unbalanced; Forrestal's decision of 9 November 1948 had reduced the number to eight. Because of loyalty to Forrestal and with the hope that the National Security Act could be made to work, Sullivan had accepted eight. With the number of carriers reduced to six, however, "the resultant unbalance of the National Military Establishment would . . . compel a complete reexamination of the structure of the entire Establishment and . . . in effect, constitute a repudiation of relevant Joint Chiefs of Staffs agreements, of your decisions, and the President's budget message to Congress."

Savings for fiscal year 1950 in operating one carrier would amount to $33 million, Sullivan went on. Since other fleet operations had already been cut to the absolute minimum, with "sacrifice of considerable basic training and morale," a further cut of $100 million could not be made "without serious effect upon naval strength, either immediately or long range."

Sullivan believed that the Navy was being attacked by the Army and Air Force because it had fared better than they at the hands of the Bureau of the Budget. The Navy had made a more sincere attempt to support the National Security Act than had the other services, he alleged, had better supported the decisions of the President and of the Secretary of the Defense, and had not publicly criticized the other services. Therefore the "unscrupulous and unjustified" attacks by the Army and Air Force were "unwarranted" and "intolerable." Forrestal should tell the public that "the air power of the United States . . . is the sum of the air strength of the Navy, the Marine Corps, and the Air Force," Air strength lay not in the 9,000 planes of the Air Force but in a total of 16,500 aircraft.

In order to comply with Forrestal's decisions and instructions, Sullivan had carefully readjusted naval strength. A cut of $100 million, he repeated for emphasis, would require "a complete reexamination of the entire [defense] structure," a process that could not be completed in time to enter the 1950 fiscal year. It was Sullivan's hope that talks he had held with Forrestal since 15 January would save both two carriers and the $100 million for the Navy.[65]

In addition, Sullivan was unhappy with the Hoover Commission report on the Organization of the Executive Branch of the Government, for it generally followed the conclusions of the Eberstadt Committee with respect to strengthening the authority of the Secretary of Defense. Were the recommendations adopted, Forrestal would have not merely "general direction" over the military establishment but would be responsible for exercising "direction, authority and control over the Departments and agencies of the Military Establishment." Nevertheless, his attempt to control the hydra-headed interservice conflict caused him to suffer from such extreme tension that, as his naval aide Herbert Riley stated, in the end "he really did go off his rocker."[66]

As Hanson Baldwin put it:

> He had no peace. That was the trouble. He had no peace at home and he got no satisfaction in the office because Symington was constantly after him, and he had no support from his boss, the President. He had been urged by a number of friends, including Fred Eberstadt . . . to . . . resign well before he actually did so. He didn't know, of course, that Johnson was going to replace him as I understand it, until after the event. I don't think that Truman told him. Or he may have been told and had forgotten it. I think he was in such a state then and that he didn't know.[67]

After a "shattering experience" on 1 March at the White House, which he described to his staff, Forrestal resigned as Secretary of Defense, effective on or about 31 March.

Drew Pearson wrote in his diary for 13 January 1949, in part:

> Louis Johnson . . . took the bit in his teeth and went to see Truman regarding Secretary of Defense Forrestal. He told Truman that Marquis Childs had reported in his column that he, Johnson, was waging a vendetta against Forrestal, and he wanted Truman to know that this was not the case. This

touched Truman off in a diatribe against Forrestal in which he resorted to Missouri mule-team language, calling him a "God-damn Wall Street bastard" and other names too foul to print. He said he wasn't going to tolerate Forrestal around very long, but that the "son of a bitch" came in and took "advantage of me and put me on the spot." I suspect this is partially true. As Louis was about to leave, Truman said, "Now, about this job of Secretary of Defense. . . ." Louis says that he held up his hand and said: Mr. President, I don't want to talk about that. . . . You don't owe me anything. I just want to tell you some time how Forrestal tried to cut your throat during the campaign.[68]

According to the recollections of Riley, Truman's whistle-stopping about the country before the elections of 1948 was made possible only because Johnson raised the needed money, which he gave on condition that if Truman won he could have any job in the administration. Truman had agreed. On 1 March Truman told Forrestal that Johnson had come "to get his pound of flesh . . . and wanted to be the Secretary of Defense right away." Truman had demurred, saying that the Department of Defense had been a going concern for only a short time and that Forrestal had been accepted unanimously by the military services as the ideal man to be its first Secretary. Would not another job, like being Secretary of the Treasury, be acceptable? Johnson would have no other; Truman must keep his promise. Truman had then told Forrestal to resign forthwith, because his resignation would be announced publicly that evening.[69]

As Drew Pearson put it on 1 March:

> Louis Johnson and Forrestal lunched with Truman today. I saw Louis afterward. He said he was as nervous as a schoolboy. He said that Truman had promised him Secretary of Defense. Forrestal doesn't want to get out until May 1 but Truman suggested April 1. Louis said that April 15 would be O.K. Louis still has his fingers crossed but the announcement is supposed to be made on Friday.[70]

On 3 March Truman announced that Johnson would be the new Secretary of Defense. He then warmly praised Forrestal's ability, loyalty, and devotion to duty. Asked whether the service secretaries would be changed also, he said they would not. On 28 March, at Pentagon ceremonies, Royall, Sullivan, and Symington congratulated their new chief and promised him support. At a second ceremony, at the White House, Truman pinned the Distinguished Service Medal on Forrestal's coat.

During the nine months from the creation of the Eberstadt Committee in May 1948 until the resignation of Forrestal in March 1949, the Navy fought to retain the position it enjoyed under the National Security Act of 1947 and the definition of roles and missions in the Key West and Newport conferences. With both the Air Force and the Army objecting to its further development of capability for the air delivery of atomic bombs, its spokesmen persistently stated that the Navy was more capable of conducting atomic air warfare than the Air Force, which as yet did not have truly intercontinental bombers. These spokesmen stated their case with such vehemence as to call down upon them the wrath of Forrestal's office. To the demand by Symington that the authority of the Secretary of Defense over the military services and the defense budget be strengthened, that the military departments be merged under a single chief of staff, and that the Air Force take over naval aviation, both Sullivan and the Eberstadt Committee interposed a veto. As that committee indicated, the single-service ambitions of the Navy and the Air Force still prevented additional unification. However, carrier air power was still needed.

Because the Air Force was developing bombers with extended ranges and had a stockpile of atomic bombs, and because Truman placed great restrictions upon the defense budget, this branch of the Armed Forces claimed that strategic air atomic warfare was the quickest and most economical way of retaliating to aggression, all of which the Navy denied on the ground that strategic bombers were ineffective and could not depend upon the use of overseas bases. Although a supercarrier was being built, pending budget reductions for fiscal year 1950 would result in the operation of fewer carriers, among other major combatant ships, to the point where the Navy believed it could not meet its commitments. Morale consequently suffered.

The Navy thought that the Secretary of Defense had sufficient authority and opposed additional unification if such unification would deny it its role as defined in the original National Security Act. Unable to settle the interservice squabble, greatly irked by what he considered to be Truman's niggardly treatment of the services, and nervously prostrate, Forrestal resigned, leaving the solution of budget, unification, and roles and missions problems to Louis A. Johnson.

NOTES

1. "Reminiscences of Hanson Weightman Baldwin," transcript of oral interview by John T. Mason (Annapolis, Md.: U.S. Naval Institute, 1976), p. 469.

2. U.S. Commission of the Executive Branch of the Government, *National Security Organization* (Washington: GPO, 1949), pp. xi-xii.

3. Secretary's Committee on Unification to M[ore] T[han] O[ne], 22 June 1948; John L. Sullivan to Secretary's Committee on Unification, 22 June 1948; M.E. Andrews, Acting, to Ferdinand Eberstadt, 13 August 1948, SNP; Sullivan to all Bureaus, Boards, and officers USN and USMC HQ, 28 July 1948, NHD: OA, OP-23 Files.

4. In addition to using the members of his board, Chairman C.H. Morris had called for advice from such active duty officers as ADM H. Kent Hewitt, VADM Harry W. Hill, and RADMs Daniel V. Gallery, Charles T. Joy, and Ralph A. Ofstie, and from such retired officers as Chester W. Nimitz, Thomas C. Hart, Dudley W. Knox, Ben Moreel, William H. Standley, John H. . Towers, and also from Hanson W. Baldwin.

5. Top Secret, General Board File 425, Serial 315, dated 25 June 1948, SNP. Sullivan distributed copies of the report on a "need to know" basis and on 27 July directed the board to forward an updated report annually on 1 July and also to submit complete or partial reports either at his request or on its own initiative. SECNAV to Chairman, GB, 27 July 1948, SNP. The General Board's report of 21 November 1947, e.g., had covered 225 pages.

6. *Supporting Study*, p. 45.

7. John L. Sullivan to Distribution List, 29 July 1948, SNP.

8. Richard F. Hayes, *The Awesome Power: Harry S. Truman as Commander in Chief* (Baton Rouge: Louisiana State University Press, 1973), p. 112. For example, Royall wrote Forrestal on 21 May:

> The set-up of the Hoover Commission to study unification does not impress me. It seems to be based on an effort to coordinate and obtain an agreement between the three departments.
> I believe that our experience to date has shown that this approach—which tends to lead to reconciliations and compromises which are in themselves unsound—will not be successful. Personally, I doubt whether the study is worthwhile under these circumstances, and I would be inclined to ask Mr. Hoover not to study unification at all.
> If you do not agree, I would like permission to discuss with him any ideas of the approach to this problem.

(Royall, Memorandum to the SECDEF, 21 May 1948, NHD: OA, OP-23 Files).

9. Walter Millis, ed., with the collaboration of E.S. Duffield, *The Forrestal Diaries* (New York: The Viking Press, 1951), pp. 463-64.

10. Robert Frank Futrell, *Ideas, Concepts, Doctrine: A History of Basic Thinking in the United States Air Force 1907-1964* (Maxwell Air Force Base, Ala.: Air University, 1971), pp. 122-23.

11. Top Secret. Symington to Sullivan, 21 July 1948; Top Secret. Sullivan to Symington, 9 August 1948, copies to Forrestal and Royall, SNP. Sullivan's ammunition was derived in part from a dry run before him of the testimony to be given by his leading civil and naval assistants to the Eberstadt Committee. Fitzhugh Lee to Messrs. Brown and Andrews, admirals Radford, Carney, Russell, Mills, and Wellborn, and captains Karig, Opie, Parks, and Thackrey, 26 July 1948, and H.G. Beauregard to Sullivan 25 July 1948. Moreover, Sullivan himself briefed some of the naval officers who would testify. Sullivan to admirals Blandy and Cooke, 10 July 1948, NHD: OA, OP-23 Files.

12. John L. Sullivan, Memorandum to the SECDEF, 1 September 1948, SNP.

13. Ibid., 22 September 1948; J.N. Brown, Acting SECNAV, Memorandum for the SECDEF, 30 September 1948, SNP.

14. Secret. Kenneth Royall, Memorandum to the SECDEF, 7 September 1948, copies to Symington and Sullivan, SNP.

15. John L. Sullivan, Memorandum for the SECDEF, 17 October 1948, SNP.

16. RADM Paul Pihl, USN (RET), to the writer, January 3, 1974.

17. Conf. H.G. Beauregard to CAPT Paul Pihl, 1 October 1948, SNP.

18. H.G. Beauregard to CAPT Paul Pihl, 7 October 1948, ibid.

19. CAPT Thackrey to ADM Price, ca. 5 October 1948, CAPT Thackrey to Secretary's Unification Committee 9 October 1948, CAPT Thackrey to Sullivan, 11 October 1948, Eberstadt to Radford, record of telephone conversation, 7 September 1948, NHD: OA, OP-23 Files; Secret. CNO to Distribution List, 29 October 1948, pamphlet entitled *Naval Air Power*, dated 18 October 1948, SNP: Dean Acheson, *Present at the Creation: My Years in the State Department* (New York: W.W. Norton and Co., 1969), pp. 243-44; John C. Ries, *The Management of Defense: Organization and Control of The U.S. Armed Forces* (Baltimore, Md.: Johns Hopkins Press, 1964), pp. 126-27; Calvin L. Christman, "Charles A. Beard, Ferdinand Eberstadt, and America's Postwar Security," *Mid-America* 54 (July 1972)' 187-94.

20. Symington to Eberstadt, copy to Forrestal, 25 October 1948, Secretary of the Air Force Files. NARG 340, "Special File No. 48—Hoover Commission—Reorganization of the National Military Establishment" (courtesy Richard Haynes).

21. Millis, ed., *Forrestal Diaries*, p. 223.

22. "The Reminiscences of VADM Herbert D. Riley, USN (RET)," transcript of an oral interview by John T. Mason (Annapolis, Md.: U.S. Naval Institute, 1972), pp. 325-32.

23. *National Security Organization*, vol. 2, Appendix G, p. 37 (successive references to this source are hereafter given in the text).

24. Ibid., pp. 97-98. In forwarding a fifty-nine page analysis of the report, CAPT Thackrey suggested to Kenney that it be sent to OP-23 "for coordination with the offices and bureaus of the Navy Department until it represents a true cross section of Navy Department opinion." Thackrey found three areas in which the Navy was in distinct disagreement with the report. To eliminate the

"delegated power" concept of the National Security Act of 1947 would give definite impulse to a single department, with consequent loss of balance and flexibility in the National Military Establishment. Second, the appointment of a chairman of the JCS from among its membership would establish a dangerous precedent. Last, it would be in error to broaden the powers of the chairman of the Research and Development Board and of the Munitions Board. Conf. CAPT L.A. Thackrey, to Kenney, ca. 10 November 1948, SNP. See also Conf. H.C. Beauregard to CAPT Parks, 1 January 1949, ibid.

25. H.C. Beauregard, Memorandum for the SECNAV, 10 November 1948, SNP. See also W. Stuart Symington, "Our Air Force Policy," an address delivered at Maxwell Air Force Base, 17 July 1949, in Eugene M. Emme, ed., *The Impact of Air Power: National Security and World Politics* (Princeton, N.J.: D. Van Nostrand Co., 1959), p. 727; Arthur O. Sulzberger, *The Joint Chiefs of Staff, 1941-1954* (Washington: U.S. Marine Corps Institute, 1954), pp. 59-63.

26. National Military Establishment. *First Report of the Secretary of Defense, 1948* (Washington: GPO, 1948), pp. 9-12, 64-66.

27. Newspaper opinion cited in ANJ 86 (1 January 1949): 514.

28. "Forrestal Speaks to the [Pittsburgh, Pa.] Chamber of Commerce," ANJ 86 (22 January 1949): 605.

29. GEN J.T. McNarney, Actg. Chairman, USAF Senior Officers Board, Memorandum for SECAF, subj: Final Report of Board of Officers, 13 January 1949; McNarney, Memorandum for SECAF, 13 January 1949; Symington, Memorandum for SECDEF, 25 February 1949, cited in Futrell, *Ideas, Concepts, Doctrine*, pp. 124-26.

30. "The Aviation Week," AW 49 (November 15, 1949): 7.

31. "Air Force Strategy," *ibid.* 49 (December 20, 1948): 7.

32. Elias Huzar, *The Purse and the Sword: Control of the Army through Military Appropriations, 1933-1950* (Ithaca, N.Y.: Cornell University Press, 1950), pp. 184-88.

33. Millis, ed., *Forrestal Diaries*, p. 498; "Annual Budget Message to the Congress, Fiscal Year 1950," [19 January 1949], in U.S. President, *Public Papers of the Presidents of the United States: Harry S. Truman*. 8 vols. (Washington: GPO, 1961-66), 6: 44-96.

34. Harry S. Truman, *Memoirs of Harry S. Truman*. 2 vols. (Garden City, N.Y.: Doubleday, 1955-56): 2: 204-5; "Global Strategy: An Interview with Fleet Admiral C.W. Nimitz," USNWR 26 (28 January 1949): 32-35. On 24 June the Air Force continued funding the original contract for 95 B-36s. By purchasing almost two-thousand aircraft and stretching its personnel, it had achieved a sixty-group strength by the end of 1948. Futrell, *Ideas, Concepts, Doctrine*, p. 124.

35. Futrell, *Ideas, Concepts, Doctrine*, p. 127.

36. Truman, *Memoirs*, 2: 305-6.

37. See "Findings and Conclusions," *National Security Organization*, vol. 2, Appendix G, pp. 27-30.

38. "Special Message to the Congress on Reorganization of the National Military Establishment, March 5, 1949," *Papers of Harry S. Truman*, 6: 163-66; Warner R. Schilling, "The Politics of National Defense: Fiscal 1950," in Warner R. Schilling, Paul Y. Hammond, and Glenn H. Snyder, *Strategy, Politics, and Defense Budgets* (New York: Columbia University Press, 1962), pp. 54-55.

39. Demetrious Caraley, *The Politics of Military Unification: A Study of Conflict and the Policy Process* (New York: Columbia University Press, 1966), pp. 223-24.

40. "The Reminiscences of VADM Fitzhugh Lee, USN (RET)," transcript of oral interview by CDR Etta Belle Kitchen, USN (RET), (Annapolis, Md.: U.S. Naval Institute, 1970), p. 186.

41. Ibid, pp. 185-86.

42. See Samuel P. Huntington, "Strategic Planning and the Political Process," FA 38 (January 1960): 285-99.

43. ARSN, 1947, p. 82; Samuel P. Huntington, "Interservice Competition and the Political Roles of the Armed Services," in Harry L. Coles, ed., *Total War and Cold War: Problems in Civilian Control of the Military* (Columbus: Ohio State University Press, 1962), p. 194; LTJG P.W. Rairden, "Navy Public Information," USNIP 73 (January 1947): 47-53.

44. Armin Rappaport, *The Navy League of the United States* (Detroit, Mich.: Wayne State University Press, 1962), pp. 190-95; "Navy Drive," AW 50 (21 February 1949): 7.

45. *Baltimore Sun*, 1 May 1949.

46. Vincent Davis, *Postwar Defense Policy and the U.S. Navy, 1943-1946* (Chapel Hill: University

of North Carolina Press, 1962), pp. 59-60, 65-67, and *The Admirals Lobby* (Chapel Hill: University of North Carolina Press, 1967), pp. 251-85; "Lee, "Reminiscences," pp. 190-91.

47. Davis, *Admirals Lobby*, p. 285.

48. Ibid. pp. 286-87.

49. *New York Times*, 27 October 1948, "What the Budget Means to Procurement," AW 50 (17 January 1949): 12-13; "Symington Says," AW 50 (17 January 1949): 14-15; "House Leaders Set Air Aid Strategy," AW 50 (24 January 1949): 15-16; Robert B. Hotz, editorial, "Air Power Is Everybody's Business," AW 50 (24 January 1949): 42; James H. Strauble, "The Case Against the Flat-top," AF 32 (February 1949): 11, 14-16.

50. John L. Sullivan, Memorandum for ADM Dennison, with enclosure, 1 February 1949, SNP; Martin E. Holbrook, "Naming the New Carrier," USNIP 75 (February 1949): 227-28.

51. Ned Root, "The Finletter Report—a Year later," AF 32 (April 1949): 15-16, 20, 22, 24, 27.

52. "Super-carrier United States," AF 32 (April 1949): 5.

53. W. John Kenney, Acting SECNAV, to the Secretary AF, 29 December 1948, SNP.

54. Secret. CNO to John L. Sullivan, 21 January 1949; Secret. John L. Sullivan, Memorandum for the SECDEF, 26 January 1949, Washington, NHD: OA, Papers of the Chiefs of Naval Operations (hereafter cited as CNO Papers).

55. John L. Sullivan to Kenneth McKellar, Chairman, Senate Appropriations Committee, 2 February 1949; OP-01, various letters to various committees of Congress, 2 February 1949, SNP.

56. U.S. Senate, Subcommittee on Appropriations, *National Military Establishment*, Hearings before Subcommittee, 81st Cong. 1st Sess. (Washington: GPO, 1949), p. 2 (successive pages refs. hereafter given in text).

57. Ibid., p. 60. For the role of Congress in writing the fiscal year 1950 defense budget, see Schilling, "The Politics of National Defense: Fiscal 1950," in Schilling, Hammond, and Snyder, *Strategy, Politics, and Defense Budgets*, pp. 54-134; for the role of the executive branch, pp. 135-214.

58. Acheson, *Present at the Creation*, pp. 249-53; Paul Y. Hammond, "NSC-68: Prologue to Rearmament," in Schilling, Warner, and Snyder, *Strategy, Politics, and Defense Budgets*, p. 280. Truman said of Pace, "Well, I've told you how he was. He was all right when there wasn't any trouble, but the minute there was . . . he'd be hiding in a goddam tent someplace" (Miller, *Plain Speaking*, p. 311).

59. As Truman said on one occasion, with clear reference to Pearson, "No S.O.B. could tell him what changes to make in his cabinet" (Arnold A. Rogow, *James Forrestal: A Study of Personality, Politics, and Policy* [New York: Macmillan, 1964], p. 309).

60. Baldwin, "Reminiscences," p. 461-62.

61. Abell Tyler, ed., *Drew Pearson Diaries 1949-1959* (New York: Holt, Rinehart and Winston, 1974), p. 9, hereafter cited as *Pearson Diaries*.

62. Ibid., p. 25.

63. "Navy '48 Report Presented by Sullivan," AW 50 (31 January 1949): 11-12; "Congress May Settle for 57-Group Air Force," AW 50 (14 February 1949):11.

64. Robert L. Smith, "The Influence of U.S.A.F. Chief of Staff General Hoyt S. Vandenberg on United States National Security Policy," Ph.D. diss., American University, 1965. Xerox. Ann Arbor, Mich., University Microfilms, 1973, pp. 178-83.

65. Secret. John L. Sullivan, Memorandum for the SECDEF, 26 January 1949, CNO Papers.

66. Riley, "Reminiscences," p. 308.

67. Baldwin, "Reminiscences," p. 464.

68. *Pearson Diaries*, p. 9.

69. Riley, "Reminiscences," p. 308-10.

70. *Pearson Diaries*, p. 27.

6

Louis A. Johnson,
Scrapping of the Supercarrier,
and the Resignation of
John L. Sullivan

A West Virginia lawyer with experience in the state legislature, Louis Johnson was big—250 pounds—tough, a stump spellbinder, and politically ambitious. His personal ambition, according to his first naval aide, Herbert D. Riley, "colored everything [he] thought or did. Johnson ran hard for President all the time he was Secretary of Defense."[1] Fifty-eight years of age in 1949, he had served as an Army officer in France in World War I, helped organize the American Legion, of which he was National Commander in 1932, and served as Assistant Secretary of War from 1936 to 1940. Although engaging in a running feud with Secretary of War Harry H. Woodring, who appeared to him to be "a sincere pacifist," and trying "to cut Woodring's throat and get his job,"[2] he so improved the industrial preparedness of the United States that it was said he shortened World War II by eighteen months. He pushed the first big expansion of the Army Air Forces and also the development of the B-17. He did not, however, earn the affections and loyalties of the armed forces. Both Woodring and he resigned in 1940, when President Franklin D. Roosevelt, in order to end their quarreling, asked them to leave. They were succeeded by Henry L. Stimson and Robert P. Patterson, respectively, and Johnson returned to law practice. When he became Secretary of Defense, Woodring commented that Johnson was a very clever man, adding, "There is but one weakness I have observed in him. Louis Johnson is over-ambitious in the same way that some men are over sexed."[3]

In his iconoclastic way Rear Admiral Daniel V. Gallery said that "as Secretary of Defense [Johnson] was . . . a fair-to-middling fund raiser for the

No major Army or Air Corps leader personally witnessed carrier operations during World War II. As part of its indoctrination program following the establishment of the Air Force, the Navy invited top defense leaders to do so. Shown below on the *Midway*-class carrier, the U.S.S. *Franklin D. Roosevelt, from left to right,* are the Secretary of the Navy, Francis P. Matthews; the Chief of Staff of the Air Force, General Hoyt S. Vandenberg; and the Secretary of Defense, Louis A. Johnson.

COURTESY THE NATIONAL ARCHIVES

wielding McNarney Board, now on temporary duty with him as his prime adviser on administration and organization. He would accelerate the unification timetable, said Johnson, eliminate scores of interservice committees including the Committee of Four Secretaries, decide soon upon the correct role of naval aviation for both defense and offense, and summarily dismiss those "who do not work wholeheartedly for unification." "A-Day," or "Ax-Day," had arrived, quipped Pentagon people. In sum, in great contrast to the cooperative manner of Forrestal, Johnson would "show who was boss," in consequence

Democratic Party," [4] a thought echoed by Captain Robert L. Dennison, Truman's naval aide. Asked in 1971 why Johnson was chosen as Secretary of Defense, Dennison replied, "Well, I don't really know. I think the principal reason was that he was a prominent, very active member of the Democratic Party. But he certainly wasn't a Secretary of Defense." [5] According to Dennison, "Johnson was terrible. Anybody, he thought, who opposed unification was just beyond the pale." Did the Navy fear that Johnson would deprive it of its aviation and of the Marine Corps? Dennison knew many naval and Marine officers who thus believed. [6] Said Herbert Riley, "Johnson viewed the military establishment and the Navy in particular as his personal and deadly enemy." [7] Moreover, his two primary ambitions were "to take Naval Aviation out of the Navy and put it in the Air Force . . . " and "to take away their distinctive uniforms and put [Marines] in the Army." [8] Newspaper reporters like Hanson W. Baldwin, who had known Johnson earlier, also evaluated his appointment as "disastrous" because he would sacrifice military efficiency in the interest of his political objectives. Although he had many political friends in Washington, Johnson knew little about defense matters and was thoroughly unpopular with military men. Everything Johnson did, Baldwin concluded, "was approached from a political point of view." [9]

Because Johnson was an old Army man and an outspoken exponent of air power and of unification—Riley spoke of "his really bitter loathing of Naval Aviation and the Marine Corps," and General Clifton B. Cates, commandant of the Corps, stated that he was "thumbs down on us" [10]—the Navy knew it stood to lose the somewhat preferred position it enjoyed under the first Secretary of Defense, James V. Forrestal. The Navy had two tasks: to prevent the transfer of the Marine Corps to the Army and to convince Johnson that the Navy rather than the Air Force was the nation's first line of defense. Well knowing that no service would accept a subordinate role in national defense or submit to a reduction in its funds in order to boost those of another, Johnson acknowledged that it was "primarily over the apportionment of funds that disagreements among the services arise." [11] To persuade him that it was more efficient than the Air Force, the Navy offered a study of the costs of an airlift from the United States to Europe, as reported in the press on 1 April. A total of 4,500 tons daily carried by C-124As loaded with 36 tons of cargo each over a round trip of 7,728 miles would require 2,651 C-124As, with the planes themselves costing $11.7 billion—or $23.4 billion if jets were used. They would consume 34,917,000 gallons of gasoline daily—or more than the total produced in the United States and half of the total oil production of the nation, with $10 million more for each of at least thirty-six new airfields that would be needed. While this air armada could provide the supplies for six or seven divisions in Europe, or an equivalent load in bombs, the study concluded that the United States lacked sufficient aircraft fuel for the undertaking and that only surface ships could transport the supplies efficiently, that is, economically. [12]

Whereas Forrestal and the Secretary of State, George C. Marshall, had cooperated, Johnson and the new Secretary of State, Dean Acheson, were antipathetic. Johnson publicly criticized the State Department's China policy and reputedly gave material critical of Acheson to at least two of Acheson's Senate enemies.[13] Johnson erred in trying to rigidly compartmentalize "political" and "military" factors. By directing that no contacts be made between the Defense and State Departments except through their secretaries, he made coordinated policy impossible and delayed agreement on a decision to build a hydrogen bomb until 30 January 1950.[14] Unlike Forrestal, who used a small staff and tried to get the services to cooperate, Johnson would build up a large staff and have the Department of Defense direct the services. The budget for Forrestal's office in 1949 was $9 million. For 1950, Johnson's first year, it was $150 million.

Johnson would most likely begin his duties with enlarged powers and with an Under Secretary, three Assistant Secretaries, and a new chairman for the Joint Chiefs of Staff. Could he, even with this help, bring order out of chaos? " . . . he was not a very patient listener to the military points of view. He had his own decisions pretty well organized, and wasn't much interested in hearing other points of view," recalled Admiral Charles Wellborn.[15] Unable to please each of the services, he must, he said, crack heads together to win agreement. Because his way was to urge, insist, drive, and prod impatiently regardless of whose toes he stepped upon, one writer noted that a new secretary and his staff always enjoyed a pleasant honeymoon and then concluded that "Johnson's was the shortest honeymoon on record."[16] Another stated that Johnson became preoccupied "with managerial problems to the exclusion of substantive issues," while syndicated columnist Marquis Childs wrote that "Johnson began with a bold statement that he would knock some heads together. He had not been in office long before the suspicion arose that he was knocking his own head against an implacable wall of opposition."[17]

In a special message to Congress on 5 March 1949, Truman urged the prompt enactment of legislation to strengthen the authority of the Secretary of Defense over the military departments but did not concur with the Hoover Commission proposal that the service secretaries be demoted to Under Secretaries. Instead he suggested that they retain their current titles but administer their departments under the direction and authority of the Secretary of Defense and be denied their present right to appeal to the President or the Director of the Budget.[18] While Captain Arleigh Burke advised the Chief of Naval Operations, Admiral Louis E. Denfeld, on the few advantages and many disadvantages the suggested Defense Department reorganization held for the Navy and while Forrestal directed the service secretaries to support Truman's recommendations, the Senate gave a tribute to Johnson by taking up his nomination out of order by unanimous consent and then confirming him. A few days later Forrestal was being treated at the Naval Hospital, Bethesda, Md., for what physicians said was "occupational fatigue" caused by excessive work. A period of rest and medical treatment, said the physicians, "will result in recovery." He seemed to improve, but at three o'clock on the morning of 22 May he fell to his death from an unguarded window. "Sym-

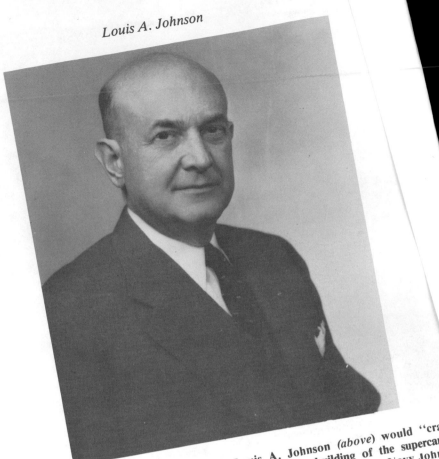

Louis A. Johnson

Big, tough, and politically ambitious, Louis A. Johnson (*above*) would "crack heads" to make unification work. His scrapping of the building of the supercarrier U.S.S. *United States* without consulting him provoked Secretary of the Navy John L. Sullivan to resign in anger.   OFFICIAL U.S. ARMY PHOTOGRAPH

ington, as you know," Hanson Baldwin told an interviewer, "was the only Secretary of the services who was not asked to be a pall-bearer at Forrestal's funeral, and that was purposefully done because some people, including, as I understand it, Forrestal's family, really felt that Symington had contributed to Forrestal's death. I almost felt that way, because the man was a goad, a real goad in a nasty way."[19]

Johnson took office on 28 March, the same day that the North Atlantic Treaty was agreed to. Although Truman would not submit the treaty to the Senate until 12 April, the Senate would not approve it until 21 July, and Truman would not sign it until 25 July, it had already spawned argument between those who would increase American military power instead of building up the very poor defenses of Western Europe.[20] In any event, on the evening of 28 March Johnson was the honored guest at a dinner attended by President Truman. Close by him sat General Joseph McNarney, USAF, formerly head of the ax-

The North Atlantic Treaty, pledging twelve nations to the principles of collective security and nonaggression, was signed on 4 April 1949. Signing for the United States is Secretary of State Dean Acheson. Standing behind Acheson are President Harry S. Truman and Vice President Alben W. Barkley. With NATO bases in the offing, the U.S. Air Force saw less need for naval aviation than ever before.

OFFICIAL U.S. ARMY PHOTOGRAPH

of which he lost the friendship and support of his staff except for the new people, often called "gauleiters" or "flunkies" he brought in. On 4 March Drew Pearson wrote that Johnson "is surrounding himself with various old cronies from the American Legion, plus some friends from big business. His hardest job is going to be to save himself from his friends."[21]

Among Johnson's old cronies were such American Legionnaires as Paul Griffith and Louis Renfro. Johnson touted Griffith, technically a Republican, to show that he was nonpartisan, yet made him in essence his patronage chief. Soon Griffith was assigning Legionnaires jobs in Johnson's office or in the military departments, telling their secretaries what civil service ratings to give them and, if necessary, to move people out to make room for them.[22] Renfro, a Reserve Army dental officer who was Harry Vaughan's civilian assistant, had served in Battery D with Captain Harry S. Truman in World War I. Disliking Johnson and knowing of his burning ambition to succeed him as President, Truman shifted Renfro to Johnson's staff as an unofficial political aide, with the understanding that Renfro would report to Truman on Johnson's doings.[23] When Renfro showed up in the uniform of an Army colonel on which was displayed the insignia of Aide to the Secretary of Defense, Robert Wood, the Army Assistant to the Secretary of Defense, exploded and told him he was wearing the uniform and the insignia illegally and to take them off. He then charged into Johnson's office to report the incident. Johnson bluntly told him to leave, to ask the Army for reassignment, never to darken his door again, and to tell "what's his name—Riley I think—" that he would be the acting aide until ordered otherwise. Wood told the story to the Chief of Staff of the Army, who could do nothing but swallow the first act Johnson made as Secretary of Defense.[24] On the next day, after the Chief of Naval Operations, Louis E. Denfeld, met with Johnson, he told Riley that Johnson wished him to remain as his aide. Riley, who preferred to attend the National War College, asked if he had any choice. Denfeld went back to Johnson, who agreed that Riley could stay until classes began and that he would find another aide.[25]

On 7 April Truman nominated Stephen T. Early, one of his secretaries and a staunch friend of Johnson, to be the Under Secretary of Defense. A former journalist and press secretary for Franklin D. Roosevelt, Early was expected to give Johnson a good press. On 2 April, on the advice of McNarney, Johnson had abolished nine interservice boards and directed the three service secretaries to report by 1 May which committees were necessary and which should be abolished. At the end of two months Johnson had abolished 68 committees; by October, 134; by the end of the year, 141. He also vetoed the suggestion of John L. Sullivan, Secretary of the Navy, made originally to Forrestal, that the Commandant of the Marine Corps meet with and inform and advise the Joint Chiefs of Staff on matters affecting the Corps. In addition he kept the consolidated National Military Establishment public relations office that Forrestal had created on 31 March. The new office was charged among other things with security review and clearance of any written or oral presentation prepared by Department of Defense personnel containing information on the performance or capabilities of new weapons or new equipment. As one commentator put it, military men must now "think in synchronization with the Air Force."[26]

On 30 March, Denfeld, who had been embarrassed by several leaks by naval personnel, asked his deputies to remind their people that any statement or writing must be cleared by his public relations office, which would then coordinate releases with the public relations offices of the Secretary of the Navy and Secretary of Defense. That the other services were also at fault was revealed when the House Armed Services Committee charged that "persons within the National Military Establishment are endangering the country's security through their efforts to sell the public their own particular views regarding air power.'' [27] Taken to task by Carl Vinson with respect to naval statements on the views of the House Armed Services Committee, a contrite Dan A. Kimball, Assistant Secretary of the Navy for Air, told Vinson he had issued "to all personnel . . . reaffirmation of nondisclosure policy,'' a matter given servicewide dissemination on 14 April in an Alnav emanating from Sullivan's Public Relations Office. On 14 April Johnson furnished the services a list of the material subject to review; on the twenty-eighth Sullivan directed that no public statements be made by naval personnel without prior reference to him for explicit policy clearance by the Office of the Secretary of Defense.

Although it worked hard and late, the Joint Chiefs of Staff budget advisory group headed by Vice Admiral Robert B. Carney was unable to agree unanimously on the defense budget for fiscal year 1951. While Johnson acceded to Sullivan's request that he ask Congress for $10.5 million with which to complete two experimental submarines authorized in 1947, the House of Representatives passed the largest military appropriations bill in peacetime history and gave the Air Force $851 million more than Truman recommended in his budget but only slight increases to the Army and Navy. Of the nearly $16 billion approved by the House Appropriations Committee, the Air Force would receive $6.216, the Army $4.481, and the Navy $5.019 billion. In debate on the measure, an attempt to add $300 million to naval aviation was decisively defeated, whereas the Air Force, with NATO European bases from which to operate against Russia, would grow from forty-eight to fifty-eight groups. In consequence of the funds allotted him, Sullivan reiterated that he must cut both his operating forces and personnel. What the fate of the USS *United States* (CVA-58), whose keel had already been laid, would be was not yet clear, for Johnson said "No comment" to newspaper reporters' questions and expressed surprise upon learning that Congress had funded her building, and particularly when told that it would take an act of Congress, not just an executive decision, to stop her construction.

That working with Johnson was difficult was revealed early. Herbert Riley stated that "he wasn't a man you could argue with or to whom you could make a logical presentation. Usually he would get up and walk out on you. Or, if he listened he would throw you out of his office when you finished—without a word."[28] On 13 April, John T. Koehler, the Assistant Secretary of the Navy, sponsored a presentation of "Industrial War Mobilization." Present were the Secretary of the Air Force, W. Stuart Symington, Generals McNarney and Omar N. Bradley, and from one hundred fifty to two hundred high ranking officers predominantly of the Army and Air Force. Captain M.G. Vangeli, of the Bureau of Ships, the first speaker, "spoke of the tremendous deficiencies to be faced if war were to come suddenly." As he took his seat, Johnson remarked that "he presumed the other speakers would bring out the same deficiencies. He remarked that his time was being wasted. He stated that he was not interested in perfect defense, but in the best defense we could provide with what we can produce. Planners in this instance have taken a wholly unrealistic

and impossible view and are not considering the other departments."
Nonplussed, Koehler suggested that another meeting be arranged at which
Johnson would be briefed "along the lines he indicated." Captain Richard W.
Ruble, who was present, then told Sullivan that "I think it just as well that you
were not present for the event."[29]

Two more examples of Johnson's terrible temper must suffice. After calling
on Johnson, Vinson left him with an expression on his face that indicated that
the meeting had been less than palatable, and he told others waiting to see
Johnson that he hoped their visit would be more pleasant than his had been.
When Major General A.W. Vanaman, USAF, Commandant of the Industrial
College of the Armed Services, began to brief Johnson about the college,
Johnson suddenly bellowed: "To Hell with all that. What I want to know is
whether you or your officers have any doubts about who is the boss of this
establishment?" Vanaman replied: "Well, I don't think so, Sir." Johnson
retorted: "You don't *think* so. . . . Well, let me tell you that any one who
doesn't cooperate with me won't have his job when the sun comes up in the
morning." He then asked the name of the Chief of Naval Operations. When
told it was Denfeld, he said, "Yes that's the fellow. They told me he wouldn't
cooperate. Well, he's cooperating, all right."[30]

On 21 April the Secretary of the Army, Kenneth C. Royall, resigned, saying
that he had stayed on as long as he did in order to help Johnson make the transition from Forrestal. Sullivan meanwhile asked Johnson to approve supplemental appropriations of $1.25 million per month to cover the Navy's costs
of participating in Operation Vittles during fiscal year 1949 and of $44.253
million during fiscal year 1950.[31] In addition to directing Rear Admiral
Ruthven E. Libby to succeed Robert B. Carney as the Navy member of the
Budget Advisory Committee that would correlate the fiscal year 1951 budget,
he spoke about the importance of sea power before the House Appropriations
Committee.

Without mentioning potential enemies, geographic area, overseas bases he
had much in mind, or the Air Force, Sullivan told the committee that control
of the sea was vital to the national economy and to national defense as long as
war remained a possibility. The daily well-being and the livelihood of many
Americans depended upon the uninterrupted flow of various critical materials
from overseas. To keep the sea lanes open both in times of peace and in times
of war was the function of sea power. He concluded that

> these considerations explain in part why we cannot abandon our naval
> strength, and why we cannot predicate our naval needs on a mere relative
> comparison with the navies of other powers. . . .
> It is my conviction that today, and in the world as it exists today, the
> Navy is more important to this country than it has ever been in time of
> peace in our entire history.[32]

In a speech to a Reserve Officers Association conference at Corpus Christi,
Texas, on 23 April, Sullivan stated that the armed services "are working in full

harmony" and that the Navy proposed to organize and operate strictly within the agreements reached at Key West and Newport. "Unfortunately," he added, "harmony and accomplishment do not make news. Dissention and frustration do make news." At this moment, in Washington, Johnson sent him a two-sentence memorandum already made public. He had received the views of the Joint Chiefs of Staff and of the President on the matter of the *United States,* Johnson wrote, and had given it his careful consideration. He then ordered Sullivan to discontinue construction on the ship. The immediate and violent explosion provoked in the Navy by Johnson's order began with Sullivan's flying back to Washington. After listening to a short briefing by Denfeld, he called Captain Dennison, at the White House, to come to his office. As Dennison recalled, it was about six o'clock in the evening. He found Sullivan, who was "absolutely furious," dictating his letter of resignation addressed to the President, "and it was a pretty strong letter." Dennison telephoned Charles Ross, who told Sullivan that he should not, or could not, send such a letter to the President and that if he was going to resign he should send a letter to Johnson. Sullivan retorted that the President, not Johnson, had appointed him. Ross, Dennison, and others pointed out that Sullivan was a good friend of Truman and that nothing should interfere with their personal or political relationship. Sullivan knew that Truman had twice approved building the carrier and that he now backed Johnson. He wrote another letter, to Johnson, then switched letters so that the bitter and indignant one would go to Johnson and the sweet one, which did not give any reason for his action beyond saying that "circumstances" prevented his further public service, to Truman. He thus did not impair his good relations with the administration but made his resignation irreversible.[33]

In his letter to Johnson, which he made public on 26 April, Sullivan asserted that neither he nor Denfeld was consulted about canceling the carrier and that the President had twice approved her building. He had surrendered $307 million that could have gone to complete other ships in order to fund her. Her construction had been approved by both houses of Congress in June 1948, and Congress had appropriated funds for the first year of construction. He had then surrendered another $57 million in building funds for her construction; additional funding for her was carried in the budget for fiscal year 1950. On 18 April, he went on, Johnson had asked him about the carrier. Before he could say much, Johnson rushed off to some meeting. On the next day he sent Johnson some data justifying the building of the carrier and a request for a personal meeting.[34] He then heard nothing about the subject until the twenty-third, when his office called him in Corpus Christi and told him that Johnson had ordered him to cancel the carrier's construction. Sullivan continued by saying:

> I am, of course, very deeply disturbed by your action which so far as I know represents the first attempt ever made in this country to prevent the development of a powerful weapon system. The conviction that this will result in a

renewed effort to abolish the Marine Corps and to transfer all Naval and Marine Aviation elsewhere adds to my anxiety.

However, even of greater significance is the unprecedented action on the part of a Secretary of Defense in so drastically and arbitrarily changing and restricting the operational plans of an Armed Service without consultation with that Service. The consequences of such a procedure are far-reaching and can be tragic.

Sullivan concluded by noting that he evidently could provide no further useful service to the Navy Department and had forwarded his resignation to the President.[35]

Upon learning of Sullivan's resignation, Johnson said, "Sullivan has joined the aircraft carrier issue on personal grounds, and I believe that he . . . will soon regret his action of today."[36] During testimony he gave to the House Armed Services Committee on 10 October 1949, at hearings concerning unification and strategy, he delivered another blow by stating that Sullivan had not resigned on 23 April but about a month earlier "because he was unwilling to support unification."[37] The truth was that Sullivan had submitted a perfunctory letter of resignation four days before Johnson succeeded Forrestal and that Johnson interpreted it to please himself. By retaining the letter he had a weapon to use against Sullivan if Sullivan did not go along with his evident desire to augment the powers of the Secretary of Defense.[38]

On 21 October 1949, after Chairman Vinson chided him on the brusque and abrupt manner in which he canceled the *United States*, Johnson denied that he had ever been discourteous to Sullivan, adding:

Mr. Sullivan was not for unification, would not support unification and . . . on March 26 . . . he tendered to the President . . . his resignation . . . and knew it was accepted, because he was not in accord with unification and because I had told him there was no room on my team on the civilian side for anybody who wouldn't loyally and enthusiastically support unification.[39]

Johnson's reasons for scrapping the carrier could have been to save money, to impress the leaders of the military departments that he could exercise "direction, authority and control" over them, and to favor the Air Force.[40] Admiral Dennison, who had been close to the event, was interviewed in 1971.

[Jerry N.] HESS: How much responsibility should be borne by Louis Johnson for the reduction in the armed forces at this time, and for the cancellation of the aircraft carrier? Was that *his* action, or was it just something that was inescapable for him because of the budget limitations? . . .

DENNISON: Well, remember I was in the White House. I wasn't in the Pentagon, so I don't know what the budget figures were or whether this was indeed a factor. But it appeared from the way Johnson made these decisions . . . that if the decision were indicated by financial pressure of some kind, Sullivan should have been told about it. I just can't believe that the budget all of a sudden appeared and there wasn't enough money for the carrier . . . . But in these decisions that Johnson made he gave me the impression of being arbitrary. *He* was the one who was doing this. The damned armed forces were too greedy and he was very much opposed to the Navy. The Navy was really a terrible outfit because they were anti-unification, the whole damn Navy. His prejudices were very strong.[41]

Herbert D. Riley was more blunt, saying that Johnson's political ambition

was evident in his many speeches, his publicity machine and most of all in his deliberate slashing of our Presidentially-approved and Congress-approved military programs, in the belief that if he slashed approved military programs under the guise of "cutting fat—not muscle," he could curry public favor—and votes. He wanted the SecDef job simply because the Defense Department budget was the largest increment of the National budget and would, therefore, give him the greatest opportunity to "save the taxpayers" mammoth sums and thereby form his election platform. Korea crossed him up—and forever out of the government, thank God.[42]

John F. Floberg, the Assistant Secretary of the Navy for Air, saw Johnson in a somewhat different light:

I found Louis Johnson a very tough nut, a very hard-boiled, uncompromising and fearless decision maker; but, at the same time, I found him to be absolutely fair and a straight shooter with me. I had quite a few matters in which I personally came into conflict with him in his office, and I always found him open-minded and fair but also positive and firm in his decisions and in his anticipation that once he had made them, I would conform with them. His biggest weakness, in my observation, was his tendency to snap judgment. I have always said that, if you and I were on opposite sides of a position and it was Louis Johnson's responsibility to settle it, he would be absolutely impartial in letting us state our respective cases—for 30 seconds each—and then would decide in absolute sincerity, according to his best judgment, which of us was right. . . . My criticism is that he made those decisions on the basis of less thorough exposure and debate than he should have.

Floberg also has commented on Johnson and the budget, saying.

I joined the Pentagon during the heaviest part of the defense budget retrenchment days and Johnson was the hatchet man and very much the target of criticism for defense cutbacks. While I was not privy to White House counsels in those days, I was always convinced in my own mind that Johnson was being a good soldier; and whether or not his heart was in the budget slashes for the military services—and I suspected then and still do that it was not—he had his orders from the President and was carrying them out with all the vigor and personal loyalty of which he was capable . . . . If there was one weakness he did *not* have, it was a tendency to procrastination; and that is why his bareback riding made him so conspicuous. It is certainly true that in the Navy at that time, and by tradition even to this date, he was utterly despised. I think that the CVA-58 decision was the basis for the deep seated hatred, but I really believe that Johnson was absolutely sincere and thought he was doing precisely the right thing and was explicitly carrying out the President's orders when he made the decision.[43]

Although economy affected Johnson's thinking, it was more likely that his conclusion to scrap CVA-58 was based on strategic considerations.[44] It may have been coincidence, but on 25 April it was publicly announced that the 509th "Atom Bomb" Group of thirty B-36s would fly the Atlantic to a front-line NATO base in England and thus be in the position to drop atomic bombs anywhere in Europe on short notice,[45] and the *New York Times* heralded the scrapping of the supercarrier with the headline "Air Force Triumphs in Strategy Fight."[46] On the twenty-sixth, writing in the *Times* under the heading, "In the Nation," pundit Arthur Krock noted that it was Johnson's main responsibility to decide how defense funds would be spent. His lawyers certainly must have assured him of his authority to cancel the carrier even though Congress had appropriated funds for her, said Krock, who stated that the weakest point in the argument for her was that while bombers could take off from her, they could not land on her. It may be added parenthetically that if such bombers had to land on friendly overseas bases, then the Navy's argument against Air Force bombers was turned against itself. In any event, Johnson had the decision of the Joint Chiefs of Staff and at least the tacit agreement of its presiding officer, Eisenhower, and did not need the advice of the civilian leaders of the services, including Sullivan. "If ever a decision was properly a military one," concluded Krock, "this was it."[47]

According to Walter Waggoner, writing also in the *New York Times:*

No one in the Truman administration has left his post with so frank a statement of the reasons, and probably not since the departure of Jesse H. Jones, who was asked to leave by President Roosevelt to make way for the appointment of Henry A. Wallace as Secretary of Commerce, has an official of sub-cabinet rank, raised such a storm with his protest.

Waggoner concluded that impartial observers saw Sullivan's protest and resignation "as the biggest setback to unification since the Army, Navy, and Air Force were put on an independent and co-equal basis."[48]

Johnson's manner in scrapping the *United States* was clever. He had opposed the carrier from the beginning and told his staff that he meant to cancel her construction, but in a very official way. He knew that Bradley, who "loathed the Navy with a passion," and Vandenberg would vote for, and Denfeld against, cancellation. Since it was his duty to resolve "split decisions," he merely had to go along with the majority and completely disregard the dissenting report from Denfeld. Herbert D. Riley, who carried the papers from the Joint Chief's "think tank" to Johnson, said to Johnson, "I have the Chiefs' paper on the *United States,*" Johnson said, "Of course. Get the Press Chief in here right away." Having already had duplicated a press release on the cancellation of the ship and stuffed in into the reporters' boxes, all he now had to do was to tell the Press Chief "Let it go."[49] Whatever the reason Johnson used to scrap the carrier, Sullivan evaluated the move as a major victory for the Air Force, which saw the carrier and its long-range planes as an invasion of its primary responsibility for strategic air warfare.

Did the scrapping of the carrier contain other portents? Would the Navy, which for half a century was the first line of defense and enjoyed the greater share of defense funds, be relegated to an antisubmarine role and be shorn of offensive power? Were the lessons of history—the failure of the independent British Royal Air Force to provide air power at sea, Germany's reliance upon air power and neglect of sea power in World War II, the stupendous accomplishments of United States carrier forces and of the Marine Corps in the Pacific World War II—to be forgotten? How would the Air Force, if denied overseas bases, perform its strategic mission? If the Air Force had bases abroad, who would provide air cover for supplies bought to them and hunt down intruding submarines? How could the Navy obtain the weapons it needed to carry out its missions when the Chiefs of Staff of the Army and Air Force could veto those weapons?[50] Given the financial straitjacket of a $15 billion budget, each service competed for funds to develop those weapons it believed would win wars. The Air Force had torpedoed the supercarrier in order to spend $3 million for each of an additional seventy-five B-36s that the Navy still persisted its fighters and those of Russia could shoot down and that would be obsolete in five to ten years. The Air Force wanted $200 million with which to develop guided missiles with a five-thousand mile range; the Navy instead wanted money to develop countermeasures to the snorkel submarine.[51] As for the Marine Corps, best estimates gave it a fifty-fifty chance of being absorbed by the Army, and it was whispered that Johnson was holding up an order transferring its aviation to the Air Force only until the furor in the Navy over his scrapping of the supercarrier died down.[52]

For three days Truman tried to persuade Sullivan not to resign. Finding him obdurate, he accepted the verdict "with deep regret." Sullivan could leave at his convenience.[53]

On 28 April, five days after the carrier had been killed, Arleigh Burke summed up the situation for Denfeld:

> It appears that one of the Air Force objectives is to take over the Navy's roles and missions of control of the sea. There are rumors that additional naval units such as Marine aviation, attack carriers, naval shore-based aviation units, amphibious units, etc., may be drastically reduced or eliminated, and also that there is a strong possibility that a National General Staff Corps will be created. If these rumors are based on fact, the Navy will be unable to perform its primary role of control of the seas. If this should come to pass, it is possible that the Navy's roles may be reassigned, all or in part, to one of the other services whether or not those services have the actual capability of carrying out those roles.[54]

And on the twenty-ninth Ofstie not only questioned the Air Force's premises and promises for strategic atomic warfare—"the principal misconceptions which have been foisted on the American people and their representatives in

Congress"—but strongly suggested that the Navy stop being on the defensive and shift to the offensive, saying, "Whatever our position is to be, let us immediately lay it down in black and white and stick to it." As he saw it, the Air Force's plans for conducting strategic atomic warfare were too narrowly conceived. The Air Force would moreover destroy enemy cities rather than military installations. He wanted the Navy to assist the Air Force with its own atomic capability "as a purely secondary function," yet naval air must also be employed "against targets of direct and immediate military importance." Naval air "considers these targets to be military forces (land, sea, and air), military installations (land, sea, and air bases), and lines of communication (ocean, and inland shipping, rail, and road transport, and the fuel therefore (oil)."[55]

Truman's prompt acceptance of Sullivan's resignation made it appear that he backed Johnson. Johnson, meanwhile, talked Kimball, who wanted to resign also, into staying on, saying, "You and I can fight without it becoming personal."[56] Sullivan stayed on until 24 May, when he sent the Navy a sincere farewell message.[57]

On the day he resigned, Sullivan attended a cocktail party. He was greeted by Secretary of State Dean Acheson, who shook his hand and said "Welcome to the most exclusive club in America."

"What club is that?" Sullivan asked.

"The club of men in public life who have resigned in the cause of conscience."

"Who are the other members of the club?" Sullivan asked.

"Just you and me and Lew Douglas," Acheson replied.[57]

Acheson erred. Although he had resigned from the Roosevelt administration in 1933, he was merely one of 389 persons in the rank of assistant secretary or in senior White House posts who had left these posts between 1900 and 1960. Moreover, of these only 8.7 percent made a public protest when they resigned, and 35.8 percent of those who resigned were later rewarded with full or part-time posts.[58]

Although some representatives on both sides of the aisle disliked the manner of his action, both Vinson and Tydings, Chairman of the Senate Armed Services Committee, agreed that Johnson had made a "courageous and momentous decision," that he had acted under presidential authority, and that the President could retire an appropriation at any time. Tydings added that he would hold no hearings on the matter because the Joint Chiefs of Staff had decided against the carrier by a vote of two to one and the Senate would not go over their heads, and Vinson felt the same way.[59]

Sullivan and Denfeld had backed the supercarrier all the way. Three members of the Joint Chiefs of Staff had supported it in March 1948 at Key West. On 28 May 1948 the Air Force representative dissented. After Johnson on 15 April 1949 asked the Joint Chiefs to review their decision, Bradley reversed his vote.[60] Air Force leaders and Bradley later questioned Denfeld's asserting that the Joint Chiefs had tacitly accepted the carrier but not approved the long-range planes with which she was to be equipped.[61] But the vote by the Joint Chiefs was unimportant to Johnson. As he said, "Whether the Joint Chiefs of Staff vote two-to-one or unanimously, they are only advisers to the Secretary of Defense and the President who do the deciding."

Vinson believed that a two-ocean Navy was still needed to perform its historic mission of controlling the seas. But if war came, it would be with a land power. As he saw the problem,

> It is simply a matter of the proper allocation of war missions between the Navy and Air Force. It is the business of the Air Force to use long-range bombers in time of war. And yet, this carrier was to accommodate such long-range bombers. We cannot afford the luxury of two strategic air forces. We cannot afford an experimental vessel that, even without its aircraft, costs as much as 60 B-36 long-range bombers. We should reserve strategic air warfare to the Air Force.[62]

The result of Johnson's cancellation of the *United States* and of Sullivan's resignation was that Johnson became the center of a controversy that emphasized service disagreements, as illustrated by the "revolt of the admirals" that had begun even before he stopped the carrier's construction, bedeviled his entire tenure, and continued under Sullivan's successor, Francis P. Matthews.

Cancellation of the building of the supercarrier drastically altered the Navy's shipbuilding program for fiscal year 1950. In consequence, Sullivan put funds allotted to the supercarrier into conversion work on two attack carriers, five experimental destroyer escorts, and two killer submarines, and into the building of two mine countermeasures ships, all at a cost less than the total estimated for the supercarrier.

The Navy was so greatly upset with Johnson and with the reduction in its air capability that on 19 April Sullivan pondered requests that he seek permission to let a Navy F2H fighter intercept a B-36, which he was told by Vice Admiral John Dale Price, Chief of the Bureau of Aeronautics, and others, had a true air speed of 337 knots (390 miles per hour) and could reach thirty-seven thousand feet with a ten thousand-pound bomb load.[63] On 10 May Price would relieve Vice Admiral Arthur Radford as Vice Chief of Naval Operations, while Radford, promoted to Admiral, would become Commander in Chief Pacific Fleet. On 6 May, after referring to a new Title IV being proposed as an amendment to the National Security Act, Price provided an excellent summary of the Navy's view toward the impending Defense Department reorganization:

> (3) Concentration of authority to the marked extent contemplated in the proposed legislation is contrary to the basic philosophy of a democratic government and completely at variance with the agreed-upon concept of unification, rather than merger, of the air services. Naval and Marine Aviation are vitally interested in any proposal which might result in a subjugation of the air elements of the Navy to the control of the other two services. The real question

at issue is whether aviation shall continue to be an integral element of the Naval Establishment, free to progress along lines best suited to naval strategy and objectives.

(4) Carrier aviation, as developed by the U.S. Navy, is without peer in the world today. As an instrument of national policy, it is unparalleled, but its only prospects for the future are complete and utter frustration if the proposed legislation should become law.

(5) The Bureau of Aeronautics views with no little alarm the fast-moving trends toward a centralization of authority so complete and so far-reaching that naval operations would be inescapably subject to the decisions and view of those who are not in a position to evaluate its requirements with competence or without prejudice. . . .

(6) The Bureau has grave fears, particularly, for the future of *Naval* and *Marine* Aviation which are well known to be the targets of attack.[64]

That Sullivan was not unhappy with Price's comment was revealed in his expressing his "genuine appreciation of the cooperation you have given to me at all times" and wishing him a successful tour as Vice Chief of Naval Operations.[65]

The humanity of the man is also illustrated in his saying good-bye to his old friend Nimitz. Sullivan, who stopped at La Guardia airport on 3 May, telephoned the admiral, who was then serving on the United States Military Commission to the United Nations. When Nimitz arrived at the airport, Sullivan had him sit in a car with him and told him the details of the scrapping of the *United States* and of his fears that other Johnson plans boded evil for the national defense.[66]

Evidently Sullivan had told Johnson that the Air University was teaching the doctrine of "ONE Air Force," for on 10 May he sent him a reference to Hanson Baldwin's article on the subject in the *New York Times* for 27 May 1947, adding that "there has been no evidence during the past year of a change in this doctrine."[67] It was also evident that he tried hard to cooperate with Symington, for on the same day he wrote Symington that certain Air Force officers had been given training by the Navy in carrier landings and that naval and Marine air groups had operated with the Air Force in various exercises. He thought the exchange between the services to be "most beneficial in promoting a better understanding between the services" and suggested that "a continuing plan for a temporary exchance of officers on a larger scale would lead to an even greater appreciation of one service for the other." However, he was most painfully aware as he prepared to leave office that the scrapping of the supercarrier left only the Air Force to enjoy a strategic air arm. He was similarly aware of the anti-Air Force sentiment provoked throughout the Navy because the Air Force objected to the modernization of even *Essex* class carriers while it proceeded to modernized its B-36s so as to increase their range.[68]

Although he provided no specific example, Drew Pearson told his diary on 24 May 1949 that "the Navy has been waging a very skillful undercover campaign to play up Forrestal as a martyr and a hero. Part of the campaign is aimed against Louis Johnson, whom the Navy hates with a bitter, undying hatred which borders close to mutiny . . . . "[69] And he wrote on the twenty-ninth:

> The Navy has sworn to get Louis Johnson. It is seething with rage over the way they have become the third-rate arm of the service. Under F.D.R. the Navy ruled the roost. There was nothing they couldn't get. The admirals never hesitated to go over the head of the Secretary of the Navy to F.D.R. direct. Now Truman, a former artillery captain, is not only partial to the Army, but his bosom friend, General Vaughan, is constantly at his side, while he has appointed as Secretary of Defense an Army colonel who leans toward the Air Force. So the Navy is pulling every conceivable wire to smear Johnson. In addition, Eberstadt, and the Wall Street gang are out to get Johnson. On top of this the little group of newspapermen who were Forrestal's brain trust have also started a campaign to smear Johnson.[70]

The administration considered offering Sullivan a high government post in order to smooth ruffled feelings and gain favor with his large political following in New England. Sullivan, however, returned to law practice in Washington. He outlived Johnson, who died in 1966, and perhaps enjoyed the irony in the situation in which he was an honored guest at commissioning exercises held for the first supercarrier, the USS *Forrestal*, in 1952, and also for the nuclear-powered carrier USS *Nimitz* (CVA-68) at Newport News, Virginia, on 13 May 1972.

NOTES

1. "The Reminiscences of VADM Herbert D. Riley, USN (RET)," transcript of oral interview by John T. Mason (Annapolis, Md., U.S. Naval Institute, 1972), pp. 315-16.
2. Ibid., p. 355; *New York Times*, 24 October 1947. See Keith D. MacFarland, *Harry H. Woodring: A Political Biography of FDR's Controversial Secretary of War* (Lawrence: University of Kansas Press, 1975), and "Woodring vs. Johnson: F.D.R. and the Great War Department Feud," *Army* 26 (March 1976):36-42.
3. Riley, "Reminiscences," p. 354.
4. Daniel V. Gallery, RADM, USN (RET), *Eight Bells and All's Well* (New York: W. W. Norton, 1965), p. 222.
5. Transcript of oral interview by Jerry N. Hess of ADM Robert Lee Dennison, USN (RET) (Independence, Mo.: Harry S. Truman Library, 1972), p. 28 (hereafter cited as Dennison, "Reminiscences").
6. Ibid., pp. 17, 21.
7. Riley, "Reminiscences," p. 315.
8. Ibid., p. 310. See also transcript of oral interview by Benis M. Frank of GEN Oliver P. Smith, USMC (RET) Washington: HQ, USMC, Historical Division, 1969), p. 185.
9. "Reminiscences of Hanson Weightman Baldwin," transcript of oral interview by John T. Mason (Annapolis, Md.: U.S. Naval Institute, 1976), pp. 487-89.
10. Transcript of oral interview by Benis M. Frank of GEN Clifton B. Cates, USMC (RET) (Washington: HQ, USMC, Historical Division, 1967), pp. 228-30; transcript of oral interview by Benis M. Frank of GEN Vernon Megee, USMC (RET) (Washington: HQ, USMC, Historical Division, 1967), pp. 88-91.
11. Alfred Goldberg, "Roles and Missions," in Goldberg, ed., *A History of the United States Air Force, 1907-1957* (Princeton, N.J.: Van Nostrand Reinhold, 1957), p. 116.
12. "Limits to the Use of Air Power," USNWR 26 (1 April 1949):20-21.

13. Merle Miller, *Plain Speaking: An Oral Biography of Harry S. Truman* (Published by Berkley Publishing Corporation, Distributed by G. P. Putnam's Sons, New York, 1973, 1974), p. 236 n.; James A. Bell, "Defense Secretary Louis Johnson,'" AM 70 (June 1950):643.
14. Johnson to National Military Establishment, 3 and 31 August, 28 September and 1 December 1949, NARG 330, Papers of the Secretary of Defense; Paul Y. Hammond, "NSC-68: Prologue to Rearmament," in Warner H. Schilling, Paul Y. Hammond, and Glenn H. Snyder, *Strategy, Politics, and Defense Budgets* (New York: Columbia University Press, 1962), pp. 286-96.
15. "Reminiscences of VADM Charles Wellborn, Jr., USN (RET)," transcript of oral interviews by John T. Mason (Annapolis, Md.: U.S. Naval Institute, 1972), p. 290.
16. "People of the Week," USNWR 26 (11 March 1949):36, 38-39.
17. "The Battle of the Pentagon," *Harper's* 199 (August 1949):52.
18. Harry S. Truman, *Memoirs by Harry S. Truman*, 2 vols. (Garden City, N.Y.: Doubleday, 1955-56), 2:53.
19. "Reminiscences of Hanson W. Baldwin," p. 467.
20. Truman, *Memoirs*, 2:250-51; Hammond, "NSC-68: Prologue to Rearmament," pp. 282-84.
21. Tyler Abell, ed., *Drew Pearson Diaries, 1949-1959* (New York: Holt, Rinehart, and Winston, 1974). p. 28 (hereafter cited as *Pearson Diaries*).
22. Riley, "Reminiscences," pp. 338-41.
23. Ibid., pp. 311, 315-16.
24. Ibid., pp. 310-13.
25. Ibid., pp. 313-14.
26. "Whispers," USNWR 26 (6 May 1949):52.
27. "Chronology," *Current History*, May 1949.
28. Riley, "Reminiscences," pp. 314-15.
29. Secret. R. W. Ruble, Memorandum for Mr. Sullivan, 13 April, SNP. Bell, "Defense Secretary Johnson," p. 645, relates that Johnson called a number of congressmen to his office to announce an economy program. "The Congressmen beamed. This was what was needed—a man in the executive branch of government who believed in economy. But the smiles immediately gave way to apoplectic purple when Johnson proceeded to list the military installations he would close in order to achieve economy. Each Congressman present heard an airfield, quartermaster depot, ordnance plant or naval installation in his district dropped."
30. "An Interview with John T. Mason, Jr., Director of Oral History," USNIP 99 (November 1973):86.
31. John L. Sullivan, Memorandum for the SECDEF, 18 March 1949, SNP.
32. "Importance of Sea Power Explained by Secretary," ANJ 86 (23 April 1949):978. See also the report of the President's Materials Policy Commission, which characterized the United States as a "have-not" nation with respect to strategic and critical materials, as discussed in *New York Times*, 3 July 1952.
33. Dennison, "Reminiscences," pp. 106-9; "The Reminiscences of VADM Fitzhugh Lee, USN (RET)," transcript of oral interviews by CDR Etta Belle Kitchen; USN (RET) (Annapolis, Md.: U.S. Naval Institute, 1970), pp. 198-99. The letters were published the next day, as in the *New York Times*, 27 April 1949.
34. On 18 April Sullivan had discussed the vulnerability of carriers in World War II. On the nineteenth, he had provided supporting data (J. S. Sullivan, Memorandum for the SECDEF, 19 April 1949, SNP).
35. John L. Sullivan to the President, 26 April 1949, SNP.
36. *New York Times*, 27 April 1949.
37. "Documents Leading to the Resignation of Sec. Sullivan," ANJ 86 (30 April 1040):1033.
38. John L. Sullivan to Harry S. Truman, 24 March 1949, in U.S. Congress, House Committee on Armed Services, House of Representatives, *The National Defense Program: Unification and Strategy*, 81st Cong., 1st Sess. (Washington: GPO, 1949), pp. 622-23 (hereafter cited as NDP).
39. NDP, p. 622.
40. Mark E. Watson, "Two Years of Unification," MA 13 (Winter 1949):193-95.
41. Dennison, "Reminiscences," pp. 109-10.
42. Riley, "Reminiscences," p. 316.

43. Floberg to the writer, 31 August 1976.
44. *New York Times*, 24 April 1949.
45. Ibid., 26 April 1949.
46. Ibid., 24 April 1949.
47. Ibid., 26 April 1949.
48. Ibid., 27 April 1949.
49. Riley, "Reminiscences," pp. 349-50.
50. David Lawrence, "How to Lose a War," USNWR 26 (6 May 1949):36-37.
51. "Why the Navy Wants Big Aircraft Carriers: An Interview with Fleet Admiral W. F. Halsey (RET.)," USNWR 26 (20 May 1949):24-28.
52. "Changed Basis for U.S. Defense," USNWR 26 (6 May 1949):16-17; "Whispers," USNWR 26 (13 May 1949):64.
53. Harry S. Truman to John L. Sullivan, 26 April 1949, SNP.
54. A. A. Burke, Memorandum for ADM Denfeld, 28 April 1949, NHD: OA, OP-23 File.
55. RADM Ralph A. Ofstie, Memorandum for OP-05, "Strategic Air Warfare," 29 April 1948, Ofstie Papers, cited in *Supporting Study*, pp. 132-33.
56. K. Jack Bauer to the writer, 3 October 1972.
57. Alnav 61, Navy Department Bulletin 49-397, 24 May 1949, NDB 14 (31 May 1949):13.
58. Edward Weisband and Thomas M. Franch, *Resignation in Protest* (New York: Grossman Publishers, 1975), and "Resignation in Protest," Potomac Section, *Washington Post,* 18 May 1975, pp. 16, 21-22, 24, 26, 43.
59. *New York Times*, 27 April 1949.
60. NDP, p. 360.
61. Paul Y. Hammond, "Super Carriers and B-36 Bombers: Appropriations, Strategy, and Politics," in Harold Stein, ed., *American Civil-Military Decisions: A Book of Case Studies* (University: University of Alabama Press, 1963), pp. 474-75.
62. ANJ 86 (30 April 1949):1003.
63. Conf. Memorandum for SECNAV [on Meetings of the War Council], 19 April 1949, SNP.
64. Chief, BUAER, to Director of [Navy] Budgets and Reports, copies to SECNAV and others, 6 May 1949, SNP.
65. John L. Sullivan to John Dale Price, 11 May 1949, SNP.
66. Elmer B. Potter, MS biography of Chester W. Nimitz, Chap. 24; courtesy Professor Potter.
67. John L. Sullivan, Memorandum for SECDEF, 10 May 1949, SNP.
68. Sullivan to Symington, 3 May 1947, SNP. See also OP-05B/BC, Memorandum to OP-09, 23 May 1949, NHD: OA, CNO Papers.
69. *Pearson Diaries*, pp. 51-52.
70. *Pearson Diaries*, pp. 53-54. The newspapermen whom Pearson named included Lyle Wilson, United Press; Frank Kent and Arthur Krock of the *New York Times*, Marquis Childs, the Alsop brothers, and Tris Coffin. (Ibid., p. 42, entry of 13 April 1949.)

PART II

The Naval Administration of
Francis B. Matthews

7

The "Rowboat" Secretary, the Defense Budget for Fiscal Year 1950, and Defense Reorganization

Secretary of the Navy John L. Sullivan resigned on 23 April 1949, after Secretary of Defense Louis A. Johnson torpedoed the Navy's hope for new life in the atomic age, the supercarrier *United States*, but he remained in office for an additional month. Whoever President Harry S. Truman should name as Sullivan's successor would head a navy in which morale, especially in its air arm, was the lowest it had been since the mid 1920s. He would have to operate under Johnson's "Consolidation Directive Number 1." This forbade service personnel to make public their views about the Defense Department without prior approval, for reasons of "policy and propriety" as well as of security. The directive was immediately criticized because it used censorship to hide organizational troubles. After 10 August the new Secretary would also administer his department under the terms of a new reorganization plan for the armed services that strengthened the power of the Secretary of Defense and further limited the authority of the service secretaries. He must try to live with an administration that made *economy* a watchword. He would be involved in two major squabbles, one over the capability of the B-36, the other over whether to build a supercarrier. Last, he stood to lose the support of his service if he did not oppose Johnson's plans for transferring Marine aviation to the Air Force.[1]

Late in April, after learning that Johnson had said that there were "too many Air Forces" and that he would do away with Marine aviation, Carl Vinson, Chairman of the House Armed Services Committee, sent for him and made him swallow his words. As Colonel Robert D. Heinl, USMC, has put it. Vinson "laid down the law: Marine aviation would not be abolished or transferred, and any such future steps affecting the Marine Corps would please be referred in advance to Congress before action was taken."[2]

American naval aviators, some Air Force pilots, and British authorities on aircraft as well asserted that the lumbering B-36 lacked the range to reach targets in Russia and could easily be shot down by fighters, let alone by missiles, whereas such top Air Force leaders as George C. Kenney, Curtis LeMay, and Hoyt S. Vandenberg insisted that their tests proved that the B-36 was practically invulnerable.[3] To make a point, the Air Force had B-36s fly ten-thousand-mile flights and with inflight refueling sent a B-50 nonstop around the world early in March 1949. To make its point, on 19 March the Navy had a P2V-3C patrol bomber capable of carrying the atomic bomb fly from the carrier *Midway*, off Norfolk, to San Diego, its 4,863-mile nonstop flight being the longest ever made from a carrier.[4]

While the Air Force stalled in replying to the Navy's request for a B-36 against which to test a Chance-Vought *Corsair* F4U-5 and a McDonnell *Banshee* F2H-1, various admirals asked the Senate Appropriations Committee to agree to $43 million the House of Representatives had allotted toward the building of a supercarrier. They got nowhere.[5]

Forrestal had established an ad hoc committee, chaired by Air Force Lieutenant General H. R. Harmon and containing both Air Force and Navy members, to evaluate the results of a strategic air offensive against Russia. In its report, dated 11 May 1949, the committee noted that it had studied the results of the dropping of atomic bombs on seventy Russian cities in the first thirty days of a war but had not assessed the chances of the bombers' reaching their targets, a problem it left to the Weapons System Evaluation Group. Would the atomic attack cripple Russia to the extent that she could not advance militarily in Europe, the Middle East, and East Asia? While 30 to 40 percent of Russian industry would be permanently destroyed, the attack would not cause Russian's leaders either to capitulate or release their control over their people. Indeed, the people would be steeled to fight on. Nor would the original attack seriously impede Russian armed forces from advancing westward or eastward. Moreover, the attack would result in maximum retaliatory strikes upon the United States. In sum, early atomic strikes would badly hurt Russia, but these must be followed by "associated military and psychological operations" before Russia would submit her will to the United States." The report thus supported the Navy's thesis that strategic bombing alone could not win a war. When the Chief of Staff of the Air Force, Hoyt S. Vandenberg, tried to change parts of the report, he was opposed by Denfeld and his naval planners, and Vandenberg submitted it as written to Johnson and Truman. These gentlemen paid little attention to it, probably because the strategic air force was best in operating on a budget that had strangled the Navy—which bided its time to present its case to the American public over the head of the Secretary of Defense and of the President.[6]

On 25 May Representative James E. Van Zandt (R., Pa.), member of the Housed Armed Services Committee and a captain in the Naval Reserve, tried to interest Vinson in investigating the Air Force procurement arrangements for the B-36, including Johnson's connection with the B-36 until 7 March 1949 as a director of its manufacturer, Consolidated Vultee Aircraft Corporation. He would also cite Johnson's approving of the purchase of many B-36s soon after he assumed office and his canceling of contracts for various other aircraft, with the result that tactical aircraft used to support the Army would be short in number. And he would bring up charges of campaign contributions having been made by Consolidated Vultee and others. When Vinson demurred, Van Zandt took the floor to demand a special investigation. Rather than having Van Zandt head a special staff of investigators, Vinson undertook the task himself. Meanwhile Millard E. Tydings, a wartime Army colonel now Chairman of the Senate Armed Services Committee, asked for a detailed report on all types of planes.

In accordance with a resolution adopted by Vinson's committee, Johnson directed the Joint Chiefs of Staff to make a test between Air Force and Navy fighter planes and the B-36. Johnson added that he, Symington, the Secretary of the Navy, and the President would assess it and report it to Vinson.[7] Johnson also allegedly said that the contest between the supercarrier and the B-36 was "the issue that gave me a chance to run the [defense] department." H. Struve Hensel has noted that Johnson "assumed command and made it stick."[8] Ferdinand Eberstadt added that "when the Secretary [of defense] was in the position to cancel a project as important as that and as dear to the heart of the Navy as that—and not be successfully challenged—that his power was adequate for anything that he would probably undertake to do."[9]

Soon after Vinson announced that he was preparing to investigate the B-36 program, his committee agreed to the request of the Joint Chiefs of Staff that the tests between the B-36 and fighter planes not be carried out because of security reasons, with the Chief of Naval Operations, Louis D. Denfeld, saying that no useful purpose with respect to the value of strategic bombing would be served. However, the committee unanimously endorsed a request for a thorough investigation into the B-36 procurement program "which would be no white wash."[10] Vinson foresaw an explosive situation that involved—in addition to the B-36—politics, campaign contributions, businessmen, the Navy, two-to-one decisions by the Joint Chiefs of Staff and the newcomer Johnson, whom he had already criticized to his face for the abrupt manner in which he cancelled the supercarrier and for seeking additional power with which to speed unification. In any event, in mid-June he offered a seven-point agenda for hearings to begin in July: (1) Was it a "sound" decision to have cancelled the *United States*? (2) Was the Air Force putting too much emphasis upon strategic bombing and not enough upon tactical aviation? (3) Should two of the armed services be able to "pass on" the weapons of a third by a two-to-one vote in the Joint Chiefs of Staff? (4) Were Van Zandt's charges true or false? (5) Identify sources of rumors and charges against the Air Force, presumably coming from the Navy and steel contractors. (6) Evaluate the performance of the B-36. (7) Evaluate the roles and missions of the Air Force and Navy, especially naval and Marine aviation.[11]

On 24 May 1949 the Irish Catholic Sullivan was piped ashore from the Pentagon. On the thirteenth, Truman had nominated as his successor Francis Patrick Matthews, another prominent Irish Catholic layman. Matthews, born

15 March 1887, was a graduate of Creighton University, a financier, corporation executive, and attorney in Omaha, and a director of the Chamber of Commerce of the United States. For special wartime work with the USO, President Truman in 1946 conferred upon him the Medal of Merit; in 1946 and 1947 he was a member of the President's Commission on Civil Rights. In 1948, he raised funds, helped swing the Nebraska delegation to Truman, and became friendly with Louis A. Johnson, chairman of the Democratic Party Finance Committee. According to Robert D. Heinl, Jr., a candidate for the top Navy position must give "advance assurance that he would not oppose eventual abolition of the Marine Corps or transfer of naval aviation to the Air Force."[12] Others said that Truman wanted someone who lacked contact with anything larger than a rowboat and would not antagonize Johnson. His nomination of Matthew took the press, Congress, and even Matthews by surprise. "I didn't lift a finger to get it," Matthews told reporters.[13] Supported by Nebraska's

The "rowboat" Secretary. A prominent Irish Catholic layman, lawyer, banker, and businessman, Francis P. Matthews was selected by President Harry S. Truman to serve as Secretary of the Navy because he had raised funds for him in the elections of 1948 and, because he knew nothing about the Navy, would not antagonize Secretary of Defense Louis A. Johnson as the latter "cracked heads" to obtain greater defense unification.

OFFICIAL U.S. NAVY PHOTOGRAPH.

Republican senators, he was easily confirmed and took office on 25 May. Completely unversed in the ways of the Navy and of Washington, and reportedly having strong isolationist views, he broke the chain of competent men James V. Forrestal trained under his own eye while he was Secretary of the Navy and then Secretary of Defense. He was "so narrow," said Hanson Baldwin.[14] As an "outsider," moreover, he would be easier to school in the political patterns of the Department of Defense than in military matters, a point Truman thought so important to the progress of national security unification that it was said that Matthews became Secretary of the Navy "with the assignment of persuading that service to yield to the administration's unification policies."[15]

In the presence of Mrs. Mary Claire (Hughes) Matthews, whom he had married in 1914, and their six children, Matthews was sworn in at the same time that Dan A. Kimball, the Assistant Secretary of the Navy for Air, was

John F. Floberg met Secretary of the Navy Francis P. Matthews at a party and was talked into joining his secretariat as Assistant Secretary of the Navy for Air. Trained as a lawyer, and a naval veteran of World War II, Floberg was one of the few people closely associated with Matthews who supported him even though he was aware of his various weaknesses. At this writing, Mr. Floberg is vice-president and legal counsel for the Firestone Company.

COURTESY OF MR. FLOBERG

sworn in as Under Secretary of the Navy. Not until November did Truman name as Kimball's successor as Assistant Secretary of the Navy for Air a Chicago lawyer named John F. Floberg, a naval veteran of World War II.

Matthews met Floberg at a party held on a Sunday late in October. He asked Floberg to have lunch with him at his dining room in the Pentagon on the next day. During the lunch, which lasted three hours, he discussed the problems that he and the Navy faced and pressured him to join his secretariat. Floberg agreed. Floberg, incidentally, married a sister of the wife of one of Matthews's sons, so that there was a relationship at least by marriage. That fact aside, Floberg was one of the few people closely associated with Matthews in the Navy Department who supported him, even though he was aware of his various weaknesses.[16]

Reporters called Matthews "the rowboat secretary" because a rowboat was the only craft he had ever sailed, and warned him that while he got "the high hat and the limousine," admirals ran the Navy. Matthews admitted that he had "little prior training or preparation" to guide him in his new post, but said that he expected to learn quickly. He approved legislation strengthening the authority of the Secretary of Defense and said that, while integration was the "big problem," it could be achieved "without impairing Navy prestige."[17] His statement revealed that, as one writer put it, "he thought Louis Johnson was the finest thing that had ever happened to the United States."[18] Another stated that "Mr. Matthews was only the voice of Mr. Johnson."[19] As a scholar has said, "Matthews was a man whose entire loyalty was to the President, and whose knowledge of, and affection for, the Navy was negligible."[20] As retired Admiral Arthur W. Radford expressed it to this writer in wonderfully mixed metaphor, "Matthews was badly miscast—a Cinderella in Wonderland,"[21] and Rear Admiral Joseph J. Clark held that Matthews "had no interest in promoting anyone who had been opposed to unification."[22] Moreover, he was so skeptical about advice offered him by naval officers that, as Admiral Charles Wellborn, Jr., recalled, "Anything you told him had to be very thoroughly documented and before it was accepted had to undergo very careful scrutiny."[23]

On 14 June, after the House Committee on Armed Services had approved Vinson's seven-point agenda, already noted, Vinson asked Matthews to send him his detailed views on it as soon as possible.[24] Matthews reply, sent five weeks later, was no doubt greatly influenced by the attitude of Denfeld and of the General Board of the Navy toward the carrier program and the attempts being made by the Army and Air Force to emasculate naval power. On 23 May, for example, Denfeld had approved an explanation by a high-ranking aviation expert in his office of the need to convert two old *Essex*-class carriers each year. Ten years earlier these carriers could handle all carrier-based aircraft; unless they were modernized, however, they were useless for war, and modernization took two years. Denfeld was told by his aviation experts that

The Air Force is modernizing its B-36's for one reason—to make its long-range bombers more effective. The Army is engaged in a tank modernization program to make its tanks more effective. . . .

It all boils down to this one simple statement. The Essex conversion program is a military necessity. Without this program the Navy cannot accomplish its assigned missions. I am responsible for the Navy's war readiness. You cannot expect me to try to operate 1951 aircraft from 1939-model carriers.

I insist that our carrier modernization program proceed as planned.[25]

On 25 May the Senate rejected by a vote of forty-six to twenty-six an amendment to the National Security Act that gave the Secretary of Defense authority to reassign combat personnel from one armed service to another. On the next day, however, it unanimously passed a bill introduced by Chairman Tydings of the Senate Armed Services Committee that would increase the stature of the Secretary of Defense over the entire military establishment by making him a cabinet member and the director of an executive department in which the existing service departments would be subordinate agencies of the whole. Among others, Symington avidly agreed.[26] During his last days, too, Forrestal had concluded that there were enough checks and balances in the defense structure to obviate fear of dictatorial direction by its head and that amendments would merely "convert the military establishment from a confederacy to a federation."[27] Yet Vinson believed the Secretary of Defense already had enough power to unify the services. "What has been troubling me," he told Johnson on 28 June, "is that the Congress is frozen out, kept at arms' length, from the problems of the three Departments. I cannot reconcile this with the constitutional responsibility of the Congress, and I think this bill should be amended to keep Congress a part of the team."[28]

On 31 May Matthews asked the General Board and Denfeld to make a study of "the present status of unification development" and to recommend steps to increase such unification.[29] On 27 July the chairman of the board replied with a twelve-page staff study. Unification was proceeding satisfactorily ". . .criticism of progress stems from publicity which develops over honest differences of opinion regarding national security requirements. The publicity given these differences of opinion is misinterpreted as lack of progress in unification." The Navy was making a conscientious effort to carry out the provisions of the National Security Act and the Key West and Newport Agreements. Reasonable progress was being made in reducing duplication of service facilities. "It will require persistent interservice education to eliminate the prejudices and suspicions of the members of one service against another service sufficiently to achieve more harmonious cooperation . . . . Despite criticism, the Navy must continue to protect its vital interests, including naval aviation and the Marine Corps, for the sake of national security." The report recommended keeping the public informed of Navy policies with respect to unification; exchanging officers between the services; resisting "merger" under the guise of "unification"; firmly holding onto naval and Marine Corps aviation as effective combatant components of the Navy; and the education of everyone on the value of sea power.[30] Denfeld later wrote Matthews that the conclusions of the board were sound and that he was directing the implementation of those recommendations which lay within the scope of his office.[31]

In May Johnson and the Joint Chiefs of Staff agreed upon force levels supportable on a budget of $14.4 billion. In July, however, Truman had his budget director tell the defense community that the budget must be reduced to $13 billion, the difference of $1.4 billion being about equal to the amount Truman had requested for mutual aid assistance. Said Johnson, "I was sick about it. The climate on the Hill, the climate of the President's economists and all the rest of the economists, the climate of the world at that moment—the [Berlin] airlift having been successful—the climate was there was going to be peace." He tried to get the figure raised but failed to do so. In consequence each service must still further reduce its forces.[32]

On 27 July Denfeld submitted to Johnson via the Joint Chiefs of Staff the Navy's requirements for fiscal year 1951. Denfeld took umbrage at Johnson's allocation of funds because the Navy would suffer more than the other services and naval aviation would bear the brunt of the shortages. Because the number of carriers had been reduced in November 1948 from eleven to eight and it was proposed to reduce them to only four, the 36.4 percent reduction of strength since November 1948 made it impossible for the Navy to counter significant air opposition and reduced it to the conduct of defensive operations alone—and he considered "an offensive naval force as equal in importance to the atom bomb force." Such reduction of force violated the Key West Agreement and resulted in an imbalance of military forces. Just consideration must be given to the provision of naval forces in a war with Russia in which the Navy must hold the Japan-Formosa-Philippines line while the Sixth Fleet, in the Mediterranean, acted as "a visible instrument of peace," that is, a deterrent to war. As he had stated many times, the minimum number of carriers needed to oppose significant air resistance was eight. On the one hand, he would accept a reduction in the number of operating air groups in order to save the carriers. On the other, he urged Johnson to reverse his reduction of antisubmarine patrol squadrons from thirty to twenty and increase the number to twenty-eight, an increase of only seventy-two planes. In conclusion, he asked for ten thousand extra men and an additional $170 million for the Navy.[33]

Given this background information, Matthews told Vinson that he wished to establish the truth of all charges brought by Van Zandt and to locate the sources of such charges. The speed of the B-36 was inferior to that of "shorter legged aircraft of comparable bomb-carrying capacity." In case of war the United States might lose land bases abroad, but it could use naval aircraft as long as the Navy commanded the seas. Therefore "the equipment of the Air Force at this time against such a contingency should not be an overriding factor in its procurement program." Was the decision to cancel the supercarrier sound? Here Matthews hedged, saying that although Johnson cancelled the ship, his permission to modernize two additional *Essex*-class carriers "establishes the principle that the Navy's aircraft development will not be brought to a halt." Matthews believed the Air Force unbalanced in favor of strategic air power and opposed the arrangement in which two of the three services passed on the weapons of a third. Last, he hedged also on the question whether strategic bombing was the most effective weapons system in the American armory, saying that the question was under study by military men and that Vinson's committee should give it "most careful consideration."[34]

On about 5 June Matthews and Denfeld had spoken with Johnson about modifying the Navy's shipbuilding and conversion program for fiscal year 1950. Following cancellation of the supercarrier, Matthews noted, Secretary Sullivan had submitted an alternative program. Because the Joint Chiefs of Staff had divergent views concerning it, Johnson must make the decision. Matthews opposed the Army and Air Force viewpoint that six carriers were more than enough for the Navy to perform its assigned missions. *Essex*-class conversions were definitely needed to accommodate the types of planes best suited to oppose the forces of potential enemies. Were the work curtailed, the Navy must operate obsolescent planes, "a procedure obviously militarily unsound." Last, what was at stake was not merely the carrier modernization program of fiscal year 1951 but "WHETHER OR NOT THE NATIONAL MILITARY ESTABLISHMENT DETERMINES AT THIS TIME TO LIMIT THE POSSIBLE PEAK EFFORT OF THE NAVY IN PERFORMANCE OF ITS APPROVED ROLES, MISSIONS, AND RESPONSIBILITIES BY RESTRICTING THE MODERNIZATION PROGRAM FOR ESSEX-CLASS CARRIERS."[35]

In quick succession Johnson announced that the President had approved his decision to modernize two additional carriers of the *Essex* class so that they could handle heavy bombers and that the Air Force would be kept at forty-eight rather than the fifty-eight groups the House had already approved. Then he told Kimball that naval aviation should be "beefed up."[36] He seemed thus to favor the Navy. Meanwhile Matthews told Johnson that he would forward his views on the Vinson agenda to Stephen Early, the Under Secretary of Defense, by 15 July, as directed, and that he understood that Early would correlate the views of the service secretaries on that agenda.[37]

After only nine weeks in office, Matthews made a brief annual report for the fiscal year 1948-49 in which he stated that he had largely followed policies and programs instituted by his predecessor. The First Fleet in the Pacific, Second in the Atlantic, and Sixth in the Mediterranean had supported U.S. interests in the Far East and in the Mediterranean. Navy transports had evacuated the families of naval personnel from China, torn by civil war. The Naval Air Transport Service had been merged with the Military Air Transport Service on 1 June 1948. With MATS heavily engaged in Operation Vittles, the succor of Berlin during its blockade by the Soviets, Navy squadrons had taken over domestic military air transport and also furnished two squadrons for use in

Operation Vittles. These squadrons, for the seven months after November, ranked far higher than Air Force squadrons in efficiency. Meanwhile NATS had set new records in delivering fuel oil and supplies to Europe for use in Operation Vittles and arrangements had been made for the Navy to assume responsibility for all military sea transportation for all the services on 1 October 1949.

"Considerable" progress had been made in antisubmarine warfare, Matthews continued, and in developing electronic devices for communications, navigation, and countermeasures. Three *Essex*-class carriers were being modernized, and several light carriers were being converted to antisubmarine carriers. Although "various considerations" had led to the cancellation of the *United States*, her design studies were available for future guidance.

A historic "first" during fiscal year 1949 was the appointment of women in the regular Navy. The Navy was also furthering its policy of efficient utilization of manpower by publicizing equal opportunities for all general service ratings and trying to recruit qualified Negroes for them. The number of naval personnel, which had seesawed with the ups and downs of the budget during fiscal year 1949, stood at 50,100 officers and 409,900 enlisted men on 1 June 1949, when there were 1,019,182 men in the Naval Reserve and 123,817 in the Marine Corps Reserve.[38]

Because of the cold war, the State Department had advised the Secretary of Defense in June 1948 that the "feast or famine" cycle of defense spending must be oriented toward a situation of "permanent crisis." General Omar N. Bradley, USA, the first Chairman of the Joint Chiefs of Staff, fully agreed.[39] Johnson did not, and he collided with Bradley by saying that $9 billion would suffice for the military services. Asked later why he did not resign in protest, Bradley said he had felt that he would have a better chance of increasing the budget than a new man in his office would have.[40]

The fiscal year 1950 budget was the first designed in keeping with the "permanent crisis" concept. The $15.9 billion defense budget approved in mid-March 1949 by the House of Representatives allotted $4.8 billion to the Army, $6.2 billion to the Air Force, and $5 billion to the Navy, thus keeping the armed forces "in balance." When the Senate cut the sum below $15 billion, the difference was given to a conference committee to resolve. In resolving the difference, the committee must also decide between Army-Navy and Air Force theories of war. The Army and Navy followed the "post D-day mobilization concept," namely, of heavy spending to keep up manpower and industrial mobilization strength while plans were drafted for additional mobilization to be undertaken after the nation went to war. The Air Force instead advocated the "force in being" concept. If the defense budget was split three ways, no service would be prepared for war. The D-day concept was outmoded, it argued, because there would be no time to mobilize in the traditional sense following the outbreak of war. Given sufficient funds, however, it could have long-range atomic bombers "in being" and thus ready to deter or to inflict great damage upon an aggressor. The resolution of the

the last four years. A committee of two admirals, two captains, and Karig had begun fourteen months earlier to try to carry out a national public relations program. It had bogged down in detail and finally ceased meeting. Therefore the "party line" was being established by OP-23. The Navy of the United States, Karig concluded, was what the people wanted it to be. The task of naval public relations was to educate them in what that Navy should be.[55]

Meanwhile the Navy League's publicity drive for more naval aircraft and carriers and for resistance to the loss of the Marine Corps to the Army created the impression that the Navy was opposed to everything Truman, Johnson, and Early wanted. Although Matthews told League President Frank Hecht that he was satisfied with Johnson's treatment of the Navy Department, Hecht refused to be bridled.[56]

In the meantime, too, Representative Van Zandt moved that the House Armed Services Committee set aside Tydings's bill for amending the National Security Act except for Title IV, which covered only budgetary and fiscal procedures, lest Johnson still further tighten his control over the National Military Establishment. On 12 June Vinson postponed the B-36 hearings and, after seeing Truman, announced that his committee would begin hearings on military department reorganization plans on the twenty-eighth. On 18 July Truman sent his own Reorganization Plan No. 8 for the National Military Establishment, long in writing, to Congress. Truman's plan converted the Establishment into a regular executive department named the Department of Defense. Its Secretary would exercise "authority, direction, and control" over the three military departments, which would be administered by their respective secretaries, but he would not have the right to change the statutory assignments or the combatant functions, roles, and missions of the services. A Deputy Secretary would replace the Under Secretary of Defense, three secretaries would be provided to assist the Secretary, and a Chairman would be provided for the Joint Chiefs of Staff. The last, who would have no vote or command authority, would prepare agendas, preside at meetings of the Joint Chiefs, and report split decisions to the President or Secretary of Defense. Only the Secretary of Defense, not the heads of the military departments, would have membership in the National Security Council. The name of the War Council would be changed to Armed Forces Policy Council, and a new Personnel Policy board would be established to advise the Secretary of Defense on personnel matters. While no service secretary or chief of staff could any longer appeal directly to the President or the Bureau of the Budget, he could notify the Secretary of Defense and make his views known to Congress.[57]

By deleting all but the title of the House bill dealing with military budget matters and substituting the Tydings bill on reorganization (S. 1269 on 16 March 1949), the Senate was ready to go to conference on reorganization, but the House was held up because Vinson wanted first to investigate the B-36 bomber program. Shortly thereafter, the two years of transition allotted by the unification law having expired, the Air Force stood completely independent

difference was also compounded because the services competed for nuclear power at a time of nuclear scarcity. The atomic weapons being developed by the Army and Navy were, according to the Air Force, smaller, hence less efficient than its large bombs, and whatever nuclear power was given to the Army and Navy detracted from its potential strength. Moreover, while the Army and Navy agreed with the administration that Russia would be slow to develop nuclear power and that there was therefore no urgent need to build up air defenses or strategic atomic forces, the Air Force estimated a quick Russian nuclear development that predicated the channeling of additional resources into continental air defense and strategic strike forces.[41]

If reports of secret orders to his budget planners were true, Johnson would use the new authority granted him by the National Security Act Amendments not only to shift funds toward the Air Force and away from the Navy but also to alter service roles and missions by giving the Air Force virtual monopoly over strategic air power, keeping the Army at its current strength, and reducing the Navy to an antisubmarine and transport force. He would halve naval and Marine Corps aviation funds, a reduction the Navy considered unsafe for defense purposes, and grant slightly increased funds for conventional naval forces the Navy had not asked for. In consequence, the Navy must reduce the number of its large operating carriers from eight to four, its light carriers from ten to eight, and also proportionately reduce its patrol, antisubmarine, and Marine Air squadrons. In addition to reducing the number of operating cruisers, destroyers, submarines, and auxiliary craft, the Navy must also close twenty shore installations and reduce still others, discharge 76,000 civil workers, and release 3,157 Reserve officers. While the number of Air Force heavy bombers would be quadrupled and both the Air Force and Army would gain tactical aircraft, the Navy would lose $687 million with which to buy 843 aircraft and thus lose the air parity with the Air Force that it had enjoyed.[42]

Naval aviation faced the greatest crisis in its history. By cutting its funds, Johnson placed a ceiling on technical improvements in naval aircraft. Moreover, without the supercarrier the Navy had to scrap designs for the new planes she would have carried, abandon plans for five aircraft prototypes, and suffer a year's delay in producing four others. It therefore sought bombers smaller than those planned for the supercarrier—of sixty-five-thousand rather than one-hundred-thousand pounds—to operate from the modernized *Midway*-class carriers. The loss of procurement funds, moreover, meant that the Navy would operate only three thousand planes in fiscal year 1950. By planning reductions of $1 billion in 1950 and another $1 billion in 1951, Johnson beautifully illustrated the concept in which "distributing shortages," in this case largely at the expense of the Navy, effectively substituted financial controls for adequate review of military requirements and therefore dictated strategy.[43]

Johnson's determination to make "substantial" savings in the fiscal 1950 and 1951 budgets by getting rid of "all waste, duplication, and extravagance" was laudable. To this end he would cut naval personnel from 534,023 to 446,000, civilian personnel by 154,000 and naval reserve officers by 12,500, and also cause various naval bureaus to absorb a reduction of $29 million by the end of fiscal year 1951.[44] By March 1951 he had abolished 160,000 "non-essential" civilian jobs at an annual saving of $489 million. But by this time he had made a shambles out of both the Navy and Marine Corps, having cut the latter's Fleet Marine Force by 14 percent in 1949 and an additional 5 percent in 1950 and also reduced Marine Aviation strength by 48 percent. He had even reduced his pet service, the Air Force, to forty-eight groups, even though the world knew that Russia had the atomic bomb.

Less money for the Navy meant increased reliance upon strategic bombing by the Air Force. However, the Navy questioned whether the nation could rely upon such bombing to support its interests or achieve wartime objectives. The Joint Chiefs of Staff instead concluded that less money indeed entailed increased reliance upon strategic bombing, and early in October General Joseph McNarney's Joint Chiefs of Staff Budget Advisory Committee proposed a plan that "placed sole reliance on the atomic offensive" on which to formulate the fiscal year 1950 budget. Denfeld immediately opposed the plan before Forrestal, the service secretaries, the Joint Chiefs of Staff, and McNarney's committee.[45] When on 4 November Rear Admiral Walter F. Boone, head of the Strategic Plans Division, recommended to Vice Admiral Robert B. Carney, Deputy Chief of Naval Operations (Logistics), that the Navy be permitted to keep its conventional sea control forces and also operate eight carrier task forces but that the Army be cut to 7½ divisions and the Air Force to 22 groups,[46] Carney let the letter sit on his desk because he realized the impossibility of implementing its recommendations. Forrestal now stepped in by asking the Joint Chiefs of Staff for information on the progress of planning for offensive forces.[47] The Chief of Staff of the Air Force offered the Joint Chiefs of Staff a paper on the "Strategic Bombing Concept" in which the urban industrial areas of an enemy would be subjected to an initial strategic atomic attack. Noting that a very substantial part of the nation's atomic weapons would be consumed in such an effort, Denfeld requested that "any evaluation of the risks involved and of the probable degree of success in delivering this effort should receive searching, careful, and impartial appraisal." His request, passed to the Weapons System Evaluation Group, resulted in the so-called Harmon report, already mentioned, on the anticipated effects of an atomic air offensive.

While Arleigh Burke, among others, questioned the Air Force's countercity strategy, Rear Admiral John H. Cassady, Assistant Deputy Chief of Naval Operations (Air), asked Rear Admiral Ralph Ofstie, Deputy Chief of Naval Operations (Air) whether the B-36 could do all the Air Force claimed for it. Did the Air Force have bases from which to launch an offensive, intelligence of the targets sufficient to have planes hit them in darkness and in bad weather, necessary inflight refueling capability? Moreover, would the Air Force permit the Navy to launch atomic air attacks at least as diversionary

measures? Cassady was thus among the first naval men known to have questioned the capability of the B-36[48]

Meanwhile, on 3 September, a plane functioning as part of the Air Force's Long Range Detection System collected a radioactive air sample. After other Air Force planes tracked the cloud from the Pacific Ocean to near the British Isles, American scientists determined that the Soviets had between 26 and 29 August detonated an atomic bomb somewhere on the Asiatic mainland, as the Air Force Chief of Staff, Hoyt S. Vandenberg, reported to Truman on the twenty-first. On the twenty-third Truman made the matter public and then secretly spurred American scientists to produce a "super"—thermonuclear or hydrogen—bomb.[49] Despite incontrovertible evidence that the Russians had "the bomb," Johnson refused to believe that fact. Many decried as "swashbuckling spirit" the threatened use of the B-36 against ninety-two atom bomb targets the Air Force selected in Russia and reasoned that certain retaliation by Russian atomic bombers should warn the United States to attempt to reduce friction by diplomatic and other means.[50] Others noted that canceling out atomic power shifted major emphasis to providing forces that could stop Russia on the ground in Europe and to improving the defenses of the United States.[51] Johnson merely continued to economize.

Johnson's order that all reports from the services concerning the B-36 controversy be submitted to Under Secretary of Defense Early before being sent to Vinson provoked such strong cries of censorship that he rescinded the order and sparked a reorganization of the public relations work of the Department of Defense and of the services.[52]

By 1949, Captain Walter Karig, USNR, had served in Navy public relations for nine years. As he told the Chief of Naval Operations on 21 June 1949, "The be-all of Navy Public Relations is—appropriations."[53] Two days later he suggested the transfer of the Office of Public Relations (OPR) to OP-004 in the office of the Chief of Naval Operations and that OP-004 and OP-23, the special studies group, constitute a planning group for Navy-wide public relations.[54]

About a month later, Karig noted that one man controlled the public relations of the Army, and one man those of the Air Force. "You can't peddle prestige from a push-cart," he said, adding that the Navy put public relations "on a par with garbage collecting." No wonder, then, that "naval aviation is on the way out, the fleet is shrinking to a ferry service, and Admirals are called 'brass hats' and cartooned as pompous nitwits—all products of anti-Navy press agentry, unopposed." The director of OPR, Karig asserted, should be a two- or three-star admiral nearing retirement, hence lacking any ambition other than to be a press agent, or a civilian assistant secretary who kept much more closely in touch with the Secretary of the Navy than had been the case in

and parallel with the Army and Navy as an agency in the National Military Establishment, and Johnson asked Congress to establish an Air Force Academy. Until the new Academy graduated its own men, West Point and Annapolis would continue to provide some of their graduates to the Air Force. Moreover, Johnson intended to overhaul the curricula of all academies, establish a common curriculum for them for the first two or three years, and provide for the interchange of officers among the services so that they would learn "what makes the wheels go round."[58]

On 21 June, when Johnson directed Matthews to determine the feasibility of adopting a system of organization similar to the general staff of the Army, Matthews turned the matter over to the General Board of the Navy. Vinson, however, warned against adopting a powerful general staff, and on 19 August the General Board advised Matthews that the Navy was "emphatically" and "solidly" opposed to having a general staff imposed upon it. Among its reasons for objecting the board noted that it would cause naval officers to cease striving for command at sea—their primary function—and begin to vie for general staff billets. Moreover, no navy used a general staff system; if one were adopted, the Navy might be subjugated to a landlocked theory of defense. The report sat on Matthews's desk for months without his taking action on it.[59]

When the Senate on 28 July amended the National Security Act of 1947 in keeping with suggestions from Truman and the Hoover Commission, Vinson stalled in considering the measure. It was rumored that he was more interested in getting an improved service pay bill passed than in additional unification when in effect he opposed any measure that gave Johnson additional power.

Johnson appealed for more authority for the Secretary of Defense, as did Herbert Hoover, with the latter, however, opposed to the naming of a Chairman of the Joint Chiefs of Staff to be "principal military adviser to the President and Secretary of Defense." Both Johnson and Hoover assured Vinson that the amendments to the original National Security Act would save between $1 billion and $1.5 billion per year, but neither man was able to catalogue where the savings would be made and Johnson hid behind "security reasons" for not answering plainly.[60] In the end, saying that he would grant the Secretary of Defense greater authority only under safeguards assuring Congress even greater control over his decisions and operations, Vinson offered fourteen amendments to the Senate's bill. One amendment would permit the service secretaries and the Joint Chiefs of Staff to have direct recourse to Congress with or without the approval of the Secretary of Defense. Another would require the last to consult with the armed services committees before ordering any change or consolidation of statutory functions. A third required him to report to Congress semiannually rather than annually. At hearings, Representative Felix Edward Hébert (D., La.) accused Johnson of going "beyond the law" with respect to Navy finances. Vinson asked whether Johnson would abolish the Navy's bureau system. Not having received Matthews's report on the feasibility of adopting the general staff system for the Navy, Johnson volunteered that Matthews favored the bureau system. Had Matthews initiated the general staff study on his own initiative? asked Vinson. He had, replied Johnson, thus contradicting his having directed Matthews to make the study. Noteworthy is Arleigh Burke's comment. Although he had been unable to complete a study on the subject of applying the general staff concept to the Navy because he was busy with preparations for the B-36 investigation, he forwarded a fifty-five-page report on the matter, adding that "Op-23's comments are enclosed herewith for possible use, since the subject seems to be an ineradicable one and as a result its recurrence appears inevitable."[61]

At any rate, Hébert then goaded Johnson by asserting that he had overruled the Joint Chiefs of Staff "in the matter of the flat-top [*United States*]." Another committee member wanted details on the cancellation. Johnson replied that "We took the position of the majority [of the JCS] that it did not tie in with global strategy, and therefore we cancelled it." Vinson said he had done well to do so, but Hébert alleged that Johnson had "vetoed Congress." The hearings were to end on 7 July, but the committee extended them to the eleventh so that the Joint Chiefs of Staff and the President of the Navy League could be heard.[62]

On 2 August Congress approved the new defense reorganization bill entitled the National Security Act Amendments of 1949. In summary, the Secretary of Defense would head a Department of Defense instead of the National Military Establishment and the armed services were demoted to military departments and shorn of their reserved powers. The Secretary of Defense would have "direction, authority, and control" over his department, yet the services would continue to be "separately administered" and the Secretary of Defense could not transfer or consolidate combatant functions without congressional approval, nor "merge" the services. Formerly, service secretaries could appeal over the head of the Secretary of Defense to the President or Bureau of the Budget; now they and any Joint Chief of Staff, after informing the Secretary of Defense, could appeal to Congress. A Chairman of the Joint Chiefs of Staff was created, with the limitations that he should "have no vote," should "not exercise military command," and that the Secretary of Defense rather than he would be the primary adviser to the President on military matters. The Joint Staff was increased from one hundred and forty to two hundred and ten officers. The Secretary of Defense was given an alter ego in the form of a Deputy, yet he was denied the right to appoint civilian personnel outside his own office or to exercise authority over the Joint Chiefs of Staff, Munitions Board, or Research and Development Board. One of the three Assistant Secretaries to the Secretary of Defense that were authorized was designated by Congress as the Comptroller. A new Title IV—"Promotion of Economy and Efficiency through Establishment of Uniform Budgetary and Fiscal Procedures and Organizations"—added comptrollers to each military department and emphasized a "performance budget." The Vice President was added to the National Security Council but the service secretaries were deleted from it. Since they no longer headed executive departments, they lost prestige and ranked below the Deputy Secretary of Defense. In sum, they were reduced to middle managers. The War Council, renamed the Armed Forces Policy Council, added the Deputy Secretary of Defense and the Chairman, Joint Chiefs of Staff, to its membership.[63]

After Truman signed the new defense reorganization act on 10 August, he stated that General Bradley would serve as Chairman of the Joint Chiefs of Staff for two years beginning 16 August; that the avid advocate of a single chief of staff, General J. Lawton Collins, would replace Bradley as Army Chief of Staff; and that Admiral Denfeld would be reappointed, when his assignment ended on 15 December, for another two-year term as Chief of Naval Operations.

By a memorandum dated 12 July that he sent via Johnson, Matthews reminded Truman that Denfeld was up for reappointment on 15 December and that the matter should be decided before Congress adjourned on or about 1 August. Matthews added that Denfeld was extremely cooperative, his administrative capacity made him valuable not only to the Navy but to the Department of Defense as well, and his reappointment insured continuity in the Joint Chiefs of Staff, of which he was the senior member. He then recommended Denfeld's reappointment for two years.[64]

To effect the savings Johnson promised under the new defense reorganization was the task Truman in August assigned to General Joseph "Little Caesar" McNarney, USAF. McNarney would be chairman of a National Defense Management Committee on which Secretary of the Army Gordon Gray, Under Secretary of the Navy Kimball, and Assistant Secretary of the Air Force Eugene M. Zuckert would be members. A question arose immediately: how would an Air Force enthusiast like McNarney treat the Navy when his committee, even if it did not reach conclusions by vote, could outvote the Navy by three to one? Feeling that it was not being given enough voice on the committee, the Navy asked that one of its officers be made McNarney's deputy. Johnson agreed, and the task was given to Rear Admiral Charles Wellborn, Jr., who nevertheless continued to wear another hat as Deputy Chief of Naval Operations for Administration.[65] That Johnson took "economy" to heart was illustrated by his ordering the services to cut their active duty personnel by 12,073 by 1 July 1950, an order by which the Navy would lose 3,129 men; directing Denfeld to report to him monthly on the dollar savings he had accomplished; and approving the hiring by the McNarney committee of Robert Heller and Associates to help acquire "a bigger bank for a buck" and to eliminate "unnecessary duplication and overlap."[66] According to Wellborn, McNarney was excellent in sniffing out areas where economies could be made, and he was well on his way to reducing the budget from $13 billion to $10 billion when the Korean War began and made his committee unnecessary.[67] Meanwhile Johnson made an enemy for every dollar he "saved" from the defense budget.

In his first five months in office, Johnson had come out clean in the investigation into the procurement of the B-36. However, he had stopped construction of the supercarrier and thereby also prevented development of naval aviation. He had tried to restrict the public information given out by officials of the National Military Establishment. He had found in the new Secretary of the Navy, Matthews, a loyal supporter who believed that the powers of the Secretary of Defense over the National Military Establishment should be augmented and that the unification of the armed services should be increased. Johnson persisted in economizing on the defense budget, much of it at the expense of the Navy, particularly of naval aviation, despite Russia's having exploded an atomic bomb. But there were various congressmen and others who thought that Congress instead of the executive branch of government should determine the powers of the Secretary of Defense and control the spending of appropriated monies. Navy "radicals" opposed the centralization of power in the Secretary of Defense and chafed at budgetary reductions that fell mostly upon their service and precluded its carrying out its assigned roles and missions. They opposed a national strategy depending solely upon the atomic bomb and upon a single delivery system, the B-36, which as yet was not an intercontinental bomber and was vulnerable to fighter aircraft. They felt that the Navy could get nowhere as long as the Army and Air Force chiefs of staff could overrule the Chief of Naval Operations on the Joint Chiefs of Staff, as long as the McNarney Management Committee was stacked against them, and as long as the Secretary of the Navy was a Johnson supporter. All of these explosive ingredients played a part in shaping the attitude the Navy radicals took in the Vinson investigation into unification and strategy in October 1949, in what is loosely called the "Revolt of the Admirals."

NOTES

1. *San Franciso Chronicle*, cited in ANJ 86 (21 May 1949):1082.
2. COL Robert Debs Heinl, Jr., USMC (RET), *Soldiers of the Sea: The United States Marine Corps, 1775-1962* (Annapolis, Md.: U.S. Naval Institute, 1962), pp. 527-28.
3. *New York Times,* 17 May 1949; *Washington Post,* 12 August 1949; "British Criticism of U.S. Bomber," USNWR 27 (1 July 1949):41-43; W. Stuart Symington, "Our Air Force Policy" [speech of 17 June 1949], in Eugene M. Emme, ed., *The Impact of Air Power: National Security and World Politics* (Princeton, N.J.: D. Van Nostrand, 1959), pp. 626-34; Robert L. Smith, "The Influence of U.S.A.F. Chief of Staff Hoyt S. Vandenberg on United States National Security Policy," (Ph.D. diss., American University, 1965. Xerox. Ann Arbor, Mich.: University Microfilms, 1973), pp. 116-19.
4. *New York Herald Tribune,* Oct. 7, 1949; James N. Eastman, Jr. "Flight of Lucky Lady II," *Aerospace Historian* 16 (Winter 1969):9-11, 33-35.
5. "Carrier Battle," AW 50 (23 May 1949):7.
6. Ad Hoc Committee, Report to the Joint Chiefs of Staff, "Evaluation of Effect on Soviet War Effort Resulting from the Strategic Air Offensive," 11 May 1949, copy in NHD:OA, OP-23 Files. The membership of the committee included LGEN H. R.

Harmon, USAF, chairman, and members COL W. I. Kennedy, USAF, BGEN J. K. Rice, USA, COL H. M. Roper, USA, and CAPT George W. Anderson, USN.

7. "NME Order to JCS," ANJ 86 (28 May 1949):1117.
8. H. Struve Hensel, "Changes Inside the Pentagon," *Harvard Business Review* 32 (January-February 1954):104-5.
9. Ferdinand Eberstadt, "The Historical Evolution of Our National Defense," NWCR 6 (January 1954):9.
10. "To Study B-36 Program," ANJ 86 (28 May 1949):1120; "B-36 Test Out: But Probe On," ANJ 86 (4 June 1949):1143.
11. "People of the Week," USNWR 26 (17 June 1949):34-37; "Air Strategy Probe Set for July," AW 50 (20 June 1949):13-14.
12. Heinl, *Soldiers of the Sea*, p. 526.
13. *Current Biography*, s.v. "Matthews, Francis P."; "Reminiscences of VADM Charles Wellborn, Jr., USN (RET)," transcript of oral interviews by John T. Mason (Annapolis, Md.:U.S. Naval Institute, 1972), p. 290.
14. "Reminiscences of Hanson Weightman Baldwin," transcript of oral interview by John T. Mason (Annapolis, Md.:U.S. Naval Institute, 1976), p. 524.
15. "Whispers," USNWR 26 (27 May 1949):36; Robert Greenhalgh Albion and Robert Howe Connery, *Forrestal and the Navy* (New York: Columbia University Press, 1962), p. 224.
16. Floberg to the writer, 31 August 1976.
17. *Chicago Daily News*, cited in ANJ 86 (2 July 1949):1266.
18. "Secnav Addresses Midshipmen," ANJ 86 (4 June 1949):1147; Carl W. Borklund, *Men of the Pentagon: From Forrestal to McNamara* (New York: Praeger, 1966), p. 73.
19. James A. Bell, "Secretary of Defense Louis Johnson," AM 70 (June 1950):645.
20. Vincent Davis, *The Admirals Lobby* (Chapel Hill: University of North Carolina Press, 1967), p. 274.
21. Interview, Washington, D.C., 28 July 1972.
22. ADM Joseph J. Clark, USN (RET), with Clark G. Reynolds, *Carrier Admiral* (New York: David McKay Co., 1967), p. 272.
23. Wellborn, "Reminiscences," p. 290.
24. Vinson to Matthews, 1 June 1949, SNP.
25. OP-05B/BC, Memorandum to OP-9, 23 May 1949, Washington: NHD: OA, Papers of the Chiefs of Naval Operations (hereafter cited as CNO Papers).
26. *Full Committee Hearings on S. 1843, Committee of Armed Services, House of Representatives, 81st Cong., 1st Sess.* (Washington, GPO, 1949), pp. 93, 97.
27. Robert Frank Futrell, *Ideas, Concepts, Doctrine: A History of Basic Thinking in the United States Air Force 1906-1964* (Maxwell Air Force Base, Ala.: Air University, 1971), p. 135; *National Security Act Amendments of 1949*, Hearings before the Committee on Armed Services, U.S. Senate, 81st Cong., 1st Sess. (Washington: GPO, 1949), pp. 6-10.
28. *Full Committee Hearings on S. 1843*, p. 2686.
29. F. P. Matthews, Memorandum to the CNO, 31 May 1949, SNP.
30. Secret. Chairman, GB to SECNAV, 27 July 1949, SNP.
31. Secret. CNO to SECNAV, 11 August 1949, SNP.
32. Futrell, *Ideas, Concepts, Doctrine*, p. 129.
33. Top Secret. CNO, Memorandum for the SECNAV, 27 July 1949, SNP.
34. Top Secret. F. P. Matthews to Carl Vinson, 20 July 1949, CNO Papers.
35. SECNAV to SECDEF, 5 June 1949, SNP.
36. " 'Beef Up' Naval Aviation," ANJ 86 (2 July 1949):1270.
37. F. P. Matthews to Louis M. Johnson, 16 June 1969; Louis A. Johnson to Army, Navy, Air Force Departments, 20 June 1949; Stephen Early to Army, Navy, and Air Force Departments, 24 June 1949, SNP.
38. U.S. Department of Defense, *Second Report of the Secretary of Defense and the Annual Reports of the Secretary of the Army, Secretary of the Navy, and Secretary of the Air Force for the Fiscal Year 1949* (Washington: GPO, 1950), pp. 205 35; *Chicago Tribune*, 12 September 1949; *New York Herald Tribune*, 19 September 1949.
39. Warner R. Schilling, Paul Y. Hammond, and Glenn H. Snyder, *Strategy, Politics, and Defense Budgets* (New York: Columbia University Press, 1962), pp. 9-10.
40. General Nathan F. Twining, USAF (RET), *Neither Liberty nor Safety: A Hard Look at U.S. Military Policy and Strategy* (New York: Holt, Rinehart and Winston, 1966), pp. 15-16.

41. Ibid., pp. 16-18, 23-25.
42. "Shift in U.S. Defense," USNWR 27 (12 August 1949):22-23. By Alnav 84, dated 19 Aug. 1949, Matthews released 250 Naval Reserve officers from duty and had 100 temporary regular officers revert to enlisted ratings. (NDB 15 [31 August 1949]:7). Denfeld detailed further cuts the Navy must make in "Certain Revisions of Plans and Policies of the Navy," Navy Department Bulletin 49-680, dated 12 September 1949, NDB 15 (30 September 1949):8.
43. Paul Y. Hammond, "Super Carriers and B-36 Bombers: Appropriations, Strategy, and Politics," in Harold Stein, ed., *American Civil-Military Decisions: A Book of Case Studies* (University: University of Alabama Press, 1963), pp. 502-4.
44. U.S. Congress. House of Representatives. *National Military Establishment Appropriations Bill for 1950*. Preconference Hearings before the Subcommittee of the Committee on Appropriations, House of Representatives, 81st Cong., 1st Sess. (Washington: GPO, 1949), pp. 22-48; Marx Leva, The DOD Legislative Program, 20 October 1949, SECDEF to the SECNAV, 10 July 1949, CNO Papers; "How the U.S. Will Fight Next War: Air Attack Only a Beginning," USNWR 27 (20 August 1949):11-14.
45. "Documentation of Admiral Denfeld's Testimony," 15 October 1949, in NHD:OA, ADM Arleigh Burke Personal Papers.
46. RADM Walter F. Boone, "Proposed Basis and Approximate Force Requirements for Emergency War Plan," and covering letter, 4 November 1948, OP-30 Files, cited in *Supporting Study*, p. 147.
47. ADM Louis L. Denfeld, Memorandum for the Joint Chiefs of Staff, "Evaluation of Current Strategic Air Offensive," 11 January 1949, OP-30 files, cited in *Supporting Study*, p. 148.
48. RADM John H. Cassady, Memorandum for RADM Ralph Ofstie, 19 January 1949, Ralph Ofstie Papers, cited in *Supporting Study*, p. 148.
49. Harry S. Truman, *Memoirs by Harry S. Truman*, 2 vols. (Garden City, N.Y.: Doubleday, 1955-56), 2:306-8.
50. David Lawrence, "It Could Mean Peace," USNWR 27 (30 September 1949):19.
51. "Why Air Force Wants the B-36," USNWR 26 (17 June 1949):18-19; Bernard Brodie, "Strategic Implications of the North Atlantic Pact," *Yale Review* 39 (December 1949): 193-208.
52. Louis A. Johnson to Army, Navy, and Air Force Departments, 20 June 1949, SNP; "Whispers," USNWR 26 (17 June 1949):60.
53. Walter Karig, CAPT, USNR, Memorandum for CNO, 21 June 1949, CNO Papers.
54. Karig, Memorandum for CNO, 23 June 1949, CNO Papers.
55. Karig, Memorandum for the CNO, 25 July 1949, CNO Papers.
56. Armin Rappaport, *The Navy League of the United States* (Detroit, Mich.: Wayne State University Press, 1952), pp. 196-97.
57. Timothy W. Stanley, *American Defense and National Security* (Washington: Public Affairs Press, 1956), pp. 89-91; "President's Plan for Reorganizing Defense Set-up," ANJ 86 (23 July 1949):1371-72.
58. Edward A. Miller, Jr., "The Struggle for an Air Force Academy," MA 27 (Winter 1963-64):163-73.
59. "Navy General Staff," ANJ 87 (10 October 1949):105, 135.
60. "Unification Act Amendments," ANJ 86 (2 July 1949):1281.
61. Burke to Chairman, GB, 7 September 1949, SNP. See George C. Reinhardt and William Kintner,"The Need for a National Staff," USNIP 78 (July 1952):720-27, and Philip B. Brannen, "A Single Service: Perennial Issue in National Defense," USNIP 83 (December 1957):1280-87.
62. "Powers of Defense Secretary," ANJ 86 (9 July 1949):1295.
63. Navy Department Bulletin 50-93, "National Security Act Amendments of 1949 (Public Law 216, Eighty-first Congress), NDB 16 (15 February 1950):23-30; R. Earl McClendon, *Autonomy of the Air Arm* (Maxwell Air Force Base, Ala.: Air University Documentary Research Study, 1954), pp. 94-116; Stanley, *American Defense and National Security*, pp. 92-94.
64. Top Secret. F.P. Matthews, Memorandum for the President, 12 July 1949, SNP.
65. Wellborn, "Reminiscences," p. 295.
66. Ibid., pp. 296-97.
67. Ibid., pp. 297-99.

8
The "Revolt of the Admirals"

Bitter bickering between those who favored the Navy or the Air Force and those who wanted or opposed centralizing additional power over the National Military Establishment in the hands of the Secretary of Defense proceeded throughout the late spring and summer of 1949. In mid-August, five days of hearings at the B-36 investigation conducted by Carl Vinson, Chairman of the House Armed Service Committee, made it appear that no political capital could be made out of Secretary of Defense Louis A. Johnson's former connection with manufacturers of long-range bombers. Nevertheless, angry clashes took place before packed press tables and galleries between Representative James E. Van Zandt, who based various charges against the Air Force largely upon rumors and an anonymous nine-page letter, and Secretary of the Air Force W. Stuart Symington, and between Air Force Generals George C. Kenney and his successor as Commander of the Strategic Air Command, Curtis E. LeMay. When he took over command of Strategic Air Command in October 1948, LeMay averred that "the Air Force had gone to utter hell. . . . [W]e didn't have one crew, *not one crew* in the entire command who could do a professional job. . . .The first B-36 had been delivered the previous June. That whole business was a mess too."[1] He had built up his command, but more with men and plans than with planes.[2] Acting as chief Air Force advocate of the B-36 before Vinson's committee, LeMay stated that no nation had a night fighter capable of successfully attacking the B-36 in darkness or in bad weather above forty thousand feet. He thought the cancellation of the *United States* had been "a wise decision" and that there was "no Navy plane that [could] take-off from a carrier deck, deliver an atom bomb to a target, and land again on the carrier." Retired Air Force General Carl Spaatz, now writing on air power in *Newsweek*, was among the witnesses. Regular in attendance was another witness, Vice Admiral Arthur W. Radford, Commander in Chief Pacific Fleet, flanked by two advisers, Captain Arleigh Burke and Commander Tom Davies, the latter an expert on naval bombers.

On 17 August the Senate unanimously authorized the Air Force to build toward seventy groups but did not make that number mandatory. On the twenty-ninth, however, when it sent a $14.8 billion Defense Department bill to conference with the House, it cut $22 million in cash and $578 million in contract authorization from the Air Force, thereby holding it to forty-eight groups. Because its demand for a "share" of strategic air power was being challenged, the Navy vented its wrath upon the B-36 as a plane and as a weapon system that could hit Russian targets.[3] According to naval spokesmen, it could not escape detection by ground radar and such Navy fighters as the *Banshee* could intercept it up to fifty-two thousand feet and shoot it down while it was still one hundred miles from a target. Moreover, high-altitude bombing was inaccurate; only one out of twelve bombs dropped by Army Air Forces in World War II landed near enough to damage a target. Better, then, to use escorted jet bombers from carriers to bomb targets precisely and also have carrier-borne jet fighters escort B-36s on their final run-ins.[4]

Meanwhile the Secretary of the Navy, Francis P. Matthews, applauded Johnson for doing "a phenomenal job in a short time," saying that having three service secretaries encouraged a "healthy rivalry" among their departments, and supporting Johnson's decision that there would be only one Armed Forces Day.[5]

Upon returning from Hawaii, where he spoke at dedication ceremonies for a new National Cemetery, Matthews established a court of inquiry to investigate the anonymous letter upon which Van Zandt relied. There was also a fifty-four page pamphlet entitled *The Strategic Bombing Myth*, which had emanated from the office of the Under Secretary of the Navy. Although it dealt mostly with perversions of the *United States Strategic Bombing Survey* by air power enthusiasts, in six drafts prepared between 5 March 1945 and 1 July 1946, it was also extremely critical of the B-36 as an aircraft and alleged that improper influence had contributed to its procurement.[6]

The court of inquiry, which Matthews asked Admiral Thomas C. Kinkaid to head, tried to find out whether the author of the anonymous pamphlet had had any military or civilian help with his writing and to determine what punishment, if any, he should be given. Matthews also asked Johnson if he wished to send a representative to the hearings.[7] To the court, the Under Secretary of the Navy, Dan A. Kimball, confessed to erring when testifying before the House committee investigating the B-36; he had been wrong about certain dates and admitted that he had not spoken to men to whom he said he had spoken. More important, it was ascertained that the anonymous document was prepared by one of his aides, a professional writer named Cedric R. Worth.[7] Worth had not told Kimball that he had written the document "because it would do him no good. . . . He would have to tell me not to do it." However, he had already confessed before Vinson's committee that he was the author of the document.[8]

Captain John W. Crommelin was a veteran naval aviator, carrier commander, and "outspoken crusader" due to be considered for promotion to rear admiral within a few months. Hanson Baldwin has stated that he had become "almost psychotic" over the unification issue" and that "I don't mean he was going off his rocker entirely, but he was riding a hobby in such an intense way that I think it affected him nervously."⁹

On 10 September, Crommelin revealed greater courage than political judgment by criticizing "potential dictatorship" in the Department of Defense, asserting that "the Navy is being nibbled to death in the Pentagon," and violating the rule that prohibited the release of classified information by publishing the statement he had prepared for delivery to Kinkaid's court, which had recessed the day before. He knew that he was breaking regulations and expected that his promising career in the Navy would be ended.

While the Tydings unification reorganization bill was under consideration, Crommelin continued, he learned that a document on Johnson's desk provided a schedule for the gradual reduction of naval aviation and the absorption of its remnants by the Air Force. Moreover, study of the Tydings bill convinced him that the bill "would play right into the hands of a group of zealots and opportunists who might desire to take over the operation of the entire Military Establishment and its fifteen billion dollar budget." Worth, said Crommelin, was prompted by the highest motives of patriotism to expose what he believed were the implications in the Tydings bill affecting procurement, and he had been glad to help him draft the "anonymous document" because the Air Force was "emasculating the offensive potentiality" of the Navy. The bill was passed after only two of the points on the agenda of the B-36 investigating committee were discussed. Had the other points been covered, the bill might not have passed. Crommelin concluded that

the B-36 controversy and the recently cancelled carrier contract are mere superficial manifestations of the real cause for disagreements between the Armed Services. The basic contention, in my opinion, lies with the area of the General Staff concept, and will never be resolved until it is thoroughly threshed out in conformance with the principles of democracy (equal representation and expression from the three services) before the Congress of the United States. The Navy cannot support an organization whose methods and principles violate the Navy concept of a Navy man's oath.

He referred specifically here to the Joint Chiefs of Staff, in which formerly two, now three, men "who may have a land-locked concept of national defense" could vote against the Navy.¹⁰

Among others, Fleet Admiral William F. Halsey and Rear Admiral Austin K. Doyle, Chief of Naval Air Reserve Training, supported Crommelin. Thereupon Representative Landsdale G. Sasscer (D., Md.) a top-ranking member of the House Armed Services Committee, demanded an inquiry into the roles of the three military services—just what Crommelin wanted—an inquiry made even more important by Truman's announcing on 23 September that the Russians now had "the bomb."

Matthews at first said that Crommelin had "obviously disqualified himself" for his billet on the Joint Staff but that he would take no punitive action against him. At the request of Admirals Louis E. Denfeld and John Dale Price, Rear Admiral Joseph J. Clark, a good friend of Crommelin's late brother Charles, got Crommelin to promise to keep quiet.[11] Kimball, however, publicly rushed to Crommelin's rescue, stating that he had voiced only his personal opinion and deserved no punishment. After Truman told reporters on 15 September that he believed "Secretary Matthews would handle the matter capably," Matthews transferred Crommelin to an office not involved with the other services. Matthews said that Crommelin would appear before the Kinkaid court of inquiry, that he should realize that "unification is a fact," and that "it was the duty of all hands to respect the action of Congress, to work for harmonious results under existing laws."[12] Moreover, on 16 September Matthews "requested" naval officers to stop criticizing the organization of the Defense Department in public and to send their complaints via regular Navy channels. When he told an admiral to stop arguing with the Air Force, the admiral replied, "If you issue that order, we'll resist it."[13]

Typical of the independent Navy breed was **Rear Admiral Daniel V. Gallery**, who skated on thin ice by publicizing that reliance on the Air Force predicated a strategy that could only bring on an atomic war. Moreover, "unification" was a "fraud" in which the Air Force would get everything and the Navy nothing. Insisting that the Navy was vital to both American economic and military security, he also asserted that the Navy could deliver atomic bombs better than the Air Force.

OFFICIAL U.S. NAVY PHOTOGRAPH

Typical of the independent Navy breed was Rear Admiral Daniel V. Gallery, who noted that Johnson had issued a "gag order" that prevented officers from publishing anything without his prior clearance. He realized that his taking advantage of legal loopholes in Johnson's directive could result in a reprimand from Matthews rather than a court-martial. First, therefore, via channels in a secret letter to Matthews dated 27 September, he offered his opinions on the Navy-Air Force controversy. Since Matthews would not accept "double talk," he presumed to speak "perfectly frankly." He was gravely alarmed over the status of national defense and particularly over "our gambling the future of the United States on the B-36 and the Atom Bomb, and that this is a sucker's bet." National defense and defense budgets were being so "rigged" that the country was being committed to the "ten-day atomic blitz theory of warfare." Were the policy not changed soon, the only kind of war we would be able to wage would be an atomic war. This "Quick, Cheap, and Sure Victory" was of course an Air Force concept. Unfortunately, Air Force zealots believed in it as much as Stalin believed in communism. "But the idea is dangerous to the safety of this country." A few more comments are illustrative. "The sad thing is that the Air Force has so outsmarted the Navy in Public Relations for the past four years that the country bought their bill of goods hook, line and sinker." "That word 'unification' is the greatest fraud ever perpetrated on the American public—we start with two services, wind up with three, and call it unification!" The only way to get along with the Air Force in Washington "is to accede to every demand they make. That is their idea of unification, and if we go along. . .before long there will be no Navy."[14]

Gallery then disregarded directives and published in the *Saturday Evening Post* two articles he knew Johnson would disapprove. The articles deviated from Johnson's "party line," which was that "all we need is SAC, and everything is sweetness and light in the Defense Department," but did not violate Navy Department regulations with respect to military security. However, Gallery submitted copies of his articles to the Navy Department *after* they had been accepted for publication. In the first, "An Admiral Talks Back to the Airmen," he challenged the concept of placing full reliance for security upon atomic weapons.[15] In the second, "Don't Let Them Cripple the Navy," he sought to prove that the Navy was vital to American economic as well as military security even in the atomic age.[16] When Johnson "threw a fit" over the first article and told the *Post* it could not print it, the *Post*'s editors "gave him the horse laugh." Before the second article appeared, Johnson tried to put the squeeze on Gallery, who directed the *Post* to withdraw it but relied upon an earlier understanding that such a request for withdrawal would be disregarded. Gallery pondered what Johnson might do to him—order a court-martial, send him to a billet, say, in Alaska, or send him home on half-pay—but the storm blew over in a couple of weeks. Gallery then offered an article to *Collier's* entitled "If This Be Treason," which ended with the words "make the most of it." The theme of this article, with reference to what the

Army and Air Force were trying to do to the Navy, was the question: "Who does the screaming when a rape is being committed?" Gallery argued that a gag on national defense leaders was a sure way to destroy democracy, that men called before Congress must be free to tell the truth, and that, although only the Navy had as yet felt the "iron heel of thought control, " the other services might feel it too. He also wrote a "sizzling" paragraph critical of Truman for having stricken the name of Arleigh Burke from the promotion list to admiral, in which of course he was in error.[17] When Burke's name was restored, Gallery deleted the paragraph concerning Burke, but he had said enough to warrant Matthews's writing him that "the proposed article I consider to be not only inflammatory and inaccurate, but contemptuous of and disrespectful to both the Secretary of Defense and to me. Its publication would constitute conduct to the prejudice of the good order and discipline of the Navy."[18]

Instead of sending Gallery before a court-martial, Matthews, perhaps wishing to avoid starting his tenure with a Donnybrook over freedom of speech, "tossed the hot potato" to the Chief of Naval Operations, now Forrest Sherman, who in due course sent Gallery a letter of admonition. Soon thereafter the Navy Department asked Gallery to represent Matthews at the annual convention of the Oklahoma Reserve Officers Association and Gallery had enough presence of mind to speak only of "home, mother and the American flag."[19] Throughout the altercation Gallery knew that Dan Kimball was standing behind him to such a degree that he asked him "to take it easy or he might get canned himself."[20]

In contrast to the treatment given to Gallery, on 6 October Crommelin was suspended from duty, confined to the District of Columbia, and told that he would write a letter of explanation to the Navy Judge Advocate General, who was preparing charges against him for violating "military law" in turning over classified naval documents to the press. When an editorial in the *Norfolk Virginian Pilot* asserted that the Navy had a persecution complex, Matthews approved the sending of a telegram stating that such was not the case. Many naval officers were greatly upset because national security was being threatened "by overemphasis on long-range strategic bombing. . .[and] because proponents of this technique are prosecuting a consistent program to influence Congress and the public into accepting this overemphasis on a provenly unrealistic theory of war. The Navy is not motivated or equipped to counter this program."[21]

Unrest in the Navy was further documented when Vinson resumed hearings on the B-36 on 5 October, as noted below. Symington, Vandenberg, and other high-ranking civilians and officers cooperated in preparing the Air Force presentation for the hearings. In contrast, Matthews cut himself off from the Navy's preparation, even from his own public relations people. Therefore the preparation was undertaken largely by professional officers headed by Burke in OP-23. As Burke put it to those who said he should not mention the B-36, the public press has made it obvious that they expect the Navy to have positive opinions on the B-36 as a weapon and on the concept of war of which it is a part. The expected opinions are generally adverse and the press knows it. The Navy should be prepared to give its own opinion lest the public reaction . . . be a revulsion against the Navy . . . as a service which has an unfounded, selfish, backbitting, sore-headed, obstinate determination to elevate itself at the cost of the other services and without regard to national security.[22]

As for the "controversial" Gallery, according to Gallery, he was sent to sea so that he could not be called to testify before Vinson's committee.[23]

Still more unrest was generated when Matthews, on 8 November, was notified by the Defense Management (McNarney) Committee that Navy funds for the current fiscal year would be cut by $353 million. Matthews opposed the cut but believed that he could work the matter out satisfactorily with Johnson. He therefore prohibited naval officers from complaining about the cut to Congress. He contacted Johnson, who assured him that he would be given a full hearing.[24]

As a "Johnson man," Matthews failed to win support from naval partisans. Perhaps wrongly, these partisans blamed Denfeld for the part he played in the cancellation of the supercarrier by the Joint Chiefs of Staff, for remaining quiet when Sullivan resigned, and for agreeing with the other members of the Joint Chiefs and approving the B-36 in the hearings Vinson held in August. It was also alleged, quite incorrectly, that Matthews's decision to renominate him for a two-year term was conditioned upon his deemphasizing naval aviation and emphasizing antisubmarine warfare and surface vessels.[25]

Because Denfeld was in Europe during much of the summer of 1949 in connection with making NATO a viable organization, his deputy, Radford, worked with Burke and others to prepare the Navy's case for Vinson's hearings until he became Commander in Chief Pacific Fleet. Even after he moved to Hawaii, however, he kept in close touch with his relief as Vice Chief of Naval Operations, John Dale Price.[26] When Vinson asked Matthews to have him returned to Washington in July as a technical consultant, he, rather than Denfeld, acted as the chief Navy spokesman, and Denfeld, who should have been that spokesman even if he was not articulate and by temperament was a conciliator, began to lose the confidence of Radford and his followers.[27]

On 20 September Vice Admiral Gerald F. Bogan, Commander First Task Fleet, Pacific Fleet, wrote a confidential letter in response to Matthews's request of the fourteenth to all fleet commanders to comment on Crommelin's statement. The letter was endorsed by Radford as Commander in Chief Pacific Fleet and by Denfeld as Chief of Naval Operations. An unidentified person gave a copy of the letter to the press.[28] Bogan told Matthews that he was in "hearty and complete agreement" with Crommelin and that Matthews erred in saying that Crommelin's statement embarrassed the progress of unification and harmony in the Navy Department because "the basic reason behind all of it is a genuine fear in the Navy for the security of our country if the policies followed in the Department of Defense since the National Security Act became law and are not drastically changed, and soon." Following are two of his most pointed paragraphs:

> The creation of three departments or sub departments where formerly there were but two is not unification. Under the present law it can be made to and does operate effectively in the field. But it would be sheer balderdash to assume that there has been anything approaching it among the Secretariat, the Joint Staff, or the high command of all three services. . . .

Asked by Secretary of the Navy Francis P. Matthews if Captain John W. Crommelin, U.S. Navy, was correct in stating that there was "potential dictatorship" in the Department of Defense and that "the Navy is being nibbled to death in the Pentagon," Vice Admiral Gerald F. Bogan replied that Crommelin was correct and that morale was lower in the Navy than it had been ever since he was commissioned in 1916.

COURTESY U.S. NAVAL INSTITUTE

The morale of the navy is lower today than at any time since I entered the commissioned ranks in 1916. . . . in my opinion, this descent, almost to despondency, stems from complete confusion as to the future role of the Navy and its advantages or disadvantages as a permanent career. . . .We . . . are fearful that the country is being . . . sold a bill of goods.[29]

In endorsing Bogan's letter, Radford stated that Bogan was a man of long experience who reflected the feelings of a majority of the officers in the Pacific Fleet as expressed in Crommelin's statement. Denfeld concurred with Radford in the second endorsement, which he wrote on 28 September and forwarded to Matthews. He added the words of a report Admiral King had made in October 1945: "Seapower will not be accorded adequate recognition, because the [unified] organization contemplated would permit reduction of that sea power by individuals who are not thoroughly familiar with its potentialities, as has happened in several other countries." Denfeld illustrated King's point by alluding to the history of Germany and Japan in World War II and concluded that "it follows that if the Navy's welfare is one of the prerequisites to the nation's welfare—and I sincerely believe that to be the case—any step that is not good for the Navy is not good for the nation." In a public statement he added that he was distressed by the violation of communications security that permitted Bogan's letter to go to the press, that Bogan voiced merely his own personal opinion, that Radford's endorsement did not mean that he concurred with Bogan's views, and that he himself concurred with Radford. He closed by noting that "unification of the Armed Forces of the United States is the law of the land, the principles and objectives of which I have wholeheartedly endorsed and am striving to make effective. In this effort I am fully supported by a large majority of Naval personnel."[30]

On about 22 September Admiral Richard L. Conolly opposed Radford's presentation. During the spring of 1949 Denfeld had told Conolly that Matthews had overruled his disinclination to accept a second term as Chief of Naval Operations. He went on, "I may not want to stay two years and you'll succeed me." Conolly believed that Denfeld was getting along well with Admiral William H. P. Blandy and that "Blandy wanted the job [of CNO] and should have had Denfeld's job. Then I was in due course lined up to succeed Blandy. These things got to be more or less dried, unless something happened. Something did happen. Denfeld was completely under the control of Radford . . . and he supported Radford in all of his contentions." Radford was about to state the case for the Navy before Vinson's committee. According to Conolly, however, "this thing wasn't as simple as that. Actually, what Radford was stating was the case of naval aviation."

When Conolly came to Washington to testify, he talked with both Denfeld and Radford. Radford said that he considered Conolly's testimony to be of the "utmost importance in supporting the naval position as a whole." After he had Conolly listen to his presentation, Conolly remarked that "he brought up those naval aviators one after another, and it was a hell of a good presentation."

Conolly, continuing to Radford:

This is the case for naval aviation, and I think you've got the cart before the horse. You present this, and then you present everybody also who is really supporting a broader point of view, to support this. It ought to be the other way around. This animal act of yours—that's what I called it to him, and it made him kind of mad.

RADFORD: Don't you think it's pretty good?

CONOLLY: Yes, it's wonderful. But I don't know anything about the B36s and I don't give a damn. That isn't the Navy's fight.

RADFORD: Well, it's important, because if they get this appropriation, why, they'll walk off with everything.

CONOLLY: That isn't the main issue. The main issue is the same old thing, fighting for the existence of the Navy. In other words, this all-out bombardment war, or the resistance of encroachment. Now I'm all in favor of a very strong strategic air force. I'm a supporter of SAC. I think they ought to have all the planes they can get, of the type they think they should have. But I haven't got a thing in my statement about B-36s and I'm not going to get sucked into it. I think you should start off with the Secretary of the Navy, instead of having him come last. And you should then call on the CNO, and the Chief should then call on his three commanders in chief, Blandy, myself, and Ramsey . . . and they get up and give their differnt points of view. Then you say, "Now here is the case for naval aviation," and you bring on your troops. You make the lead off speech for them and bring them on.

RADFORD: Well, I've had advice from public relations experts on how this should be done.

CONOLLY: To hell with that. I'm a public relations expert, as well as those fellows, and I'm telling you it should be the other way around. This is a matter of objective, and you're shooting at the wrong objective.

RADFORD: Well, what are you going to do, quit on us?

CONOLLY [having gone] to see Denfeld: Louis this thing is all wrong. It's cockeyed. It's going to look as if we were just presenting the case for naval aviation. We went to present the case of the Navy.

DENFELD: Well, that's just Radford's idea, but I'll talk him out of that, because I agree with you. I want to come in and talk to the Secretary of the Navy.

Conolly then told Matthews that he should be the first to testify, not Denfeld, then "the rest of us come in."

MATTHEWS: Oh, by all means.

Matthews then said he would like to talk with Conolly. When Conolly called he asked for five days' leave necessary to recover from some minor surgery. Matthews agreed. While Conolly was away, "Denfeld and Secretary Matthews had a falling out, because Louis Johnson got wind of this, and he summoned Mr. Matthews to his office and gave him hell. Johnson told him he had better straighten this out before it reached the Congressional Committee, and suppress the whole thing, or he was in danger of his job. Matthews was in a hell of a state of perturbation." Upon Conolly's return, Matthews sent for him, explained the situation, and asked for Conolly's support. Conolly said, "Well, gosh, I just work for one boss, Mr. Secretary. I work for the CNO. As far as I know we're both supporting you."

Conolly believed it "unthinkable" that Denfeld was not supporting Matthews, particularly after Matthews had talked him into accepting a second term as CNO. "The reason [Matthews] wasn't getting along with him," surmised Conolly, "was because Mr. Johnson had told him that he'd better get Louis Denfeld in line or he was not going to permit him to be reappointed." At any rate, Matthews clearly intimated that Conolly was his choice to succeed Denfeld. "He practically told me so. If Denfeld couldn't stay, he'd like to rely on me." After lunch one afternoon, Conolly rode to the Capitol with Matthews.

> This had a great effect on me. This would be confidential. He gave me to understand unmistakably that what I said in this testimony would have a great deal to do with my future career. Well, that's as near as I ever came to being offered a bribe! So I decided right then and there—first, I couldn't believe my ears, but he made it plainer yet, that Mr. Johnson was waiting to hear what I was going to have to say, and whether he could get me by Mr. Johnson as his candidate would depend on my pulling my punches in this testimony. So I decided right then that I was going to call the shots exactly as I saw them, and not pull any punches.

Through a friend Conolly got to talk with "an awfully nice guy," Deputy Secretary of Defense Stephen Early. "From then on, I was Steve Early's candidate to succeed Denfeld. Everybody knew Louis Denfeld was skating on thin ice except Louis. Denfeld thought he was going to get the support of Mr. Vinson and the people up on the Hill, and they'd keep the political scene in check, but he underestimated Louis Johnson." Soon thereafter Johnson told Conolly, "Two admirals in the Navy I have a high opinion of: one of them's you and the other is Blandy." After he testified, however, Johnson's opinion of Blandy "was completely shot, so I was the other admiral of the Navy he liked."[31]

On 3 October Matthews, Denfeld, Radford, and other naval leaders met with Vinson. Knowing that naval witnesses could not be kept from talking about the B-36, Vinson suggested postponing the resumption of hearings, slated for the fifth. Matthews agreed but added that he would take up the Navy's budget cut with Johnson and then if necessary with Capitol Hill. Denfeld also supported postponement in order that he might study the case the Navy was preparing. Vinson thereupon said he would recommend postponement until early January. But Radford argued that the question of budget reduction could not wait that long and Vinson agreed to proceed with the hearings.[32]

Later that day, Crommelin leaked a copy of the Bogan correspondence to the press, which published it on the fourth.[33] Matthews had had Bogan's letter on his desk for five days without reading it. Now, in Bogan's words, "the muck hit the fan."[34] Vinson said that the Navy could air its views at the

The major naval spokesman before Carl Vinson's investigation into matters concerning strategy and unification was Chief of Naval Operations Louis N. Denfeld. The latter is shown *(above)* leaving the Pentagon following his "firing" and retirement, when he appeared more heroic than while in office. Overruled by Denfeld when he argued that Admiral Arthur W. Radford stated the case for naval aviation rather than for the Navy as a whole was Admiral Richard L. Conolly *(below left)*. President Truman's naval aide, Robert L. Dennison *(right)*, was largely responsible for the failure of Secretary of Defense Louis A. Johnson and Secretary of the Navy Francis P. Matthews to punish Arleigh Burke because of his work in OP-23.

OFFICIAL U.S. NAVY PHOTOGRAPHS

hearings to begin on the morrow. Matthews, who held both Bogan and Crommelin in disfavor, also gave first indications of his unhappiness with Denfeld.

Matthews's recommending Denfeld's reappointment suggests that he was satisfied with his performance of duty and support of unification. Denfeld's endorsement of Bogan's letter, however, caused Matthews to tell him that his usefulness as Chief of Naval Operations had ended. Overlooking the public statement in which Denfeld had asserted that his endorsement of Bogan's letter did not indicate agreement with Bogan's views and that he whole-heartedly supported unification, he ordered Denfeld to sound out Admiral Sherman as his relief.

Before Denfeld could find out who leaked the Bogan correspondence, Crommelin admitted that he had done it. He was promptly suspended from duty, told that charges would be drawn against him, and invited to submit a written statement in his own behalf. If he did not wish to write a statement, he should say so in writing.[35] Crommelin replied that he had released Bogan's letter "in keeping with that pledge of my oath which requires me 'to support and defend the Constitution,' " adding that democracy was being challenged by the use of "the general staff concept in running the Defense establishment."[36] Not until 8 October did Matthews reply to Bogan, and then merely to say that he would discuss "your procedure in handling it." Because both Radford and Denfeld had declassified Bogan's letter, there was apparently little Matthews could do to Bogan. However, an investigation conducted by the Naval Inspector General revealed that a captain and a commander in the Office of the Vice Chief of Naval Operations had in an unauthorized manner distributed several copies of Bogan's letter and of its endorsements and therefore were subject to disciplinary action.[37]

There is no evidence that Matthews used the ample public relations machinery available to him to prepare a presentation for Vinson's committee. Whether he was aware of the work being done in OP-23 is moot, although Burke faithfully sent copies of material prepared in OP-23 to his naval aide, Captain Richard W. Ruble.[38]

In OP-23, Burke was to "prepare suggested positions for the Navy Department" not only on immediate short-range issues with respect to impending reorganization, but also on the Navy's position in future defense policy. With time short, he concentrated upon the impending B-36 hearings. In addition to gathering data to support the Navy's argument for supercarriers and against B-36 bombers, OP-23 wrote policy papers, ghosted speeches, chose the witnesses, and wrote the testimony they would offer.[39]

The Navy did not know that the Air Force had begun a similar and much better organized undertaking in mid-August 1948, thirteen months before the Vinson hearings on the B-36, when a part-time committee had begun "basic studies as a foundation for a final analysis." Included in the studies were the capabilities of the Navy in its surface, underwater, and air aspects, particularly of carriers and carrier-borne aircraft, the last with or without atomic bombs.

In November, a more permanent committee was established "to make an objective analysis of the relative position of the USAF and of the USN in the field of strategic bombing to determine a rock bottom basis for the future USAF stand." At meetings held during December, various notes were made, including one by a general who "suggested evaluation of Leyte Campaign where Navy withdrew escort carriers in face of an enemy threat and left about 600 ships in the Gulf unprotected." To this writer, who has studied and taught the Leyte campaign, this note reveals a shocking lack of information about naval operations on the part of Air Force officials. At any rate, the report was fairly complete seven months before Vinson held his hearings. It was then kept current, with men working on it even after the hearings began. The completed study, as of 25 October 1949, contained in addition two studies of the supercarrier, a study entitled "Logistic Aspects of Air Operations," and still another entitled "Comparison of Strategic Bombing Systems."[40]

After closing the investigation of the procurement of the B-36, on 5 October Vinson stated that he would ascertain the views of the representatives of the Navy and, if necessary, of the other services, on the other points on the agenda not already covered. These included:

> Item Number 3—Examine the performance characteristics of the B-36 bomber to determine whether it is a satisfactory weapon.
> Item Number 4—Examine the roles and missions of the Air Force and the Navy (especially Navy aviation and Marine aviation) to determine whether or not the decision to cancel the construction of the aircraft carrier United States was sound.
> Item Number 5—Establish whether or not the Air Force is concentrating upon strategic bombing to such an extent as to be injurious to tactical aviation and the development of adequate fighter aircraft and fighter aircraft techniques.
> Item Number 6—Consider the procedures followed by the Joint Chiefs of Staff on the development of weapons to be used by the respective Services to determine whether or not it is proposed that two of the three Services will be permitted to pass on the weapons of the third.
> Item Number 7—Study the effectiveness of strategic bombing to determine whether the nation is sound in following this concept to its present extent.
> Item Number 8—Consider all other matters pertinent to the above that may be developed during the course of the investigation.[41]

As already noted, at Vinson's request, on 20 July Matthews had forwarded his ideas on these points by a classified letter most likely drafted by Denfeld.

The Navy testified for the first seven days of hearings on "Unification and Strategy," held between 6 and 21 October. Matthews spoke first, then almost the entire high command of the Navy. Five additional days were given to Air Force and Army representatives, Louis Johnson, George Marshall, and Herbert Hoover among the approximately forty men who testified. At last Navy men could air the frustrations and fears that had beset them for the past nearly four years by indicting the philosophy and weapons of strategic air bombing, the door being opened for them especially by Item Number 7 on Vinson's agenda. Their testimony was charged with emotion because they were concerned with the continued existence of the Navy, which had behind it a splendid history of successful tradition and performance.

While at his headquarters in Hawaii, Radford had kept in close touch with friends in Washington. He had given an outline of his ideas for his testimony to a member of his staff, Captain Fitzhugh Lee, who wrote a draft from it that he changed about twenty times as he learned of new developments or new ideas came to mind. Each draft was given to a "murder board" and then taken by plane to Washington, usually by Lee. Radford's friends in Washington sent their ideas to Hawaii until Vinson had Radford called to Washington in July. Radford's statement was thus under constant revision, with Lee as a sort of general editor, almost to the time he would deliver it, with the officers in

Fitzhugh Lee served as Admiral Nimitz's public affairs officer at Guam headquarters. Using an outline provided by Vice Admiral Arthur W. Radford, he wrote the paper Radford used before Carl Vinson's inquiry into matters concerning strategy and unification late in 1949.

OFFICIAL U.S. NAVY PHOTOGRAPH

Washington who were working on it ever fearful that Matthews would ask to see it. But he did not, and Radford kept saying, "I am going up there to testify under oath, and these are my opinions and I must say them. Even if Mr. Matthews wants me not to say them I probably will have to say them at a juncture like this, even though I am contravening the orders of my immediate superior."[42]

During the evening of 5 October, Lee went to the private offices once used by the Secretary of the Navy in the old Munitions Building on Constitution Avenue. He had worked there when he had been naval aide to Sullivan and knew the civilian secretaries working there. When he asked them if they would help cut stencils and mimeograph the statement Radford would deliver, they happily complied. At about 10:30 P.M. Matthews himself called, saying to Lee, "I understand you have copies of Admiral Radford's statement." Lee replied that he was preparing copies of it. "I would like you to bring me a copy," said Matthews. Lee replied, "Mr. Matthews, I feel that I cannot do that unless I have Admiral Radford's permission to do so." Matthews retorted, "Well, get it." Lee found Radford about half an hour later. "Let him have it," Radford said, and Lee delivered it to Matthews at his apartment hotel.[43]

On the morning of 6 October Vinson called Matthews, Denfeld, and Bogan. Matthews, who was making his first appearance before the committee, tried to have the statement to be made by Radford heard in executive session because it would have "a definite effect upon the national security of our country" and "will give comfort to a possible enemy of our country," a clear dodge to keep from the public the views of Navy "partisans."[44] Vinson retorted, "We want to find out the cause of all of this unrest" and pointed out that Radford's statement was not classified. Representative Lansdale G. Sasscer (D., Md.) elicited from Matthews that Matthews gave classified security status not only to "security" matters but also to matters involving naval "efficiency," with the result that he could muzzle critics of his administration and that of Johnson.[45] Matthews then read a prepared statement. He would not attempt to censor any Navy man's testimony or prevent him from testifying, he began, but he punctuated his comments with expressions of wounded feelings and a desire to punish traitorous people. Naval aviators particularly were "insubordinate," "faithless," and "guilty." The morale of the Navy was good, he asserted, except among a few individuals who violated their oath of office and "deliberately engaged in the indefensible procedure of surreptitiously disclosing to persons unentitled to possess it documentary and other restricted information belonging to the Department of the Navy." These few would be "brought to an accounting for their guilty conduct." Moreover, these men did not monopolize the loyalty, honor, or patriotic devotion of Navy men and did not speak for anywhere near a majority of naval personnel. After quoting Johnson at length to prove that Johnson was not hostile to carrier aviation or to Marine Corps aviation, he dealt very briefly with the other items on Vinson's agenda.

On the B-36, Matthews said that he was ignorant of its technical details and that its qualities could best be ascertained by the Weapons Systems Evaluation Group. Johnson's discontinuation of the *United States* did not mean that he opposed either carriers or naval aviation. Matthews did admit that he believed that the Air Force was "unbalanced in favor of strategic bombing." On Item 6 of the agenda, Joint Chiefs of Staff procedures for determining weapons for the armed services, Matthews did not believe that a split vote should control the weapon systems of a service. If such a split occurred, the decision should be made by the Secretary of Defense. On whether strategic bombing was effective as national strategy, Matthews referred the committee to his earlier classified letter. On the organizational structure of the military establishment, he said "I have the utmost confidence not only in the organizational set-up, but I have the utmost confidence in the men who man this set-up," and he gave to Johnson the highest praise he could bestow. He concluded by asserting that both he and Denfeld would make a good case for the Navy in the budget being prepared for fiscal year 1951.[46]

His statement completed, Matthews submitted to questioning. Representative Porter Hardy, Jr. (D. Va.), wished to know "what avenue a conscientious believer that a change is necessary in the interest of national security has to make his views known if he runs into a stone wall within his own department or if he gets blocked in the Department of Defense and can't make his position known."[47] Matthews replied: "I don't know how he could become blocked"—at which his audience of naval officers guffawed and laughed jeeringly.[48]

Vinson suggested that the major problem was in the naval aviation branch. Matthews agreed. To the question, who was responsible for morale in the Navy, he replied, the Chief of Naval Operations and "the high ranking officers." How could morale be improved? By good personnel administration, additional compensation, improving living conditions, and bettering the administration of the Navy. Why had not the cut from seventy to forty-eight groups caused a similar drop in morale in the Air Force? Matthews did not know. Was it true that heavy aircraft could fly off modernized carriers but could not land on them? Matthews did not know. Said Vinson: "The services are still sniping at unification but it is now the law of the land. Doesn't the drop in morale in the Navy depend on the reduction in ship, aviation, and Marine Corps strength? This goes beyond the argument against unification." Matthews answered: "I wouldn't be able to explain that." Had Johnson cut the appropriation for naval air provided in the fiscal year 1950 budget? Matthews believed that Johnson had, but did not know by how much.

After Vinson again suggested that cuts in both the Navy's surface and air programs adversely affected the morale of the Navy, Representative Sasscer asked Matthews: "Isn't the main opposition . . . produced by the manner in which this [unification] act gives so much power to one man is being projected on a course that is gradually clipping the Navy, Navy air, and the Marine Corps?" Matthews said he could not answer. Representative Joseph A.

Anderson (R., Calif.) queried: "Doesn't Denfeld's sitting with the Joint Chiefs of Staff, on which there are three West Pointers, have an effect on the morale of the Navy?" Matthews disagreed. What was Matthews doing about morale in the Navy, especially in its aviation corps? asked Vinson. Said Matthews: "Whatever we can to make the Navy know it is not to be scrapped," probably because Vinson had alleged that Navy and Marine Aviation would lose 50 percent of the number of planes provided in the fiscal year 1951 budget. Vinson then sharply questioned Matthews on whether cuts in most categories of ships and in the number of plane groups accounted for the low morale in the Navy. Matthews was not sure. Nor did he know how many Navy flag officers opposed unification. Although he had directed that a "study or survey" of the committee's agenda be made, Matthews alleged that he had not set up a "task force" to prepare the Navy's position at the B-36 hearings and did not know whether a task force had been established within the Navy to prepare a statement on naval policy for presentation at the current hearings. When Representative Van Zandt referred to OP-23 in all but name, Matthews failed to acknowledge that he was familiar with its work, some of which remains in his official papers, but admitted that there was a "top policy committee" composed of two civilian assistants and the top military people in his office who had "discussed the matter." He would have been more honest had he admitted that a task force established by Dan A. Kimball, his Under Secretary, had produced a twenty-nine page report on how to answer the items on Vinson's agenda.[49] Crommelin had been suspended from duty and orders had been issued to draft charges against him, Matthews continued. Would that have any effect on future Navy witnesses? he was asked. Said Matthews: "Not the slightest." Nor did Matthews see any correlation between the criticism of the concentration upon the doctrine of strategic air bombing sent to him by his admirals and poor morale in the Navy, for "a man can be very much dissatisfied and yet his morale could be 100 percent."[50]

The committee then heard Radford read his statement in executive session. Upon deciding that it did not contain classified material, Vinson announced that Radford could read his statement in open session, at which press correspondents present cheered mightily, and asked the Admiral to testify publicly on the morrow.

Although he was a brilliant man with a keen sense of humor, Radford was serious about national security problems and avoided light talk. A military statesman rather than merely a military expert, he was a controversial figure because he expressed his positive views quite forcibly.[51] When he testified, on 7 October, he began by denying charges that naval officers were concerned with the future Navy only to the degree that it affected them personally, as in promotion and prestige. Nor did he stress the traditional Navy's strategic doctrine of peripheral warfare. An aviator with almost thirty years of service, he believed that national air power, the sum of land air power and naval air power, was unquestionably the dominant factor in national security. He had been a party to the Key West Agreement on roles and missions and concurred that strategic air warfare should be the primary mission of the Air Force. He was thus one of the few witnesses or committee members to see that the hearings were important less because they concerned the B-36 program than because they might determine strategy to follow both in peace and war. But he had the B-36 much in mind, saying that it "has become, in the minds of the American people, a symbol of a theory of warfare—the atomic blitz—which promises them a cheap and easy victory if war should come." He rejected that conclusion, on which the committee must pass judgment.

The B-36, he went on, was a gamble with national security not only because of its inherent inability to defend itself or to bomb accurately from great heights—and he brought a technical expert to prove his point to the committee—but also because it symbolized the unsound theory of atomic blitz warfare. If it was decided that the atomic blitz theory was correct, a more efficient plane was needed. In picking the B-36, the Air Force had made a "billion dollar blunder." In developing its strategic bombers, the Air Force had neglected planes suitable for tactical and fighter missions. Pushing the B-36 program undermined unification and prevented mutual trust, understanding, and unified planning. Any service must be permitted to bring an experimental weapon through the development, test, and evaluation stages—as the *United States* should have been by the Navy—but no weapon should be provided in quantity until it had been proved. Strategic bombing should be a primary mission of the Air Force, but the United States should not depend upon strategic bombing as a shortcut to victory.[52]

Did Radford have official Navy endorsement for his views? asked Vinson. "No," replied Radford, "because the Secretary of the Navy has not assured me one way or the other and I assumed that he represents the Navy Department. . . . I have not discussed the matter with him."[53] He had expressed his personal opinion, one developed after consultation with several other high-ranking naval officers. How many of the Navy's top officers shared his views? Almost all senior officers and every experienced officer on the active and retired list, replied Radford, and at request he named Fleet Admirals Halsey, Nimitz, King, and Leahy, and Admirals W.H.P. Blandy, Richard L. Conolly, and Denfeld, among others, adding that it was exceedingly difficult for the minority of experienced officers he represented to get their points of view across to "our sister services" and "some of the civilian secretaries" who were inexperienced in naval matters.[54]

Navy witnesses who followed Radford in person on 8, 10, 11, 12, and 13 October included a galaxy of World War II leaders—Halsey, Burke, Kinkaid, Conolly, Carney, Ofstie, Spruance, Nimitz, and Brigadier General Vernon E. Megee, Assistant Director of Marine Corps Aviation—all of whom upheld Radford in his argument against the B-36 as a plane and as symbol of the misguided strategy of atomic bombing, and both Radford and Denfeld criticized the Air Force for violating the spirit of unification by procuring additional B-36s without consulting the Secretary of Defense or the Joint Chiefs of Staff, an at least tangential blow at the Air Force's approval of the cancellation of the

United States. Although Radford did not question the budget ceiling of the Department of Defense, he countered Matthews, who had stated that morale in the Navy was good, by saying that it was low for legitimate and serious reasons, among them lack of confidence in the intentions, actions, and judgments of the other members of the unification team.

In his testimony, Conolly maintained his integrity. His *Reminiscences* details his answer when Vinson asked him whether forces allocated to him would be sufficient, then graphically describes the reaction it provoked:

"Well, Mr. Chairman—I'll have to narrow that down, before I can give an answer. Do you mean the forces that would be allocated to me under the appropriated funds, or after the appropriated funds have been curtailed?"

The old boy jumped three feet out of his chair. He said, "Admiral, you have put your finger right on the main issue here."

You can imagine, this wasn't helping me any. He said, "There it is in a nutshell. Congress appropriated these monies, after what they think after long consideration is what is needed, and along comes Mr. Louis Johnson and decides in the fullness of his strategical—" Oh boy, he was sarcastic as hell—"that he is going to cut them, and he presumes to reduce what Congress has appropriated. . . ."

Well, after that I was finished. The CNO deal went out the window.[55]

By questioning Rear Admiral Herbert G. Hopwood, the Budget Director of the Navy, and Wilfred J. McNeil, Comptroller of the Department of Defense, Vinson brought out clearly, and angrily, that Johnson usurped the powers of Congress by changing the appropriations made to the services. By asking Congress for stated funds and then reducing spending, Johnson made it appear that he was saving the taxpayers' money, thereby gaining political prestige. Johnson should economize by reducing overhead and making the Department of Defense more efficient, not by cutting combat strength. Others challenged the validity of the strategy of strategic atomic bombing and pointed to the need of forces adequate for limited war; the lack of tactical air power by the Air Force provided an apt illustration. Admiral Blandy, Commander in Chief Atlantic Fleet, not an aviator, helped develop amphibious warfare in the Pacific during World War II and then had commanded the Bikini Atoll atomic bomb tests. In contending that the Navy needed both amphibious and atomic forces, he contradicted Matthews, who had sought to blame only naval aviators for unhappiness in the Navy, as he did again when he asserted that the cuts in the current Navy budget would reduce the operating forces of the Navy "dangerously below the minimum estimate of forces I have submitted to the Chief of Naval Operations as needed at the beginning of a war."[56]

Retired Fleet Admiral Halsey upheld the Navy, as did a statement from Retired Fleet Admiral King, who was too ill to testify. After Arleigh Burke and other high-ranking nonaviators offered a systematic and complete defense of the supercarrier as a weapon system necessary for the future, the spotlight fell on Denfeld, who would summarize the Navy presentation.

Would Denfeld continue to support Matthews, as he had when he bolstered him in trying to keep Radford's testimony from the public, or would he stick by the "radicals"? Would he, as Matthews asked him to, "get him off the hook" with the press with respect to his own testimony? Would he fulfill Johnson's optimism that he would repudiate his Navy colleagues, "toe the Johnson economy line," and stop what Johnson called the Navy's "campaign of terror"?[57] He had hoped against hope that the interservice squabble could be solved without his being forced to take a rigid position and having to say things about the other services that normally would have remained unsaid.[58] Someone had to say those things, however, and as the Chief of Naval Operations he was in the best position to do it. Moreover, the longer he came under the influence of men like Burke and Radford, the more likely he was to make a stronger case than he originally might have made.[59] The tragedy of his position was that a good performance as a naval spokesman would lose him stature on the Joint Chiefs of Staff and, because Matthews was a Johnson man, would cause disaffection also with Matthews. Moreover, Matthews had asked Truman's naval aide, Captain Robert Lee Dennison, to help Denfeld prepare a statement that would not be opposed to "the President's policy."[60]

After he supported Matthews's attempt to keep Radford's testimony secret, Denfeld decided—much too late—to stop acting as a conciliator and to support the radicals. Among others who helped prepare his testimony was Captain Charles Donald Griffin, in OP-30, the Special Projects Office in the Office of the Chief of Naval Operations. Griffin's job consisted mostly of preparing position papers for Denfeld "on very very critical points." When directed to prepare Denfeld's paper for the Vinson committee, he did so, put it on Denfeld's desk, and called every day at the office to learn whether it was acceptable. He heard nothing because, as he put it, "it became quite apparent to me that Admiral Denfeld was not going to take any fast action on this because he, himself, was feeling his way along. Griffin also flew to Pearl Harbor several times to correlate matters with Radford, for, as he put it, "My job really was to make sure that there was perfect liaison between Admiral Radford'd headquarters and Admiral Denfeld's headquarters." Finally, on the day before Denfeld would testify, Griffin was called at 7 A.M., to be at Denfeld's office at 8 A.M. When he arrived he found that Denfeld had assigned Oswald C. "Ozzie" Colcough, two other officers, and Griffin to draft the statement, using Griffin's paper as a base. The four men worked on the paper all day, eating lunch and dinner in Denfeld's office.

Although Hanson Baldwin in 1976 could have missed the occasion by a day or so, he recalled that he had had dinner with the Denfelds that evening and noted that the admiral

> tried to play a cautious game. He was between the devil and the deep blue sea and he knew that he would have hard time if he took too strong a stand. . . .(Denfeld was not, in my opinion, a very strong man; he was a pretty wise one and he was a very nice guy and he knew his way politically around Washington). . . . We had dinner . . . and then I sat down and read the testimony. It was very much stronger than anything he'd said before, very

much stronger and the first time he'd really come down hard. . . . I told him I agreed with it, it was strong, it was good. . . . But I think I said, again I'm quoting from memory, that this will probably play hell, or something like that. . . . [61]

After dinner Denfeld joined Burke, Dennison, and Radford in his office. At three o'clock in the morning Denfeld approved the paper he would read at ten.[62] According to Griffin:

> The Secretary of the Navy was just wild. I use that word deliberately, because he had been trying for days to get a copy of Admiral Denfeld's statement for the committee. He had been told there was no statement, and it wasn't available. He didn't get the statement until just about an hour before it was to be made at the committee. By that time, he was on his way over to the committee, so he had no chance to read it. He sat there and listened to it being given by Admiral Denfeld.[63]

Denfeld began by saying that he would "fully support the broad conclusions presented to this committee by the naval and Marine Officers who have preceded me," then concentrated upon management in the Department of Defense that enabled the Air Force to add to its stock of B-36s, to cancel the construction of the *United States*, and to cut the Navy's budget. The Navy supported unification, but unification was not being followed. The Navy's counsel was being excluded by the Department of Defense; the Navy was not admitted to full partnership. Denfeld made a vigorous but moderate statement; unlike Radford, who had criticized the B-36 and strategic atomic bombing, he saw naval power, including air power, as part of an integrated force. But by supporting what Radford had said, he, instead of Radford, became the butt of criticism.[64] He added, in part:

> The entire Navy . . . is gravely concerned whether it will have modern weapons, in quality and quantity, to do the job expected of the Navy at the outbreak of a future war. We have real misgivings over the reductions that are taking place in the Navy today. . . .It is not so much the reduction in congressional appropriations that worries us. . . .Our concern is with arbitrary reductions that impair, or even eliminate, essential naval functions. It is not so much a question of too little appropriated money, but how we are allowed to invest that money. . . . Limitations are imposed without consultation, and without understanding of the Navy's responsibility in defense of our maritime nation.
>
> I am an advocate of air power. . . .I am also a proponent of strategic air warfare.

> There has been no objection raised by the Navy to the development of the B-36 to the point where its value as a weapon might be thoroughly evaluated . . . . However, it is illogical, damaging, and dangerous to proceed directly to mass procurement without evaluation to the extent that the Army and Navy may be starved for funds and our strategic concept of war frozen about an uncertain weapon.

Among Marine Corps leaders backstopping the Navy in its attempt to prevent the Army from taking over the Marines and the Air Force from taking over its aviation were General Alexander Archer Vandegrift, Commandant of the Corps from 1 January 1944 to 31 December 1947 *(above left)*; his successor, General Clifton B. Cates *(right)*; General Holland M. "Mad" Smith *(below left)*; and Lieutenant General Oliver Prince Smith *(right)*. The last, who led his Marines through eight Chinese armies during their withdrawal from the Chosin Reservoir, in Korea, was greatly skeptical of Air Force contributions to unification in the field.

OFFICIAL USMC PHOTOGRAPHS

The procedure leading up to the cancellation of the carrier *United States* is another exemplification of the improper operation of unification.[65]

As fellow officers congratulated Denfeld when he ended his testimony and welcomed him to the ranks of the radicals, a visibly flushed Matthews hurriedly left the room. On the next day he told Denfeld that he had been "stunned" by his presentation.[66]

Meanwhile Dennison told Truman, "I've just learned what Johnson and Matthews have done" and asked permission to visit Denfeld at the Naval Observatory, traditional site of the home for Chiefs of Naval Operations until 1974. Truman approved, and Dennison learned that Denfeld was not resentful and "was really relieved because of the intolerable situation that he'd been in with both Johnson and Matthews." On the next day Matthews sent for him. Upon entering his office, Dennison found Matthews "absolutely livid." As he recalled, Matthews asked,

> "Did you write Admiral Denfeld's speech?"
> "I certainly did not, but I was in on the drafting sessions because you asked me to be there. But I didn't see his speech."
> "I understand you went up to Denfeld's quarters yesterday."
> "Yes, I did."
> "That's the most disloyal act I ever heard of. . . ."
> "Well, Mr. Secretary, I can tell you one person who doesn't think it's disloyal."
> "Who's that?"
> "The Commander in Chief."

Upon hearing the last, Matthew's face "fell a mile." Dennison knew that "Johnson had been in on this too," but Truman again said that this was not the time to fire Johnson or Matthews, although he planned to get Matthews out by appointing him Ambassador to Ireland.[67]

The hearings, recessed for the weekend, resumed with a presentation by General Clifton B. Cates, Commandant of the Marine Corps. Cates had a think-tank, or "pots and pans division," at Quantico that included such senior officers as Victor H. "Brute" Krulak, James D. Hittle, Gordon Gayle, Merrill B. Twining, Robert D. Heinl, Jr., Angus "Tiny" Fraser, Samuel Shaw, and others who worked hard to prepare papers defending their Corps from what they perceived as the imminent danger that it would be reduced to a mere police force.[68]

The paper written by the Quantico think-tank for the B-36 "chowder," or fight, was bitter. It criticized "Lord Louie Johnson," the Joint Chiefs of Staff for having "wheels within wheels," General Dwight D. Eisenhower for wanting to cut the Marine Corps so that it would have no unit larger than a regiment, Army Chief of Staff J. Lawton Collins for holding that Marines "should be pushed down to Navy yard guards and ship detachments" and also desiring a single chief of staff. The paper documented that during World War II in Europe the Army Air Force was so busy escorting bombers that it failed

In addition to Admirals Denfeld, Radford, and Gallery and Captains Arleigh Burke and Fitzhugh Lee *(above left)*, other naval officers who questioned the Air Force's ability to deter war and to defeat Russia if war came or helped prepare the Navy's case during the "revolt of the admirals" were *(right)* Admiral John Howard Cassaday and *(below)* Admiral Charles D. Griffin.

OFFICIAL U.S. NAVY PHOTOGRAPHS

Army leaders who would build up the Army and the Air Force at the expense of the Navy and Marine Corps included Secretary of the Army Kenneth C. Royall *(above left)*, General Dwight D. Eisenhower *(right)*, General J. Lawton Collins *(below left)*, and General Omar N. Bradley *(right)*. Collins succeeded Bradley as Chief of Staff of the Army when Bradley became the first chairman of the Joint Chiefs of Staff.

OFFICIAL U.S. ARMY PHOTOGRAPHS

to provide air support for Army troops, and noted that although it could not put a squadron of B-36s into the air the Air Force "wanted to put everything into strategic bombing and nothing in anything else."[69] Cates greatly tempered the statement. He paralleled Denfeld in asserting that unification did not work well. He spoke of the "elimination" of the Marine Corps by budget cuts in fiscal years 1950 and 1951, and of the takeover of its amphibious function by the Army, which was not permitted by the National Security Act. He was upheld by General A.A. Vandegrift, his predecessor as Commandant.[70]

Air Force witnesses had at hand ample data on naval matters. The bibliography of a report made by a committee headed by Brigadier General Edmund C. Lynch, USAF, listed seventy-five sources of various kinds, while the report itself constitutes a masterly statement of the roles land-based and carrier-based air power would play in a war with the USSR.[71]

Instead of going into detail, in his testimony Symington noted that the Navy had previously offered ideas similar to those expressed by its witnesses at the hearings and that they had been rejected by those responsible for deciding upon national military policy. He refuted the Navy's charges about the B-36 and the B-36 program and the weakness of the Air Force tactical strength. In

Among Air Force leaders who demanded a seventy-group force and saw the B-36 as the weapons system that would deter war with the Soviets and win a war with them if one came were General Hoyt S. Vandenberg *(left)* **and General Curtis T. LeMay** *(right).*
OFFICIAL USAF PHOTOGRAPHS

Admiral Forreset P. Sherman—Intelligent, hard working, a bit acerbic, a pilot and carrier and fleet commander, a moderate with respect to defense unification and not involved in the "revolt of the admirals," Sherman became the youngest man to date selected as Chief of Naval Operations. He is shown *(above)* at the U.S. Naval Air Station, Pensacola, where a master jet field has been named after him. He is shown *(below)* on 22 August 1950 at the Pusan Air Strip, Korea. To his left is ADM Arthur W. Radford, Commander in Chief, Pacific and U.S. Pacific Fleet. Facing him is VADM Charles T. Joy, Commander Naval Forces Far East. He died of a heart attack while visiting Naples, Italy, on 22 July 1951.

OFFICIAL U.S. NAVY PHOTOGRAPHS

the fiscal years 1949 through 1951, B-36s made up only 2.9 percent of the number of planes, at 16.3 percent of Air Force expenditure for aircraft. He saved his greatest blows to demolish the Navy's criticism of strategic air bombing, an instrument of war approved by the Joint Chiefs of Staff and a primary Air Force mission. Characterizing it as being jealous of the B-36, especially at budget-making time, Symington took an uncompromising position against the Navy.[72]

Symington believed that 'integrated effort and unified direction" was provided in the National Security Act as amended in 1949 and that the law was "worthy of our strongest support." He was disturbed by the Navy's attack on the Air Force because the ensuing debate imperiled the security of the nation by revealing technical and operating details of the latest kinds of equipment. Instead of the forty-eight air groups Congress would provide, he believed that seventy groups were needed to defend the nation, adding that the firepower of the groups was now such that sixty-seven groups equaled seventy groups as constituted in 1948.[73]

Vinson asked whether Symington agreed with Spaatz's writing in *Newsweek* that the air strength of the nation must be pooled, and commented that "the Navy now spends more than half its total appropriation in support of naval aviation," and that "as matters stand, a complete air career in the Navy will be impossible unless naval aviation continues to be emphasized beyond its true requirements and against the decision by Congress to assign the primary airpower role to the Air Force." Symington objected to a single air force and stated that the Navy and Marine Corps should have an air service, to do with what they wished.

>   THE CHAIRMAN. Do you feel or believe that the Navy and the Marine Corps should determine what types of air weapons and what types of aircraft and what is necessary for their full use should be developed by them?
>   Secretary SYMINGTON. I do, subject to the Joint Chiefs of Staff and the Secretary of Defense.[74]

When Vinson pressed him on the Navy-Air Force debate, Symington replied: "I believe that the reason for some of the Reserve officers in the Air Force coming out for a single Air Force is because some of the Regular officers in the Navy, over a period of years, have come out for Navy participation in strategic bombing." Those who analyzed the B-36, he added, "are men of recognized military competency with battle experience and . . . know far more about the grim business of strategic bombing than any other group in the world of today."[75] Did the same reasoning apply, Vinson asked, "to men who think there should be an airplane carrier?" Symington made the amazing retort that "if there is any feeling on the part of you or the committee, sir, that the Air Force is opposed to airplane carriers, that is not true." Moreover, each service should develop weapons it believed to be necessary, he went on, with this qualification: "But I do not think that that weapon should be purchased either, if one of four people disagree with it; the Joint Chiefs of Staff, the

Secretary of Defense, the President, or the Congress."[76] Representative Sterling Cole then put the question straight: "Now, do I understand that it is your viewpoint and that of the Air Force that strategic bombing should be exclusively a mission of the Air Force." Symington fudged a bit before concluding that "if we can afford one strategic bombing force, as a layman I think that strategic bombing force should be in the Air Force." Did Symington know of another service trying to obtain a strategic air force comparable to that in the Air Force? inquired Cole. Thus pinned down, Symington replied:

> One of the things as I listened to the Air Force men talk, that kicked off this bitterness was a speech made by Admiral Nimitz in January 1948 when he started talking about the desirability of the Navy bombing Russia's heartland. It seemed to me that implied they wanted to get into the strategic bombing picture beyond the point that we felt they had wanted to get into it. . . .
> If they can help in strategic bombing with what is necessary to perform their assigned mission as given to them by the Joint Chiefs of Staff and the Secretary of Defense, I would be for it. But if they plan to build equipment in order to become strategic bombers per se, I personally don't think that the Government or the taxpayer can afford it.[77]

Cole continued to bore in: "As a matter of fact, Mr. Secretary, did not the Navy do some effective strategic bombing during the last war?"[78]

Alleging that he was ignorant of the accomplishments of carrier aviation during World War II, Symington stated: "Frankly, I don't think that carriers are much of the Air Force's business, as far as decisions—"

> Mr. COLE. That is a shocking statement for you to make.
> The CHAIRMAN. Go right ahead. That is very important. That is what the trouble is, isn't it?
> Secretary SYMINGTON. I am sorry you felt it was a shocking statement. What I was trying to say was—
> Mr. COLE. It is amazing.

> Secretary SYMINGTON. We agree 100 percent that the Navy should have carriers. Their operations of their carriers, I think, is their business, just as I think, incidentally, the operation of our bombers is our business, subject to higher authority's decisions as to whether we buy them.

> Mr. COLE. Yes, in spite of the viewpoint that you have expressed to the effect that the operation of a carrier by the Navy is not Air Force business, the representative of the Air Force on the Joint Chiefs of Staff undertook the right to negate the acquisition and construction of a carrier.

Symington then divorced his work as Secretary from that of Vandenberg as his chief of staff and member of the Joint Chiefs of Staff. He and Vandenberg worked well together, he was perfectly satisfied with Vandenberg's work, and he would leave it to Vandenberg to answer questions on military matters.[79]

Vandenberg wondered why the Navy could not concentrate on antisubmarine warfare and control of sea communications and leave strategic bombing to the Air Force, and contended that "the only force that can counter-attack the [Russian] threat at its source is the Air Force's Strategic Air Command." He asserted that the Air Force had not neglected tactical aviation and questioned whether the Marine Corps, with seven air groups, did not have too much air power to support its mere two divisions. He then made the stupendous admission that "the ultimate we can ever hope for from the point of view of destruction of forces launched against us is the neighborhood of 25 percent. That is the ultimate, and it undoubtedly would be less than that."[80]

The Army's General Omar N. Bradley followed the line that balanced forces were needed if war came with a great foreign power. While strategic bombardment and large-scale land operations could be foreseen, he said, "island hopping" would be of little use and large-scale amphibious operations would "never occur again." Moreover, the Navy's denigration of atomic power damaged the nation's security. He was upheld by the new Chief of Staff of the Army, General J. Lawton Collins, who particularly made the point that the Air Force was cooperating with the Army.

Bradley was almost always very courteous and soft-spoken. However, he mentioned Denfeld's war record which, according to Hanson Baldwin at least, was "pretty poor pool,"[81] and in ending his remarks became so emotional that he trembled; his naturally high-pitched voice became so shrill that it was difficult to understand him. He concluded that the Navy had failed to teach its people, including aviators, that its role was to wage antisubmarine warfare; that it opposed unification; and that it included "fancy dans" who, rather than being team players, would not play unless they could call the signals.[82]

Bradley of course overshot the mark and in releasing pent-up emotions exhibited service partisanship and engaged in personalities. He insulted the Navy by seeking to restrict it to an antisubmarine role. He also asserted that while he had been a member, the Joint Chiefs of Staff had not considered the supercarrier before April 1949.

Denfeld now submitted a paper showing that the Joint Chiefs discussed the supercarrier in May 1948. Seeing his error, Bradley went back to the committee to say that the Joint Chiefs did not make a *formal* decision on the carrier before April 1949. However, in discussions of late May 1948 he had agreed to its building only because of his "understanding that it had been approved by those in authority, and I accepted it as a fait accompli." In April 1949, when a formal decision had to be made, he had opposed the carrier. Denfeld had misunderstood him.[83]

Both Eisenhower and Marshall were conciliatory, with Eisenhower noting that friction came from the unified budget process, which forced the services to compete for funds within a budget ceiling.

In his testimony—thirty-five pages of blunt language—Johnson stated that "tradition, opposing interests, and fear of losing identity have all played a part in the turmoil on the subject of unification. . . . " He made much of the fact that he would save $1 billion of the fiscal year 1950 budget and $1.5 billion in that of 1951. At his suggestion the McNarney Management Committee had recommended on 8 September a cut in the Army budget for fiscal year 1950 by $357 million, in that of the Navy by $376 million, and in that of the Air Force by $196 million. Since representatives of the service secretaries sat on the committee, the secretaries must have known about the cuts and Matthews would be granted the hearing he had requested to protest them. He alleged that the naval witnesses had an "erroneous picture" of the Joint Chiefs of Staff war plans and that Denfeld erred in describing the cancellation of the supercarrier. He also revealed that Secretary of the Navy Sullivan had resigned not following its cancellation, as we have seen, but a month earlier "because Sullivan was unwilling to support unification."[84]

After the final witness, Herbert Hoover, supported Johnson's efforts to promote economy and efficiency in the Department of Defense, Vinson contradicted him by deploring the preparation of the defense budget in accordance with limits established by the Treasury Department and Bureau of the Budget instead of with the nation's defense and foreign policy requirements held uppermost.

The hearings ended, the committee promised a report and adjourned on 21 October until 3 January 1950.

Before returning to his post in London, Conolly asked Matthews if his testimony had been objectionable. It was not, said Matthews, but Conolly should have cleared it with him first. Why should he have done so when he had cleared it with Denfeld? Conolly queried. "That was not sufficient. Admiral Nimitz cleared his statement with me," Matthews replied. Conolly pointed out that Nimitz was retired, hence not a subordinant of Denfeld's. Matthews said that Conolly's statement had paralleled Nimitz's and had been quite acceptable. Conolly went on:

> He made no reference to the conversation we'd had in the automobile. He just said that my statement was satisfactory to him. Then I got it through the grapevine that Mr. Louis Johnson, when he heard what I had said hit the roof, and turned to Steve Early and said, "There goes your candidate." I saw Early before I went back to London. He thought my statement was perfectly proper. I did not have any further interviews with Johnson. I didn't want any.
> That was the end of what chance I had to be CNO.[85]

Although the hearings were held on the wrong subject—the central issue should have been how to reorganize military and diplomatic policy to deal with a Soviet Union possessed of the atomic bomb—the hearings showed that unification was still an emotionally charged and controversial issue. Naval partisans revealed that they resented the Navy's being treated as a junior partner, of having decisions it opposed imposed upon it by the other services.[86] While the committee felt that there was more than one road to unification, disagreement over the road to take did not diminish the role of Congress in determining national defense policies, the need of Congress to have the advice of military men given without fear of reprisal, or the desire of the committee to continue to assist in the progress of unification.

In Vinson's committee, naval partisans enjoyed a forum in which to point out that the "economy drive" of the Truman administration kept the services on extremely short rations. The radicals broke with Matthews primarily because the promised reduction in naval aviation favored the Air Force and gave credence to the long-held Navy position that unification would mean gain for the Air Force and loss for the Navy. In point was the charge that mass procurement of the B-36 had begun before it had been properly evaluated by the Joint Chiefs of Staff, even before the cancellation of the supercarrier, a weapon needed for future warfare—thus highlighting the need for a weapons system evaluation group.

In "the line of highest duty" and with a "sense of dedicated rightness," read a *Life* editorial, "The highest officers of the Navy . . . shook the country's confidence in the makers, the methods, the chosen instruments of military policy. They exposed difficulties in two central agencies of military policy, the Department of Defense and the Joint Chiefs of Staff." The Navy was not objecting to the new defense establishment or to the Joint Chiefs of Staff as such, continued the editorial, but to the way they had worked against the interests of the Navy thus far. Denfeld would agree to unification if it meant "coordination" rather than, as Johnson viewed it, "central direction by a central authority," and he had made it clear that coordination could not be achieved in the Joint Chiefs of Staff when two of the services had the power to make decisions binding upon the third. Nevertheless, there was no excuse or reason for the Navy to retain all the prerogatives and attitudes of its vanished past at a time when the global interests of the nation were the shared concern of three services.[87]

Some naval witnesses offered incompetent testimony; others failed to prove some of their major contentions, as that the B-36 performed poorly, that its procurement was achieved in an improper manner, that the policy of strategic atomic bombing was inadequate to provide for national security—which could not be done without the test of war—or that the supercarrier was approved by the Air Force and Army at Key West and earlier. Furthermore, the men in OP-23 had prepared their presentation without the knowledge of Matthews and assistance of Denfeld, and Denfeld might have improved or tempered important parts of it. Denfeld's testimony soon led to his dismissal as Chief of Naval Operations by Matthews and Truman. The hearings had no real impact upon the fiscal year 1950 budget, in which the Navy felt badly mistreated, and the Navy was castigated by Vinson's committee for trying to undercut the authority of the Secretary of Defense, take over strategic bombing missions, and force disclosure of secret information.[88]

The Navy suffered in various other ways in making its presentation to Vinson's committee: its demand for additional funds made it appear that it sought recompense for the cancellation of the *United States* and cuts in its budget; the highly classified nature of much of its material precluded its public dissemination; it failed to explain satisfactorily to either the public or its sister services the anguish it had felt for over four years in being in a minority position in the postwar defense organization; it had just too many complicated issues to handle in one set of hearings; and those who had spoken for it were primarily technical officers rather than broad strategists. Last, the hearings were anticlimatic because Truman announced that the Soviets had the atomic bomb just one week before the hearings began and the Navy was unable to take Soviet atomic capability into account. The Air Force's much-touted pushbutton warfare and short-wars philosophy was therefore upheld while the Navy created a negative image as an opponent of strategic and technological process.[89]

The hearings greatly influenced Johnson's conception of the authority he should have as Secretary of Defense and procedure for dealing with Congress. On 25 October he called into conference the service secretaries and his deputy and assistant secretaries "to propose additional constructive steps towards a strong Department of Defense" that he would then talk over with the President. On the agenda were three items: to establish closer and continuous working relationships with Congress, especially with the armed services committees and their staffs; to insure that no one who had testified or would testify before Congress would suffer "reprisals," although "of course there will be some changes in assignments within the Department of Defense"; and "there must be no circumvention of the roles and missions assigned to the services."[90]

In the long run, by reducing its identification with the Air Force and listening more sympathetically to the Navy, Vinson's committee helped naval morale swing upward from the nadir it had reached during the fall of 1949. Congress, meanwhile, played no favorites. In light of the $13.5 billion fiscal year 1950 budget, the Army would lose about one hundred thousand men; the Navy must reduce its operating ships, including thirty-five combat vessels, cut off fifty-six thousand men, and suffer a cut of 50 percent in its 5,658 planes by 1 July 1950; and the Air Force would keep its current strength. Only if its funds permitted would it build up from forty-eight to fifty-eight groups.

In 1971 Jerry N. Hess asked Admiral Robert L. Dennison: "One of the things [naval officers] were particularly concerned with was that the air wing might be transferred to the Air Force. Did this concern you? Did you think the Navy's role in the defense of our nation might be diminished by unification?" Dennision replied:

> Well, it wasn't quite the way I looked at it. I think the basic difficulty with the Navy was the lack of understanding of what unification was all about. It *hadn't* been defined. It was another one of those words that was a great favorite of Johnson's. You were either for unification or you weren't. But what the hell was it? Was it a merger? Did it mean the loss of service identity? This was what the Navy was fearful of, a loss of identity. We didn't want to merge with any service, obviously, because they have different roles and different missions. We have different instruments and a different uniform, and for a good reason.

So it wasn't that the Navy was opposed to the *concept* of a Department of Defense because it was apparent to everybody that the armed forces had gotten so big that something had to be done if only for management, let alone for command. But this revolt of the admirals was another emotional expression. It was really an honest difference of opinion and a questioning of what this was all about, and had Johnson not been so *terribly* extreme, it might have been different. . . .

But this revolt of the admirals, it wasn't a revolt and it wasn't just the admirals. The whole Navy was questioning what the future held, what were the policies, why? So it was a disturbing time.[91]

NOTES

1. Curtis E. LeMay, with MacKinlay Kantor, *Mission with LeMay: My Story* (Garden City, N.Y.: Doubleday, 1965), pp. 429-30.
2. As of December for each year indicated, there were 35 B-36s out of 837 tactical airplanes in the Strategic Air Command in 1948, 36 out of 837 in 1949, and 38 out of 961 in 1950. The number of officers, airmen, and civilians assigned to SAC was 51,965 in 1948, 71,490 in 1949, and 85,473 in 1950. John T. Bohn, *The Development of Strategic Air Command 1946-1971* (Offutt Air Force, *1907-1957* (Princeton, N.J.: Van Nostrand Reinhold, 1957), pp. 121-28; Ned Root, "Plans Without Planes," AF 34 (February 1951):30-33.
3. AW, 51 (22 August 1949):7.
4. "New Climax in Navy-Air Battle," USNWR 27 (2 September 1949):20-21. The Army supported the Air Force instead of the Navy. Although he would depend in part upon naval air for support of ground troops, General Jacob L. Devers, chief, Army Field Forces, would rely primarily upon the Air Force. When interviewed, Devers stated, "I am a thorough believer in unification." He thought that "we have plenty of carriers right now" and doubted that amphibious operations would be needed in the future. ("Is Air Support for Ground Army Being Neglected? An Interview with Gen. Jacob L. Dever," (USNWR 27 [9 September 1949]:32-36).
5. "Secnav Issues Navy Day Edict," ANJ 86 (13 August 1949):1430; "Encourage 'Healthy Rivalry,' " ANJ 86 (27 August 1949):1479.
6. A copy remains in SNP. Along with it is a thirty-seven page phamphlet entitled *Eighteen Principles,* in which Admiral Denfeld announced ideas not too different from Worth's which "reflect the consensus of personnel of the service as expressed by a large group of senior officers." Still another pamphlet, entitled *Analysis of Another Anonymous Attack on the Air Force and the Concept of Aerial Warfare Held by the Joint Chiefs of Staff,* thirty-three pages long, contains the Air Force critique of the Worth pamphlet. On how Truman and the Air Force doctored the USSBS, see Restricted. Arleigh Burke to R.A. Oftsie, 9 September 1949, Personal. Burke to ADM Louis DeFlores, 27 September 1949, ibid.; "The Reminiscences of VADM Fitzhugh Lee, U.S. Navy (RET)," transcript of oral interview by CDR Etta Belle Kitchen, USN (RET) (Annapolis, Md., U.S. Naval Institute, 1970), pp. 251-55; David McIsaac, "The U.S. Strategic Bombing Survey, 1944-1947" (Ph.D. diss., Duke University, 1970), and McIsaac's illuminating introductions in *The United States Strategic Bombing Survey,* 10 vols. (New York: Garland Publishing Inc., 1976).
7. SECNAV to Kinkaid, 25 August 1949, F.P. Matthews to Louis A. Johnson, 27 August 1949, SNP; Paul Y. Hammond, "Super Carriers and B-36 Bombers: Appropriations, Strategy, and Politics," in Harold Stein, ed., *American Civil-Military Decisions: A Book of Case Studies* (University: University of Alabama Press, 1963), p. 496; "The Reminiscences of Hanson Weightman Baldwin," transcript of oral interview by John T. Mason (Annapolis, Md.: U.S. Naval Institute, 1976), p. 466.
8. Walter Millis, with Harvey C. Mansfield and Harold Stein, *Arms and the State: Civil-Military Elements in National Policy* (New York: Twentieth Century Fund, 1957), p. 241.
9. Baldwin, "Reminiscences," p. 468.

10. "Reminiscences of VADM Charles Wellborn, Jr., USN (RET)," transcript of oral interview by John T. Mason (Annapolis, Md.: U.S. Naval Institute, 1972), p. 293; "Court of Inquiry," ANJ 87 (10 September 1949):27; "Kinkaid Report Under Study," ANJ 87 (5 November 1949):254.
11. ADM Joseph J. Clark, USN (RET), with Clark G. Reynolds, *Carrier Admiral* (New York: David McKay, 1967), p. 263.
12. "Capt. Crommelin's Statement," ANJ 87 (17 September 1949):51.
13. Carl W. Borklund, *Men of the Pentagon; From Forrestal to McNamara* (New York: Praeger, 1966), p. 78.
14. Secret. Gallery to SECNAV, 27 September 1949, SNP.
15. SEP 221 (25 June 1949):25, 136-38.
16. Ibid. 222 (29 October 1949):36-37, 44, 46, 48.
17. *Collier's* 125 (21 January 1950):15-17, 45.
18. SECNAV to Rear Admiral D.V. Gallery, USN, 10 January 1950. SNP.
19. Daniel V. Gallery, RADM, USN (RET), *Eight Bells and All's Well* (New York: W. W. Norton, 1965), pp. 222-28.
20. Ibid., p. 228.
21. CAPT L. A. Thackrey, telegram, *Norfolk Virginian Pilot*, 30 September 1949, SNP.
22. Letter of 28 September 1949, SNP.
23. Gallery, *Eight Bells,* pp. 234-35.
24. Hammond, "Super Carriers and B-36 Bombers," p. 511.
25. Ibid.; Hanson W. Baldwin, in *New York Times,* 15 October 1949.
26. Wellborn, "Reminiscences," p. 292.
27. Hammond, "Super Carriers and B-36 Bombers," pp. 505-7.
28. *New York Times,* 3 and 4 October 1949.
29. Conf. VADM General F. Bogan to the SECNAV, 20 September 1949, Washington: NHD:OA, Papers of the Chiefs of Naval Operations (hereafter cited as CNO Papers). In reply to Matthew's letter of 16 September, VADM H.M. Martin stated that morale in the Navy was low because, among other reasons, the Navy was being relegated to a secondary role by persons ignorant of the value of sea power; that strategic bombing, a fallacious philosophy, had been sold to the nation by aggressive propagandists. (Secret. VADM H.M. Martin, Chief, Naval Air Technical Command, to SECNAV , 28 September 2949, SNP.) VADM John W. Reeves substantiated the low morale in the Navy by citing a twenty percent dropout rate in the flight program, at a cost of $1,290,000; a sixty percent turnover in enlisted personnel at the Reserve Air Training Command; by talk of the fear that the Army would take over the Marine Corps; and by reductions in naval forces and operations, especially of carriers. He recommended more effective leadership "at the top" than that exercised by former Secretary Sullivan. He excoriated Sullivan because he had abided by Forrestal's directives and suggested that Matthews undertake a propaganda crusade such as that being carried out by the Air Force. (Secret. Reeves to Matthews, 4 October 1949.) VADM M.L. Deyo, retired, thought that morale had deteriorated so much in two years that officers could not concentrate on their work. Discouragement prevailed because the Navy's case was not being presented properly to the country and "the Army and the Air Force vote together to form a constant unbeatable majority." In consequence, the Navy was being "reduced to impotence . . . by men who are not qualified to determine its needs" (Letter to SECNAV 10 October 2949, SNP).
30. "Texts of Documents in Naval Discussion." ANJ 87 (8 October 1949):139.
31. "The Reminiscences of ADM Richard L. Conolly, USN (RET)," transcript of oral interview by Donald F. Shaughnessy (New York: Columbia University Oral History Project, 1960), pp. 393-98.
32. Hammond, "Super Carriers and B-36 Bombers," p. 511.
33. "Reminiscences of VADM Gerald F. Bogan, USN (RET)," transcript of oral interview by Etta-Belle Kitchen, USN (RET), (Annapolis, Md.: U.S. Naval Institute, 1969), p. 123; Clark and Reynolds, *Carrier Admiral,* p. 263.
34. Bogan, "Reminiscences," pp. 123-24.
35. CNO to Cromwell, 24 October 1949, SNP.
36. Cromwell to CNO, 18 November 1949, SNP.
37. Naval Inspector General to SECNAV, 7 October 1949, SNP.
38. John H. Dillon to VADM H.W. Hill, Chairman, GB, 19 September 1949; Burke to Ruble, October 5, 1949, SNP.

39. Vincent Davis, *The Admirals Lobby* (Chapel Hill: University of North Carolina Press, 1967), pp. 286-88.
40. David E. Debeau and Robert Dorfman, Operations Analysts, Memorandum for BGEN E.C. Lynch, 8 December 1848; GEN E.C. Lynch, Memorandum for GEN Norstad, 10 December 1948; COL Harlan C. Parks, USAF, Executive Deputy Chief of Staff, Operations, Memorandum for: Director of Plans and Operations, Assistant for Atomic Energy, Director of Intelligence, Director of Communications, Assistant for Programming, Chief of Guided Missile Group, Director of Training and Requirements, Chief of Civilian Components Group, 11 December 1948; David E. Debeau, Memorandum for BGEN E.C. Lynch, 16 December 1948, with enclosure, "Summary of Major Events in Connection with Study of USA Strategic Bombing System," AFSHRC. See the more extended discussion in *Supporting Study*, pp. 106-15.
41. "Rep. Vinson," in "Texts of Documents in Naval Discussion," ANJ 87 (8 October 1949):139.
42. Lee, "Reminiscences," pp. 215-16.
43. Ibid., pp. 216-17, 222.
44. U.S. Congress, *National Defense Program: Unification and Strategy,* Hearings before the House Committee on Armed Services, 81st Cong., 1st Sess. (Washington: GPO, 1949), pp. 2-3 (hereafter cited as NDP).
45. Ibid., pp. 3-4, 23-24.
46. Ibid., pp. 2-12.
47. Ibid., p. 29.
48. Ibid.; *New York Times,* 8 October 1949.
49. LCDR R. T. Swenson, Memorandum for the Record, "Notes on First Meeting of the Undersecretary's Task Force," 22 June 1949, NHD: OA, OP-23 files. The task force included rear admirals R.P. Briscoe, C.R. Brown, D.V. Gallery, M.B. Gardner, R.A. Libby, R.A. Ofstie, BGEN R.A. Robinson, USMC, and captains A.A. Burke, C.D. Griffin, W.R. Hollingworth, and A.S. McDill.
50. NDP, pp. 12-35.
51. Jack Raymond, *Power at the Pentagon* (New York: Harper and Row, 1964), p. 287; "The Reminiscences of ADM Charles Donald Griffin, USN (RET)," transcript of oral interview by John T. Mason (Annapolis, Md.: U.S. Naval Institute, 1970), p. 235.
52. NDP, pp. 39-52. At the time, although fourteen of the Air Force's forty-eight regular groups were equipped primarily for strategic air bombing, only four groups were comprised of B-36s, with the remaining groups equipped primarily for air defense and the support of land and sea operations. (Smith, "The Influence of U.S.A.F. Chief of Staff Hoyt S. Vandenberg on United States National Security Policy," pp. 111-12.) The plans of the Air Force in March 1949 to purchase additional B-36s, although approved by Forrestal and Truman, did not become known to the Navy Department until reports of the purchases appeared in the press. (Robert Frank Futrell, *Ideas, Concepts, Doctrine: A History of Basic Thinking in the United States Air Force 1907-1964* [Maxwell Air Force Base, Ala.: Air University, 1971], p. 129.)
53. NDP, pp. 52-53.
54. Ibid., pp. 53-54. Radford was invited to continue answering questions at an afternoon session. See ibid., pp. 54-107.
55. Conolly, "Reminiscences," p. 398.
56. NDP, pp. 126, 201-36.
57. Hammond, "Super Carriers and B-36 Bombers," p. 528; Borklund, *Men of the Pentagon,* p. 81.
58. Wellborn, "Reminiscences," p. 289.
59. Griffin, "Reminiscences," p. 193.
60. Transcript of oral interview by Jerry N. Hess with ADM Robert Lee Dennison, USN (RET) (Independence, Mo.: Harry S. Truman Library, 1972), p. 140 (hereafter cited as Dennison, "Remeniscences").
61. Baldwin, "Reminscences," pp. 471-72.
62. Griffin, "Reminiscences," pp. 187-90.
63. Ibid., p. 190.
64. Dennison, "Reminiscences," p. 141.
65. NDP, pp. 349-64.
66. Griffin, "Reminiscences," p. 190; ADM Louis E. Denfeld, "Reprisal: Why I Was Fired,"

Collier's 125 (18 March 1950):62.

67. Dennison, "Reminiscences," pp. 141-42.
68. Transcript of oral interview by Benis Frank with GEN Clifton B. Cates, USMC (RET) (Washington, HQ, USMC, Historical Division, 1967), pp. 230-31 (hereafter cited as Cates, "Reminiscences").
69. Transcript of oral interview by Benis Frank of GEN Vernon Megee, USMC (RET) (Washington, HQ, USMC, Historical Division, 1967), pp. 113-15, 135-36 (hereafter cited as Megee, "Reminiscences"). When Eisenhower was Army Chief of Staff after World War II, he said in the presence of Nimitz and others that "the Marines would never again have infantry divisions. The most he would permit the Marines to have would be shore brigades. In other words, if I understood his use of the term 'shore brigade' correctly . . . the Marines were going to become the logistics and support troops for the Army which would make future amphibious landings needed by our country. Admiral Nimitz was quite perturbed . . . " (transcript of oral interview by MAJ L.E. Tatem of MGEN Omar T. Pfeiffer, USMC (RET) [Washington: HQ, USMC, Historical Division, 1968], p. 388).
70. NDP, pp. 394-96; Transcript of oral interview by Benis Frank of GEN Oliver P. Smith, USMC (RET), (Washington: HQ, USMC, Historical Division, 1969), pp. 181, 184, 191.
71. Maxwell Air Force Base, Ala.: NAF I. Confidential, 2 vols. USAF Historical Archives, ASI (ASHAF-A), 1949. No. 168.15-28, vol. 2.
72. NDP, pp. 397-449. In a speech he delivered at Maxwell Air Force Base on 17 June 1949, Symington had stated that "upon mobilization, more than 80 percent of the Air Force would consist of groups primarily equipped for purposes other than strategic bombardment. On the other hand, if the composition of the Air Force did not contain enough strategic bomber groups—equipped with aircraft capable of accomplishing the required mission—then both the Air Force and the whole military establishment would be out of balance" ("Our Air Force Policy," in Eugune M. Emme, ed., *The Impact of Air Power: National Security and World Politics* [Princeton, N.J.:D. Van Nostrand, 1959], p. 631). Since B-29s, and B-50s were considered to be medium bombers, the percentage of heavy bombers, B-36s, that Symington had in 1949 was closer to four percent of his total forces. (See Bohn, *Development of the Strategic Air Command,* p. 13).
73. NDP, p. 407-9.
74. Ibid., pp. 410-11.
76. Ibid., p. 411.
77. Ibid., p. 419.
78. Ibid., p. 420.
79. Ibid., pp. 420-21.
80. Ibid., p. 1352. The Weapons Systems Evaluation Group established by Forrestal had made a study of SAC between August and December 1949. Although its report was not made public, it was generally known that it held that the B-36 had "a better than even chance of delivering its bombs to a target area . . . anywhere in the world" (Futrell, *Ideas, Concepts, Doctrine,* p. 133).
81. Baldwin, "Reminiscences," p. 472.
82. NDP, pp. 516-37.
83. Ibid., p. 567.
84. Ibid., pp. 606-35.
'85. Conolly, "Reminiscences," p. 400.
86. "Not Much Harmony Here," USAS 34 (October 1949):5-6.
87. "The Navy and Security," *Life* 27 (24 October 1949):44.
88. Timothy W. Stanley, *American Defense and National Security* (Washington: Public Affairs Press, 1956), pp. 94-95; Hammond, "Super Carriers and B-36 Bombers," pp. 538-46; CDR Richard Lane, USN, "The Navy and Public Opinion," USNIP 77 (March 1951):285-88; "Revolt of the Admirals," AF 32 (December 2949):22-27.
89. *Supporting Study,*, pp. 140-41.
90. Louis Johnson, Memorandum for SECA, SECNAV, SECAF, 24 October 1949, SNP.
91. Dennison, "Reminiscences," pp. 167-69.

9

The "Firing" of Louis E. Denfeld
and the Advent of
Forrest Sherman

On 14 October 1949 Secretary of the Navy Francis P. Matthews telephoned
Fleet Admiral Chester W. Nimitz in New York to say that he needed some
advice. They conferred on the fifteenth in the Hotel Barclay. Speaking
agitatedly, Matthews said he felt that he "was the victim of a conspiracy in
which the Chief of Naval Operations, Louis E. Denfeld, was the principle
conspirator. Something was going on in OP-23 and between Arleigh Burke
and Admiral Arthur W. Radford that had to do with the B-36 controversy and
the unification of the services, but [Denfeld] tells me nothing. . . .Is that
right?" After Nimitz admitted that Denfeld was wrong in not keeping
Matthews informed, Matthews showed his ignorance about naval matters by
asking "How can I get rid of Denfeld?" Nimitz told him to tell the President
that he could not work with Denfeld and to offer reasons for removing
him—but these reasons could not include Denfeld's testimony because
Representative Carl Vinson had guaranteed the witnesses before his committee
immunity from reprisal.[1]

Matthews then wrote the President that he was well aware of naval
opposition to unification when he entered office and vividly recalled Truman's
telling him that the success of unification was vital to the defense of the
country and that naval officers in key positions, including the Chief of Naval
Operations, must work for unification. He had recommended Denfeld for a
second term largely because of the value of his continuity of service. However,
he had found it increasingly difficult to work with him in the "harmonious
relationship which should prevail." Because of his disloyalty, as in endorsing

the letter of Vice Admiral Gerald F. Bogan, he himself could not properly perform his duties as Secretary of the Navy. Therefore a new Chief of Naval Operations should be appointed "at the earliest possible date." Truman replied that he was familiar with the problems concerning unification, approved Denfeld's removal, and gave out copies of his correspondence with Matthews at a press conference held on 27 October. He later said that he had got rid of Denfeld "in a move to restore discipline."[2]

Denfeld learned of his dismissal from radio reports about the press conference and from a telephone call from Truman's naval aide, Captain Robert L. Dennison, rather than from Matthews. "Frustrated" rather than "angry,"[3] he took his dismissal "like the man he was, no question about that, hurt that the President had seen fit to fire him without even calling him and telling him in person,"[4] But that was Truman's way.

On the relationship between Matthews and Denfeld, John F. Floberg, lately installed as Assistant Secretary of the Navy for Air, noted that "Mr. Matthews felt very strongly that Denfeld had manifested a personal disloyalty to him. The feelings of animosity between those two, incidentally, were highly reciprocal. I was on good terms with both of them, but there was certainly no love lost between them."[5]

On 1 November Matthews detached Denfeld from duty and directed him to report for further assignment; on the second he endorsed his reporting in. Hanson Baldwin says of his departure: "I remember going to see him and he was considerably crushed and Mrs. Denfeld was much upset, too. I was there on the Pentagon steps when he left and I remember how all the naval officers were standing at salute and there were some actual tears. He emerged from it more of a hero than he had been as Chief of Naval Operations."[6] Matthews was to have shared a box with Denfeld at the Navy-Notre Dame football game on the twenty-ninth. By not attending, he missed witnessing the standing ovation given Denfeld by the midshipmen.

Vinson asserted that he would tolerate no reprisals against witnesses and that Denfeld was made to "walk the plank" because he was honest enough to voice his opinion that the Navy was not accepted in full partnership in the national defense structure. Some members of his committee evaluated Matthew's action as an "insult to Congress," and "malicious retaliation," which the committee would not take "lying down." Frank A. Hecht, President of the Navy League, noted that "Admiral Denfeld is the Number 1 victim to the new thought control in the United States."[7] Columnist David Lawrence believed that Truman violated the unification law by "punishing" Denfeld for his testimony; that Matthews similarly violated law by seeking to deny Congress information it needed for legislative purposes; and that the Secretary of Defense, Louis A. Johnson, made cuts in defense funds and changes in service roles and missions not contemplated in law. Indeed, Lawrence thought a good case could be made for the impeachment of both Johnson and Matthews for those reasons and for their "intimidation" and "coercion" of military leaders.[8] So did the *Baltimore Sun* and *Washington*

News, whereas such newspapers as the *New York Times* and *Philadelphia Inquirer* spoke of the need to uphold civil supremacy and maintain unity in the armed forces.[9]

Various members of Vinson's committee held that Johnson and Matthews had removed Denfeld as a form of reprisal and that he would not have been removed had his testimony pleased them, and Vinson promised that the removal would be reflected in his committee's report on the October hearings. While some senators—among them William G. Knowland, a member of the Armed Services Committee who had lost confidence in Johnson and Matthews—called for Matthews's resignation, on 25 October Johnson spelled out his ideas on unification in a special meeting he called with the service secretaries and then wrote a number of congressmen the reasons for the removal of Denfeld.[10]

Although Matthews mentioned no successor to Denfeld, rumor had it that it would be Forrest P. Sherman. Uninformed of Matthews's choice, Truman asked Nimitz to serve again. Nimitz declined. Whom would he recommend? Nimitz suggested Richard L. Conolly and Sherman, the latter at the moment flying to the United States from Lebanon at Matthews's order. On 1 November Matthews told Sherman that he would be the new Chief of Naval Operations.[11]

Sherman, who graduated second out of the 203 men in the Naval Academy class of 1917, was fifty-three years of age. He was an aviator who had commanded carriers, served as Deputy Chief of Staff to Nimitz during World War II, and helped work out compromises that led to the writing of the original unification act. Since 1948 he had commanded the Sixth Fleet, in the Mediterranean. He would be the first naval aviator and the youngest man ever to be Chief of Naval Operations. However, his selection by Johnson and Matthews without consultation with top naval officers and the armed services committees of Congress raised several questions. Moreover, the leaders of the Marine Corps feared that he would absorb the corps into the Navy, abolish it, or, as Secretary of the Army Kenneth C. Royall demanded, transfer it to the Army. Could he undertake the human relations task of making the Navy like unification? Could he gain the confidence of those naval and Marine Corps officers and congressmen who opposed additional unification?[12] In his favor was the fact that naval aviators had led the fight against the Air Force and that he was an extremely capable officer.

Of him John F. Floberg has said:

> I would say that Forrest Sherman was one of the truly great people I have met in my life. His intellectual capacity was enormous and his studious habits were intense so that he had a background of knowledge which made him uniquely qualified to be Chief of Naval Operations. . . . I knew that Mr. Matthews always considered that the biggest thing that he had ever done for the Navy or could do for the Navy was to bring Sherman in as its senior Naval officer, and I must say that I agree with him. . . It was

perfectly obvious, not long after I had assumed my duties in the Navy Department, that Louis Johnson had implicit confidence in him. I think the obvious confidence which Johnson, and very shortly thereafter President Truman, manifested in Sherman and the well-known major responsibilities which they vested in him rather than in the other members of the joint chiefs caused even the most skeptical senior Naval officers to realize that Sherman was a gem and that he was accomplishing by his quiet manner and his talent at intelligent persuasion infinitely more than all the bombast, Congressional hearings, and protest which the ablest of them could make. Unqualified support and loyalty to Sherman were relunctantly forthcoming in some cases; but I think that self-interest made it apparent that it had to be the universal Navy position, and it was not long before that was the fact.[13]

Admiral Richard L. Conolly, Sherman's superior in Europe, saw the selection of Sherman in a somewhat different light, saying, with an aside on Matthews:

Louis Johnson put Sherman in as CNO . . . because he had to go way down the list before he found somebody who had not participated in the presentation to the [Vinson] Committee. There were several people who were very friendly to Sherman. He had had a great deal of duty in Washington, and he was a good compromiser and temporizer, and that is what Louis Johnson wanted. Actually, by the time they got him there, he was in a position, being Johnson's choice, where Johnson had to like what he did no matter what it was. He had to back Sherman up. He put him in there. . . .
I'd say Matthews was one of the less effective Secretaries of the Navy we've had in the last twenty-five years, without any question. I don't think he was a highly intelligent man, nor a very forceful man. . . . He didn't want any part of a fight. He welched on the Navy, I'd say—for which the Navy will never forgive him.[14]

Hanson Baldwin's view of Sherman is somewhat colored by the fact that Sherman, before he became Chief of Naval Operations, once cautioned naval leaders not to divulge information to him for an article he would write for the *New York Times*. "He had a reputation for great brillance of mind but I, as a newspaperman," said Baldwin,

found him not as easy to get along with as many of the other naval officers. He was terse, sometimes, little acerbic, sardonic, and what troubled me about him was that he was not as straightforward as others that I knew. . . . I think his strategic judgments were probably quite sound and far-seeing, and I may be quite unfair to him in saying that he was a manipulator. But he handled power like that.[15]

Although Vinson had got Johnson to promise that he would not transfer the Marines or Marine aviation to another branch of the service without congressional sanction, the Chief of Naval Operations had the power to detach operating Marine forces from the Navy. Notwithstanding the Sullivan-Vandegrift understanding that the Corps' direct responsibility to the Secretary of the Navy would remain unchanged, Sherman demanded military command over the corps and its commandant and from Johnson obtained permission "to have a free hand in the interior organization of Marine divisions." By thus interposing himself between the commandant and the Secretary of the Navy, he sought to reduce the Corps' Headquaters to a technical bureau like the Bureau of Naval Personnel. Doom for the corps seemed to impend when General Omar N. Bradley testified before Vinson's committee that the future foretold no more amphibious landings; Sherman, "the Navy's most extreme advocate of unification," succeeded Denfeld; and Sherman, for 1950, allocated naval shipping to Army-Navy amphibious exercises and virtually froze Marine Corps amphibious training.

After the Senate approved him for an interim appointment, Sherman was sworn in on 2 November, when Mathews announced that he had offered Denfeld the post of Commander in Chief U.S. Naval Forces Eastern Mediterranean and Atlantic, but that Denfeld declined the post, saying that the "embarrassment" he had suffered would place an "undesirable restraint" upon his dealing with other governments.[16] As has been said, "the discord between the Secretary and the Chief of Naval Operations led to a premature ending of the career of one and an inability for any further effective exercise of his office by the other."[17] To Sherman, thus, fell the task of restoring morale in a Navy shaken by the congressional hearings on the B-36, by the Cedric Worth document and John Crommelin's disclosures, by the removal of Denfeld, and by the injunction by Johnson that he support his economy program by forwarding monthly reports on "Progress in Unification in Planning and Operational Fields" and a directive to Matthews to deactivate certain naval forces and facilities and also to reduce naval flight time.[18]

Sherman assumed his unenviable duties at a time when President Truman had impounded in the Defense Department funds Congress had appropriated to add ten groups to the Air Force, and Johnson so cut the Navy's funds that it had to drop thirty-five aircraft squadrons, inactivate an air facility, reduce maintenance on five air bases, inactivate sixty-five training ships, and reduce the modernization program.[19] When Crommelin, who had been transferred to a West Coast billet, violated Sherman's directive to stop criticizing the Defense Department, Matthews furloughed him at half pay. Crommelin thereupon resigned.[20]

If the Crommelin case was closed, the unification controversy continued to rage because Denfeld had been ousted, Arleigh Burke's promotion had been endangered, and Vice Admiral Gerald F. Bogan had been demoted. Moreover, the Secretary of the Air Force, W. Stuart Symington, asked Matthews to give him his thoughts about an outburst by Blandy. As chairman of the international planning group for the North Atlantic region of the North Atlantic Treaty Organization, Blandy had asserted that the member nations of the organization "are vitally concerned with the safety of shipping in the Atlantic and its contiguous waters. They show little enthusiasm for the concept that the atomic bomb is going to render unnecessary the use and control of the sea in war."[21] On 8 December Johnson directed that only his office would release information on NATO, the military assistance program, and other international programs, and on 28 January 1950 Truman directed Admiral William N. Fechteler to relieve Blandy, who was placed on the permanent disability list.[22]

Of course Symington said nothing about *Air Force* magazine, which continued to criticize the Navy,[23] or about a series of newspaper articles being published by retired Air Force General H.H. Arnold that denigrated the Navy and therefore impeded service unification. Nothing came of a suggestion to have Matthews ask the War Council to request the Air Force to repudiate Arnold's articles, of Representative Sterling Cole's asking Nimitz to reply to Arnold, or of Captain Walter Karig's asking Fleet Admiral William F. Halsey to sign articles ghosted for him.[24] "This continuous sniping and needling by Air Force propaganda against the Navy is the most disruptive factor in attempts to achieve workable unification," Karig wrote Sherman. "Overwhelming sentiment in the Navy is to call off the shooting and all hands get to work, but, unless some influence can curb the inspired attacks on the Navy's reasons for being, unification will continue to be impaired."[25] Sherman's attitude, shared by Matthews, was that the Air Force attacks were disturbing but that somehow something would be done to quiet them.

But the issue would not down. Representative Cole asked the 308 flag and general officer in the Navy and Marine Corps whether they agreed with the views Denfeld expressed before Vinson's committee. He then made public the replies but not the names of his correspondents. A Naval Reserve officer, he strongly loaded his questions against the Department of Defense and in favor of Congress and of the Navy, and Matthews authorized his addressees to reply only on condition that they omit classified information and send a copy of their letters to him.[26] Cole's summary of the 170 replies, copy to Vinson, included 117 that emphatically supported Denfeld's views and 15 that approved them "in general" or "in the main"; only 26 were noncommittal.[27] Matthews, meanwhile, said that the Navy would suffer further "financial cramps" but that it was being "equitably treated," that Johnson and the Deputy Secretary of Defense, Stephen T. Early, had no favorites among the services, that officers were not gagged, and that Denfeld had not suffered retaliatory action. As for unification, Matthews predicted that it would "ultimately be universally regarded as one of the most constructive developments in the evolution of our system of government."[28] On 6 February 1950 Matthews assured the Navy League of the full cooperation of the Navy Department in its championing of the Navy cause.[29] However, on 20 January 1950 Sherman cautioned the naval service that organizations seeking to establish chapters in ships and other naval activities for the purpose of affecting legislation or public opinion violated *Navy Regulations, 1948*.[30]

In the meantime Johnson had made a trip to Europe, stopping in London for just one night. Conolly planned to give him a cocktail party and asked the American ambassador, Lewis Williams Douglas, to give him a dinner. Saying

"I hate his guts," Douglas did so anyway. At the cocktail party, Johnson, as Conolly put it, "tried to make a monkey out of [him]" by saying that the Vinson committee business was "all settled" and by adding: "We're going ahead and we're going to build up the Air Force. I started to build up the Air Force when I was Assistant Secretary of War. I'm a great friend of the Air Force." On the next day he said to Conolly:

> Admiral, the Navy is on its way out. Now, take amphibious operations. There's no reason for having a Navy and a Marine Corps. General Bradley . . . tells me that amphibious operations are a thing of the past. We'll never have any more amphibious operations. That does away with the Marine Corps. And the Air Force can do anything that the Navy can do nowadays, so that does away with the Navy.

Said Conolly:

> I will say without reserve that Bradley doesn't know what the hell he's talking about. I know a hell of a lot more about amphibious operations than Bradley does, and I've commanded a number of them when Bradley was either a passenger or witness . . . and I tell you that it's a technique we can't afford to abandon. It might be very useful, certainly during the next ten years.

Conolly could hardly have been more prophetic, because U.S. Marines would be landing in Korea within six months. "But he backed right down," Conolly added, thereby agreeing with John F. Floberg that Johnson did so when proved wrong.[31]

To the second session of the Eighty-first Congress, which convened on 3 January 1950, Truman sent a military budget of $13.5 billion for fiscal year 1951, $1.2 billion less than in fiscal year 1950, suggested that the services transform their "fat" into "muscle", and kept impounded the aviation procurement funds voted by the first session of the Eighty-first Congress. While Johnson hoped to economize on the 1951 budget as he had on that for 1950, Matthews told Vinson's committee that the $350 million cut Johnson meant to make in the Navy's budget for 1950 would imperil the security of the nation. He also let Truman know that the Navy, operating largely out of reserve stocks with obsolescent equipment, was unable to support developments in jet aircraft and guided missiles.[32]

The $3.9 billion allotted to the Navy for fiscal year 1951—$450 million less than in 1950—meant that it would have to drop 31,000 men and 15 combatant ships including a reduction in large carriers from eight to six and in small carriers from eleven to eight; reduce carrier air groups from fourteen to nine, patrol squadrons from thirty to twenty, and Marine Air squadrons from sixteen to twelve; and undertake no new ship construction or conversions. Funds were provided for the development of both defensive and offensive submarine warfare, including an atomic-powered submarine, but nothing could be done about naval air, which on 30 June 1950 would have 42.8 percent of its fighters, 40.8 percent of its attack planes, 59.3 percent of its patrol planes, 89.2 percent of its transports, 74.4 percent of its utility craft, and 74.4 percent of its training planes over five years old.[33] Last, instead of spending an estimated $28 million to expand facilities at the Naval Academy, into which 3,400 midshipmen were crowded into space designed for 2,150, Matthews planned to ask Congress to cut congressional appointments thereto from five to four.[34]

At a press conference attended by the service secretaries and the Joint Chiefs of Staff, Johnson stated that the budget provided "sufficiency of defense for the hour." Matthews added, and Sherman agreed, that a proper balance between combat forces and support would be maintained, but that both operations and support would be kept at "a minimum level consistent with Military readiness,"[35] Symington, however, told Truman that "I can't accept that man [Johnson]. I don't mean to make a mess . . . but I want out." Rather than have Symington "make a mess," Truman shifted him to head the National Security Resources Board.[36]

The Senate Armed Services Committee approved Sherman's nomination as Chief of Naval Operations on the morning of 12 January rather than holding it up until Vinson released his report on the B-36 investigation. In the afternoon, Matthews told the committee that he thought very highly of Sherman and that he assumed full responsibility for the ouster of Denfeld. Various senators threatened to hold hearings on Denfeld's "firing," however, if Vinson's report did not give the Navy "constructive" handling. The report, issued on the tenth, exonerated the Air Force of any irregularities in the selection and procurement of the B-36 but postponed reporting on the other changes proferred by the Navy until further studies were made, including an investigation of the treatment given Denfeld. Shortly before Matthews ousted Denfeld, and without informing Arleigh Burke, Matthews ordered the Naval Inspector General to investigate OP-23. Investigators and Marine Corps guards impounded Burke's files; he and his staff were placed under technical arrest and held incommunicado for a time. Nothing incriminating was found. The following day Burke demanded that Matthews charge him with having committed some offense so that he could "enjoy the rights of a criminal" and defend himself in a court-martial. "If you wanted to know what I had in my files, I would gladly have told you. We are all on the same team here," he told Matthews.[37] Matthews retorted that Burke was making a mountain out of a molehill and that OP-23 would continue to operate. It did, until Matthews had the group disbanded and all the "useful files" placed in the central files of the Chief of Naval Operations. Matthews apologized to Burke for having had him investigated—and then gave the Navy's public information agency its first major overhaul since 1945 by creating the billet of Chief of Information, which would be filled by a rear admiral who would supervise both public relations and the information service and work for both the Secretary and the Chief of Naval Operations.[38] Nevertheless, under the title of Progress Analysis Group (OP-09D) created by a memorandum of November 1950 from the Deputy Chief of Naval Operations for Administration, the Navy continued its attempt to burnish its image before both Congress and the public, a task made much easier when the Navy proved its utility in the Korean War.

It had been widely rumored that Matthews had dropped Burke's name from the list of twenty-three captains considered for promotion to rear admiral and that at Sherman's objection his name was restored. The truth was that Johnson and Matthews had violated the law that required a selection board's report to go directly to the President by convening the board that recommended Burke and causing it to delete his name. When Truman asked his naval aide, Captain Robert L. Dennison, if any "injustice" had been done, Dennison explained what had occurred and Truman directed that Burke's name be added to the list.[39] Despite their violating the law and assuming the President's power of appointment, a touchy point with Truman, Truman added, "You know, I don't wish to fire Johnson or Matthews now."[40] On 16 June Matthews recommended Burke's promotion to Under Secretary of Defense Early, who on the twentieth transmitted the nomination to Truman, who approved. After Burke was promoted and appointed to the nonsensitive post of Navy Secretary of the Research and Development Board in the Department of Defense, Matthews replied to questions about him by saying merely that he had been promoted and that "newspaper forecasts to the contrary have lost their significance."[41]

In part because of a supposed scarcity of fissionable uranium, the Air Force had built only large atomic bombs instead of a family of weapons suitable for a long range of targets. Although its chairman, Admiral Lewis L. Strauss, wished to develop a thermonuclear or "H" Bomb, the Atomic Energy Commission could not reach agreement on doing so and laid the problem before Truman on 25 November 1949, about two months after the United States detected the Soviet explosion of an atomic device. After Truman agreed on 31 January, the AEC not only developed an H-bomb but an entire family of nuclear weapons and the capability of producing A-bombs on an assembly-line basis. Among the last were A-bombs small enough to be carried in fighter aircraft and useful for tactical as well as strategic warfare by both the Air Force and the Navy. On the other hand, the United States had little in the way of defense against intruding aircraft carrying nuclear weapons, and some students of the defense problem could see no solution to stopping such intruders beyond destroying their launching sites—or a preventive war to which Truman, and Symington's successor as Secretary of the Air Force, Thomas K. Finletter, were opposed but, as noted below, appealed to Secretary Matthews. Vitally concerned with defense, Vandenberg asked a committee headed by Professor George Valley, Jr., of the Massachusetts Institute of Technology, to recommend a defense system. In March 1950 the Valley committee recommended new sensor and communications systems, to cost $1 billion, that would alert fighter interceptors and missiles to destroy any intruders. In consequence of developing the new defense system, the Air Force had to reduce its tactical air force and rely more heavily upon its strategic air as a deterrent and second striking force.[43]

After the first test of an H-bomb, on 1 November 1952, the Air Force emerged more than ever as the primary organization to exercise the function of strategic deterrence. Not to be overlooked, however, was the suggestion by Secretary of State Acheson, Johnson, and the Chairman of the AEC, now David E. Lilienthal, that a thorough reexamination be made of the nation's foreign policy and strategic plans, as the Policy Planning Staff of the Department of State had suggested in September 1949 because the Joint Chiefs of Staff had persuaded it that budgetary limitations might seriously impair national security.[44] On 5 January 1950, when the National Security Council began a strategic reappraisal based on American commitments, the State Department created a group to work with it. The actual work was accomplished by an ad hoc joint State-Defense group that began work in mid-February and reported late in March, as will be noted below, in a paper known as NSC-68.

Matthew's first full semiannual report, for the period 1 July-31 December 1949, dated 24 February 1950, was not only short but one of the most vapid on record. He waxed optimistic even though he acknowledged that "drastic changes" had caused a "general downward adjustment" that required "a re-evaluation and restatement of some current Navy plans and policies and reduction in both the operating forces and shore establishment." Following a narration of routine matters, he hailed the adoption of a performance type budget system.[45] However, he failed to state that naval aviation was forced to assume a new role. No longer prestigious as the quarterback of the defense team, and squeezed for three years in a row in its budget, the Navy was forced to shift from large carriers and heavy bombers to an antisubmarine role, to stress quality rather quantity, to develop speedy medium-bombers and turboprop rather than long-range turbojet aircraft as complements to the intercontinental Air Force bombers, and to develop only prototypes that could be produced in quantity when needed.[46] Meanwhile, upon learning that the *Missouri*, which had been run aground off Norfolk, had been refloated, Vinson suggested that she be mothballed and that a carrier be reactivated and added to the fleet in her stead. Johnson directed that the *Missouri* be used as a training ship for midshipmen and Naval Reserve personnel and that an additional carrier be retained in operation. When Vinson asked whether a new supercarrier, to be named in honor of James V. Forrestal, would be built, Johnson replied that there was no immediate prospect of such construction.[47]

Early in February Matthews directed that internal must parallel external unification. He forbade the use of such terms as "black shoe" (nonaviation personnel), "trade school boys" (Naval Academy graduates), and "airedales" (aviators). Moreover, no discrimination would be made between reserve and regular personnel.[48] The directive was observed at first more in the breach than in the observance, and in November Matthews made it "policy" that no Naval man would "utter any comment reflecting upon" the Army, Air Force, or

Marine Corps. While Navy personnel cold speak and write freely, they must refrain from "belittling" and "adverse" comments, and from speaking on subjects that were "controversial between the services."[49]

In mid-February came the report of the Service Academy Board of which Robert L. Stearns, president of the University of Colorado, was chairman, and of which General Eisenhower was vice chairman. The report urged the establishment of an Air Force Academy but did not offer changes in the basic structure of the academies. No evidence of interservice friction and jealousy was found among the students or instructors at West Point and Annapolis, but controversy was noted among higher commanders, particularly those who had not had the benefit of joint education and joint command experience. [50]

The report of the House Armed Service Committee on the B-36 and unification and strategy hearings, issued on 1 March 1950, was fifty-six pages long and contained a thirty-three point summation. The committee agreed on the objectives of the national security establishment but suggested that the National Security Council provide firm statements of principles upon which the Joint Chiefs of Staff and other agencies in the National Military Establishment could undertake their strategic planning. The report took note of the Navy's opposition to indiscriminate atomic bombing as the only strategy to follow in a future war and its demand for conventional forces that were mobile, flexible, and tailored to perform a given task. Read the report:

> Strategic bombing (high-altitude bombing attacks on area targets in the hinterland of an enemy), Navy strategists contended, will not serve any of [a number of] requirements, for the giant, high-altitude bomber cannot defend the United States, seize or hold advance bases, defend western Europe, or maintain control of the seas. It was held that tactical air power rather than strategic air power, plus ground troops and sea power, are the only military instrumentalities that can meet these elementary requirements.

Conversely, air power advocates stressed the deterrent effect of long-range, atomic-laden strategic bombers, that strategic bombing could lay waste the productive heartland of an enemy, and that strategic bombing was "the only alternative available to the United States as a balance for the vast numbers of ground troops available to a potential enemy." Because the committee had not heard witnesses on the value of strategic bombing, it reached no "finding" on the point but suggested that the Defense Department consider the question and reach a conclusion on it "so that all services will have confidence in the decisions rendered and that the Nation may have confidence that the decisions represent a meshing of views, not the imposition of a one-service or two-service concept upon a third service. This committee holds the view that the existing national defense structure does not insure this result. . . ."

The committee agreed that only the test of war could determine the capability of the B-36, that the Air Force was unbalanced in favor of strategic air power rather than tactical air power, and that errors had been made in the cancellation of the *United States*. While the committee accepted the advice of

Air Force "experts" that the B-36 was the best weapon for strategic bombing missions, it felt that such "experts" as the Chief of Staff of the Air Force and the Chairman of the Joint Chiefs were not qualified to determine for the Navy the best weapons needed for control of the seas. Johnson had erred in "summarily" scrapping the *United States* without having conferred first with Secretary Sullivan and with the congressional military and appropriations committees, thereby exacerbating debate over the unification of the services, and a supercarrier should be built when the budget permitted. As for the military budget, "this whole process appears to be disjointed and uncoordinated. . . ." With respect to the outster of Denfeld, the report asserted that

> the committee is convinced that this act was a reprisal—that the frank and honest testimony of Admiral Denfeld in respect to national defense planning and the administration of the unification law, not some more distant cause, produced his removal from office. . . .The removal of Admiral Denfeld unquestionably tends to intimidate witnesses for the executive branch. It greatly aggravates the ever-present difficulty of obtaining uninhibited testimony upon which to base legislative decisions. The committee is convinced that the removal of the Chief of Naval Operations . . . violated promises made to witnesses by the committee and the Secretary of the Navy, and by the Secretary of Defense.

If the committee learned of similar reprisals in the future, it would "ask the Congress to exercise its constitutional power of redress."[51]

A dissenting report signed by eight members of the committee agreed with the entire report except the characterization of the transfer of Denfeld as a "reprisal." In any event, new legislation the committee would call for included adding the Commandant of the Marine Corps to membership on the Joint Chiefs of Staff, a cheerful note to friends of the Navy; rotating the chairman of the Joint Chiefs of Staff after a two-year term; and requiring the Secretary of Defense within certain limits to confer with congressional appropriations committees before withholding appropriated funds by administrative act.

Naval men who hoped that the Vinson hearings would reduce budget pressures on their service and improve the status of naval aviation were disappointed. "Radical" Navy witnesses, however, had revealed their loss of confidence in the President, Secretary of Defense, and Secretary of the Navy. By airing the rivalry and points in dispute between the services, they cleared the way for closer working relations among the Joint Chiefs of Staff and among Sherman, Matthews, and Johnson. Moreover, by tarring Matthews with a breach of faith in removing Denfeld, they isolated him from his Department.[52]

After saying that he knew nothing about published reports that he was to be appointed as the United States Ambassador to Eire, Matthews alleged that Sherman had "brought back to the Navy the brilliant administration of its military side which characterized the period when Admiral Nimitz was C.N.O." Although only five months in office, Sherman had "restored discipline, reestablished good order, and renewed confidence throughout enlisted and officer personnel."[53] Matthews also instructed that the Kinkaid report on the Worth investigation be published.

It may be recalled that Matthews had appointed the Kinkaid court of inquiry to investigate the circumstances surrounding preparation of the once "anonymous" B-36 document subsequently known to have been written by Cedric Worth. The court convened in August 1949, heard testimony for two months, took two additional weeks to prepare its findings, and sent its report to Matthews in mid-October. The report, which Matthews approved, stated that Worth had "incurred serious blame" for violating the trust inherent in his position, but that he had implicated no other person. Since Worth had long left the government service, no disciplinary action against him was recommended, and Matthews dissolved the court.[54]

Having retired from the Navy—after forty years of service—Denfeld lost no time in striking back at Matthews in articles written for *Collier's*. In one, entitled "Reprisal: Why I Was Fired," he asserted he knew he would be the first target of Johnson and Matthews but had not expected the "contemptuous treatment" he received. Loyalty should work both ways, down as well as up, and loyalty included "politeness." The supercarrier was canceled, and he was fired in such an arbitrary way that he feared that control of national defense would pass from the people's representatives. Vinson, Matthews, and Johnson had promised that there would be no reprisals—but he had "offended the secretariat."

Denfeld then wrote that Matthews's deletion of Burke's name from the admirals' promotion list had caused such a public and congressional uproar that he had restored it. Bogan was the third victim of Matthews's vengeance; Blandy, who retired in part because of discouragement over his future prospects, was the fourth. Denfeld hoped Matthews would not visit his ire upon Radford, "this splendid officer, the Navy's number one aviator."[55]

The purport of Denfeld's second article is clear from its title: "The Only Carrier the Air Force Ever Sank." Men like Bradley and Vandenberg, he asserted, never boarded an aircraft carrier at sea until 1949, yet they, and others equally ignorant of the Navy's vital role, took it upon themselves to decree how naval warfare would be fought in the future. Denfeld added bluntly: "Strategic bombing was never a factor in the plans for the carrier *United States*." However, the Air Force imagined that the Navy posed a danger to its prime function of strategic air warfare and gathered enough pilots and lay supporters to "sink the *United States*." Denfeld had been forced to conclude that the Air Force wanted to abolish or acquire all combat naval aviation and the Army all the amphibious functions of the Marine Corps and reduce the latter to a mere security force. The twin ambitions resulted in a working agreement, the two-to-one votes against the Navy in the Joint Chiefs of Staff.[56]

Neither Matthews, Bradley, Eisenhower, nor the congressional armed services committees were happy with "the minimum essential for effective

Navy participation in an adequate security program." By "economizing" on defense, Johnson had not "transformed" fat into muscle but "cut" into muscle. Bradley told the Senate Appropriations Committee that the armed forces were insufficient to fight a major war and would not be ready to do so by the end of the next fiscal year, whereupon the committee suggested adding $385 million to the defense budget. On 25 April Sherman asked the House Armed Services Committee for authority to build a nuclear-powered submarine, and on the twenty-seventh for a sixty thousand-ton carrier. "This ship was the personal triumph, as were so many things, of Forrest Sherman. He had persuaded Johnson, before Johnson's departure, that the ship should be included in the budget and Johnson's implicit faith in Sherman made his support of the ship unreserved—a fact not too many people even in the Navy realized," John F. Floberg has written the writer. Floberg went on:

> Getting the Joint Chiefs of Staff to approve the ship after the fracas over CVA-58 was a masterpiece of diplomacy which no one but Sherman could have handled. By this time, I think the other members of the Joint Chiefs realized both that Sherman was smarter than the rest of them and that Sherman had become the President's fair-haired boy; I think that none of them would have had the stomach to challenge him with regard to the ship because it was better to avoid a confrontation with him than to be clobbered by him in debate.[57]

Motivated by what it termed a "pressing need" for new naval vessels in the atomic age, the House Armed Services Committee voted unanimously early in May to add $350 million to the defense budget, including funds for the construction of 112 new ships and craft and a nuclear-powered submarine (to cost $40 million) and for the conversion of 29 existing ships, one of them to be a powerful guided-missile cruiser. The bill "authorized and directed" the President, not the Secretary of Defense or the Navy Department, to undertake the new construction. Because the 1951 budget was almost ready, the new funds would be sought in the budget for fiscal year 1952.[58] Perhaps in keeping with Eisenhower's suggestion—backed by Vinson, the departing Symington, and Symington's successor, Thomas Knight Finletter, an exponent of a seventy-group Air Force—that half a billion extra dollars be provided, Johnson capitulated. On 9 May the House had voted unanimously to add $85 million to defense funds. Of the total, $100 million would go toward the procurement of ninety-five additional naval aircraft and $50 million for the Navy antisubmarine program.[59]

Although Matthews would neither confirm nor deny the story that the Navy had secretly developed two air squadrons with a primary mission of carrying the atomic bomb, in mid-May it was publicly reported that this was the case. About half of the thirty-two planes were P2V-3C Neptune patrol bombers, and half AJ-1 attack bombers, the AJ-1 being the first carrier plane able to handle atomic weapons even though it weighed less than half of a B-29.

The Navy's development of aircraft, small atomic bombs, and of a supercarrier able to service the aircraft started in a very small way with those officers and civilian employees who worked in the Los Alamos laboratories in the Manhattan District Project, in the Naval Research Laboratory, in the Naval Ordnance Group at Dahlgren, Virginia, and naval officers who helped conduct Trinity Test, the first explosion of an atomic weapon, at Alamogordo. Others directed the assembly of planes and of the "Little Boy" and "Fat Man" atomic bombs and the crews that would drop them on Japan. In September 1945 Forrestal created OP-06, Deputy Chief of Naval Operations for Special Weapons, and charged it with developing atomic weapons and assessing "the capabilities and inherent advantages of aircraft operating from mobile bases, in attacks on vital targets." Vice Admiral Blandy had designed and carried out the Bikini tests to find out how atomic weapons affected naval warships. The charge by the Air Force that the tests proved the Navy to be obsolescent stimulated some naval officers to disprove the charge in part by acquiring for the Navy the means to deliver atomic bombs, with the formidable task undertaken by the thirteen men in OP-06.

In the fall of 1946 OP-06 was dissolved in favor of two agencies, OP-36, tasked with developing atomic bombs and delivery systems, and OP-57, tasked with guided missile development. Rear Admiral W. A. Parsons, who had worked in the atomic field since the days of the Manhattan Project, headed OP-36; Daniel V. Gallery, OP-57. Some of Parsons' subordinates talked with North American Aviation (now Rockwell International) about the suitability of their XAF-1 Savage to carry atomic weapons and came away convinced that it could handle the "Fat Man." Although Forrestal was asked to obtain presidential approval to proceed with the project, he himself gave the green light on the ground that the design of a Navy plane was within the purview of his department. Needed design changes in the XAF-1 prototype were approved in a contract with North American on 26 June 1946. A first step had been taken.

Various naval officers served on the Atomic Energy Commission, which Truman created on 1 August 1946 and charged with the administration of all atomic projects. Commander F. L. Ashworth and Admiral Ofstie became members of the advisory Military Liaison Committee, and Commander John T. Hayward was a member of the Armed Forces Special Project. These men were thus able to alert the Navy Department on how the Air Force sought to monopolize atomic weapons. Hayward, who realized that the Air Force could keep its monopoly if atomic bombs remained large and that there was more nuclear energy available than it would admit, tackled bomb size reduction. With progress being made, what was needed was to determine how to handle atomic weapons in ships and how to deliver them from carriers. The handling problem was solved by modifying *Midway*-class carriers; the delivery system by the XAJ-11.

The minute it has taken to tell this story covers almost four years of history, however. Moreover, because Sherman, while Deputy Chief of Naval

Operations (Operations) in 1947, declined to ask Congress to endorse development of a naval atomic delivery capability, Hayward and others had to work with what they had. They refined the atomic bomb, had *Midway*-class carriers modified to handle the bomb, and originally used the Lockheed P2V Neptune bomber, designed for long-range maritime patrol from shore bases, as a delivery system, even though it exceeded the weight of the AJ-1 by twenty thousand pounds. Although both the Neptune and *Midway*-class carriers were modified, it was seen that only ten feet of space existed between the tips of the wings of the plane and the carrier's island. Furthermore, Neptunes and AJ-1s could lift off carriers but could not return to them, which meant that they must either ditch after delivery and be rescued or fly to a land base. In any event, flights of Neptunes from the *Coral Sea* on 27 April 1948, 7 March 1949, and thereafter proved that the Navy had an atomic bomb delivery capability. Then, in September 1949, Hayward piloted a P2V-3C from the *Midway* with Secretary of the Navy Matthews on board. Members of the Joint Chiefs of Staff were then taken in other AJs on flights from the *Midway* and *Franklin D. Roosevelt*. By January 1950 the Navy had proved its atomic air capability and had established two atomic air squadrons, one at Norfolk and one at Moffett Field, California, with VC-5, at Norfolk, ready for deployment and VC-6, at Moffett, to continue experimental and training work. VC-5 training paid off when Hayward piloted the first AJ-1 from the *Coral Sea* on 21 April 1950 and on 21 August not only took off but landed on her.[60] "It is not important, but," John F. Floberg told this writer,

> Chick Hayward and I were the two in the cockpit for the first deck to deck flight of the AJ-1. The squadron was VC-1 under Hayward's command, and it flew out from Oceana to a carrier off Norfolk—I think it was the *Coral Sea* but the records would show the fact. Admiral Felix Stump, who was then Comairlant, rode in the right hand seat. When they landed on the ship, Stump climbed out and I climbed in and Hayward and I made the first circuit. After that, the carrier qualifications of the squadron took place, and Stump and I witnessed them from the carrier's island.[61]

Even if the Navy was not ready to employ her VC squadrons operationally —the AJ had very poor radar, for example, and good information on Russian targets was unavailable—it had broken the Air Force's monopoly on atomic power. The final step was soon forthcoming—approval of a supercarrier in an atomic-age naval appropriations bill.

The Rules Committee of the House of Representatives paved the way for early consideration of Vinson's bill that authorized the building of 173 new vessels and converting of 291 others at a cost of over $2 billion. Among the new ships were a fifty-seven-thousand-ton carrier to replace the cancelled *United States* and an atomic-powered submarine. Although Truman repeated his opposition to a seventy-group Air Force, saying that the country could not afford such expansion, on 29 June, four days after North Korea invaded

South Korea, the Senate granted authority but not funds for seventy groups and also approved of 837,000 men for the Army.

In his semiannual report covering the period 1 January-30 June 1950, Matthews noted that the inexorable grinding of budget limitations had caused the Navy to cut active duty personnel by 33,464, reduce by twenty-four the number of operating combatant ships and auxiliaries, and aircraft from 5,047 to 4,303. Ships operated with merely 67 percent of combat complements. Both Fleet Marine Divisions and their Air Wings were in reduced strength. Although jet fighters now operated from carriers, the first of the five *Essex*-class carriers to be modernized would not join the fleet until late in the year. On the brighter side, the conversion of submarines to the snorkel type had moved steadily forward and both aircraft and helicopters were being adapted to antisubmarine warfare; the Navy was the prime developer of the turbo-prop type of plane; rockets and guided missiles were being provided to ships, submarines, and aircraft; enough progress had been made on a submarine nuclear power plant to warrant a request to Congress to authorize the building of a nuclear submarine in fiscal year 1952; and the membership in the Naval Reserve had grown rapidly, with 17,000 out of 1,120,000 Reservists on active duty. Nevertheless, Matthews concluded that additional funds beyond those provided in the fiscal 1951 budget would be needed to bring the fleet to a satisfactory state of combat readiness. Were Korea the only danger zone, the problem would be relatively simple, but the communists might contemplate an attack on the United States "if all our normal forces are occupied elsewhere."[62]

During the nine months from the close of the Vinson hearings on unification and strategy in October 1949 to the outbreak of the Korean War in June 1950, interservice disputes greatly impaired the progress of defense unification. Matthews had supported Johnson's demand for additional unification, whereas Denfeld, consistently outvoted in the Joint Chiefs of Staff, felt that the Navy was being denied the weapons systems it needed to accomplish its assigned missions, if not being "whittled down to impotence"; and he resisted what he perceived as an Air Force attempt to acquire control over all military aviation and the Army's attempt to acquire the amphibious functions of the Marine Corps. The devoted efforts of a small number of naval officers working with whatever was available to them, had nevertheless broken the monopoly of the Air Force on atomic weapons. Denfeld's dismissal as Chief of Naval Operations, moreover, was made in an utterly gross manner, as was Matthews's investigation of Burke and OP-23. For speaking out honestly in answer to requests for information from Matthews, furthermore, it appeared that Bogan too had suffered reprisal. Last, in their attempt to deny Burke his promotion, Matthews and Johnson impinged upon the President's prerogative of appointment. In the end, civilian authority triumphed over the military, but Matthews had lost the confidence of the Navy and the low state of morale in his service demanded a successor to Denfeld who could restore that morale while still toeing the line on unification.

Compounding the confusion over unification was the administration's economizing in defense funds, disagreements between the Navy and the Air Force over roles and missions, and the continued Air Force propaganda campaign against the Navy which Matthews, by disbanding OP-23, indicated he would not counter.

The fiscal year 1950 defense budget cut funds from all the services but particularly hurt the Navy, which could undertake no new ship construction outside of antisubmarine types, was expected to carry out its air missions with terribly outdated planes, and was being relegated to a defensive antisubmarine role. Johnson's stating that the budget provided "sufficiency for defense for the hour" notwithstanding, the report of the Vinson committee on its unification and strategy hearings, issued on 1 March 1950, at least questioned the capability of strategic air bombing. It also held that the Air Force was unbalanced in favor of strategic bombing, noted that the scrapping of the supercarrier *United States* had been in error, and asserted that two chiefs of staff ignorant of naval needs should not be permitted to determine the weapons the Navy needed. The report castigated Johnson for administratively altering the expenditures of defense funds provided by Congress, and Johnson and Matthews for having intimidated witnesses and thereby made it impossible for Congress to obtain the honest testimony it needed for legislative purposes.

In September 1949 the Department of State had reiterated a demand of 1948 that a reexamination be made of the nation's foreign policy and strategic plans because the Joint Chiefs of Staff, several leading Army generals, and the Navy radicals had assured it that budgetary limitations seriously impaired the national security. Late in March 1950 a State-Defense study group recommended additional defense spending over a period of years. Truman had just directed Johnson to estimate the cost of funding the study as revised in NSC-68 when war in Korea began. The war would show that Matthews was incorrect in thinking that the "critical period" of unification was over and would test the philosophy of relying upon a single weapon, doctrine, or military staff, and the placing of a tight curb upon military spending including funds for research and development. The war would also prove the correctness of those who demanded balanced and flexible forces, and uphold those who questioned the centralization of power in the Office of the Secretary of Defense at the expense of the service secretaries.

NOTES

1. Professor Elmer B. Potter, memorandum to the writer, 24 September 1975, and MS biography of Chester W. Nimitz, chap. 24.
2. Harry S. Truman, *Memoirs by Harry S. Truman*, 2 vols. (Garden City, N.Y.: Doubleday, 1955-56), 2:53.
3. "The Reminiscences of VADM Charles Wellborn, USN (RET)," transcript of oral interview by John T. Mason (Annapolis, Md.: U.S. Naval Institute, 1970), p. 287.
4. "The Reminiscences of ADM Charles Donald Griffin, USN (RET)," transcript of oral interview by John T. Mason (Annapolis, Md.: U.S. Naval Institute, 1973), p. 191.

5. Floberg to the writer, 31 August 1976.
6. "The Reminiscences of Hanson W. Baldwin," transcript of oral interview by John T. Mason (Annapolis, Md.: U.S. Naval Institute, 1976), p. 474.
7. Armin Rappaport, *The Navy League of the United States* (Detroit, Mich.: Wayne State University Press, 1952), p. 197.
8. "Contempt of Congress," USNWR 27 (4 November 1949):34-36.
9. Newspapers cited in ANJ 87 (5 November 1949):250. See also "Ax for the Admiral," *Newsweek* 34 (7 November 1949):27; E. K. Lindley, "Denfeld Firing: A Turning Point?" *Newsweek* 34 (7 November 1949):26.
10. Johnson to Army, Navy, Air Force, 24 October, 1949, Atlanta Chapter, RONS-ROA, to Johnson, 21 September 1949, Washington: NARG 330, Box 6, vol. 7 (hereafter cited as SECDEF Papers). For the letters to congressmen, see SECDEF Papers, 2 November 1949; for the letter of 10 November 1949, see ibid., in G41 (16.B4).
11. Potter, Memorandum to the writer, 24 September 1975, and MS biography of Chester W. Nimitz, chap. 24.
12. "The Reminiscences of VADM Herbert D. Riley, USN (RET)," transcript of oral interview by John T. Mason (Annapolis, Md.: U.S. Naval Institute, 1972), pp. 295-99; "The Reminiscences of LGEN Victor H. Krulak, USMC (RET)," transcript of oral interview by Benis M. Frank, (Washington, D.C.: HQ, USMC, Historical Division, 1973), pp. 114, 120-21; USNWR 27 (11 November 1949):40.
13. Floberg to the writer, 31 August 1976. Reprinted by permission.
14. "The Reminiscences of ADM Richard L. Conolly, USN (RET)," transcript of oral interview by Donald F. Shaughnessy (New York: Columbia University Oral History Project, 1960), pp. 405-6.
15. Baldwin, "Reminiscences," pp. 481-82.
16. F. P. Matthews, Memorandum for the SECDEF, 3 November 1949, SNP.
17. Paul Y. Hammond, "Super Carriers and B-36 Bombers: Appropriations, Strategy, and Politics," in Harold Stein, ed., *American Civil-Military Decisions: A Book of Case Studies* (University: University of Alabama Press, 1963), pp. 547-48.
18. Johnson to SECNAV, 7 November 1949, Johnson to MTO, 12 December 1949, SNP: File E. "Economy Program," Johnson to *Readers Digest* on "Economy in the Department of Defense," and Memorandum to SECDEF for SECNAV, 23 November 1949, SECDEF Papers; SECDEF Memorandum to all Department of Defense agencies, 17 November 1949, "The Department of Defense Supply System," Navy Department Bulletin 50-121, in NDB 16 (15 January 1950):7-8; "Continuing Survey of the Shore Establishment," 5 January 1950, NDB 16 (28 February 1950):9.
19. "Johnson on...Program for the 2d Session of the 81st Congress," 4 October 1949, Johnson to Truman, 6 and 9 December 1949, SECDEF Papers.
20. CNO to Crommelin, 7 November 1949, SNP. "Crommelin Case Closed," ANJ 87 (4 November 1949):335; "Furlough Capt. Crommelin," NAJ 87 (18 March 1950): 761; "The Reminiscences of Arleigh A. Burke," transcript of oral interview by John T. Mason, Jr. (Annapolis, Md.: U.S. Naval Institute, 1973), p. 164; *Christian Science Monitor*, 21 January 1950.
21. Symnington to Matthews, 6 December 1949, SNP.
22. OP-010 to Alnav 113, dated 8 December 1949; Truman to Fechteler, 28 January 1950; Kimball to Blandy, 2 February 1950; Matthews to Blandy, 6 February 1950, SNP.
23. See, for example, "The Revolt of the Admirals," AF 32 (December 1949):25; "The Navy's Basic Charges," ibid.; and "Where Do We Go From Here?" ibid., p. 28.
24. Cole to Nimitz, 1 December 1949; H. E. Sears, Acting Chief of Public Relations, to CNO, 2 December 1949, SNP.
25. Karig to CNO, 1 December 1949. SNP.
26. SecNav, Alnav 108, dated 9 November 1949, SNP.
27. *New York Times*, 11 November 1949; *Washington Post*, 11 November 1949; "Survey of Navy Views," ANJ 87 (17 December 1949):413.
28. "Further Navy Reductions," ANJ 87 (3 December 1949):372, 379.
29. Navy Department Bulletin 50-90, "Naval Policy Concerning Navy League of the United States, 6 February 1950, NDB 17 (15 February 1950):17; Rappaport, *Navy League of the United States*, p. 198.
30. Navy Department Bulletin 50-56, 20 January 1950, NDB 16 (31 January 1950):9.
31. Conolly, "Reminiscences," pp. 404-5.

32. "Soviet Adds to Navy: U.S. Navy Cuts Back," USNWR 27 (30 December 1949):18-19.
33. John F. Floberg to F. P. Matthews, 18 March 1950: F. P. Matthews to Louis A. Johnson, 21 March 1950; SECNAV to SECDEF, 20 April 1950, SNP.
34. "Explain Military Budget," ANJ 87 (14 January 1950):506, 526; Walter Millis, "Our Defense Program: Master Plan or Makeshift?" *Yale Review* 39 (March 1950):385-401.
35. Carl W. Borklund, *Men of the Pentagon: From Forrestal to McNamara* (New York: Praeger, 1966), pp. 85-86.
36. *Congressional Quarterly Almanac* 6 (1950):322.
37. Ben Jones and Hubert Kelley, Jr., *Admiral Arleigh (31-Knot) Burke: The Story of a Fighting Sailor* (New York: Chilton Books, 1962), pp. 149-50.
38. Vincent Davis, *The Admirals Lobby* (Chapel Hill: University of North Carolina Press, 1967), p. 274-75, 288-89; Jack Raymond, *Power at the Pentagon* (New York: Harper and Row, 1964), p. 200.
39. Special Assistant, Memorandum to CAPT W. J. Stewart, 6 January 1950, SNP.
40. Transcript of oral interview by Jerry N. Hess of ADM Robert Lee Dennison, USN (RET), 1972 (Independence, Mo.: Harry S. Truman Library, 1972), pp. 136-40(hereafter cited as Dennison, "Reminiscences.")
41. F. P. Matthews, Memorandum for SECDEF, 16 January 1950; Stephen Early to The President, 20 January 1950, F. P. Matthews to Senator Herbert L. Lehman, 18 January 1950, SNP.
42. "Admiral Bogan to Retire," ANJ 87 (7 January 1950):482, and "Admiral Bogan Relieved," ANJ 87 (14 January 1950):510.
43. H. Struve Hensel to Robert Anderson, 20 March 1953, SNP; Robert Frank Futrell, *Ideas, Concepts, Doctrine: A History of Basic Thinking in The United States Air Force, 1907-1964* (Maxwell Air Force Base, Ala.: Air University, Aerospace Studies Institute, 1971), pp. 140-44; Truman, *Memoirs*, 2:306-7; James R. Shepley and Clay Blair, Jr., *The Hydrogen Bomb* (New York: David McKay, 1954), pp. 80-89, 137; LCOL Harry M. Pike, USAF, "Limitations of an Air Defense System," AUQR 3 (Hall, 1949):46-48.
44. Harland B. Moulton, "American Strategic Power: Two Decades of Nuclear Strategy and Weapons Systems, 1945-1965" (Ph.D. diss., University of Minnesota, 1969. Facsimile. Ann Arbor, Mich.: University Microfilms, 1973), pp. 46-47.
45. *Semiannual Report. . .July 1 to December 1, 1949,* pp. 165-95. See also RADM Julius A. Furer, USN (RET), "The Structure of Naval Appropriations Acts," USNIP 74 (December 1948): 1517-27.
46. "Navy's Role in Air Power," AW 52 (27 February 1950):15. By the end of 1950, the Strategic Air Command had among its 961 tactical aircraft 38 B-36s, 282 B-29s and 195 B-50s. (John T. Bohn, *The Development of Strategic Air Command, 1946-1971* [Offut Air Force Base, Neb.: HQ, SAC, 1972], p. 17).
47. "No Supercarrier," ANJ 87 (18 March 1950):754.
48. "Navy Slang Barred," ANJ (11 February 1950):627.
49. Alnav 126, "Public Comments on Other Branches of Armed Forces," NBD 16 (15 November 1950):17; "SECNAV Sets Policy," ANJ 87(11 November 1950): 283.
50. Dan A. Kimball, USECNAV, Memorandum for SECDEF, 20 October, 1949, SNP.
51. "House B-36 Report May Stir New Laws," ANJ 87 (4 March 1950:693, 722 and "Report Urges Restudy of Defense Concepts: Scores Denfeld Relief [complete text of report]," ibid., 708-13, 723-34; *New York Times*, 2 February 1950.
52. Hammond, "Super Carriers and B-36 Bombers," pp. 553-54, and "NSC-68: Prologue to Rearmament," in Warner II. Schilling, Paul Y. Hammond, and Glenn H. Snyder, *Strategy, Politics, and Defense Budgets* (New York: Columbia University Press, 1962), p. 295; Eugene A. Wilson, "A Basis of Unity," USNIP 76 (September 1950):961-67.
53. "Service News and Gossip," ANJ 87 (4 March 1950):707; "Mission of the Navy," ANJ 87 (18 March 1950):755; "CNO's Accomplishment," ibid., p. 759.
54. "Report on Cedric Worth Inquiry," ANJ 87 (February 1950):655; "Report on Cedric Worth Investigation," ANJ 87 (18 March 1950):766; and "End of Cedric Worth Case," ANJ 87 (6 May 1950):959.
55. Denfeld, "Reprisal: Why I Was Fired," *Collier's* 125 (18 March 1950):13-15 62, 64.
56. "Denfeld Strikes Back," ANJ 87 (18 March 1950):766; ADM Louis T. Denfeld, "The Only Carrier the Air Force Ever Sank," *Collier's* 125 (25 March 1950):32-33, 46-47, 50-51.
57. Floberg to the writer, 31, August 1976.

58. "House Group Backs 112 New Navy Ships," ANJ 87 (6 May 1950):957.
59. "House Unanimously Votes More Funds," ANJ 87 (13 May 1950):1005; "Naval Aircraft Purchases," ibid., p. 1001. The B-17 of World War II cost $238,000 each; a B-36 in 1950 cost $5,757,584 each. The B-29 of World War II cost $640,000 each; the Navy's AJ carrier attack which could deliver an atomic bomb, cost $1,105,599—and the Navy had ordered 15 of the last in 1950 alone. The Navy figured it was still short 435 first-line planes, which would cost $650 million to acquire.
60. The development of the Navy's air atomic capability has followed closley *Support Study*, 150-62, and the historical reports of Composite Squadron Five dated 31 December 1948, 1 April 1949, 30 January 1950, and similar reports by Composite Squadron Six dated 31 December 1950 and 15 January 1951, NHD: OA. Insights into the operational problems of carriers and their aircraft were provided in CAPT William C. Chapman, USN (RET), to the writer, 27 September 1975.
61. Floberg to the writer, 31 August 1976.
62. *Semiannual Report . . . for 1950*, pp. 107, 109-26; *New York Times*, 8 February 1950; ANJ 87 (1 July 1950):1181-83.

10
Korea:
Time of Testing,
June 1950-September 1950

On 25 September 1947 the Joint Chiefs of Staff told President Harry S. Truman that "from the standpoint of military security, the United States has little strategic interest in maintaining the present troops and bases in Korea."[1] After the U.N. General Assembly at American request took up the Korean unification problem, the United States sought to train and equip Republic of Korea armed forces so that they could provide security "against any but an overt act of aggression by North Korean or other forces," but by 29 June 1949 it had withdrawn its own occupation forces. Thereafter General Douglas MacArthur, Commander Far East Command, excluded Korea from his mission, saying that "our line of defense . . . starts from the Philippines and continues through the Ryukyu archipelago which includes its broad main bastion, Okinawa. Then it bends back through Japan and the Aleutian Island chain to Alaska."[2]

The defense of Formosa was also deemed to lie outside the American military sphere. On 12 January 1950 Secretary of State Dean G. Acheson said that those subjected to attack outside the perimeter as established by MacArthur must rely initially upon their own strength and then turn to the United Nations for aid. Small wonder the Soviets believed that no American military response would be made to a North Korean invasion of South Korea.

For want of a better definition of national security policy by the National Security Council, "containment of communism" served a useful purpose. In accordance with it, military and economic aid had been granted in 1947 to such nations as Greece and Turkey and to Berlin and Trieste. With such expenditures in mind, on 7 May 1948 Truman had cautioned the Secretary of Defense, James V. Forrestal, that his expenditures must not cut too deeply into the civilian economy or exceed the firm budget limits he himself established.[3]

Forrestal's successor, Louis A. Johnson, would not take orders from the

Department of State and permitted only top leaders in his department to conduct relations with the Department of State because, he alleged, diplomatic arrangements would cause the expenditure of defense dollars and so counter his mandate to economize.[4] His compartmentalization of defense duties is very well expressed in his stating that "When foreign policy is determined, then our line is determined. Within that foreign policy it is our duty to work."[5] In consequence of Johnson's divorcement of military from foreign policy, the Joint Chiefs of Staff avoided expressions about foreign policies and restricted themselves to merely answering questions about their military implications. What was vitally needed, therefore, was a great improvement in the correlation of foreign, domestic, military, and economic policy.

The outbreak of war in "the land of the morning calm" at 0400 on 25 June 1950, Korean time, caught all agencies of the American national security system utterly unawares and unprepared.[6] The United States had no war plan for Korea on 25 June nor time to prepare an estimate of the situation for one.[7] The attack on South Korea gave the Department of Defense its first combat role as a new organization and provided an acid test for the unification of the services and for the policy of containment as well.[8] The test revealed that the national security system did not permit executive effectiveness by the Secretary of Defense nor abate endless argument between the military departments. Indeed, "unification of the Armed Forces, despite its avowed aims, divided the Services into suspicious and viperishly hostile factions."[9] Even with the addition of a chairman, it has been said that the Joint Chiefs "remained primarily a corporate command body asserting authority superior in many fields to that of the Secretaries of the military departments; and secondarily a debating society for the airing of service views (instead of a vigorous strategic planning body) and a sort of staff organization for the Secretary of Defense which was overloaded with minor problems (for instance, expressing a military opinion as to how many coffee roasting plants should be operated by the Army)."[10] By acting as commanders instead of planners, the chiefs weakened the authority of both the Secretary of Defense and the military secretaries to the extent that they only casually cleared their decisions with the Secretary of Defense.[11]

The Korean War upheld the contention of the Navy radicals and of General Omar N. Bradley, who had appealed for a continuing program of military readiness during the cold war, instead of the economizing demanded by Truman, Johnson, and Secretary of the Navy Francis P. Matthews. One admiral snapped, "Louis [Johnson] said we could lick the Russians. He didn't say anything about the North Korean."[12] Asked if he were going to fire Johnson, Truman replied, "He'll be Secretary of Defense as long as I'm President."[13] Truman might talk tough; the point is that the United States had not adopted an effective policy on the Far East, evaluated properly the intelligence reports about the massing over a long period of time of a powerful North Korean force near the border of South Korea,[14] nor spent its defense funds in such a way as to procure military forces adequate to support its interests. Most of the $50 billion spent for defense since the adoption of the National Security Act had gone to the Air Force. Of that sum, $33 billion had gone for military and civilian salaries and only one dollar in seven for arms. Moreover, little had been done to mobilize industry for war or to defend the populace from enemy bombing.[15] With the meat-ax blows delivered by Truman and Johnson, the Navy had its back to the wall. Its 610 amphibious ships in 1945 were reduced to 362 in 1947 and to 81 in 1950—with a 40 percent cut coming during 1950 alone, Johnson's first year as Secretary of Defense. The Marine Corps similarly fought for existence. On Johnson's order, its enlisted strength was cut from 78,715 on 30 June 1949 to 67,025 on 30 June 1950, which meant that it could barely field a brigade and one air group out of two supposedly full divisions and two air wings. Also, the Fleet Marine Force of 35,086 men in 1948 was reduced by Johnson to 23,952 officers and men in 1950, or from two divisions to six infantry battalions in ground fighting strength. And in February 1951 the Chief of Staff of the Air Force, General Hoyt S. Vandenberg, frankly stated that in a determined attack against American defenses, 70 percent of the bombers would reach their objectives.[16] American strategic atomic air power had not prevented an attack on South Korea. If the United States was ready to retaliate against an enemy with the Strategic Air Command, it was unprepared either for following up a strategic attack that did not produce decisive results or for a limited war fought with conventional forces, for Pentagon preparations had aimed at a global war centering in Europe. While the Strategic Air Command could pulverize parts of Russia, American military power would find it extremely difficult to check the veteran and battle-hardened North Korean army in a limited war on the ground in Korea.[17]

On the morning of 25 June 1950 General J. Lawton Collins, Army Chief of Staff, who was the executive agent for the Joint Chiefs of Staff in the Far East, consoled himself by thinking "how fortunate it was for us that the Soviets had picked for this venture the one area in the world where the United States military forces of all arms were well positioned if we should decide to intervene." Although the United States had only a Military Advisory Group in Korea, Army and Air Force elements were stationed in Japan and the Navy had ships in Japanese and other Western Pacific Waters.[18] Similarly, Thomas K. Finletter, Secretary of the Air Force, said that "the enemy came down right under our noses, where we had the greatest concentration of military power outside the United States."[9] Collins and Finletter, and MacArthur and Army Secretary Frank Pace as well, knew, however, that Army troops were tragically short in number, untrained for the type of war they must fight, equipped with obsolete and unserviceable combat weapons and vehicles, lacking the means to knock out the Russian-built T-34 tanks used by the North Koreans, and bereft of training in amphibious operations.[20] MacArthur had asked the Navy and Marine Corps to provide amphibious training for the Eighth Army. In consequence, Colonel Edward S. Forney, USMC, in April 1950 had taken a sixty-seven-man team from San Diego to Japan. In May there arrived Rear Admiral James H. Doyle, Commander Amphibious Group 1, with his headquarters ship, the *Mount McKinley*, and four other ships that carried a tactical air control squadron and detachments of air and naval gunfire liaison teams. A month later the North Koreans attacked.

Far East Air Forces, short of conventional aircraft, troop transports, reconnaissance aircraft, and trained personnel had been concentrating upon the internal security and air defense of Japan but also had responsibility for the air defense of Okinawa, the Philippines, and the Marianas. Moreover, its F-80 jet fighters had a combat radius of only one hundred miles; all planes had to use fields in Japan until South Korean fields were provided with fuel and maintenance facilities by the Army; and ground-to-air communications had to be established for use with frontline troops.[21] It was time to reconsider the national strategy recommended by the Air Force and note that·conventional forces would be needed if a nuclear stalemate portended the fighting only of limited wars, and perhaps to substitute nuclear-tipped guided missiles for manned bombers.

On 12 June Johnson and Bradley had begun a thirteen-day inspection tour of the Far East. While in Tokyo Bradley asked Rear Admiral Doyle what he was doing there. Doyle explained that he was there at MacArthur's request to give amphibious training to units of the Eighth Army. "Bradley simply looked scornful." Shortly thereafter, during a visit with Rear Admiral Charles Turner Joy in MacArthur's office, Doyle mentioned Bradley's attitude, which was in keeping with his having told Carl Vinson's House Naval Affairs Committee in October 1949 that amphibious operations were passé. "It was then MacArthur's turn to be scornful. He said: 'Bradley is a farmer.' "[22]

Upon his return to Washington on 25 June Johnson told newspapermen that "we have seen all our important commands in the Far East and I think we've got the facts."[23] Meanwhile Truman had left the capital for a visit to Independence, Missouri. While he was in flight, about 110,000 North Korean soldiers with over 1,400 artillery pieces and 126 Russian-made T-34 medium tanks and supported by about a hundred Yak and Stormovik tactical aircraft, crossed the 38th parallel into South Korea, which had only 98,000 men under arms, no tanks, no heavy guns, and no supporting aircraft. About a third of the Republic of Korea Army was on leave; most of the American advisory group—five hundred strong—were spending the weekend in Seoul. The American ambassador to Korea, John J. Muccio, cabled word of the attack at about 0930 (0830 Washington time) to Washington and also to MacArthur in Tokyo. One can only surmise the dismay of Johnson, who had not learned while in the Far East that a North Korean assault was imminent.

After notifying the United Nations of the North Korean attack, Secretary of State Acheson telephoned Truman the "bad news." Truman replied, "Dean, we've got to stop the sons of bitches no matter what."[24] Truman flew back to Washington and was briefed by Acheson and Johnson during the ride from the airport into town. At a meeting held at the temporary White House, Blair House, Truman sat with the service secretaries, Johnson, the Joint Chiefs of

Staff, and Acheson and other leaders in the Department of State. At Truman's request and much to Johnson's displeasure, Acheson presented the views of the Joint Chiefs. It was decided to evacuate the approximately fifteen hundred civilian Americans in Korea by sea and air, start the Seventh Fleet north from the Philippines to establish a neutrality patrol between Formosa and the Chinese mainland, and increase the flow of American ammunition and supplies in Japan to South Korea. Then the Joint Chiefs prepared directives for MacArthur, which were dispatched following presidential approval.[27]

On the morning of the twenty-sixth Johnson conferred with his deputy, Stephen T. Early, his Special Assistant for Military Affairs and Assistance, Major General James H. Burns, USA, the service secretaries, and the Joint Chiefs of Staff. Although Korea was central to their thought, for they discussed the pros and cons of permitting operations north of the 38th parallel, they indicated that "they were not losing sight of what they regarded as the larger theater of the 'cold war'—Europe."[28] After Acheson prepared recommended courses of action for Korea, Truman called for a second meeting, at 0900 at Blair House, of essentially the same men who had conferred the previous evening, with Matthews, however, not appearing until after the meeting adjourned. By the time the U.N. Security Council had branded North Korea as an aggressor, Acheson's recommendations to give naval and air support to South Korea, increase military aid to the Philippines and to Indochina, and neutralize Formosa had been adopted and MacArthur was so informed. MacArthur was also directed to use his naval and air forces to aid South Korea, but these must remain south of the 38th parallel in order to keep the action limited and not invite Soviet or Chinese intervention.[27]

The Chief of Naval Operations, Forrest Sherman, and Vandenberg felt that sea and air power would suffice to halt the North Koreans, even though some air power devotees would rely upon that power alone. The former Secretary of the Air Force, W. Stuart Symington, advised the prompt settlement of problems with the Soviets while the United States still enjoyed an advantage in atomic air power. However, as Truman put it, the Joint Chiefs of Staff "did not feel that atomic advantage was a sufficient guarantee to deter the Soviets,"[28] If, MacArthur said, Formosa could be used, the United States would have a chain of air bases in the Western Pacific that would "permit the United States to dominate with air power every Asiatic port from Vladivostok to Singapore."[29] The Commander of the Far East Air Force Bomber Command, Major General Emmett O'Donnell, Jr., believed that five groups of B-29s using incendiary bombs could destroy everything in North Korea in three months. His superior, General George E. Stratemeyer, vetoed his suggestion because of overriding political and diplomatic considerations.[30] Most outspoken was Major General Orvil Anderson, Commandant of the Air War College, already on record as an advocate of preventive war against Russia, who reportedly told a newspaperman that "We're at war, damn it. Give me the order to do it and I can break up Russia's five A-bomb nests in a week." He was immediately suspended from duty and shortly thereafter he

During the early days of the Korean War, Truman's major advisers on diplomatic and military matters were the Secretary of State, Dean C. Acheson; the Secretary of the Navy, Francis P. Matthews; the Secretary of the Army, former Director of the Bureau of the Budget Frank Pace, Jr. *(above)*; and the Chief of Naval Operations, Forrest Sherman. Commanding United Nations forces in the Far East was General of the Army Douglas MacArthur *(below left)*. General Matthew B. Ridgway, USA, was in command of Operation Killer until he became Supreme Allied Commander, Europe *(right)*.

OFFICIAL U.S. ARMY PHOTOGRAPHS

requested retirement.[31] After the war Lieutenant General Albert C. Wedemeyer, USAF, asserted that he thought that "we Americans are surface-minded. We think in terms of the Army and Navy, and not up in the air with the new weapons that science has given us. I think that punitive action should have been taken with the Air Force, instead of putting ground forces in Korea."[34] General Collins, however, had stated that American ground forces would be needed if the army of the Republic of Korea was badly hurt, and his advice was taken into consideration by the administration.

On Tuesday, 27 June, Truman had representatives of the State and Defense departments brief selected congressional leaders. Among other things, the congressmen were told that no consideration was being given at the moment to the use of ground troops. On the twenty-eighth the service secretaries and Joint Chiefs of Staff considered courses of action that Russia and perhaps Red China might take.

On Thursday, the twenty-ninth, Johnson asked the National Security Council, which Truman called into session at his request, to advise the President to authorize MacArthur to extend his air and naval operations to North Korea, to employ Army service forces in South Korea, and also to use combat infantrymen to protect Korea's main southern port, Pusan. The commitment of ground troops was aimed at the preservation of public order and the evacuation of Americans. Meanwhile, however, after visiting the front lines and suggesting the employment of ground troops, MacArthur read his orders as permissive rather than restrictive and ordered naval and air action against North Korea. Johnson supported MacArthur and Truman approved the limited use of ground troops and the extension of naval and air activity to North Korea. A few hours after he had done so, MacArthur recommended the use of troops for offensive action in the combat area. At about 0500 on the thirtieth, Truman approved the use of a single regimental combat team and told MacArthur that he would seek advice on providing the two divisions he wanted. General Collins talked with Admiral Sherman and General Vandenberg. Sherman hesitated to commit infantrymen against Asiatics on the Asiatic mainland but said that their use in Korea was "unavoidable" and "sound" and recommended the extension of a naval blockade north of the 38th parallel. Truman called another full-scale conference for 0930. On the day before, Chiang Kai-shek had offered the use of thirty-three thousand men. Truman's advisers counseled spurning the offer, and Truman, by rescinding his orders to MacArthur of the twenty-ninth, approved the use of Army forces in Korea. At the end of one week, thus, the United States was fully committed in Korea.[33]

Truman had not as yet consulted the National Security Council with respect to Korea because it had no contingency plans for that country, and its formal processes were too cumbersome to permit the reaching of speedy decisions. After 6 July, however, he directed that all recommendations on Korea be forwarded to him via the council.[34]

Early in 1950 Truman had agreed with the service secretaries on the need to reexamine the "entire military posture" for dark days ahead in light of the Soviets' possession of the A-bomb, even though the budget people in the Office of the Secretary of Defense rather than they or the Joint Chiefs of Staff "unified" the military budget. Similar feelings in other high quarters resulted in the writing of National Security Council paper No. 68. Its authors considered four possible courses of action to follow during the next five years that would provide the United States with security against the Soviets: maintain the status quo with the slow-paced defense programs at hand; the Fortress America concept, or isolationism; preventive war designed to preclude the Soviets from building a nuclear arsenal; and political, psychological, economic, and military programs to reach, "if possible, a tolerable state of order among nations without war and of preparing to defend ourselves in the event that the free world is attacked." The resulting paper called for increasing annual defense spending from the approximately 6 percent of the national income in 1949 to 20 percent by 1954, or from $17 billion to $18 billion up to a level of $35 billion to $50 billion. It was the work of a State-Defense study group in which neither Johnson nor the service secretaries had been involved, and only a delegate from the Joint Strategic Survey Committee of the Joint Staff represented the Joint Chiefs of Staff. When briefed on the paper, Johnson became infuriated because his subordinates had not kept him informed and had undercut him. When Truman was alerted to the study, however, he ordered it continued. Having secured approval for their paper from all the service secretaries and the Joint Chiefs of Staff, the study group had outmaneuvered Johnson, who very reluctantly signed the document and sent it to Truman on 4 April.[35] On the twelfth Truman approved and forwarded it to the National Security Council with the request that the council estimate the forces needed to implement it and what it would cost. On 1 July Johnson ordered studies made of the estimates called for in NSC-68 to be completed by 1 November, since the deadline for submitting the fiscal year 1952 budget was 1 December. Because of the danger that the Russians might break out into central Europe, Truman directed on 10 December that the buildup suggested by NSC-68 be moved back to 1952.[36]

In consequence of his looking at the Korean War not as an isolated instance but as part of a global problem, early in July 1950 Vandenberg tripled the strength of the Strategic Air Command in England. Between July and October he sent an atomic B-29 group to Guam and another to bases in Newfoundland and Labrador and 180 F-84Es to Germany in addition to dispatching four B-29 groups to Korea. With the exactly eighteen large industrial targets in North Korea destroyed, two of the last were returned to the United States in October, although the appearance of MIGs caused the sending of a Strategic Air Command F-84 jet fighter escort wing and a Far Eastern Air Defense Force F-86 fighter-interceptor wing to Korea. It was the exploitation of its maritime supremacy, however, that enabled the United States to furnish the men, weapons, and supplies needed by all of its military services in Korea.

On 30 June, as already noted, Truman approved the use of the Eighth

Army. In consequence of advice from the Joint Chiefs of Staff, moreover, he directed that the Seventh Fleet, which was based in the Philippines, be placed under MacArthur's operational command and prevent a communist invasion of Formosa and also a Nationalist Chinese attack upon the China mainland. In addition he agreed to the strengthening of American forces in the Philippines and to the giving of increased aid to the French in Indochina.[37]

The American naval chain of command in the Pacific included, under the Chief of Naval Operations, Arthur W. Radford as Commander in Chief, Pacific Fleet, and Joy as Commander U.S. Naval Forces Far East. On 2 February Sherman had told reporters in Tokyo that he would build up the Navy in the Pacific "within the means available," yet in June the Seventh Fleet consisted of only one carrier, one cruiser, a destroyer squadron, and a submarine division.

When notified of the North Korean attack, Sherman radioed Radford: "Be ready to move Seventh Fleet north on short notice when and if directed." Radford replied that the Seventh Fleet would be ready to move on six hours' notice.[38]

On 25 June Admiral Joy had on loan from the Seventh Fleet only a light cruiser, four destroyers, five small amphibious ships, and six mine-sweepers. Upon learning of the North Korean attack, he ordered his ships readied for sea. He had no naval air because naval aviation was centered at Guam with certain elements of the Seventh Fleet. However, he needed not worry about the North Korean Navy, comprised only of light craft and fishing boats, and could assure command of the sea about Korea to United Nations forces. Radford had only three carriers. He ordered the *Boxer*, loaded with 145 F-51s to supplement Far East Air Forces aircraft, to proceed from the west coast of the United States to Korea and directed other ships in the continental United States to prepare for extended operations with the Seventh Fleet. The latter, under Vice Admiral Arthur Dewey "Rip" Struble, from a base in Okinawa established the neutrality patrol in Formosa Strait, starting 29 June. To help defend Formosa from invasion by Communist Chinese, who had 250,000 troops and 5,000 small ships on the mainland opposite Formosa, Far East Air Force contributed three jet squadrons. Since the jets were ordered to Formosa by MacArthur without the knowledge of the Pentagon, Acheson quickly had Truman send him orders that emphasized the limits of American policy with respect to Formosa. When MacArthur then planned to send to the annual convention of the Veterans of Foreign Wars a message stressing the strategic importance of that island, Truman directed Johnson to order him to withdraw the message. When Johnson said that the order would embarrass MacArthur, Truman told him to send the order forthwith.[39] When certain military operations, such as the air bombing of Racin, seventeen miles from the Russian border, violated directives "to stay well clear" of the Soviet border, Johnson upheld the military and refused prior consultation with the Department of State on such operations. Acheson was out of town but, in Johnson's words, "I got quite a strong letter . . . from Jim Webb as the Acting

Secretary of State.''[40] Thereafter Truman himself brought Acheson and Johnson into consultation.

Because it was assumed that the attack on South Korea was only a *ruse de guerre* designed to draw American power away from Europe, where the Russians might launch a major thrust, a second carrier task force was sent to the Mediterranean, four divisions were dispatched to bolster NATO, the production of American guided missiles and of nuclear weapons was greatly accelerated, and negotiations were begun for airfields for SAC bombers in French Morocco and Greenland and for air and naval bases in Spain. By the end of the year, moreover, it was arranged that an integrated NATO force would be put under the supreme command of an American officer. Upon request, Truman named General Dwight D. Eisenhower to be Supreme Allied Commander Europe. Greece and Turkey were admitted to NATO in September 1951. Although France kept West Germany out of NATO, NATO had greatly improved its position for carrying out its "forward strategy," that is, to repel a Soviet invasion as far to the east as possible, by the time the Korean War ended. Meanwhile the air defenses on the West Coast of the United States and of Canada as well were improved by the creation of the North American Defense Command.

To Johnson's request for the views of the Joint Chiefs of Staff on legislation adding the Commandant of the Marine Corps to the Joint Chiefs of Staff and rotating its chairman, Bradley had replied that the Joint Chiefs were unanimously opposed on both points. Johnson and Matthews agreed wholeheartedly and in addition opposed the creation of an Assistant Secretary of the Navy to handle Marine Corps Affairs.[41] Following the outbreak of war in Korea, the Commandant of the Corps, General Clifton B. Cates, noted that Secretary of the Navy Matthews had canceled the daily meetings held with him and others. When Matthews resumed his meetings, he failed to call Cates. Cates therefore went to Sherman, saying, "Forrest, it looks like the Army's 24th Division is in a pretty bad spot over there. We can furnish a brigade by draining our two divisions." Sherman asked, "How soon could you have them ready?"

"We can have them ready as quickly as the Navy gets the ships," Cates replied.

"All right," said Sherman, who said he would notify Admiral Joy and MacArthur that the Marines could send a brigade and an air group.[42]

A few days later MacArthur requested the Joint Chiefs of Staff to send not a brigade but a division, adding, "Earliest arrival here imperative." When the Joint Chiefs telegraphed to San Diego, they were told that a battalion landing team could sail in forty-eight hours and a regimental landing team in five days. The Marines in San Diego were bluffing because they lacked enough men, but Cates showed up uninvited at a meeting of the Joint Chiefs of 3 July and won approval for the use of his Corps even at the risk of leaving the East Coast and the Atlantic Fleet practically denuded of Marines. He directed some units to proceed from Camp Lejeune, Virginia, to Camp Pendleton, California, formed a brigade of 6,800 men including air and ground, and had them sailing out of San Diego on 14 July. Although the Joint Chiefs of Staff obtained Truman's approval to mobilize the Marine Corps Reserve, on 19 July, Admiral Sherman and General Vandenberg tried to prevent the use of the Marine Corps's thirty aviation squadrons. Vandenberg's thinking is easy to follow. Although he gave no reasons for disliking the Marines, Sherman may have gone along with Vandenberg because he had been denied command of the Marine Corps by the veto of Secretary Matthews. At any rate, it took "a plain, forceful, and harsh" meeting on 31 July among Vinson, Sherman, and Matthews before Sherman announced not only that the reserve aviation squadrons would be mobilized but that the Corps would grow to two war-strength divisions and eighteen squadrons.[43]

A similar battle was fought over whether the First Marine Division would be comprised of two regiments, as Johnson and the Joint Chiefs of Staff desired, or of three, as MacArthur and Cates wished. Carl Vinson, chairman of the House Armed Services Committee, again entered the breach—and in early August Sherman directed that the First Marines would be comprised of three regiments. For its commander, Cates chose the Assistant Commandant of the Marine Corps, Major General Oliver Prince Smith. It was Lieutenant General Lemuel C. Shepherd, Jr., Commanding General, Pacific Fleet Marine Force, who directed Major General Field Harris to move his First Marine Aircraft Wing Headquarters to Korea and assume command of Marine tactical aircraft operations therein.[44]

The First Marines landed at Pusan on 2 August. Five days later they saw their first action, just west of Masan, with Marine fighters from the escort carriers *Badoeng Strait* and *Sicily* providing them close ground support. Foresightedly, the Marines had reconditioned surplus World War II jeeps, tanks, trucks, and amtracs and stored them in dry climate near Pendleton and San Diego. Since the Marines were never picky about gear they "liberated," they occasionally used some green paint to obliterate Army OD and Navy gray.[45]

On 2 July, before the First Provisional Marine Brigade and its aviation, Marine Air Group 33, could arrive in Korea to reinforce the Army's 24th Division, and before the First Cavalry could be transported thereto by the Navy from Japan, Far Eastern Air Force Major General Earle M. Partridge committed one medium and one light bomber wing and eight fighter squadrons to Korea and Truman ordered a close naval blockade of the entire Korean peninsula. On the eighth, in consequence of the creation by the United Nations of a unified Korean command, Truman named MacArthur its supreme commander but disapproved his urgent call for additional troops, arms, and supplies. Indeed, Truman would spend less for Korea than for improving mobilization and deterrent strength in the United States and in Western Europe, as already indicated. For three months after the war began,

Johnson was still trying to "economize," and his relations with the Department of State, it has been said, "remained as cold as if they represented opposite sides in a war."[46]

Only sixteen of the sixty member nations of the United Nations sent armed contingents to Korea, most of them small. At any rate, British, Australian, and Canadian fleet units joined American naval forces in patrolling the fifty-four hundred miles of Korean coastline, enforcing the blockade, attacking enemy naval vessels and shore installations, bombarding shore targets, and preventing enemy amphibious operations. Particularly effective were air strikes flown from American carriers. Each carrier had three fighter-bomber squadrons and one attack or dive-bomber squadron, the latter equipped to carry torpedoes, bombs, or rockets. The fighters were the old propeller-driven, bent-wing F4U *Corsairs*, F9F *Panther* jets, and the newer F2H *Banshee* jets, with the jets being launched for the first time in combat from aircraft carriers. The *Corsair* was also used by two Marine air squadrons flying from two escort carriers, beginning 2 August. The rugged propeller-driven, single-engine carrier plane that could carry more bombs than a B-17, the AD Skyraider, first battle-tested in Korea, became the workhorse of the air war. Also, patrols were flown by the new land-based P2V-5 "sub-killer" and new P5M-1, along Korea's coasts, where both submarines and surface craft were expected to lurk.[47] Naval men in addition conducted commando raids, minesweeping operations, shore bombardment, and amphibious landings, and provided vital tactical air support for Army and Marine forces on the ground while the Military Sea Transportation Servce bridged seven thousand miles of ocean with ships that funneled huge amounts of supplies to ports in Japan, Okinawa, and Korea. Escort carriers brought replacement aircraft and spare parts. By 15 August 1950, MATS had transported forty-thousand men, five-hundred thousand tons of military cargo, and two million barrels of petroleum products to Korea alone. By May 1951 seven-hundred thousand tons of supplies per month were reaching Korea.

American troops sent to Korea from Japan were soon pressed southward by their more numerous and powerful foes, eventually to a fifty-mile perimeter about the port of Pusan. While Seventh Fleet naval gunfire and carrier aircraft helped protect the perimeter, additional Army and Marine Corps men landed in safety and held the enemy at bay until they were ready to break out.

To keep the war limited, Truman not only spurned the offer of troops by Chiang Kai-shek but announced on 27 July that he would not permit the use of atomic bombs.[48] Having alerted Red China that he would not use his most powerful weapon, he changed the course of the war in Korea and in addition may have changed the course of history in Southeast Asia.

After ten months of squabbling over the size and composition of the Air Force and the Army, Congress finally reached agreement on 22 June 1950. The Army and Air Force Authorization Act of 1949 that Truman signed on 10 July authorized the Army to have 837,000 officers and men and the Air Force 502,000 officers and men and seventy-group strength (or 24,000 aircraft so long as they did not exceed 225,000 tons of airframe weight). To keep tabs on all phases of the national war effort, the Senate on 27 July created a special preparedness subcommittee of the Senate Armed Services Committee, Lyndon B. Johnson chairman. Among the duties of the subcommittee were "to keep a continuous watchfulness on the rearmament program, explore bottlenecks and shortages, and eliminate duplicating investigations."[49]

Truman originally did not contemplate calling reservists to active duty. At his request, however, Congress removed the budgetary ceiling on military personnel strength, then extended Selective Service for a year, to 9 July 1951, extended enlistments for twelve months, and also authorized the involuntary recall of reserve and retired military personnel for a maximum of twenty-one months. With time short for training new men and with mothers protesting the drafting of their eighteen-year-old sons for combat duty, many veterans of World War II were again dislocated from their civilian careers. By mid-April 1951 40 percent of the First Marine Division in Korea, 30 percent of the First Marine Air Wing, and 25 percent of the men in Navy ships and planes in the Far East were reservists. In the Air Force 71 percent of its officers on active duty and 72 percent of those on duty with Far East Air Forces were reservists. On 19 June 1951 Selective Service was extended to 1955, leaving universal military training for future consideration. By that time the Army had been increased from 592,000 to 1.6 million men.[50]

At a meeting of the Joint Chiefs of Staff with the Senate Armed Services Committee, Chairman Millard E. Tydings commended the Navy for its prompt action in strengthening American forces in the Far East. The commendation was amply warranted, for the Navy responded quickly in its first expansion since World War II by demothballing forty-eight combatant ships and taking out of storage and rehabilitating a number of carrier-based aircraft. In the eighteen months prior to the outbreak of war in Korea, the Navy had lost about sixty-five thousand officers and enlisted men and about 10 percent of its combatant ships. Now the ships it had wisely mothballed during the demobilization following World War II—"fighting ships on the leash"—proved to be a "secret weapon."[51] Between June and October 1950 it added 1 light carrier, 1 escort carrier, and a cruiser to the Atlantic Fleet and 2 heavy carriers, 1 escort carrier, 1 battleship, and 2 cruisers to the Pacific Fleet and increased the number of destroyers from 172 to 200. By June 1952 it had added 4 battleships, 12 aircraft carriers, 6 cruisers, more than 100 destroyer types, 25 submarines, and auxiliaries for a total of 500 ships, with an additional 140 under construction. The only photography aircraft in the Far East Command when the war started, incidentally, was a pair of "photo jo" Marine Corsairs on the carrier *Valley Forge.*[52]

General Shepherd was among the first to see a number of paradoxes in the air war in Korea. As he reported,

> B-29's are employed against tactical targets to the dissatisfaction of all
> concerned—the Air Force because of misemployment of its planes, and the

ground forces because of the results achieved. Carrier aircraft, despite the wealth of close support targets available, were committed against deep and semi-strategic targets. Jet fighters, with little enemy air to engage, have been assigned to close support work despite a fuel restriction which holds them to no more than 15 minutes in the combat zone. Only a very limited number of aircraft adaptable to tactical support missions are available (F-51 and B-26) and there appears to be urgent need for suitable close support aircraft along with competent air-ground liaison units.[53]

Until they were provided with wing tanks, Air Force jet fighters operating from Japanese fields could spend from five to twenty minutes over a Korean target area, and their pilots were untrained in the support of combat troops, whereas Navy and Marine fighters from nearby carriers could stay over a target for almost two hours and performed well in support of ground units. The Army clearly preferred Navy and Marine Corps to Air Force air support.[54] As has been said, "Lack of target information for the [Air Force] bombers and the limited capabilities of Air Force fighters placed great premium upon carrier-borne aviation. Never, perhaps, had the virtues of free movement upon the face of the waters shone so brightly, even to those who had long derided this instrument of war."[55] Marine Corps divisions with their own integrated air support became important bulwarks of defense. These were the same Marines that the Army's Bradley and Collins had called obsolete a year earlier and Sherman had wished abolished. Indeed, 97 percent of the casualties to be suffered in Korea were accounted for by the Army and Marine Corps. Among the American forces that fought in Korea, it has been said, only the Marines went "the North Koreans one better in morale, esprit de corps, and the ability to travel light—and fast. . . ."[56]

To examine the feasibility of the amphibious landing at Inchon that MacArthur proposed on 4 July, which Bradley strongly opposed because he believed amphibious operations to be obsolete, the Joint Chiefs of Staff planned to send Admiral Sherman and General Collins "not so much to discuss but to dissuade him," as MacArthur put it, and to talk also with such others as Admirals Struble, Joy, and Doyle, Major General Oliver P. Smith, USMC, Lieutenant General Shepherd, and General Stratemeyer. Collins and Vandenberg flew to Tokyo on 13 July; believing that he was needed in Washington, Sherman asked Radford to represent him. Because the Pusan perimeter was not yet secure, MacArthur's plan for an amphibious landing at Inchon on 22 July, Operation *Bluehearts*, was canceled.[57] Collins opposed the use of Marines and alleged that the lack of shipping would make it impossible to bring the Marine Division offered by Shepherd to Korea. The commander of the Military Sea Transportation Service, however, stated that shipping was available. Moreover, Shepherd suggested that MacArthur use the First Marine Division, which he said he could have ready to be lifted out of Pusan on 1 September. Worried about a Russian breakout in central Europe, Collins told MacArthur, "General, you are going to have to win the war out here with the troops available to you in Japan and Korea." MacArthur replied, "Joe, you are going to have to change your mind." Assured by Radford and Shepherd that a complete Marine division would reach Korea and could be used at Inchon, Collins did change his mind.[58]

On 23 August, among others, Collins, Sherman, and Lieutenant General Idwal H. Edwards, USAF, representing the Joint Chiefs of Staff, Admirals Radford, Doyle, and Joy—but no leading Marine Corps representative—had "an audience" with MacArthur, who realized that it was Sherman he must convince to provide the ships, troops, and professional naval skill that would spell success at Inchon. Since Sherman had already told "Rip" Struble that he was "going to back the Inchon operation completely,"[59] he was not convinced to do so by the fervid oration in which MacArthur may have won others over to support Operation *Chromite,* which he characterized as a "5000-to-1 gamble."[60]

Chromite was planned by the Joint Strategic Plans and Operation Group of Far Eastern Command Headquarters, an agency discussed briefly in the next chapter. Enough to say at this point that naval and Marine Corps leaders were keenly aware of the myriad difficulties that they would face while Army leaders who had amphibious training, experience, or even an understanding of amphibious operations were rare indeed. For example, Major General Edward M. Almond, MacArthur's chief of staff, saw the amphibious landing as "a simple mechanical operation that led to the desired objective, the overland capture of Seoul" and, as MacArthur told General Shepherd on 24 August, a capture that "would quickly end the war." However, MacArthur told General O. P. Smith that the Marines would win the war and that there could be no question as to the future of the Corps after such a victory. Upon Collins's return to Washington, he and Sherman briefed Bradley and Vandenberg; on 28 August, with Johnson's blessing, the Joint Chiefs of Staff sent MacArthur their approval for operation *Chromite.*[61]

After the brilliant Inchon operation, Matthews provided input into a proposed surrender message that MacArthur would deliver to the North Koreans. Considered were terms for surrender, occupation, and political action in the post-hostilities period.[62] He also noted a memorandum from the Department of State that stated that while Inchon might cause the North Koreans to agree to an armistice or surrender, it might also provoke Soviet or Chinese communist intervention, and he asked for consideration of what the United States must do in such case.[63] MacArthur had won a military victory in the field. However, the announcement that the United States would not use atomic weapons in Korea told the Chinese communists that UN forces would use only conventional weapons if the decision was made to unify Korea by military operations north of the 38th parallel.

During his eighteen months in office, Johnson was subjected to a great deal of criticism. Representative Anthony F. Tauriello (D., N.Y.), for example, in late August 1951 told him that he should resign because he had bungled the job of national defense through false economy . . . lost the confidence of the American people, and . . . [embarrassed] the Chief Executive." When interviewed in 1971, Admiral Robert L. Dennison was asked how he would rate Johnson as a Secretary of Defense.

> DENNISON: Just about as poor as you possibly could.
> [Jerry N.] HESS: Why would you give him such a low rating? What did he do, or not do?
> DENNISON: Well he nearly wrecked the armed services. And one thing he did, cutting down on money and running them downhill much too fast. Of course, he couldn't foresee Korea, but that's the kind of a situation we're supposed to be ready to handle.
> HESS: In his reduction of the armed forces, do you think he was just carrying out the orders that had been handed him and had been formulated by others, or was he carrying this out with the zeal that might indicate that he felt the services should be cut back?
> DENNISON: Oh, I think the latter is undoubtedly the case.[65]

As noted below, Johnson resigned in September, and Matthews was not to enjoy his own position much longer. As Truman stated, "Every decision I made in connection with the Korean conflict had this one aim in mind: to prevent a third world war and the terrible destruction it would bring to the civilized world. This meant that we should not do anything that would provide the excuse to the Soviets and plunge the free nations into full-scale all-out war."[66] Matthews did not take the hint and ended his usefulness to the administration on 25 August by demanding a preventive war in an address before one hundred thousand people at the celebration marking the sesquicentennial of the Boston Naval Shipyard.[67] According to Hanson Baldwin, Matthews's speech was a trial balloon in behalf of Johnson, who had been "selling the doctrine of preventive war in private conversation around Washington."[68] At any rate, viewing Matthews's departure as certain, naval aviators hoped he would be succeeded by the former Army pilot Dan A. Kimball, the Under Secretary of the Navy.

Truman "fired" Johnson before he did Matthews. Johnson, on a speaking tour, learned that a "White House spokesman" had disclosed that he was through. He rushed back to Washington to tell Truman that without his backing the Pentagon would not follow his orders. "Well, Louis, if you feel that way about it, in your resignation, mention George Marshall as your successor."[69] As a newspaperman told it, "Grim, white-faced, with tears in his eyes, Johnson returned to the Pentagon, picked up a pencil and did as instructed."[70] Ironically, although American military forces were unprepared for the Korean War largely because Truman and Congress cut defense funds, Johnson wrote his resignation while MacArthur planned to outflank the communists with an amphibious landing at Inchon just three days later. But Johnson was fired less for his misdirection of the military effort at the Pentagon than, as Representative Vinson saw it, his being too steeped in politics to put defense first, and for foot-dragging and such unbelievably crude actions in working with Secretary of State Acheson and other officials that he received a bad press and Truman came to see him as an expendable liability.[71] He was also beautifully set up as a fall guy for Truman. Acheson believed that he was mentally ill. "Johnson's behavior," he said, "had passed beyond the peculiar to the impossible."[72] Several years later Johnson underwent an operation for a brain malady that eventually proved fatal.

On 12 September, Truman accepted the resignation offered by Deputy Secretary of Defense Early, who had served much longer than the year he had bargained for. On that very day Johnson also submitted his resignation, saying that while the unification of the armed forces was accomplished to a great degree and the nation was rearmed to fight in Korea, "the country should have a Secretary of Defense who does not suffer under the handicap of the enemies I have acquired." He then recommended that his successor be General of the Army Marshall—"a man of such stature that the very act of naming him will promote national and international unity."

To many Americans and particularly to its military men, Johnson's relief by Marshall was considered a blessing. "Everybody seemed happy," declared General Shepherd, and MacArthur thought the choice of Marshall a good one.[73]

On 15 September, Congress approved Truman's request to exempt Marshall from the provision of the National Security Act that forbade the appointment as Secretary of Defense of any regular officer who had been on active duty within ten years. With the change of the top defense leaders, the service secretaries and others were expected to offer their pro forma resignations. Truman, however, stated that no decisions on changes would be made until he had talked with Marshall.[74]

Marshall, approaching seventy years of age, was sworn in as the third Secretary of Defense on 20 September, but he said nothing about bringing new men into the defense establishment. On 28 September Truman named Robert A. Lovett as Deputy Secretary of Defense. Lovett, a naval aviator in World War I and for twenty years a businessman, had also served as Assistant Secretary of War for Air in World War II, when Marshall had been Chief of Staff of the Army, and as Assistant Secretary of State when Marshall had been the Secretary of State. While Pace and Finletter were expected to stay, rumor had it that Matthews would grasp the occasion to resign in order to accept a diplomatic post. He did not do so. Neither did he say anything about the hope that with Marshall as Secretary of Defense and the end of defense fund cutbacks the building of a supercarrier might follow. It was Vinson who obtained Truman's approval and introduced a bill to build one.[75] With her atomic-laden, long-range bombers, the Navy would break the monopoly the Air Force had on strategic bombing even though strategic bombing would remain a secondary rather than primary mission.

While Marshall temporarily continued in effect all the official actions and organizational framework of Johnson, it was suspected if not hoped in some quarters that he would decentralize somewhat the various prerogatives

Johnson had taken from the service secretaries and put under the Office of the Secretary of Defense and also would permit the Joint Chiefs of Staff, through him, to tell the President and Congress what they thought the military budget should be. By getting rid of the "gauleiters" with whom Johnson had surrounded himself and acquiring a staff of experienced and cooperative men, Marshall soon restored morale in the Pentagon and also renewed cooperation between the Department of State and the Department of Defense, for Acheson revered and loved his former chief.[76]

Whereas Secretary of Defense Louis A. Johnson divorced military concerns from diplomatic matters and failed to win the loyalty of his workers, General George C. Marshall, his successor, quickly restored morale in the Department of Defense. Moreover, while Johnson and Secretary of State Dean G. Acheson were antipathetic, Acheson got along well with his former chief in the Department of State. Shown having lunch at the Pentagon on 12 October 1950 are Marshall *(to the left)* and Acheson *(to the right)*.
OFFICIAL DEPARTMENT OF DEFENSE PHOTOGRAPH

During its first three years of operation, the National Security Act had failed to provide the desired unification either among the agencies charged with developing national security policies or among the armed services. For these deficiencies Louis A. Johnson was most culpable, for he separated military from foreign affairs and so economized in the Department of Defense that the armed services were incapable of supporting national policies. A restructuring was also needed so that the Joint Chiefs of Staff would deal with policies and plans instead of command functions. Reliance upon a single weapon and single delivery system—atomic bombing by the Air Force—failed to prevent aggression against South Korea, and Truman's vetoing the use of atomic bombs in Korea predicated that only a conventional war would be fought there—a point of great interest, particularly to Red China.

The outbreak of war in Korea showed that the U.S. Army was unready for war and sadly lacked training in, and the capability to conduct, amphibious operations, and that the Air Force was unable to provide adequate tactical air support for ground troops. By obtaining and maintaining control of the sea, the U.S. Navy made Air Force and Army operations possible in Korea. Despite opposition to them by the Army and Sherman, the Marines were called upon to land amphibiously at Inchon—and to fight elsewhere. Marine carrier-based and later land-based air vied with naval air in providing the kind of tactical air support relished by ground troops. Aircraft carriers again proved their great worth, and the building of the *Forrestal* would greatly increase the Navy's strategic bombing capability, a strength useful in case of war with the Soviet Union. If the unification of the military services caused more controversy than cooperation during the first year of the Korean War, the replacement of Johnson and Marshall presaged cooperation between the Department of State and the Department of Defense necessary to define and implement national security policy.

NOTES

1. Robert Frank Futrell, *Ideas, Concepts, Doctrine: A History of Basic Thinking in the United States Air Force 1907-1964* (Maxwell Air Force Base, Ala.: Air University, 1971), p. 139.
2. Ibid., pp. 136, 149; U.S. Department of State. *The Record of Korean Unification, 1943-1960* (Washington: Department of State Publication 7084, 1966), pp. 1-15; Allen S. Whiting, *China Crosses the Yalu: The Decision to Enter the Korean War* (New York: Macmillan, 1960), p. 39.
3. U.S. Congress. Senate Committee on Foreign Relations and Senate Committee on Armed Services, *Hearings on the Military Situation in the Far East*, 5 parts. 82nd Cong., 1st Sess. (Washington: GPO, 1951), 2:1110, 3:1672; 4:2612-13 (hereafter cited as MSFE).
4. Ibid., 4:2594-95, 2687-95, 2690.
5. U.S. Congress. House of Representatives. *Department of Defense Appropriations for 1951*, 81st Cong., 2d Sess. (Washington: GPO, 1951), pt. 1, p. 66.
6. Top Secret. James S. Lay, Jr., Memorandum for the National Security Council, July 6, 1950, SNP; transcript of oral interview by Benis M. Frank of GEN Vernon Megee, USMC (RET) (Washington: HQ, USMC, Historical Division, 1967), pp. 147-49 (hereafter cited as Megee, "Reminiscences"; J. Lawton Collins, *War in Peacetime: The History and Lessons of Korea* (Boston: Houghton Mifflin, 1969), pp. 83, 113, 239, 312-13.
7. *New York Times*, 8 December 1949; MSFE, 4:2671.
8. Samuel Stratton, "Korea: Acid Test of Containment," USNIP 63 (March 1952):237-49.
9. COL Robert Debs Heinl, Jr., USMC (RET), *Victory at High Tide: The Inchon-Seoul Campaign* (Philadelphia and New York: J. B. Lippincott, 1968), p. 4.
10. H. Struve Hensel, "Changes Inside the Pentagon," *Harvard Business Review* 33 (January-February 1954):105.
11. Ibid.
12. Carl W. Borklund, *Men of the Pentagon: From Forrestal to McNamara* (New York: Praeger, 1966). p. 86.

13. Ibid., p. 87.
14. MGEN Charles A. Willoughby and John Chamberlain, *MacArthur, 1941-1951* (New York: McGraw-Hill, 1954), pp. 351-54; Alexander L. George, "American Policy Making and the North Korean Aggression," *World Politics* 7 (January 1955):209-32; Editorial, "As for Korea," USAS 35 (August 1950):5. On 20 June 1950, Assistant Secretary of State Dean Rusk told the House Foreign Affairs Committee that a North Korean attack was not imminent and that "we believe that the kind of force being developed in South Korea at the present time could meet creditably the kind of force which the North Koreans have established" (*Washington Post*, 17 October 1976).
15. "Congress Is Determined to Find Out Three Essential Things," USAS 35 (August 1950):12; Eugene E. Wilson, "What Has Happened to American Air Superiority?" USAS 37 (January 1952):9-10. Secretary of Defense James V. Forrestal had created an Office of Civilian Defense in 1948. In March 1949 Truman shifted the responsibility for defense to the National Security Resources Board. After the outbreak of the Korean War, the board's chairman, W. Stuart Symington, suggested the establishment of a Federal Civil Defense Administration. This was done by Executive Order of 1 December 1950, then regularized by legislation of 12 January 1951. The law provided that the federal government would coordinate civil defense measures undertaken by "the several states and their political subdivisions," thus vesting primary responsibility in the states. The Defense Production Act of 1 September 1950, however, conferred authority for defense mobilization upon the President. (Donald W. Mitchell, *Civil Defense: Planning for Survival and Recovery* [Washington: ICAF, 1966], pp. 19-20).
16. Heinl, *Victory at High Tide*, p. 7, and *Soldiers of the Sea: The United States Marine Corps, 1775-1962* (Annapolis, Md.: U.S. Naval Institute, 1962), pp. 526-27; Megee, "Reminiscences," pp. 5-19, 154; GEN Hoyt S. Vandenberg, USAF, "The Truth About Air Power," SEP 223 (17 February 1951):20-21 ff.
17. In "An Exchange of Opinion," William Stauck writes on "Cold War Revisionism and the Origins of the Korean Conflict: The Kolko Thesis," and Joyce and Gabriel Kolko respond," PHR 42 (November 1973):537-75. See also Robert E. Osgood, *Limited War: The Challenge to American Strategy* (Chicago: University of Chicago Press, 1957), p. 151; Eric Larabee, "Korea: The Military Lesson," *Harper's Magazine* 201 (November 1950):52-54. After the Soviet, the North Korea Peoples Army was the best armed and equipped army of its size in the Far East.
18. Collins, *War in Peacetime*, pp. 1-4.
19. Robert Frank Futrell, Lawson S. Moseley, and Albert F. Simpson, *The United States Air Force in Korea 1950-1953* (New York: Duell, Sloan and Pearce, 1961), pp. 23-27.
20. MSFE, 1:237-38; Collins, *War in Peacetime*, pp. 66-67; Heinl, *Victory at High Tide*, p. 9.
21. Matthew B. Ridgway, GEN, USA (RET), *The Korean War* (Garden City, N.Y.: Doubleday, 1967), pp. vi, 11, 13, 34; James F. Schnabel, *Policy and Direction: The First Year* (Washington: OCMH, 1972), pp. 41-80; Harry S. Truman, *Memoirs by Harry S. Truman*, 2 vols. (Garden City, N.Y.: Doubleday, 1955-56), 2:316-22; GEN Otto P. Weyland, USAF, "The Air Campaign in Korea," AUQR 6 (Fall 1953):3-41.
22. Heinl, *Victory at High Tide*, p. 10.
23. *Washington Post*, 25 June 1950.
24. Merle Miller, *Plain Speaking: An Oral Biography of Harry S. Truman* (Published by Berkley Publishing Corporation, distributed by G. P. Putnam's Sons, New York, 1973), p. 273.
25. MSFE, 2:1049-50; Glenn D. Paige, *The Korean Decision, June 24-30, 1950* (New York: Free Press, 1968), pp. 125-43; Dean G. Acheson, *The Korean War* (New York: W. W. Norton, 1971), pp. 15-21; Beverly Smith," The White House Story: Why We Went to War in Korea," SEP 224 (10 November 1951):76.
26. MSFE, 2:1475; *New York Times*, 27 June 1950.
27. MSFE, 1:534-36, 2:1475, 1651; Paige, *The Korean Decision*, pp. 161-82; Acheson, *The Korean War*, p. 22; Albert L. Warner, "Why the Korean Decision Was Made," *Harper's* 122 (June 1951):99-106. During the year of active fighting in Korea, the United States granted military aid in the sums of $3 million to the Philippines and $12 million to Formosa. Between June 1949 and June 1951 it also gave $54 million to Indochina. (MSFE, 2:1345-46.)
28. Truman, *Memoirs*, 2:383; "Orvil Anderson and Our Tradition," AF 33 (October 1950):5.
29. Truman, *Memoirs*, 2:383.

30. Futrell, *Ideas, Concepts, Doctrine*, p. 147.
31. Ibid., p. 148.
32. Ibid., p. 147; Acheson, *Korean War*, pp. 24-26.
33. MSFE, 1:235-36, 2:1476, 1751, 4:2609-11, 2621; Acheson, *Korean War*, p. 26; Richard F. Haynes, *The Awesome Power: Harry S. Truman as Commander in Chief* (Baton Rouge: Louisiana State University Press, 1973), pp. 170-72.
34. Haynes, *The Awesome Power*, p. 185. How the Joint Chiefs of Staff made their decisions about the Korean War is revealed in JCS File 1776 and in the Papers of the Chiefs of Naval Operations (Washington: NHD: OA.). The latter are henceforth cited as CNO Papers.
35. NSC-68, "The Report by the Secretaries of State and Defense, on United States Objectives and Programs for National Security, April 7, 1950," was declassified by the Assistant to the President for National Security, Henry A. Kissinger, on 27 February 1975. It appears in toto in NWCR (May-June 1975):51-108. The NWC has also published it separately.
36. Paul Y. Hammond, "NSC-68: Prologue to Rearmament," in Warner R. Schilling, Paul Y. Hammond, and Glenn H. Snyder, *Strategy, Politics, and Defense Budgets* (New York and London: Columbia University Press, 1962), pp. 271-328; GEN Nathan F. Twining, USAF (RET), *Neither Liberty nor Safety: A Hard Look at U.S. Military Policy and Strategy* (New York: Holt, Rinehart, and Winston, 1966), pp. 44-52.
37. Top Secret. Joint Secretaries Meeting on NSC-101, 4 July 1950: Top Secret. Draft Statement of U.S. Policy on Indochina, for NSC Coordination, 18 October 1950, SNP: Douglas MacArthur, *Reminiscences: General of the Army Douglas MacArthur* (New York: McGraw-Hill, 1964), pp. 331, 335-36; Truman, *Memoirs*, 2:337, 341, 346; Willoughby and Chamberlain, *MacArthur*, pp. 356-57.
38. CAPT Walter Karig, USNR, CDR Malcolm W. Cagle, USN, and LCDR Frank Manson, USN, *Battle Report: The War in Korea* (New York: Rinehart, 1952), pp. 78.
39. Acheson, *Korean War*, pp. 43-46.
40. MSFE, 4:2591.
41. Bradley to SECDEF, 22 March 1950, Johnson to Vinson, 5 May 1950, Johnson to Tydings, 18 April 1950, Matthews to Vinson, 18 April 1950, SNP.
42. Transcript of oral interview by Dr. Benis M. Frank of GEN Clifton B. Cates, USMC (RET), (Washington, HQ, USMC, Historical Division, 1967), pp. 232-34 (hereafter cited as Cates, "Reminiscences"); *U.S. Marine Corps Operations in Korea, 1950-1953*, 5 vols. (Washington: HQ, USMC, Historical Branch, G-3, 1954-1972), 2:3-4, 9-11, 18-35.
43. Top Secret. Memorandum to Truman signed by the three service secretaries, the Army and the Air Force Chiefs of Staff, and Admiral Sherman, 13 July 1950, SNP; Heinl, *Victory at High Tide*, pp. 17, 21-22.
44. Cates, "Reminiscences," pp. 234-35; transcript of oral interview by Benis M. Frank of GEN Oliver P. Smith, USMC (RET) (Washington: HQ, USMC, Historical Division, 1969), p. 193 (hereafter cited as O. P. Smith, "Reminiscences"); transcript of oral interview by Benis M. Frank of LGEN Victor H. Krulak, USMC (RET) (Washington: HQ, USMC, Historical Division, 1973), pp. 147-49 (hereafter cited as Krulak, "Reminiscences,"); Heinl, *Victory at High Tide*, pp. 36-37, and *Soldiers of the Sea*, p. 537; Karig, Cagle, and Manson, *Battle Report: Korea*, p. 71.
45. Heinl, *Victory at High Tide*, p. 37.
46. BGEN S. L. A. Marshall, USA (RET), "Our Mistakes in Korea," *The Atlantic* 192 (September 1953):46.
47. Joseph J. Clark, ADM, USN (RET), and Clark G. Reynolds, *Carrier Admiral* (New York: David McKay Co., 1967), pp. 274-75; Karig, Cagle, and Manson, *Battle Report: Korea*, p. 77; Gerald E. Wheeler, "Naval Aviation in the Korean War," USNIP 83 (July 1957):762-77.
48. JCS File 1776/15, 5 July 1950, CNO Papers; Miller, *Plain Speaking*, pp. 282-83; MacArthur, *Reminiscences*, pp. 339-44; Truman, *Memoirs*, 2:332-33, 348.
49. *Congressional Quarterly Almanac*, 1950, pp. 303, 320.
50. MSFE 2:1309; Haynes, *The Awesome Power*, pp. 86-87; Alnav 66, Involuntary Extension of Enlistments, July 7, 1951, in NDB 19 (15 July 1951):13.
51. CAPT Harley Cope, USN, "Fighting Ships on the Leash," USNIP 73 (February 1947): 161-65.
52. Secret. Louis Johnson, Memorandum for the Service Secretaries and Chairman JCS,

25 August 1950, CNO Papers; Heinl, *Victory at High Tide*, p. 34.

53. CGFMF Pacific, Memorandum to CMC, 11 July 1950, cited in *U.S. Marine Corps Operations in Korea*, 2:13.
54. "The Reminiscences of ADM Charles Donald Griffin, USN (RET), transcript of oral interview by John T. Mason (Annapolis, Md,: U.S. Naval Institute, 1973 "The Reminiscence of VADM Fitzhugh Lee, USN (RET)." transcript of oral interview by CDR Etta Belle Kitchen, USN (RET), (Annapolis, Md.: U.S. Naval Institute, 1970), pp. 211-13; Md.: U.S. Naval Institute, 1970), pp. 211-13 (hereafter cited as Lee, "Reminiscences"); CDR Malcolm W. Cagle, USN, "Errors in the Korean War," USNIP 84 (March 1958): 33-34; Top Secret. Marine Corps SG2, *Intelligence Study of the Air Support in Korea, Oct. 19, 1951*, copy in SNP.
55. James A. Field, Jr., *History of United States Naval Operations: Korea* (Washington: GPO, 1962), p. 60.
56. Karig, Cagle, and Manson, *Battle Report: Korea*, p. 72
57. Collins, *War in Peacetime*, pp. 114-15.
58. Heinl, *Victory at High Tide*, p. 22.
59. Ibid., pp. 38-41.
60. Willoughby and Chamberlain, *MacArthur*, pp. 365-73.
61. Heinl, *Victory at High Tide,* pp. 38-45. For the planning stages and landings at Inchon, see *U.S. Marine Corps Operations in Korea*, 2:37-280.
62. Top Secret. H. Freeman Matthews to Francis P. Matthews, 26 September 1950; Top Secret. Pace, Matthews, and Finletter, Memorandum for SECDEF, 27 September 1950, SNP.
63. Top Secret. GEN James H. Burns to Pace, Matthews, and Finletter, 16 September 1950, SNP.
64. "Secretary Johnson Replies," ANJ 88 (2 September 1950):17.
65. Dennison, "Reminiscences," pp. 29, 31.
66. Truman, *Memoirs*, 2:345.
67. *New York Times*, 26 August 1950; Truman, *Memoirs*, 2:383.
68. See Bert Cochran, *Harry Truman and the Crisis Presidency* (New York: Funk and Wagnalls, 1973), p. 325; David Rees, *Korea—The Limited War* (New York: St. Martin's Press, 1964), pp. 76-77; Whiting, *China Crosses the Yalu,* p. 96.
69. Borklund, *Men of the Pentagon*, p. 87.
70. Ibid., pp. 87-88.
71. Haynes, *The Awesome Power*, p. 193; Wilbur Hoare, "Harry S. Truman," in Ernest R. May, ed., *The Ultimate Decision: The President as Commander in Chief* (New York: George Braziller, 1960), pp. 196-97.
72. Dean Acheson, *Sketches from Life* (New York: Harper and Bros., 1959), pp. 162-63. See also Gaddis Smith, *Dean Acheson* (New York: Cooper Square Publishers, 1972), pp. 128-29, 155-62, 241, 291-93, 364-65, 370, 393, "What's Ahead in Congress," AW 52 (28 August 1950):16, and "Washington Roundup," ibid., (4 December 1950):16.
73. Heinl, *Victory at High Tide*, p. 87.
74. "Letter Accepting Resignation of Louis Johnson as Secretary of Defense, Sept. 12, 1950" [followed by the letter], in *Public Papers of the Presidents of the United States: Harry S. Truman*, 8 vols. (Washington: GPO, 1961-66), 7:632-33; "Letter to Committee Chairman Transmitting Bill to Permit General Marshall to Serve as Secretary of Defense," ibid., 7:633-34.
75. "Drive for Big Carrier," ANJ 88 (4 November 1950):251.
76. Gaddis Smith, *Acheson*, pp. 215,293.

11
Korea: Fighting with
One Arm Tied,
September 1950-September 1951

President Harry S. Truman originally intervened in Korea in order to restore South Korea to its antebellum status. On 11 September 1950, however, he decided to attempt the political unification of the entire peninsula by conquering the north. In consequence, on 27 September Secretary of Defense George C. Marshall and Secretary of State Dean Acheson agreed on new orders authorizing General Douglas MacArthur to conduct operations against North Koreans north or south of the 38th parallel. Although the objective of unifying Korea was blessed on 7 October by a resolution of the General Assembly of the United Nations and no major Soviet or Chinese forces had intervened or threatened to do so, the possibility of such intervention caused the administration to limit MacArthur's operations. He must not cross the Manchurian borders of Russia and China, use non-Korean troops near the Russo-Manchurian border, nor conduct air and naval action against Manchuria or Soviet territory, and he must submit his plans for future operations for approval by the Joint Chiefs of Staff.[1] By 7 October, with Chinese intervention presumed imminent, Marshall and Acheson agreed that MacArthur should counter the Chinese as long as his action promised "a reasonable chance of success." Moreover, "in any case you will obtain authority from Washington prior to taking any military action against objectives in Chinese territory."[2] So important did Truman consider the situation that he flew to Wake Island, where MacArthur told him that North Korean resistance should end by Thanksgiving and that the Eighth Army would be withdrawn to Japan by Christmas. Truman asked if the Chinese or Russians would intervene. MacArthur thought not, adding that "if they tried to get down to Pyongyang there would be the greatest slaughter."[3] In public speeches on 30 September and 1 October, however, Chou En-lai, China's foreign minister, had stated that China would resist foreign aggression against

251

North Korea, and on 3 October he asserted that China would enter the war if Americans advanced north of the 38th parallel.[4]

The Secretary of the Navy, Francis P. Matthews, discussed the possibility of Chinese intervention with the Secretary of the Air Force, Thomas K. Finletter, just before he himself left Washington for a twenty-day tour of the Far East. At Pearl Harbor he was briefed by Admiral Arthur W. Radford, Commander in Chief, Pacific Fleet. After inspecting naval installations at Guam, he went via the Philippines and Okinawa to Japan, where he conferred with MacArthur prior to visiting naval activities in the forward area in Korea, into which Chinese troops had begun to cross from Manchuria on 27 October, and returned via Adak and Kodiak. On 16 November Truman said that the United States would not invade China, thereby enabling China to continue the war in Korea from the privileged sanctuary of her territory.

While the Navy conducted its remarkably efficient amphibious operation in reverse at Hungnam, beginning 13 December, Matthews offered advice on a speech Truman would make declaring a national emergency and asking for additional military appropriations and for a doubling of military personnel to 2.7 million by 30 June 1951.[5] Before Congress could act on defense proposals Truman had already made, on 16 December Truman, because of the Chinese intervention in Korea, proclaimed a national emergency and called for increasing armed personnel strength to 3.5 million "as soon as possible." The proclamation gave Matthews a host of new powers. He could, for example, recall retired enlisted men and officers of the Navy and of the Coast Guard to active duty, authorize contracts without calling for bids and make contracts on a cost-plus basis in certain cases, and disregard limits placed upon the number of admirals of the Navy and of generals of the Marine Corps. Meanwhile, to help plan for the orderly growth of the navy in a projected five-year preparedness program, he furnished Congress a table showing how long it would take to activate and repair, and to train the crews, for every type of combatant and auxiliary ship.[6] He also discussed various problems with the other service secretaries and with Robert A. Lovett, the Under Secretary of Defense. Among these were NATO planning and possible reorganization; appraising the Korean situation particularly in the light of the Chinese intervention; East-West trade; position of the United States with respect to the Philippines; the foreign information program and psychological warfare; the guided missile program; universal military training; peace and defense treaties with Japan; and European defense and defense forces.[7] On 16 January 1951 he considered a National Security Council paper entitled "A Concrete Program for Action Against Communist China." On 23 January he disagreed with a National Security Council paper that advocated unilateral policies toward both Europe and Asia, but he agreed with the other service secretaries that various U.N. members be pressed to furnish additional forces for service in Korea.[8] Although he preferred to have Spain admitted to the United Nations than to try unilaterally to acquire more naval and air bases therein, Acheson, backed by Truman, General Omar N. Bradley, Chairman of the Joint Chiefs of Staff, and Finletter strongly opposed negotiating with Spain. Thereupon Matthews, Assistant Secretary of the Navy for Air John F. Floberg, Chief of Staff of the Air Force General Hoyt S. Vandenberg, and Chief of Naval Operations Admiral Forrest Sherman urged a change in policy, with Sherman probably winning Bradley over to what Floberg called "a piece of unification that worked."[9] Last, Matthews would support any measure that would prevent Italy from falling under communist domination, mollify French fears of a resurgent Germany, and gain the adherence of West Germany to the defense of Western Europe.[10] Hanging over the head of Secretary of Defense Marshall was a directive from the Bureau of Budget dated 7 January 1951 to initiate a review of his department and report by the twenty-third on how its organization and administration could be improved in keeping with the National Security Act Amendments of 1949.[11]

Legislation to provide more than $50 billion for defense in fiscal year 1952, for the increase in military personnel Truman had suggested, and for a five-year preparedness program that would stress the defense of Western Europe against Russia were priority items to be considered by the first session of the Eighty-second Congress, which convened on 3 January 1951. There was also the suggestion made in the report of the House Naval Affairs Committee on Unification and Strategy and revived by a former Marine in the Senate, Paul H. Douglas (D., Ill.), former Marines in the House like Mike Mansfield (D., Wy.), and other congressmen aware of the favorable publicity well earned by the Marines in Korea, to almost triple the Marine Corps strength to four divisions of up to four hundred thousand men and two air wings, and to give the commandant membership on the Joint Chiefs of Staff.[12] In addition there was a bill introduced by Carl Vinson, Chairman of the House Armed Services Committee, to build a supercarrier. Despite objections from General J. Lawton Collins, Chief of Staff of the Army, to having "representation by a specialty" on the Joint Chiefs of Staff, the Commandant of the Marine Corps had met with the Joint Chiefs once in April, July, August, and November 1950, and once in February 1951. Although the Senate approved, Marshall opposed the Douglas-Mansfield bill. Sherman added that the Marine Corps "is in no danger of dissolution" and that the bill "is an unnecessary device to safeguard it."[13] Douglas argued that "events in Korea bear out the absolute necessity of such legislation," but Matthews opposed the interposing of the Commandant of the Marine Corps between a naval secretary and the Chief of Naval Operations. He also sharply contradicted Sherman when the latter said he commanded the Marine Corps. In great part because Lovett and the Joint Chiefs of Staff, especially Bradley, also opposed the expansion of the Marine Corps and adding its commandant to the Joint Chiefs, no bill on the subject reached the House floor for debate in 1951.[14] It would not be until 28 June 1952 that Truman would sign a bill that authorized the Commandant of the Marine Corps to sit with the Joint Chiefs (but then only when Marine Corps matters were considered), set the strength of the Corps at three combat divisions and three air wings and a personnel strength of not more than four hundred thousand men, and recognized the corps as a separate service even though it was part of the Navy.[15]

Neither the Air Force nor the Navy objected to an Army desire that an additional Assistant Secretary be provided for the Army, with Dan A. Kimball, as Acting Secretary, adding the the Navy had no present requirement for another such office. Moreover, Sherman was consolidating his administrative overhead. Believing that the Assistant Chiefs of Naval Operations should be reduced from eighteen to nine, he recommended that nine be approved and that the others be known merely as directors of their offices.[16] Moreover, since war planning, the formulation of principles of strategy and tactics, and the determination of ships' characteristics, number of naval personnel, and material requirements of naval forces had gravitated from the General Board to the Office of Chief of Naval Operations, he recommended that the former, which was not a statutory board, be abolished. But he offered the suggestion to Matthews only after he had wisely notified Vinson, who thought the suggestion "warranted and in the interest of national defense." In consequence of Matthews's approval, the board was dissolved effective 10 March 1951.[17] Under discussion at the highest levels, too, was a proposal made by the fiscal people in the Department of Defense that a Defense Supply Agency be established to replace the supply systems of the three services. The Navy's position on the subject was that there was no proof that such a system would save either time or money.[18]

Testimony on Vinson's naval construction bill was offered by Sherman and Admiral David H. Clark, Chief of the Bureau of Ships, rather than by Matthews. Among the 173 ships were a supercarrier capable of accommodating heavy bombers that could carry atomic bombs and numerous minesweepers and amphibious craft. In response to dramatic revelation of the need for combat ships in Korea, it took Vinson's committee only two hours to approve a program to cost about $3 billion, and only two hours of debate on the floor before the House approved it by unanimous vote on 17 January. Both the Senate Armed Services Committee and the full Senate heartily agreed, and Truman signed the bill into law on 10 March.

Knowledge that the Navy had deployed its first carrier-based aircraft detachment to Port Lyautey, Morocco, in February, and that atomic bombs could be flown to them from the United States to Lyautey, thence to carriers in the Sixth Fleet, may also have helped the bill to pass. The high regard held for Forrest Sherman may have helped too, for he supported unification even though as an aviator he had advanced the nuclear attack capability of carriers. In addition, he was more politically oriented in his strategic outlook than Denfeld had been. To put it another way, he placed less reliance upon nuclear warfare by the United States and downplayed the possession of atomic weapons by the Soviets. Moreover, even before the scrapping of the *United States*, the Navy had restudied the contributions carrier aircraft armed merely with conventional weapons could make.

As Commander in Chief, U.S. Naval Forces Eastern Atlantic and Mediterranean, Admiral Richard L. Conolly, at a request dated 4 October 1948 from Vice Admiral Arthur D. Struble, Deputy Chief of Naval Operations (Operations), had had his staff make such a study. The report, which was forwarded to Denfeld in January 1949, went little beyond what Fleet Admiral Chester W. Nimitz had envisaged was necessary for the defense of the Mediterranean during his last days as Chief of Naval Operations late in 1947—three carrier task groups in that sea with one group in the Atlantic Fleet ready to join up if needed.[19] A second study, made by OP-55, Air Warfare Division, which was still headed by Rear Admiral Edwin A. Cruise, was forwarded on 22 August, at the height of the B-36 hearings. Although it should have concerned only the development of follow-on carriers and carrier-based planes, it included strategic considerations yet avoided interservice bickering. It held that carrier aviation must be maintained at strength in order to be able to support the Navy's functions, that the air threat was greater than the submarine threat, and that overemphasis on the latter might cause naval aviation to assume merely an antisubmarine warfare role. To carry a wide range of aircraft types, a large, flush-deck carrier was imperative, as was also a 15,000-ton antisubmarine escort carrier—the last a precursor of the Surface Control Ship. Cruise stated that it was wrong to depend upon only one weapon system and that the Navy should use any weapon available to it. It was also wrong to equate the use of atomic weapons with "strategic bombing." Yet he recommended that only a limited number of long-range, heavy attack planes be placed in carriers and that these be considered a special organization, one set apart from the ordinary air group. The composition of the carrier air groups of the early 1950s followed the recommendations of Conolly and Cruise. Rather than being loaded with strategic bombers they included numerous types of planes capable of conducting the conventional kind of warfare needed in Korea—with the strategic bombers lying in wait as the Navy's "Sunday punch."[20]

In contrast to their negative vote on a supercarrier in 1949, the Joint Chiefs of Staff now unanimously supported building one, with the General Board of the Navy limiting her size in order not to jeopardize her life, hoping that she would be flush-deck in design, and recommending that nuclear propulsion for her be "extensively examined."[21] The importance of minesweeping was reflected not only in the authority to build nonmagnetic minesweepers but in the reactivation of the Pacific Fleet Mine Force as a separate command organization. Truman meanwhile told Congress that military expenditures in fiscal year 1952 would approximate $42 billion and perhaps reach $61 billion. After being considered by the Senate Armed Services Committee, now chaired by Richard Russell (D., Ga.), a conference committee reached agreement. Lovett told the Senate Committee on Appropriations that the budget was formulated on military requirements and not on an allocation of dollars, as had been the case in recent years. In his testimony, given shortly before the first anniversary of the beginning of the Korean War, Matthews stated that naval gunfire support had been an important factor in Korea, as at the Inchon landings and Hungnam withdrawal, and that combat action in the Korean "proving ground" had demonstrated "generally successful equipment design policy."[22] MacArthur went a step further in saying that "the amphibious landing is the most powerful tool we have."[23] The naval construction bill authorized the Navy to build half a million tons of new construction and to modernize 291 vessels, of one million tons, at a cost of $2 billion. New construction included a supercarrier and seven submarines; conversion work included 6 *Essex*-class carriers, 12 cruisers, 2 guided missile cruisers, and 194 destroyers. The Navy thus would be expanded to 1,066 ships by 30 June 1952, including 18 large carriers when all modernization work was completed. In addition it would increase its operating aircraft from 8,161 to 8,739 and its personnel from 664,200 to 735,000, with 204,029 in the Marine Corps.

The detailed defense budget for fiscal year 1952 that Truman sent to Congress on 30 April 1951 called for $60.6 billion, with the Navy allotted $15.1 billion in new obligational authority and authorized to operate 1,161 ships and raise its personnel limit to 790,000 men. Part of the funds, however, would be eaten up by the marked inflation following the outbreak of the Korean War.

Pursuant to a resolution introduced by Lyndon B. Johnson, in the summer of 1950 the Senate Armed Services Committee had created a Preparedness Subcommittee which, like the Truman Committee of World War II, would oversee Pentagon readiness and spending procedures. Its chairman was Johnson, who was anxious to get both the physical and mental fat out of the armed services. When the Korean War started, he demanded the development of long-range global defense plans and the immediate mobilization both of manpower and of the economy in order to halt "delay—defeat—retreat." Truman promised the complete cooperation of the Executive Department to Johnson's seven-man subcommittee, as did Matthews, and the committee produced forty-four unanimous reports, thirty-two of them in 1951 alone. On 22 August 1950 it reported that the $14.4 million needed to equip an infantry division in 1944 had risen to $74 million, the $30 million to equip an armored division to $199 million. The destroyer that had cost $7 million in 1939 cost more than $40 million in 1950. A B-17 bomber before World War II had cost $300,000; the B-36s coming off the assembly line in 1950 cost more than $3 million. The committee looked into the synthetic rubber production program, with consequent saving to the taxpayer of $1 billion; into price-gouging practices of tin producers that, when corrected, saved another $500 million: and into Air Force personnel practices. On 18 February 1951 Johnson severely criticized the Air Force for "hoarding," that is, using an enlistment policy that siphoned off the best recruits to the detriment of the other services. Its action was therefore "irresponsible and merits censure." The Air Force mended its ways. Reports on poor Army personnel practices also resulted in corrections that permitted the addition of two combat divisions without increasing the size of the Army. When the committee looked into a "slowdown" in the expansion of air power, it learned from Vice Admiral John W. Cassady, Deputy Chief of Naval Air Operations, the the Navy would soon be able to deliver small or large atomic bombs on most targets and from others that the United States jet plane production program was far behind the Russian. Most shocking to the American public was the charge by General James A. Van Fleet, former commander of the Eighth Army in Korea, of critical ammunition shortages, a charge upheld with the conclusion that such shortages had resulted in the "needless loss of American lives." It has been estimated that Johnson's committee, which lasted to February 1953, saved the taxpayer between $3 billion and $5 billion at a cost of $275,000. The committee also made its voice felt in criticizing the administration's decision to stretch out completion of the Air Force's proposed 143-wing program from 1954 to 1956, about which more later.[24]

The first session of the Eighty-second Congress provided a statutory basis for the organization of the Air Force, which hitherto had rested upon the National Security Act of 1947. Vinson's bill on the subject would have turned over its medical service and several other units to the Army and Navy. When Secretary Finletter objected vigorously, Vinson told his staff to rewrite the bill so that the Air Force would be "in charge of its own housekeeping."[25] In consequence of the bill, which Truman signed on 19 September, the Air Force would have three major divisions under the command of its chief of staff and a new Tactical Air Command.

If Matthews was happy with the Navy and Congress, the same cannot be said of the Air Force. On 22 February 1951 top Air Force officials told the Senate Armed Services and Foreign Relations committees that they lacked sufficient planes for "minimum defense" of the nation. Senator Henry Cabot Lodge, Jr., demanded 150 groups; retired General Carl Spaatz, 250, adding that the use of American ground troops in Europe would follow "the wall of flesh philosophy." Vinson suggested a compromise by building the Air Force to 138 wings, with 25 troop carrier wings, and expanding naval aviation by building three supercarriers instead of one, each capable of handling the heaviest long-range bombers.

The Navy and Marine Corps were to participate with the Air Force in early August in the largest joint training exercises to be held since the end of World War II. Service differences over the system of air control to be used caused their cancellation, which informed sources indicated represented a by-product of far broader service differences than those arising out of systems of controlling air support furnished ground troops in Korea. Such influential congressmen as Sterling Cole declared that interservice disagreements had reached a point at which congressional intervention was necessary, and various service spokesmen said that the proposed increase in the Air Force was provoking a bitter three-way service split. As Matthews verged upon leaving office, therefore, the Air Force's personnel policies' demand for a tremendous increase in its strength and differences over air control systems threatened to provoke the most controversial interservice fight since the congressional investigation into unification and strategy that engulfed him upon his entering office in July 1949. Aware of the possibility, Truman wisely directed the Pentagon to "keep this fight in the family."[26]

Two spectacular congressional hearings were held early in 1951. The first grew out of a challenge of 8 January by a number of isolationist Republican senators led by Kenneth S. Wherry, of Nebraska, to Truman's constitutional authority to send ground troops to bolster the defenses of Western Europe.[27] The second grew out of Truman's recalling of MacArthur. The intervention of China in Korea had drastically changed the character of the conflict. Among other things, MacArthur would bomb Manchurian targets, blockade the Chinese coast, and use Chiang Kai-shek's troops, thus perhaps starting an expanded new war with China and Russia that the administration and America's U.N. allies wished to avoid. Believing that "there is no substitute for victory." MacArthur had tried to bring the administration to his way of thinking. Truman resented the challenge to civil supremacy and the making of foreign policy in the field instead of in Washington. On the advice of the Joint Chiefs of Staff—none of the civilian service secretaries, nor the National Security Council, nor the chairman of the congressional armed services committees was consulted—on 11 April he summarily relieved the general of all his commands.[28] He thereby provoked another "great debate" and additional hearings that ranged more widely than earlier ones and probed deeply into strategic problems, political-military and civil-military relations, the unification of the armed services, and the relations of the Joint Chiefs of Staff with a field commander.[29]

Recognition of the inseparability of political and military affairs was revealed in the fact that the hearings, printed under title of *The Military Situation in the Far East*, but popularly called the MacArthur hearings, were conducted jointly by the Senate Armed Services and Foreign Relations committees. Since their objective was to obtain information necessary to draft legislation providing for the national security, the senators probed not only into the Korean War but into the adequacy and strength of the American defense organization in light of the global situation. The hearings were held between 3 May and 17 August; their public version, daily purged of information that might be of use to an enemy by the Director of the Joint Staff of the Joint Chiefs of Staff, included the words of thirteen witnesses that ran to 3,691 pages.

MacArthur had returned home to a tumultuous reception in San Francisco and the adulation of crowds everywhere. He had delivered an emotion-filled address to a joint session of Congress, then enjoyed a ticker-tape parade in New York. As the first witness at the hearings, he testified for three days. Whether misinformed or ignorant of the true status of the effectiveness of the unification of the armed services, he alleged that "in the Far East the integration of the three fighting services has been as complete as I could possibly imagine. They have worked as a team. The responsiveness of each service to the desires and wishes of the other has been almost perfection.''

> The CHAIRMAN [Richard B. Russell]. That includes the cooperation between the air in support of ground forces as well as all of the other phases of activity, tactical activity?
> General MacARTHUR. Yes, sir. What I am referring to is the coordination. I am not referring to the efficiencies; I am referring to basic amalgamation of the services and their efforts in support of each other.[30]

He added, however, that the naval and air forces at his disposal had operated at only a fraction of their efficiency. Confined as they had been to the narrow area of the battleground, they had performed merely as tactical support of the infantry line. They had not been permitted to follow the strategic concept of interdicting enemy supply depots, transportation lines, and the buildup of troops at the front. "All of the uses which over the years and centuries the Navy and Air are supposed to do are not permitted over there." But, "If you would take off and permit them their full capacity, I do not believe it would take a very great additional component of ground troops to wind this thing up." (1:10).

Had he not been denied the right of "hot pursuit" of enemy aircraft across the Yalu and the right to bomb Chinese troops as they formed to cross it from Manchuria into Korea, MacArthur continued, he could have thrown back those troops. Moreover, could he have had his way, he would have warned China that if she did not agree to discuss a cease-fire, "the entire force of the United Nations would be utilized to bring to an end the predatory attack of her forces on ours." Anything less than the full use of American force in Korea—about 10 percent of the nation's potential—would "introduce a new concept into military operations—the concept of appeasement, the concept that when you use force, you can limit that force," and a political control over military operations "such as I have never known in my life or have ever studied." (1:12-68).

> Senator GREEN: You have dealt with these questions in both countries. [China and Korea] on a purely military basis. But isn't our government required to give consideration and decide upon it on both a military and a political basis? Can you separate them so distinctly and say that a military victory is a political victory?
> General MacARTHUR: I think that it is quite impossible to draw a line of differentiation and say this is a political and this is a military situation.
> The American Government should have such coordination so that the political and military are in coordination. (1:45).

In introducing Secretary of Defense Marshall, Senator Russell referred to MacArthur's having voiced a ''point of view of a policy . . . which appears to challenge the basic concepts—or at least some of the basic concepts—of our nation's foreign policy'' (1:322). Confessing that he was distressed at the necessity for doing so, Marshall said that he was "in almost direct opposition to a great many of the views and actions of General MacArthur'' (1:322). While there had been no disagreement since the beginning of the Korean war among the President, Secretary of Defense, Secretary of State, and the Joint Chiefs of Staff, there had been differences between all of these and MacArthur. As Marshall put it, the men in Washington had all sought "to confine the conflict to Korea and prevent its spreading into a third world war. . . . Our efforts in Korea have given us some sorely needed time and impetus to accelerate the building of our defenses and those of our allies against the threatened onslaught of Soviet imperialism'' (1:324-25). Asked how top administration leaders had been brought into unison, Marshall stated that he had reversed Secretary Johnson's procedure and encouraged Defense talks with the Department of State on the lower as well as on the top echelons (1:379, 384). Agreeing with J. William Fulbright that the policy of unconditional surrender followed in World War II had not restored world peace, Marshall believed that new concepts for ending war on terms other than unconditional surrender should be devised (1:644-52).

General Bradley, named by Truman on 25 July for a second term as chairman of the Joint Chiefs of Staff, stated that the National Security Act, as amended, empowered him to give the President, Secretary of Defense, and National Security Council the advice and recommendations of the Joint Chiefs of Staff. The chiefs, of course, could be overridden by higher political authority, but they wished the war restricted to Korea. Following MacArthur's advice would cause it to blossom into a global war. "Red China is not the powerful nation seeking to dominate the world. Frankly, in the opinion of the Joint Chiefs of Staff, this strategy would involve us in the wrong war, at the wrong place, at the wrong time, and with the wrong enemy." In other instances—as in Berlin and Greece—the United States had acted with a restraint that nevertheless did not represent "appeasement" or aggression. (2:729-33).

Would air and sea power alone stop the Chinese hordes from "coming over us in Korea?" Bradley did not think so, saying:

> Normally, you think of strategic bombing as going after the sources of production. The sources of production in this case are very largely out of reach of any strategic bombing because they are not even in China.
> We think that such action could not be decisive, by itself.
> That has been proved many times, that air, by itself, is not decisive.

While the U.N. naval blockade had denied the enemy use of the sea and caused him to move supplies by road and railroad, air power had not been effective because he moved at night. Moreover, thirteen of the U.N. nations fighting in Korea had vetoed the "hot pursuit" of enemy fighters advocated by the Joint Chiefs of Staff, the Secretary of State, and the President (2:744-88).

Had any lessons been learned from Korea? Yes. Realization of the needs of global defense had caused defense appropriations to quintuple in a year, from $13 billion to $60 billion. Second, experience had been gained about a "guerrilla warfare" in which the enemy infiltrated through American lines and assembled in their rear. Third, "I think we have improved the cooperation of our three services. I don't think we have ever reached, before, the perfection, almost, of the cooperation of the three services in working together" (2:1009).

Why had MacArthur been relieved of his commands? Not because he held different views from the administration but because he had made them public, "and before our country and before our allies and before the United Nations we found ourselves speaking with two voices—that of the Government in Washington and that of General MacArthur in Tokyo" (2:1024).

On the last point, General Collins was in complete accord with Bradley. While Collins also agreed that the limitations placed upon MacArthur's waging of war were correct and would avoid World War III, he noted that great improvement was needed in the employment of tactical air power on the battlefield (2:1187-1262).

Admitting that their jet engines were superior to American ones, General Vandenberg accounted for the destruction of MIGs by American superiority in tactics, technique, training, and armament. He objected to the strategic bombing of Manchuria and of the cities of China and Russia because the use of even the full power of the Air Force might prove inconclusive and because attrition would preclude the application of full power elsewhere. "The fact is that the United States is operating a shoestring air force in view of its global responsibilities." American air power "is the single potential that has kept the balance of power in our favor. . .[and] has kept the Russians from deciding to go to war." Nevertheless, "in my opinion, we cannot afford to . . . peck at the periphery [of the Sino-Soviet border] as long as we have a shoestring Air Force." Moreover, when Russia acquired a long-range air force and atomic weapons, the Air Force would have two tasks in war: to defend the United States and to lay waste Russia's industrial productivity. If the air defenses of the United States were adequate today, they might not be tomorrow (2:1379-80).

Vandenberg had a higher estimate of the effectiveness of air power in Korea than Bradley and Collins. The Air Force had immediately obtained and then maintained air superiority in Korea. Reports from the field told him that "the support furnished by Air was more complete and more efficient than had ever been provided before in the history of ground warfare." Rather than providing for balanced forces, however, the nation should balance its air forces against the threat posed by a potential enemy. Rather than using the full power of the Air Force against China and Russia, he would "kill as many Chinese Communists as is possible without enlarging the war at the present time in Korea." As for air bases in Europe, England, and North Africa from which to strike Russia, they would be "desirable" but were not "essential" because the Air Force was rapidly assuming a position in which it would not require overseas bases (2:1383-86).

Could air power have stopped the Chinese who intervened in Korea even if "hot pursuit" had been permitted? "In my opinion," replied Vandenberg, "it would have assisted somewhat. . .but would not have been in any way decisive." But to carry out MacArthur's program would call for a doubling of American strategic air power, which simply could not be accomplished in less than about three years. Indeed, the current ninety-five-group goal "is simply a stepping stone toward the force that we believe is necessary." The number of groups, now called wings, that he thought necessary was classified information. Moreover, "we would probably have to increase our fleet in order to carry out the naval recommendations" (2:1388-1440).

Admiral Sherman began his testimony by referring to how rapidly conditions had changed in Korea: the intervention of Red China in late October 1950, the President's proclamation of a national emergency on 17 December, the Hungnam withdrawals completed on Christmas Day, MacArthur's new strategy for winning the war. In December 1950 and in January 1951, the Joint Chiefs had considered lifting the restrictions placed on MacArthur, which had been designed to deter Chinese intervention and, among other things, to place a naval blockade on Red China. Such a blockade, which presumed the existence of war, would badly hurt China but would also subtract at least initially from the naval forces in Korea. Because the American economic blockade of China established in December 1950 was not being respected by various other U.N. nations, it would be better if the United Nations imposed such a blockade. Sherman agreed that MacArthur should have been dismissed and that the United States should continue to fight in Korea, even if "with at least one arm tied behind our back," until attrition forced the enemy to end the war. Any extension of the war, he feared, would "jeopardize our long-term national security on a global basis." Like Vandenberg, Sherman thought that military power was relative; he could not say whether the nation had sufficient naval strength to support its global responsibilities. However, the Navy could, if necessary, join the Air Force in attacking Russian or Chinese targets in case of war, with carrier-based aircraft playing an especially important role if overseas bases were denied the Air Force (2:1510-87). In consequence, however, American naval power would be reduced in the Far East if war with Russia was undertaken in Europe and the Middle East (2:1584-85, 1594-95).

After Acheson reiterated the administration's wish to keep the war limited, former Secretary of Defense Louis A. Johnson offered no prepared statement but said he would answer questions.

Had he visited the Far East while he had been in office? Yes, beginning 12 June 1950, he had visited installations in the Pacific, conferred with General MacArthur, and received briefings from representatives of the three services on MacArthur's staff. He had returned to Washington about noon on the twenty-fifth, the day the Korean War started. As for American military forces in the Far East, "we found them in good shape" as occupation forces went, for they were not trained or equipped for offensive war. He had heard nothing about the immediacy of a North Korean attack on South Korea.

The Department of State, not the Department of Defense, Johnson continued, had responsibility for Korea, but with the outbreak of war he had attended the meetings of 25, 26, 27, and 30 June in which the administration decided upon its Korean policy. Acheson, not the military leaders, had suggested going into Korea, and Truman had supported Acheson.

> Senator [Alexander] WILEY. Now, you are the one that carried through the unification policy, are you not?
> Mr. JOHNSON. I like the way you phrase that question. I did my best sir.
> Senator WILEY. How do you believe that has been carried out in Korea.
> Mr. JOHNSON. I think that if there had not been unification directed by the Congress, and as made permissible by your amendments after I came into office. . .we would never have gotten into Korea, and never had done the good job that our military forces have done in Korea; and I think, secondly, . . .that if you had not had unification, and the new thing on the finances that you authorized in the unification bill, you would have been pouring money down the rat hole in furnishing money for the United States for defense at the present time.

Johnson agreed that MacArthur should have been dismissed and, lest the war be expanded, would adopt only one part of his program—a naval blockade of China.

Asked about the defense budget for fiscal year 1951, Johnson said that it had been drafted when the climate of the world presaged peace. It had been "thrown out" to him by the President, and he had gotten nowhere in trying to get it increased from $13 billion to at least $14.6 billion. To have given the services more money before the reforms he was instituting were completed would have been pouring it " 'down a rat hole.'. . .I believe, therefore, the $13 billion was good."

Was it not strange, asked several senators, that he should have resigned just four days after the Inchon landings presumed that the United States would take the initiative in Korea? On oath, Johnson replied he did not know why he had been ousted. Although General Collins had opposed, Johnson had supported MacArthur on the landing at Inchon. But his dismissal had been decided upon several days prior to the landings, which "might have cleared up much of the criticism." Could the resignation have resulted from differences with Acheson over foreign policy, particularly Far Eastern policy? Johnson stated that he "had the complete support of the President in the things that were purely defense." For the rest, he was not sure or did not know.

> Senator WILEY. Do you feel that in the National Security Council the recommendations originating from the Department of Defense were given equal weight with those of the Department of State?
> Mr. JOHNSON. May I pass?

Was there not a great similarity in the ouster of both him and MacArthur? Johnson answered: "I don't know about that." Believing the reasons for Johnson's ouster germane to the subject of the hearings, Senator Harry P. Cain pressed Johnson to give them. Johnson said he had already told the truth—he did not know—and refused to speak further on the matter.

Had the Air Force so concentrated on strategic bombing that it lacked capability for tactical support of ground forces to the degree that the Navy and Marine Corps had been called in to provide that support? Johnson praised naval and Marine aviation, saying only: "I know that General Vandenberg and General Collins are profiting by the Korean experience," and that the Air Force would soon face up to its responsibilities. On the other hand, the Air Force had been built up "to deter, to defend, and defeat." That was why Russia hesitated to go to war. How about Vandenberg's comment about his "shoestring" Air Force"? Johnson did not believe it, for Vandenberg dramatized his ways in the "usual approach of the Air Force to getting more money for the things they want to get."

Senator [Lyndon B.] Johnson asked: "Is our preparedness goal . . . sufficiently high in the light of world conditions, 3,462,000 Armed Forces, 95-group Air Force, 1,100 ships?" Johnson's amazing reply was that to prepare the United States for all-out war at a moment's notice would bankrupt it. "Any very substantial increase above the three million five [manpower] mark will border on that," as would a 150-group Air Force.

When asked about the preparation of the military budgets for fiscal years 1949, 1950, and 1951, Johnson replied in terms that contradicted much of what had happened at the time. When he entered office, the budget for 1949 had already been reduced from $30 billion to $15 billion. For the 1950 defense budget the President approved merely $13 billion. No defense leader objected, but Johnson was "sick about it." When Truman would approve no increases, Johnson had then had "the most soul-searching couple of weeks I ever had in my life" in trying either "to make that thing work or resign." Only because the service secretaries, the Joint Chiefs of Staff, Eisenhower, and a number of congressmen insisted that he remain, did he not resign, and "we went in to do the best job we could with the 13 billion." He had been hurt by lies about his cutting defense appropriations, had "caught hell on that score," when the truth was that he "never made a cut."

Soon after Truman announced the explosion by the Soviets of an atomic bomb, on 23 September 1949, Johnson went on, the President had ordered a reevaluation of the national security program. From that reevaluation, in part, the President had given the green light to the development of an H-bomb, buildup of NATO, and an increase in the military aid program—all of which called for enlarged appropriations. However, Johnson had determined that the new defense appropriations for fiscal year 1950 would be used to increase and improve combat forces and not be drained off in the form of unnecessary overhead, as they had been up to a year before. When the President set the defense budget for fiscal year 1951 at $13 billion, the services tailored their strength to fit that figure. However, Johnson concluded that sum would "provide a sufficiency of defense during the period covered by this budget" (4:2571-3250).

On 3 March 1950 Johnson had said that "the forces we already have in being, plus what our potential allies are developing, should tend to discourage aggressive action by any potential enemy." In less than three months the outbreak of war in Korea had caused him to eat these words, and in less than six months he had been ousted as Secretary of Defense.

What had the hearings accomplished? The chairman won unanimous agreement to a "Statement Affirming Faith in the Country" that proved reassuring to Americans and their allies. Eight Republican senators issued forty-eight "findings" on which four other Republican senators disagreed. The war in Korea continued, with less strain between leaders in Washington and those in the field. Thus the greatest importance of the published hearings was to reassert the tradition of civilian control over the military. The secret portions of the hearings, which were declassified in 1973, even further demolished MacArthur's policy of attacking in Manchuria. Bradley in particular believed that the Soviets had ample forces with which to compel the U.N. to evacuate Korea. Others thought that extending the war to China would incur such aircraft attrition that the Strategic Air Command would lose its credibility as a deterrent. Moreover, it was pointed out that the communists were also engaged in a limited war in Korea, for they did not use their air power against U.N. front line troops or naval forces, Korean ports, Japan, Okinawa, or Formosa.[31]

The National Security Act, as amended, had provided organizational arrangements presumably adequate to mesh foreign, domestic, military, and economic national policy. The MacArthur hearings revealed that the arrangements did not work well, that while a good deal of energy was expended in planning to increase the defenses of Europe against a possible Russian onslaught, insufficient thought was given to the policies and forces needed in the Far East. Particularly in Korea, a vacuum was permitted to exist. Truman's ordering of the divorcement of foreign from military policy countered both the letter and spirit of the National Security Act. The feuding between Johnson and Acheson, Truman's failure to consult the National Security Council, and the inability of the council to move speedily precluded furnishing the kind of advice the President needed. Not until after the Korean War began did Truman rely upon the Council to exercise the functions assigned it in the National Security Act. And not until Marshall succeeded Johnson and Lovett relieved Early did such harmony exist between the State and Defense Departments that political and military policies were brought into better coordination.

Second, the hearings revealed that the President and Congress, not the agencies established by the National Security Act, were responsible for the poor military posture of the United States when the Korean War began. It was Truman, using the "remainder method," who set the limits on the defense budget; it was Congress, in the 1949 amendments to the National Security Act, that demanded proof of economizing from the Department of Defense; and it was Congress that went along with Truman's small defense budgets. Many months before the Korean War started, as NSC-68 indicated, certain State and Defense officials realized the shortfalls of the defense program and called for a realistic, long-range preparedness schedule that would almost quintuple for five years the defense budget levels of 1949, 1950, and 1951. Moreover, the defense budget would be drafted to support America's global responsibilities rather than merely keep the military forces "in balance."

Despite Johnson's apologia at the hearings, American armed forces were in an unfavorable position in the summer of 1950 to repel aggression either in the West or in the East. All force levels were too low for that; especially because of cuts in its air, the Navy felt that it was too weak to support national policies; the Marine Corps believed it was on the verge of being abolished; the Air Force cried about its "shoestring" character. In addition, the Joint Chiefs of Staff had not yet sufficiently divorced themselves from uniservice concepts and from operational details to become what they should be, a corporate advisory and planning body. They loyally obeyed their instructions from the President, who wanted the Korean War limited. They supported the philosophy of civil supremacy and, although it pained them personally to do so, answered Truman's request for advice by agreeing unanimously that MacArthur should be relieved because his policies did not square with those of the administration.

The hearings showed that the United States had fought a new, guerrilla type of war in Korea with one arm tied. Truman's order that atomic weapons not be used was in keeping with his desire to keep the war "limited," a concept defying exact definition. The enemy, the terrain, and weather had rendered ineffective or inapplicable various Army, Navy, and Air Force weapons. What irked MacArthur and especially Air Force leaders was the confining of air power to Korea itself. Denied "hot pursuit," the Air Force was doomed to providing tactical support to a battle line confronted by enemy troops coming and supplied from an untouchable sanctuary. In the end, despite its naval and air superiority, the United States had to depend upon its infantry to determine the issue of victory or defeat.

The hearings revealed the inefficacy of the U.N. as an agency that by punishing aggression could maintain world peace. They also demonstrated a divergence of American opinion over what constituted peace. To MacArthur and his followers, peace came when war achieved the objectives for which the nation offered battle; to Truman and his followers, peace came when a war ended on terms less than unconditional surrender. To MacArthur, the Truman way spelled the abandonment of historic principle in favor of appeasement, opportunism, and defeatism; to Truman, the MacArthur way spelled World War III. The State Department had determined that national policy was to contain communism. Truman supported that policy in extremely anomalous ways. He said he would not use atomic weapons in Korea, not even tactically. He refused to take on Red Chinese on their own soil. And he did not try to punish the main instigator of aggression, Russia. Being defensive and passive, containment accepted the status quo. It contained no positive policies for settling the conflict with the Sino-Soviet bloc. It denied the United States the initiative, as in affirming that it would fight to hold a line. It pulled the teeth of its greatest deterrent and striking force, strategic air power. It thus lessened the credibility and prestige of the United States. Building upon earlier actions in which full American military power had not been used, as in Greece, Turkey, Berlin, and Trieste, containment as practiced in Korea reinforced those precedents and heightened the conviction that in the future the communists could continue their aggression by proxy and that, if it fought at all, the United States would fight only limited wars—again "with at least one arm tied behind our back," as Sherman put it at the MacArthur hearings.

NOTES

1. Top Secret. SECDEF Marshall to the President, 27 September 1950, SNP; Roy E. Appleman, *South to the Naktong, North to the Yalu, June-November 1950* (Washington: OCMH, 1960), pp. 607-8; Dean Acheson, *The Korean War* (New York: W. W. Norton, 1971), pp. 55-56.
2. Top Secret. Robert Lovett to the President, 7 October 1950, SNP.
3. Top Secret. Substance of Statements Made at Wake Island Conference, on 15 October 1950, compiled by General of the Army, Chairman of the Joint Chiefs of Staff [Bradley], SNP.
4. J. Lawton Collins, *War in Peacetime* (Boston: Houghton Mifflin), pp. 149-55; Dean Acheson, *Present at the Creation: My Years in the State Department* (New York: W. W. Norton, 1969), p. 452; Harry S. Truman, *The Memoirs of Harry S. Truman*, 2 vols. (Garden City, N.Y.: Doubleday, 1955-56), 2:261-62; John W. Spanier, *The Truman-MacArthur Controversy and the Korean War* (Cambirdge, Mass.: Harvard University Press, 1959), p. 85.
5. Secret. F. P. Matthews, Memorandum for Mr. Leva, 14 December 1950, SNP.
6. NDB 50-1001, "Procurement During the Period of the Present National Emergency," NDB 17 (31 December 1950):5-6; Secret. F. P. Matthews to Kenneth McKellar, 30 December 1950, SECNAV to Justice Department, 5 January 1951, SNP.
7. These items are selected from the agenda of the Joint Secretaries meetings held between 31 July and 29 December 1950, SNP. See also Department of the Navy, *History of Administrative Problems of the Korean War*, 5 vols. (Executive Office of the Secretary), copy in NHD: OA.
8. Top Secret. F. P. Matthews, Memorandum for SECDEF, 23 February 1951; Top Secret. F. P. Matthews, Memorandum to SECDEF, 20 March 1951; Top Secret. Pace, Matthews, and Finletter, Memorandum to SECDEF, 20 March 1951, SNP.
9. Robert L. Smith, "The Influence of U.S.A.F. Chief of Staff General Hoyt S. Vandenberg on United States National Security Policy" (Ph.D. diss., American University, 1965. Xerox. Ann Arbor, Mich.: University Microfilms, 1973), pp. 162-65. See also Theodore Lowi, "Bases in Spain," in Harold Stein, ed., *American Civil-Military Decisions: A Book of Case Studies* (University: University of Alabama Press, 1963), pp. 667-705.
10. Top Secret. Pace, Matthews, and Finletter, Memorandum to the SECDEF, 26 January 1951, SNP.

11. BGEN Marshall S. Carter, Director, Executive Office of the SECDEF, to Secretaries of the Army, Navy, and Air Force, with enclosure, 7 January 1951, SNP.

12. Senator Paul H. Douglas to SECNAV, 12 January 1951, SNP.

13. *Congressional Quarterly Almanac* 7 (1951):297.

14. JAG, Memorandum to SECNAV, 3 November 1950, with negative endorsement by Sherman dated 18 September; Douglas to Matthews, 12 January 1951; Matthews to Douglas, 23 January 1951; Matthews to Senator Estes Kefauver, 19 April 1951; Statement of Admiral Forrest Sherman, CNO, on Bill S. 677, in House of Representatives, 23 May 1951; CAPT H. C. Bruton, USN, Director, Legislative Division, Memorandum for SECNAV, CNO, Chief BUPERS, Commandant Marine Corps, JAG, 25 June 1951; Matthews, Memorandum for DOD, 11 July 1951; DOD, Memorandum to SECNAV, 23 July 1951, SNP.

15. PL 416, 82d Cong., 2d Sess., 1951. See transcript of oral interview by Benis M. Frank of GEN Clifton B. Cates, USMC (RET) (Washington: HQ, USMC, Historical Division, 1967), p. 236; COL Robert D. Heinl, Jr., USMC (RET), *Soldiers of the Sea: The United States Marine Corps, 1775-1962* (Annapolis, Md.: U.S. Naval Institute, 1962), pp. 580-82; COL Angus M. Fraser, USMC (RET), "The Marine Corps as a Separate Service," USNIP 101 (November 1975):1925.

16. CNO to SECNAV, 12 April 1950, 15 February 1951, CNO Papers.

17. Carl Vinson to Forrest Sherman, 15 November 1950, CNO to SECNAV, USECNAV, ASECNAV, copy to Vinson, 5 December 1950, SNP.

18. ASECNAV to SECNAV, 11 January 1951, John H. Dillon, Administrative Assistant to SECNAV, to Assistant CNO (Logistics), 11 April 1951, SNP.

19. *Supporting Study*, pp. 165-71.

20. Ibid., pp. 172-73. See also Operations Evaluation Group, Study No. 34, "Some Factors Affecting the Feasibility of Very Long Range Bombing from North American Bases, 12 July 1949," copy in SNP.

21. Secret. Chairman GB to CNO, 31 October 1950, SNP.

22. "Korean Proving Ground," ANAFJ 88 (16 June 1951):1162.

23. CDR Malcolm W. Cagle, USN, and LCDR Frank A. Manson, USN, *Battle Report: The Sea War in Korea* (New York: Rinehart, 1952), p. 77.

24. In April 1951 the Navy noted that the price to it of wool melton used in dress jumpers had risen from $3.22 to $8.10 a yard, and that of peacoat kersey from $5.45 to $13.62 a yard, and that the allowance for an enlisted man's full bag had been increased from $118.35 to $254.75 (NDB 51-266, in NDB 18 [15 April 1951]:29-30.) See also Stephen R. Chitwood, ed., *Economic Policies for National Strength: The Quest for Sustained Growth and Stability* (Washington: ICAF, 1968), pp. 75-76; Harry B. Yoshpe, ed., *Emergency Economic Stabilization* (Washington: ICAF, 1964), pp. 69-76; Benjamin H. Williams and Harold J. Clem, eds., *United States Foreign Economic Policy* (Washington: ICAF, 1965), pp. 46-48.

25. *Congressional Quarterly Almanac* 7 (1951):298.

26. "Chronology," CH 21 (September 1951):188.

27. See U.S. Congress. Senate Committee on Foreign Relations and Senate Committee on Armed Services. *Hearings, Assignment of Ground Forces of the United States to Duty in the European Area, on S. Con. Res. 8*, 82nd Cong., 1st Sess. (Washington: GPO, 1951).

28. U.S. Senate Committee on Foreign Relations and Senate Committee on Armed Services, *Hearings on the Military Situation in the Far East*, 82nd Cong., 1st Sess., 5 parts (Washington: GPO, 1951) (hereafter cited as MSFE), 1:558-62. Said Truman of Mac-Arthur: ". . .there was never anybody around him to keep him in line. He didn't have anybody on his staff that wasn't an ass kisser. He just wouldn't let anybody near him who wouldn't kiss his ass . . . . I fired him because he wouldn't respect the authority of the President . . . . I didn't fire him because he was a dumb son of a bitch although he was, but that's not against the law for generals. If it was, half to three quarters of them would be in jail." (Merle Miller, *Plain Speaking: An Oral Biography of Harry S. Truman* [Published by Berkley Publishing Corporation, distributed by G. P. Putnam's Sons, New York, 1973], pp. 287, 291. Acheson has said: "As one looks back in calmness, it seems impossible to overestimate the damage that General MacArthur's willful insubordination and incredibly bad judgment did to the United States in the world

and to the Truman Administration in the United States . . . . The General was surely bright enough to understand what his Government wanted him to do. General Ridgway, who succeeded him, understood perfectly and achieved the desired ends.'' (Acheson, *The Korean War*, p. 111.)

29. Collins, *War in Peacetime*, pp. 267-87; Arthur M. Schlesinger, Jr., and Richard H. Rovere, *The General and the President* (New York: Farrar-Strauss, 1951); Spanier, *The Truman-MacArthur Controversy and the Korean War;* Trumbull Higgins, *Korea and the Fall of MacArthur* (New York: Oxford University Press, 1960).
30. MSFE, 1:3-4. Further MSFE citations are given in the text.
31. Declassified Hearings-Transcripts, NA, Records of the United States Senate, Records of the Senate Foreign Relations Committee, RF 46. The gist of these transcripts appears in John Edward Wiltz, ''The MacArthur Hearings of 1951: The Secret Testimony,'' MA 39 (December 1975):167-73.

PART III

The Naval Administration of Dan Able Kimball

12
Unification and Korea

Defense unification caused controversy in the field as well as in Washington. Three of the four chiefs of staff—Omar N. Bradley, J. Lawton Collins, and Hoyt S. Vandenberg—had a common background from West Point and subsequent service in Europe during World War II and preferred a single chief of staff to the federated organization provided in the National Security Act.[1] The question thus may well be raised whether the use of the word *joint* for task forces that operated in Korea was not merely a mask used in numerous instances by the Army and Air Force to camouflage a desire to bypass well-established naval and amphibious doctrines, terminology, and command relations and to call "joint" certain operations in which the Navy and Marine Corps contributed much more than did the Army and Air Force.[2]

For example, under pressure for "jointness" by the Joint Chiefs of Staff, in 1949 General Douglas MacArthur established a Joint Strategic Plans and Operations Group in his headquarters. This elite group was headed under a second hat by Brigadier General Edwin K. Wright, USA, Assistant Chief of Staff for Operations. Wright's group had prepared Operation Chromite by 12 August 1950. On the fifteenth, MacArthur assembled a planning staff for the operation and also asked the Department of the Army to activate X Corps headquarters. Meanwhile Admiral James H. Doyle and his Amphibious Group I were trying to fill in the details of Wright's plan and the top Marine Corps leaders worked to flush out the Second Marine Division at Camp Lejeune while transferring the First Division and its air wing to Korea. Marine ground and air were to seize the port of Inchon and Kimpo airfield, cross the Han River and seize, occupy, and defend Seoul, and then join the Seventh Infantry to smash the North Korean invaders. General Field Harris's First Marine Air Wing, temporarily called "Tactical Air Command, X Corps," would operate from its carriers until it could provide tactical air support from Kimpo Airfield. In sum, the "joint" operation, less the Seventh Infantry and some Korean Marines, was wholly Navy and Marine Corps.

Take another example. Rear Admiral Charles Turner Joy, Commander U.S. Naval Forces Far East, on 20 August 1950 formed Joint Task Force 7 for

Secretary of the Navy Dan A. Kimball.

the Inchon operation. Though called joint, JTF-7 was nothing more than the U.S. Seventh Fleet commanded by Rear Admiral Arthur D. Struble, who as the joint commander would control all forces used in the operation, including any Air Force elements provided. MacArthur, however, directed the use only of naval and Marine air, leaving the Fifth Air Force to support the Eighth Army. Though well versed in the naval and amphibious doctrines of World War II, Struble was ready, he said, "to throw the book away [and forge] a damn good unified command." He obtained gunnery and air officers for his joint task force headquarters from the Seventh Fleet and in talks with Joy and General Lemuel C. Shepherd wondered whether MacArthur would give command of the X Corps to Shepherd, as Chief of Naval Operations Forrest Sherman suggested. Logic favored Shepherd, who commanded the Pacific Fleet Marine Force. His headquarters was organized for amphibious warfare, and he was a veteran amphibious commander who as a lieutenant general had corps-command rank. General Wright and MacArthur's deputy chief of staff supported Sherman, but the Chief of Staff, Major General Edward M. Almond, did not. On 15 August MacArthur designated Almond, who would remain as chief of staff, to command the operation. The reason MacArthur chose him, Almond said, was that *"Chromite* was definitely a land operation, once the landing was made. . . . The real essence of the Inchon landing was not merely to land and form a beachhead but to drive across difficult terrain and capture a large city and thereafter properly outpost and protect that city."[3] Although he had attended the Air Corps Tactical School and the Naval War College, Almond knew nothing about amphibious operations and "didn't understand Marines." As Hanson Baldwin has put it, "Almond was commanding that corps . . . but also still acting chief of staff, which was a hell of a note. He was wearing two hats. . . . Which was absurd."[4]Instead of joining Struble on his flagship the *Rochester* as "commander, expeditionary troops," Almond went with MacArthur in the *Mount McKinley* and sent his X Corps headquarters to an MSTS transport. He thus deprived himself of the excellent communications available on the *Rochester* and of the opportunity to personally conduct liaison with the top naval commander. Not until 21 September—a full six days after the landings—did X Corps Headquarters land at Inchon and assume command of operations ashore, whereupon Struble dissolved JTF-7 and became Commander Naval Support Force, in which role he subordinated himself to the requirements of a land campaign. X Corps Headquarters should never have been activated, for the record it made was poor. Shephard's Fleet Marine Force Headquarters, a going concern that knew how to conduct amphibious operations, should have been used instead.

Was the victory in the Inchon-Seoul operation due to unification? President Harry S. Truman spoke of "the splendid cooperation of our Army, Navy, and Air Force" but never mentioned the Marine Corps or its field leaders. "The truth is," Colonel Robert D. Heinl, Jr., USMC, has said, "the fact of unification was virtually irrelevant at Inchon, and very nearly so for the rest of the [Inchon-Seoul] campaign."[4] Administratively, the Marines remained under Shepherd. When they operated ashore, however, they were under Army direction, an arrangement that did not always please Marine Corps field officers such as O. P. Smith. Although called the Tactical Air Command, X Corps, and headed by a Marine Corps brigadier general, that command consisted of Marine Air Group 33 and headquarters and service units from the First Marine Air Wing. Standing by to help on the jeep carriers *Badoeng Strait* and *Sicily* was Marine Aircraft Group 12. No unification here.

Unification created a host of problems in the field in Korea. Although he had attended the Air Corps Tactical School and the Naval War College, General Edward M. Almond, USA *(above)* knew nothing about amphibious operations and "didn't understand Marines," yet General MacArthur put him in charge of the X Corps and of the Inchon landing. While Air Force commanders such as General Earle E. Partridge *(below, left)* wanted the Air Force to control all aircraft in Korea, General Mark W. Clark, USA *(right)*, among many other Army officers, preferred the close support provided troops on the ground by the Navy and Marine Corps to that of the Air Force.

OFFICIAL U.S. ARMY PHOTOGRAPHS

Admiral Joy declined the request of 8 July 1950 by General George E. Stratemeyer, Commanding General, Far Eastern Air Forces, for operational control over all naval aircraft. While the Navy would gladly use whatever strength the Air Force would give it, experienced naval commanders like Struble preferred to avoid complicated command arrangements that always resulted when the Air Force was involved; in a stormy meeting he told Stratemeyer that Air Force planes coming from bases in Japan would have little time over target and could carry only small bomb loads compared to the Navy and Marine aircraft on carriers just off Korea's coast. With MacArthur's approval, it was arranged that naval and Marine air would support the Inchon landings while the Air Force, for three days prior to the landings, would support a deception operation at Kunsan. It may well be, as has been suggested, that naval and Marine Corps pilots were determined to perform at their absolute best in order to prove the unsurpassed capabilities of naval aviation for precision attacks and perhaps ease the pressure against naval air applied since unification had gone into effect.[6]

What coordinated air planning was undertaken in Korea was not greatly successful because Far East Headquarters failed to assign areas of responsibility for the air interdiction campaign. By default of directives, the Navy took over the eastern half and the Air Force the western half of Korea. In its half the Navy coordinated the use of naval surface and air power. Navy and Air Force coordination, however, was poor. As the commander of the First Marine Division, Major General O. P. Smith, put it:

General [Earle E.] Partridge commanded the 5th Air Force, and he'd been raised on the Joint Operations Center business where everything had to be cleared through the Joint Operations Center [JOC] at Taegu. At Inchon we hadn't had to worry about that kind of business, but at Wonsan they put that in effect, and it worked for a while. . . . Then, even their Air Force saw that when we got up to Chosin Reservoir this business of clearing things through Taegu over the mountains would just not work at all. . . . Partridge agreed to let Field Harris run the show, and tell him what he did afterwards. And Field Harris, in order to handle the control of the air up there with these rugged mountains, got a transport plane and fitted it up with a tremendous amount of radio gear, and it flew continuously over the Chosin Reservoir area and communicated with the squadrons and with the liaison parties down on the ground, and we got excellent support.

Again:

when we went into Operation Killer, the 5th Air Force system went into effect—the JOC—and what I was trying to do was to have our Marine Air support us. We brought the Marine Air Wing out there, and we figured that we should get some priority out of our Air Wing.
I went to Gen. [Matthew] Ridgway about it and I said, "I realize of course that I can't ask for all the Marine Air Wing to work for the Marines; as a matter of fact we don't need all this all the time. But I

would like to have one squadron that we could have on station at all times, that we could call. . . ." He said, "Smith, I am sorry, but I don't command the Air Force." The 5th Air Force didn't recognize the 8th Army Commander as their chief. They went back direct to MacArthur. Well, then we argued back and forth, and I talked a lot to Field Harris—he was sympathetic to us, but he had to play ball with the Air Force. Finally we got Gen. Partridge to come up to our CP [Command Post], when we were somewhere up near Hongchong, to discuss this close air support. And he came up and told me, "Smith, close air support frankly doesn't pay dividends." I said, "We don't agree with that; we figure it pays a lot of dividends." He wanted to use most of our air to go up the line and bomb the railroad tracks and all that kind of thing—this Operation Strangle—which never worked.

While we were talking, somebody had requested an air strike, and they were trying to raise Taegu to go through the JOC. It took 45 minutes to get the call through, and I told Gen. Partridge, "You see what this involves?" He said, "Well maybe you've got something." But it wasn't changed, and what it meant was that our people up in the front lines, finding that it took so long to get any air, just. . .tried to get the artillery to do the job. . . .

[The Air Force's] main objection was philosophical: they didn't want anybody on the ground telling a plane what to do. We got around that in the Marine Corps by having an air liaison party where one of these officers was a pilot. There were two officers with this group, and the other officer might have been an artilleryman. And when a request went up to the Air for support, those people up there knew that some aviator down on the ground had checked that over and they were not going to have to do something impossible. We never had any complaints from our aviators.[7]

Heinl noted that "the timely, precise, unfailing [Marine Corps] close air support. . .didn't just happen. It resulted from sound doctrine, from superb training and airmanship, and from a tested control organization on the ground, spearheaded by young aviators as muddy and exposed and as far forward as any rifle platoon leader."[8] According to the official Marine Corps history of Marine Corps operations in Korea,

The close coordination of aviation with the ground forces in the Chosin campaign was due in large measure to the assignment of additional pilots to the 1st Marine Division as forward air controllers. .. .Air units frequently had to rely upon charts with place names, grid coordinates, and scales different from those in the hands of the ground troops. Here the Marine system of the man on the ground talking the pilot onto the target by reference to visual landmarks paid off.[9]

Captain John S. Thach, USN, commanded the jeep carrier *Sicily*, in which VFM-214 was embarked. As he put it:

The U.S. Air Force wasn't too interested in close air support. The people in high command in the Air Force were primarily hepped on the big bomber idea—that you didn't even need troops to win a war. Just fly over and bomb them, and then wait for a telegram saying that they surrender. So they were utterly unprepared to do close air support the way it had to be done if you were going to help the troops at the front lines. And it wasn't a matter of just curing a communications problem. It was a matter of education over a long period and experience and doctrine built up.

Air Force F-80 jet fighters had a range of only one hundred miles. Flying from bases in Japan, they could remain over a Korean target for only about fifteen minutes and their pilots were not trained in ground support. From his escort carrier, the *Sicily*, in which VFM-214 was embarked, Captain John Smith Thach, USN, sent pilots trained in ground support to deliver that support "right on the button."

OFFICIAL U.S. ARMY PHOTOGRAPH

In contrast, speaking of Marine pilots, he remarked: "They knew the business of close air support. Every one of those pilots had had infantry training, and so the ground-air team of the Marine was really proficient. . . . The Marine forward air controller on the ground was often an aviator. He and the ground troops knew each other's business because they trained at it." That was why, Thach concluded, Marine close air support in Korea could put it "right on the button."[10]

The X Corps liked the Navy-Marine Corps air support system, was taught how to use it by Marines from the First Division, and found that it worked well. An Army regimental commander who had seen the Marines in action about the Pusan perimeter wrote directly to Washington:

> The Marines on our left were a sight to behold. Not only was their equipment superior or equal to ours, but they had squadrons of air in direct support. They used it like artillery. . . .We just have to have air support like that or we might as well disband the Infantry and join the Marines.[11]

And Brigadier General Homer W. Kiefer, USA, of the Seventh Division, recommended that the Army adopt the Navy-Marine Corps way.

Until the Chosin Reservoir episode, Marine air had supported Marine ground troops as an air-ground team. Early in 1951, however, MacArthur specifically directed that Marine air be assigned to the Fifth Air Force and be employed in support of the Eighth Army as a whole. Fifth Air Force gave Marine Air groups many tasks that did not call for their specialty—close air support—and the Fifth Air Force prevailed,[12] thus illustrating that in this instance unification, as represented in the Joint Chiefs of Staff and theater command organization, separated rather than integrated ground and air.

Evaluations of the effect of air power in Korea differ widely. Some writers have held that it was "the decisive factor."[13] MacArthur said in May 1951 that "the support that our tactical air has given to our ground troops in Korea has perhaps never been equalled in the history of modern war." However, he went on,

> I believe that perhaps too much was expected of their air. The air alone has certain limitations as compared with ground troops. . . .It is quite evident to anybody that is acquainted with war that determined ground troops cannot be stopped alone by air. I think it is well understood now, certainly by the Congress that passed the unification law, that modern war must have all the components working together in unison, and that it's quite silly for anyone to say that the artillery fire is more effective or less effective or equally effective with the fire from a plane. The two things are quite different. Both are important; both are absolutely necessary for victory in modern war.[14]

General Matthew B. Ridgway stated that without airmen the war would have been over in sixty days, with all Korea in communist hands, a statement echoed by General Walton Walker, commander of Army troops in Korea after the capture of General William F. Dean. Moreover, Chinese officials were keenly aware that aerial attacks by Russian MIGs on American troops in Korea might provoke Air Force bombing of their own territory. China as well as Russia therefore wanted to keep the war limited. Air Force planes quickly transported supplies and men to, from, and about Korea and destroyed large quantities of enemy equipment and numbers of troops. The Air Force flew more missions in Korea than the Navy and Marine Corps, and the F-86 successfully hammered MIGs into the rice paddies of Korea, for the kill ratio as of May 1952 was seven to one—147 MIGS to 20 F-86s and would rise to nine to one at the end of the fighting. However, because it was forced to live with the political limitations placed upon it, the Air Force could not exploit its strategic and tactical power to the full, for the logistic base of the enemy lay in the privileged sanctuary, Manchuria. On the other hand, the enemy, unable to maintain air bases south of the Yalu, could not attack U.N. beachheads and ports, or deny to the U.N. control of the air over Korea. In part for this reason, the communists became amenable to suggestions for peace.[15]

A Marine Air Intelligence study credited the F-86 with being the only American plane that compared favorably with the MIG-15, but offered several additional interesting observations. As of 19 October 1951 the sole F-86 interceptor group in FEAF rotated its squadrons between Japan and Korea, with the result that only between thirty and forty were ever combat ready. No Air Force night fighters were in Korea, and only two of five F-82 (twin *Mustangs*) based in Japan were combat ready. Moreover, B-29s could not be protected by escorting jets against MIG-15 attacks. While enemy fighters based in Manchuria were roughly two-and-a-half times the number of U.N. jets in Korea, naval and Marine aircraft on American and British aircraft carriers brought the numbers into balance. "These forces, although they vary from time to time, are particularly important because their mobile bases allow their range endurance factor to be multiplied by sudden shifts of the carriers near to the battle areas. The friendly and enemy air forces . . .are thus about equal by virtue of the presence of the naval air units."[16]

Few if any chroniclers of Air Force exploits in Korea—and they have religiously detailed the number of troops, tanks, vehicles, freight cars, locomotives, barracks, buildings, gun positions, and the like that were destroyed—mention the fact that all the planes, pilots, fuel, supplies, and ammunition were provided the Air Force because the U.S. Navy, in control of the seas, made it possible also to command the air about Korea.[17]

Naval leaders considered the Air Force effort in Korea extremely disappointing. Vice Admiral Joseph J. Clark, Commander Seventh Fleet, said that "the interdiction program was a failure. It did *not* interdict."[18] To naval leaders, the Air Force shibboleth that he who controls the air controls all below had been refuted. Indeed, the war gave striking proof of the great dependence of air power on events taking place on the ground, particularly upon adequate single service and joint communications, Marine aviation being a notable happy example, and taught some Air Force leaders at least the beneficial lesson that air power had limitations.[19] The Secretary of the Air Force, Thomas K. Finletter, accounted for the failure of tactical air power to stop the North Korean ground attack in this way:

> Tactical air power must be in relationship to Ground forces. Tactical air power alone cannot win a war—any more than Ground Forces alone could win a war. . . . A force of ground troops is a kind of composite power of ground elements and air elements which support them. . . . [W]here there is such gross disproportion as there is and has been in Korea between the ground elements, tactical air superiority of its own cannot win the immediate battle.[20]

While reminiscing in 1976, Hanson Baldwin recalled that "the Air Force boasted. . .that they had initiated Operation Strangle and it was bound to cut off the Chinese from their sources. I wrote several pieces saying that Operation Strangle wasn't strangling and hadn't strangled, which incurred the ire of the Assistant Secretary of the Air Force, who wrote to *The [New York] Times*. . . .They couldn't possibly stop men with ammunition on their backs from filtering through the hills. You can't do it by air power."[21]

Collins, MacArthur, and Ridgway agreed that tactical air power alone could not isolate a battlefield or completely interdict enemy troops and supply lines, and the Joint Chiefs did not pursue MacArthur's suggestion made during a visit to him by Collins and Vandenberg in early July 1950 that atomic bombs be used to interdict enemy supply routes.[22]

In October 1950 Bradley made it clear that in the Air Force what was needed was "a *balance* between strategic and tactical air power."[23] On 30 November, although he said that "every weapon" should be used in Korea, Truman vetoed the use of atomic arms. When MacArthur, in December, was faced with Chinese intervention and sought "political decisions and strategic plans. . .adequate to meet realities involved," Truman tersely told him that "we consider that the preservation of your forces is now the primary consideration."[24] MacArthur wanted authority to bomb military targets in Manchuria and to launch an air and naval campaign against China, but on the matter of "hot pursuit" of enemy aircraft across the Yalu, thirteen of the nations fighting with the United States in Korea cast a veto against it. Atomic bombs were as yet designed for strategic rather than tactical employment, but Truman's decision not to use them was based on other factors: the lack of suitable strategic targets in China, whose great strength was in manpower; doubt that the issue involved was vital to the security of the United States; and a well-based fear that their use would result in the explosion of World War III. Although the Air Force's "ace in the hole," the atomic bomb, had been found to be "uneconomical," it had proved its efficacy through inaction and, as a deterrent, had avoided Armageddon.[25]

Not until November 1950 did the Strategic Plans Division ask the Office of Naval Intelligence for target data on the Soviet Arctic, Baltic, Black, and Far

East fleets for naval nuclear weapons. These targets were to be within one-hundred miles of waters in which carriers would operate. Late in November a request was made for Soviet targets six-hundred miles inland from waters about the Soviet Union. This target information proved useful in establishing priorities until about 1956, but it never entered into the operation plans of the Navy's Composite Squadrons. Moreover, those squadrons remained in the Mediterranean, where they sought to overcome various operational difficulties. Not until nuclear weapons were made smaller so that they could be carried by standard Navy attack aircraft, the *Forrestal*-class carriers were commissioned, and the *Midway* and *Essex* classes were modernized could it be said that the Navy had a respectable atomic air capability. The fact that VC-6 was not fully operational at Atsuki Naval Air Station, Japan, until early 1953 showed that the Navy had made no effort to use its atomic weapons in Korea.[26]

Because many problems had arisen since the Hoover Commission had submitted its report on the organization of the Executive Department, Truman asked all executive agencies for proposals for improvement that he would submit to the next Congress.[27] Secretary of Defense Robert A. Lovett in turn asked the military services to forward "a review of organization and activity with a view toward improvement in accordance with the Reorganization Act of 1949."[28] The Under Secretary of the Navy, Francis P. Whitehair, conferred with civilian and military leaders of the Navy Department and by 23 November concluded that, since the Department continually tried to improve its organization and administration through its Navy's Improvement Program and occasional special management surveys and audits, "it is not considered necessary or desirable to recommend any substantive changes of such magnitude as to require special legislation or internal reorganization."[29] Meanwhile, in response to the investigations of the Navy Department by the Senator Lyndon B. Johnson's Preparedness Subcommittee, Secretary of the Navy Dan A. Kimball initiated Operation Austerity, designed to make everyone in the Navy "cost conscious."

After the Korean armistice was signed, on 27 July 1953, fuller assessments could be made of the military operations of the Korean War and of how well the National Security Act, as amended, had served to "manage" those forces. According to Lieutenant General Laurence S. Kuter, USAF, air power employed at the beginning of World War II had operated under two errors: "it failed to recognize that air forces must be commanded and employed as entities, and that the first task of air forces in war is to win the air battle."[30] General H. H. Arnold had voiced a new doctrine in 1943, one that called for air superiority as the first requisite to success in any major land battle. He demanded that the control of air forces be centralized and insisted that command be exercised through the air commander.[31] A new Air Force publication, FM 31-35, *Air Ground Operations*, 1946, stressed the coequality of air forces, adding that "the basic doctrine of air-ground operations is to integrate the effort of air and ground forces, each operating under its own command, to achieve maximum effectiveness, as directed by the theater commander, in defeating the enemy." In April 1951 General Otto Weyland followed Air Force doctrine in demanding that "all aircraft operating in a theater, except those performing Naval missions, be placed under the command of the air commander." In his *Far East Air Force Report*, however, he said that most interservice problems with respect to the use of air power in Korea had lain in the lack of a joint headquarters at the highest level. As a careful student of the air war in Korea has put it,

> While carrier-based air forces represented an important theater air force potential, Navy commanders in the Far East were slow to commit themselves positively to the collateral missions which they believed might hinder their ability to maintain control of the seas. Thus the agreement for air coordination in defense of the Far East Theater signed on 26 March [1951] gave the Far East Air Forces air defense commander operational control over all shore-based Navy and Marine fighter aircraft in an air defense emergency, but it provided that carrier-based fighter aircraft were an integral part of the fleet and could not normally be pre-committed to any emergency operational control of the air defense commander. Marine land-based aircraft were successfully integrated into the Fifth Air Force-Eighth Army air-ground system, but Seventh Fleet aircraft could not be positively committed to ground support as long as the Naval Forces Far East had a mission in the Taiwan Straits. When relieved of this mission, the Seventh Fleet established a naval member in the Joint Operations Center in Korea in June 1953 and thereafter participated integrally in the support of the ground forces in Korea.[32]

Aviation Week commented caustically that the "Navy's carrier-borne jets were assigned the task of ground support, tangled infrequently with enemy aircraft, scored few victories and produced no aces," adding that this drew Navy charges that Air Force was hogging the war."[33]

How about Air Force-Army cooperation? From its studies of Korea, the Air Force decided that tactical air power could be divorced from mere troop support. Given the improvement in its capabilities, tactical air would not only support troops on the ground but operate directly against enemy forces in the field where no friendly ground forces were present. The result would be a divorcement of tactical from the strategic air arm and also a separation of tactical air from direct troop support. Indeed, new Tactical Air Command regulations of 29 June 1953 suggested that "it [was] quite reasonable to say that we should look for a modification in our tactics and in our concepts of war. . .which would point toward the exploitation of tactical air atomic attacks by highly mobile ground forces."

Although the Army preferred to have its own organic close-support aircraft, it had managed to live with approved doctrine in accordance with which the Air Force would provide air support for its troop and cargo operations. A joint agreement of 20 May 1949 had set the maximum weight of Army aircraft at twenty-five hundred pounds, of its helicopters at four thousand pounds.

When the Army sought heavier aircraft, the Air Force refused because of the infringement upon its transportation mission. On 2 October 1951 Finletter and the Secretary of the Army, Frank Pace, lifted the limits on Army aviation and defined the combat zone to be an area from sixty to seventy-five miles deep behind the battle line. When the Army suggested allocating helicopter battalions to a typical field army, the Air Force again objected, on the ground of the duplication of services it should perform. It took the intervention of Secretary of Defense Lovett to reach an agreement, on 4 November 1952. The Army could use fixed-wing aircraft weighing up to five thousand pounds and helicopters of any weight to transport men and supplies within an area fifty to one hundred miles deep behind enemy lines and leave the transportation of Army troops and supplies outside that zone to the Air Force.[34]

One might assume that the Air Force was happy with the new funds allotted it for fiscal year 1951. Apparently it was not. In May 1951, when rumor had it that the administration wanted to build up to ninety-five groups in fiscal year 1952, General Vandenberg, it may be recalled, testified at the MacArthur hearings that "the United States is operating a shoestring Air Force in view of its global responsibilities" and spoke of the need of a 150-wing strength. He based his demand for such increased strength upon the acquisition by Russia of the atomic bomb in August 1949, use of force by North Korean and Chinese Communists in Korea to achieve foreign policy objectives, the need to bolster the defenses of Western Europe, and the estimate that by 1954 Russia would have sufficient atomic power to destroy the military and industrial centers of the United States.

The attitude of the Navy toward the Air Force's demand for 150 wings is well expressed by James W. McConnaughhay, who worked in the Office of the Under Secretary, who told his chief, Kimball:

> the Air Force now wants 138 wings, groups, or whatever they choose to call it, instead of 150. However, these are to be combat wings and will include troop carrier and strategic transport units. In addition to the 138 combat groups, they will want 20 to 25 troop carrier and transport units, and they plan to have 4 squadrons per wing instead of the present 3. . . .
>
> On the basis of the figures I obtain from OP-05 I would guess that they want to have approximately 40 to 50 thousand aircraft in their active inventory. . . .
>
> I have come to the conclusion that trying to predict the total number of aircraft desired by the Air Force at this stage of the game is almost as easy as trying to predict what my wife will come home with on her next trip to the local department store.[35]

On 8 August Kimball put it to Finletter straight with respect to a congressional resolution that sought to increase the Air Force to 150 groups:

> The Department of the Navy. . .is opposed to the adoption of subject resolution. If this resolution is adopted it would place an obligation on

the House of Representatives to initiate the appropriate measures to carry out its provisions. Such action should be an attempt to legislate the strategic direction of the armed forces since, in view of the appropriations available to the Department of Defense, it could be taken only at the expense of the other military departments. The concept of the resolution is contrary to the intent of Congress as stated in the National Security Act, as amended.[36]

Meanwhile, in light of doubts cast upon Air Force capabilities for air defense and tactical air warfare by such men as Carl Vinson in the House, Paul Douglas in the Senate, and lessons learned about air warfare in Korea by a number of tactical airpower evaluation groups, Vandenberg reorganized the internal field structure of the Air Force. The Strategic Air Command, for example, would be strengthened—but naval air would also have a part in any expanded air offensive.[37]

One day earlier the issue had practically been settled when Vinson suggested augmenting both the Air Force and naval air power. While air power, combined with new weapons of mass destruction, had changed "the entire strategic situation," he desired not a crash air program but one for the long pull, one that he believed industry could handle without expanding its base. Although he would increase the Air Force from 95 to 138 wings, plus 25 troop carrier wings intended primarily for joint Army-Air Force operations, he would also augment naval aviation by adding "as promptly as possible" two additional supercarriers to the one already authorized.[38]

Vandenberg wanted 150 air groups, Collins more ground forces and more tactical air power. While he said he had no intention of creating a tactical air force or of taking over the Tactical Air Force of the Air Force, Collins wanted the Army to have aircraft specifically designed for close support roles and authority to control such aircraft down to corps level, leaving to high-performance Air Force fighters the mission of protecting them from enemy aircraft. While multipurpose fighters were adequate, these had frequently been diverted by the Air Force from a support role. The Army's demand for a light aircraft useful only for support and always available when needed was seconded by the House Armed Services Committee, which said that the Army was not being provided sufficient tactical air support by the Air Force. The Air Force faced a problem: an all-purpose fighter with the supersonic speed needed to seek and destroy enemy jets would not have the slow speed and endurance needed for ground air support. Its answer was to transfer the Ninth Air Force to the Tactical Air Command, which it said would "provide for Air Force cooperation with land, naval, and/or amphibious forces." On 25 January 1951 command was given to Lieutenant General John K. Canon, who opposed the Army's demand for integrated tactical air support. Moreover, the Army's demand for control of close support aircraft countered Air Force doctrine, which called for Air Force control of any object that flew under the principles of concentration of force and centralization of control. These were the same principles that had steeled the Air Force to demand the JOC system in Korea in opposition to the integrated ground air support system used by the Navy and Marine Corps. General Mark W. Clark, chief of the Army Field Forces, told Collins:

> I consider that the traditional Air Force doctrine, which provides for co-equal command status between ground and air at all but theater levels constitutes a fundamental defect in command relationship. This doctrine of command by mutual cooperation is unacceptable because it reserves to the supporting arm the authority to determine whether or not a supporting task should be executed. The theory of divided command in the face of the enemy is foreign to the basic concept of warfare wherein the responsible commander exercises undisputed directive authority over all elements essential to the accomplishment of his missions.

Unable to win agreement with the Air Force, Pace and Collins agreed with Finletter to set the Army's demands aside until the Air Force could provide the tactical air forces capable of performing the missions required of tactical air power. Similarly, General Cannon's demand that his Tactical Air Force be authorized to deliver atomic weapons did not sit well with the leaders of Strategic Air Force. However, the Joint Chiefs of Staff approved the establishment of several tactical divisions to serve in Great Britain and in Germany in support of NATO ground troops. As for the air defense of the United States, an arrangement agreed upon earlier continued in effect under which the Army controlled antiaircraft artillery and the Air Force provided aircraft to defend target areas decided upon jointly by the Army and Air Force Departments.[39]

Still to be settled was the demand by the Army, backed by the Navy, for the channeling of fissionable materials into such tactical weapons as small bombs, guided missile warheads, and atomic artillery, thus breaking the Air Force's monopoly on giant atomic bombs transportable only by large strategic aircraft. Moreover, the Army wanted to end the procedure in which it channeled its aircraft acquisitions through the Air Force and also demanded guided missiles and rockets that would lessen the role of piloted aircraft on the battlefield.[40]

On 28 April 1952 Truman had named General Mark Clark as Commander in Chief U.N. Command and Far East Command to succeed Ridgway, who became Supreme Allied Commander Europe. Clark believed that Air Force and naval air power could exert sufficient pressure to affect not only the truce negotiations being conducted at Panmunjom but the attitude of the Soviets and of the Red Chinese. The Eighth Army's Lieutenant General James A. Van Fleet wanted to control aircraft assigned to Army troops for close support purposes. Although Clark declined to make any radical change in Army Air Force Doctrine, he established a joint headquarters staff served by men of all three services who would plan and supervise combined operations. While a Navy representative was not a formal member of the FEAF Formal Target Committee established by General Weyland, the theater air commander toward the end of the war, a naval aviator was invited to attend its meetings. Meanwhile the Navy was kept informed of the targets to be attacked. A subsequent conference of Air Force, Army, Navy, and Marine Corps air representatives that assessed the air war effort found that that doctrine, already adopted, had worked well in Korea.

What lessons were learned in Korea? The first lesson the Air Force learned was that a limited war in an area containing few strategic objectives obviated the employment of its Strategic Air Command. Second, although it violated its doctrine by using medium bombers such as the B-26 and B-29 in a tactical role and escort fighters for ground support, the preponderance of evidence upheld its contention that control of the air is a prerequisite for successful ground action. Most likely because they feared atomic retaliation if they did so, the communists did not use their full air power in Korea. Therefore the most potent air weapon in the American armory, even if it was merely "in being," may have been the Strategic Air Command. As General Maxwell D. Taylor, an Eighth Army commander in Korea put it, "in the U.S., the ultimate effect of the Korean experience, oddly enough, was not to weaken faith in atomic air power but rather to strengthen it."[41]

American tactical air strikes in Korea were most successful when launched against concentrated troop, supply, and transportation targets behind the lines, least successful when enemy troops were scattered along the front lines. Navy men evaluated the Air Force's railroad interdiction campaign, Operation Strangle, to have been a failure; General Shepherd called it a "fizzle." Tactical air support was seen to be at its best when used to isolate the battlefield when friendly troops were on the move, at its poorest when these troops were static and subject to attack.

Unification of the doctrines, weapons, and tactics of the three services had proceeded extremely slowly because it took the Air Force six years to determine its doctrine and even longer to publish its doctrinal and tactical manuals, because it remained deaf to the lessons of Korea, and because the Army, Navy, and Marine Corps opposed much of what it proposed. An Ad Hoc Committee for Joint Policies and Procedures established by the Joint Chiefs of Staff had reported in October 1949. Its Army member suggested the creation of four joint centers to devise joint doctrines, tactics, techniques, training, and equipment testing for airborne, tactical air support, air defense, and amphibious operations. The Marine Corps feared being despoiled of its amphibiouis responsibilities; the Air Force bridled at the thought that ground officers should be permitted to evaluate air operations, reiterated that air power was "indivisible," and gagged when it heard it said that tactical air power existed merely to support ground forces. Both Navy and Air Force members declined the proposal, saying that it meant the transfer of service roles and missions to new agencies. However, the Air Force had agreed to an Army proposal that it review current tactical air doctrine and established a Board of Review for Tactical Air Operations on 10 June 1949. Before this board, General Collins argued that tactical air should be used to aid the ground force commander to achieve his missions and that a Tactical Air Support Center should be established. But the Air Force would rewrite tactical air doctrine only if it could be the sole judge of its tactics, techniques, and equipment. It preferred to emphasize the phrase *theater air forces* instead of *tactical air forces*, and *the tactical employment of air force* rather than *the employment of tactical air force*. In the end, Collins was pleased when the Tactical Air Command and the Army Field Forces concluded that the Army and Air Force should work together to devise doctrine for joint training, airborne and close support operations, and the development and testing of equipment. Although most of the paper work had been completed by March 1950, the outbreak of the Korean War introduced pressure for revisions in joint air-ground doctrine. The result was the Joint Training Directive for Air-Ground Operations dated 1 September 1950. Although the Army and the Tactical Air Force accepted the doctrines it set forth, the latter did so only on the basis that it must be approved and made official by higher authorities and refused to cooperate with the Army to the degree the Army desired.

The Army took the position that the principle of unified command should be followed in the establishment of joint centers operated under the immediate jurisdiction of the Joint Chiefs of Staff. One of the Joint Chiefs would be the executive agent for each center, which would be headed by a commander who would have a joint staff. Although the Navy and Air Force opposed the establishment of joint centers, the Joint Chiefs eventually agreed to a paper that spelled out the "Principles Governing the Functions of the Armed Services," "Functions of the Individual Services," "Principles Governing Joint Operations of the Armed Forces," and "Principles and Doctrine Governing Joint Aspects of Special Operations of the Armed Forces." The *Joint Action Armed Forces* paper was published in September 1951 as Army Field Manual 110-5, Navy JAAF, and Air Force Manual 1-1. Each manual reflected an individual service; none provided for complete integration and unification. Nevertheless, JAAF provided for the establishment of a number of joint boards under the service that had a primary interest in a matter. The Air Force was made responsible for the Joint Air Defense Board, Joint Tactical Air Support Board, and Joint Air Transportation Board; the Army for the Joint Airborne Troop Board; the Commandant of the Marine Corps for the Joint Landing Force Board; and the Chief of Naval Operations for the Joint Amphibious Board. Once doctrines these boards recommended were approved by the Joint Chiefs of Staff, they would supersede single service doctrines.

Unable to agree on terminology describing the employment of air power, the Air Force referred the problem to Secretary Finletter. After visiting Korea during the summer of 1951, he directed that the Air University's concept—the "indivisibility of air power"—be adopted by the Air Force. The concept made no great distinction between "strategic" and "tactical" uses, thus freeing tactical air from merely a ground support role. Late in the summer of 1951 the Air University was directed to "function as an Air Force doctrinal, educational, and research center." Should the term *theater air forces* replace *tactical air forces* in the manuals it would write? Should *theater air forces* include Navy and Marine air units assigned to a theater? Did *air superiority* mean superiority only in the local area of operations or include the entire air power complex of an enemy? Was an Air Force-Army Joint Operations Center really *joint* when the Army merely provided liaison personnel to choose targets and the Air Force did all the planning and performed the strike function? Not until mid-March 1953 did General Vandenberg approve Air Force Manual 1-2, *United States Air Force Basic Doctrine*, which held that air forces were most likely to be the dominant forces in war, and then only with the comment that "the dynamic and constant changes in new weapons makes periodic substantive review of this doctrine necessary."

The Air Force published various operational manuals between September 1953 and December 1954. Thus it was not until the end of 1954, seven long years after it had become an independent entity, that the Air Force finally adopted a basic doctrine and wrote its operating manuals. Would its doctrine and procedures be acceptable to the Army and Navy with respect to joint procedures? As already noted, in response to JAAF a number of joint boards were established in the fall of 1951 to deal with tactical air support, air transportation, airborne troops, and amphibious operations. While the Army, Navy, and Marine Corps advocated the decentralization of the command of air support to the supported unit, the Air Force demanded the retention of the existing system, with "unified command at theater level only, and co-equal status of component command at all echelons." On 1 February 1954 the Air Force formally recommended the discontinuance of the joint boards because they were expensive, used manpower better utilized elsewhere, duplicated the work of other agencies, and were unable to fulfill their purpose effectively. By the end of the year the Navy and Marine Corps agreed to their disbandment; when the Army also approved, the Joint Chiefs of Staff discontinued them. In 1955 the Joint Chiefs directed the Air Defense Command to assume the responsibilities of the Joint Air Defense Board. The responsibilities of the Joint Tactical Air Support Board and the Joint Air Transportation Board were assumed by the Tactical Air Command, which would develop joint doctrines with the aid of liaison members furnished by the Army, Navy, and Marine Corps. The Tactical Air Command would in turn provide liaison officers to the Army Field Forces, Amphibious Forces Atlantic Fleet, and Marine Corps Development Center to aid in the development of joint airborne troops and amphibious operations.[42]

Although it took six years for the diverse attitudes toward air power held within the Air Force to be codified into acceptable terms, the result—a statement of the "indivisibility" and utter supremacy of air power—proved indigestible to the Army, which held that "Army forces as land forces are the decisive component of the military structure" even though they "might need support from time to time by other military components." Even though the Navy's statement of doctrine in *U.S. Naval Warfare Publication 10* fairly paralleled that of the Air Force, the Navy believed that "air strategy, designed to seek a decision primarily by air action. . .is in the process of historical development and. . .will become more clearly definable with the passage of time."

The Army and Navy contended for unity of command at the scene of battle. The Navy, particularly, wanted to use functional task forces containing all the military components needed to complete their missions. Air power thus would help land power or naval power. The great increase in the speed, range, and firepower, and thus in the flexibility of aircraft, caused the Air Force to object to the fragmentation and subordination of this flexibility at the scene of battle and to demand the centralized control of this awesome power. In the end, attempts to use joint boards to draw the three services closer together in their doctrinal thinking and procedures not only failed to do so but resulted in widening their divergences.

NOTES

1. J. Lawton Collins, *War in Peacetime: The History and Lessons of Korea* (Boston: Houghton Mifflin Co., 1969), p. 38.
2. COl Robert Debs Heinl, Jr., USMC (RET), *Victory at High Tide: The Inchon-Seoul Campaign* (Philadelphia and New York: J. B. Lippincott Co., 1968), p. 50.
3. Ibid., p. 61.
4. "The Reminiscences of Hanson W. Baldwin," transcript of oral interview by John T. Mason (Annapolis, Md.: U.S. Naval Institute, 1976), p. 498.
5. Heinl, *Victory at High Tide*, pp. 263-64.
6. Ibid., pp. 57-59; ADM John S. Thach, USN (RET), " 'Right on the Button': Marine Close Air Support in Korea," USNIP 101 (November 1975):56.
7. Transcript of oral interview with GEN Oliver P. Smith, USMC (RET), by Benis M. Frank (Washington: HQ, USMC, History Division, 1969), pp. 274-75 (hereafter cited as O. P. Smith, "Reminiscences").
8. Heinl, *Victory at High Tide*, pp. 221-22.
9. *U.S. Marine Corps Operations in Korea, 1950-1953*, 5 vols. (Washington: HQ, USMC, Historical Branch, G-3, 1954-72), 3:346-47.
10. Thach, " 'Right on the Button,' " 54-56.
11. COl Robert Debs Heinl, Jr., USMC (RET), *Soldiers of the Sea: The United States Marine Corps, 1775-1962* (Annapolis, Md.: U.S. Naval Institute, 1962), p. 576.
12. Ibid., pp. 576-79.
13. See for example, BGEN Benner Fellers, USAF, *Wings for Peace: A Primer for a New Defense* (Chicago: Henry Regnery, 1953), and COL James T. Stewart, USAF, ed., *Air Power: The Decisive Factor in Korea* (Princeton, N.J.: D. Van Nostrand, 1957.)
14. U.S. Congress, Senate Armed Services Committee and Senate Foreign Relations Committee *Hearings on the Military Situation in the Far East*, 82nd Cong., 1st Sess., 5 parts (Washington: GPO, 1951), 1:309.
15. Testimony of GEN Vandenberg, ibid., 1:507, and of MGEN Emmett O'Donnell, Jr. USAF, ibid., 4:3061-3115; "How the Air-Ground Team Operates in Korea," AF 34 (March 1951): 56-58; Donald W. Coble, "Air Support in the Korean War," *Aerospace Historian* 16 (Summer 1969):26-29; Harold C. Stuart, "The New Look in Korea," AF 34 (December 1951):22-24, 64-67.
16. Top Secret. Marine Corps SG2. *Intelligence Study of the Air Support in Korea, Oct. 19, 1951, copy in SNP.*
17. See, for example, GEN Otto P. Weyland, *"The Air Campaign in Korea,"* AUQR 6 (Fall 1953):5-13; Robert Frank Futrell, *Ideas, Concepts, Doctrine: A History of Basic Thinking in the United States Air Force, 1907-1964* (Maxwell Air Force Base, Ala.: Air University, 1971), pp. 149, 152, and "The United States Air Force in Korea," in Alfred Goldberg, ed., *A History of the United States Air Force 1907-1957* (Princeton, N.J.: Van Nostrand Reinhold, 1957), pp. 285-345.
18. CDR Malcolm W. Cagle, USN, and CDR Frank A. Manson, USN, *The Sea War in Korea* (Annapolis, Md.,: U.S. Naval Institute, 1957), p. 270.
19. Robert Frank Futrell, Lawson S. Moseley, and Albert F. Simpson, *The United States Air Force in Korea, 1950-1953* (New York: Duell, Sloan and Pearce, 1961), pp. 243-58; GEN Hoyt S. Vandenberg, USAF, "Air Power in the Korean War," in Eugene E. Emme, ed., *The Impact of Air Power: National Security and World Politics* (Princeton, N.J.: D. Van Nostrand, 1959), pp.400-406, and GEN Otto P. Wayland, USAF, "The Air Campaign in Korea," ibid., pp. 388-400.
20. U.S. Congress. House. *The Supplemental Appropriation Bill for 1951*, 81st Cong., 2nd Sess. (Washington: GPO, 1951), p. 10.
21. Baldwin, "Reminiscences," p. 509.
22. Matthew B. Ridgway, *The Korean War* (Garden City, N.Y.: Doubleday, 1967), pp. 25, 76-77, 82.
23. GEN Omar N. Bradley, "U.S. Military Policy: 1950," *Readers Digest* 47 (October 1950): 143-54.

24. Futrell, *Ideas, Concepts, Doctrine*, p. 149; Futrell, Moseley, and Simpson, *The United States Air Force in Korea*, pp. 225-27; Harry S. Truman, *The Memoirs of Harry S. Truman*, 2 vols, (Garden City, N.Y.: Doubleday, 1955-56), 2:391-96.

25. Truman, *Memoirs*, 2:395-416; MacArthur's testimony in *Military Situation in the Far East*, 4:3072; Douglas MacArthur, *Reminiscences: General of the Army Douglas MacArthur* (New York: McGraw-Hill, 1964), pp. 378-80; Eugene E. Wilson, "Air Power and Foreign Policy," USAS 37 (June 1952):18-19; Donald J. Mrozek, "The Transformation of the United States Military Establishment, 1940-1972," MS, courtesy Dr. Mrozek.

26. *Support Study*, pp. 174-77.

27. Director of the Budget of SECDEF, 1 November 1951, WNRC, Suitland, Md., RG 80, Papers of the Secretary of the Navy (hereafter cited as SNP).

28. Department of Defense Memoranda to Army, Navy, Air Force, 7 and 24 November 1951, SNP.

29. Whitehair to SECNAV, 25 November 1951, SNP.

30. U.S. War Department, Field Manual 30-35, *Aviation in Support of Ground Forces;* "No Room for Error," AF 3 (November 1954):29.

31. Army Field Manual 100-20, *Command and Employment of Air Power*.

32. Futrell, *Ideas, Concepts, Doctrine*, p. 178.

33. "The Air Lessons of Korea," AW 58 (25 May 1953):21-30.

34. "Weight Limits Upped for Army Aircraft," AW 57 (8 December 1953):17.

35. McConnaughhay, Memorandum for Mr. Kimball, 31 July 1951, SNP.

36. Kimball, Memorandum for SECAF, 8 August 1951, copies to SECDEF and SECA, 18 August, 1951.

37. U.S. Congress. Senate Armed Services Committee, *Study of Air Power: Subcommittee on the Air Force*, 84th Cong., 2nd Sess., 23 parts (Washington: GPO, 1956), pt. 1, pp. 126-27; Futrell, *Ideas, Concepts, Doctrine*, pp. 153-55.

40. "Washington Roundup," AW 57 (20 October 1952):12.

41. *The Uncertain Trumpet* (New York: Harper and Bros., 1959), p. 16.

42. The material in this section is derived from Futrell, *Ideas, Concepts, Doctrine*, pp. 182-207; "The Air Lessons of Korea," p. 28; "The Tactical Air Command," AF 37 (August 1954):37, 39-42; and I. B. Holley, *An Enduring Challenge: The Problem of Air Force Doctrine* (Colorado Springs, Col.: U.S. Air Force Academy, 1974).

PART IV

The Naval Administration of
Robert B. Anderson

13

Korea Calls for Changes

Until North Korea attacked South Korea and crammed into America's consciousness that her containment policy was being challenged, the watchword of the Truman administration was *"economy"* for her military defenses. A civilian colleague once referred to Secretary of Defense Louis A. Johnson as "Secretary of Economy, not Secretary of Defense." General J. Lawton Collins thought the appellation perhaps unfair, because Johnson "probably" was carrying out the orders of President Harry S. Truman.[1] In any event, the war in Korea cost a great deal of money. The new fiscal year 1951 began on 1 July 1950, but by mid-July 1950 the defense appropriations bills had not yet passed. Johnson therefore directed the service secretaries, who were dunning him for funds, to spend what they needed out of the fiscal year 1951 budget and submit revised supplementary estimates for that year.[2] On the nineteenth Truman directed him to exceed his budget, draft what men he needed, and also call up reservists. Johnson thereupon informed Congress that he had only enough funds to carry on until 31 July. To be considered by Congress in addition to defense appropriations was legislation providing for the transfer of a number of antisubmarine ships to allies in Europe and Latin America and for the loan of sixty-eight ships to Japan—the first step toward creating the Japanese Maritime Self-Defense Force permitted by the Japanese Peace Treaty. By September the transfers and loans were approved.[3]

Although the Senate Appropriations Committee added $383 million to his budget for fiscal year 1951, Johnson stated that he would ask for an additional $1 billion. Francis P. Matthews, however, asked for a doubling of the 1951 naval budget to $6.657 billion.[4] On 22 July, when the Army asked for $3.055 billion, the Navy for $2.466 billion, and the Air Force for about $5 billion, Johnson emphasized that he would not ask for more than $10.5 billion,[5] a total that Truman approved on the twenty-fourth and Congress on the twenty-eighth. In a little over thirty days, thus, the services were granted $25 billion in cash and contract authorizations. No one spoke now about the "crushing bur-

Robert Bernerd Anderson obtained his legal training at the University of Texas Law School. In addition to serving in the state legislature and as an assistant attorney general of the state, he managed the Waggoner Estate, a ranching and oil empire in northwest Texas. He is shown discussing matters on 3 November 1953 with representatives of the Department of Defense Construction Forces.

OFFICIAL U.S. NAVY PHOTOGRAPH

den of a fifteen billion dollar military budget'' or suggested that economic collapse would result from military spending. Instead, demands were heard to make good deficiencies of the last five years by passing mountainous military appropriations and expanding the industrial mobilization program. In any case, Truman greatly outdid Johnson by calling upon an approving Congress to add still another $10 billion to defense funds, as the service secretaries and the Joint Chiefs recommended. Carl Vinson, Chairman of the House Armed Services Committee, told the House of Representatives that this sum should be the minimum rather than the maximum, and that the statutory limit of two million servicemen should be removed. Of the additional $10 billion, the Air Force would get $4.5 billion, the Army $3.3 billion, and the Navy $2.2 billion.

Although the defense budget for fiscal year 1951 reached $41.8 billion and called for a doubling of military personnel to 2.7 million by 30 June 1951, Truman said that this was not a "war budget" but "a step toward putting the United States in a position to move speedily into an increased state of

Robert A. Lovett—World War I naval aviator, businessman, Assistant Secretary of War for Air, Assistant Secretary of State, and Secretary of Defense, 1951-1953. Feeling that civilian control in the Department of Defense should be strengthened, Lovett in 1951 brought the secretaries of the armed forces back into the policy-making process rather than depending solely upon the Joint Chiefs of Staff. His greatest contribution in defense reorganization was his suggestion of reforms which were studied by the President's (Rockefeller) Advisory Committee on Government Organization and which finally resulted in Reorganization Plan No. 6, effective 30 June 1953.
OFFICIAL DEPARTMENT OF DEFENSE PHOTOGRAPH

mobilization if the situation grows worse." The results were that for fiscal year 1951 the Army received $19.26 billion, the Navy $12.46 billion, and the Air Force $15.85 billion. Such was the pressure of added work in the Navy that on 15 February 1951 Matthews lengthened the official work week from five to five-and-a-half days for chiefs of bureau and of major officers including the assistant secretaries.

That relationships at the highest administrative level were good in the summer of 1951 was revealed by the Secretary of State, Dean Acheson, who said that "during early June the White House, the State Department, the Pentagon, and the Supreme Command in Tokyo found themselves united on political objectives, strategy, and tactics for the first time since the war started."[6] Moreover, the Joint Chiefs of Staff, after initial disagreements, reached unanimity on the expansion of the services. Robert A. Lovett, who succeeded George C. Marshall as Secretary of Defense on 12 September 1951, early in October asked a committee chaired by James M. Killian of the Massachusetts Institute of Technology to evaluate the force structure recommended by the Joint Chiefs. He approved Killian's report and won assent to it from both the National Security Council and the President. The new force structure provided for 20 Army divisions, 409 major combatant ships, a Marine Corps of 3 divisions and 3 air wings, and a 143-wing Air Force, including 126 combat and 17 troop carrier wings. Matthews had asked for $17.3 billion in new obligational authority for the Navy in fiscal year 1952.[7] The defense appropriations for that year, in the amount of $57.2 billion, were completed on 12 October 1951, with $13.2 billion going to the Army, $12.6 billion to the Navy, and $20.6 billion to the Air Force. Although he said that 143 wings left no "fat," the Secretary of the Air Force, Thomas K. Finletter, hailed the authorization of that number as "a decision of great moment" because it deviated from the earlier pattern in which funds were fairly evenly divided among the services.[8] Meanwhile the Commander in Chief Atlantic Fleet announced the development of a miniaturized atomic bomb that could be carried by carrier aircraft and the Atomic Energy Commission began testing small tactical nuclear weapons at its Nevada test site.

On 10 March 1951 Truman signed Vinson's "atomic Navy" bill that called for 125 new ships. In addition to an atomic-powered submarine, a guided missile cruiser and a supercarrier capable of handling strategic bombers would be built. Between 20 August and 12 October, contracts were let for a prototype atomic-powered submarine to be named the *Nautilus* and the second supercarrier, the *Saratoga*. In mid-1950, with the first naval atomic bombing unit, VC-5, on board, the Atlantic Fleet finally acquired a carrier-borne atomic capability. In December the Pacific Fleet followed suit.

The truce negotiations that began in Korea on 10 July 1951 were destined to continue for more than two years. The negotiations had barely begun when it was rumored that Matthews had accepted Truman's appointment of him as Ambassador to Ireland. Matthews had declined to accept such appointment during the Navy-Air Force controversy in the fall of 1949 lest it appear that he was being forced out. By the summer of 1951, however, the Navy was being administered much better than it had been when he had taken office twenty months earlier, largely because of the effective work done by Admiral Sherman.

A great admirer of Louis Johnson, Matthews had supported the latter's economy drive in the Department of Defense instead of abetting top professional naval leaders who saw that their service was being cut to the point where it could not support the nation's interest and was unable to take advantage of technological programs that promised improved weapons systems. After the Korean War began, however, he worked hard to augment the forces to be employed not only in the war but in a preparedness program revised in the light of the Russian threat and of the global situation. An avid supporter of the unification of the services, he left no record of his attitude toward Air Force policies and doctrines that threatened to provoke a second "revolt of the admirals." Nor did he make any comment on Truman's relief of General Douglas MacArthur or upon changes in defense appropriations that favored the Air Force over the Army and Navy. He commented upon advice the National Security Council proposed to offer the President on foreign policy but made no observable impact upon that policy beyond stressing the need to augment forces that could oppose communism. By letting his hatred of communism and lack of good judgment sweep him along the path of preventive war against Russia, he ended his usefulness to the administration.

For all practical purposes, Matthews's tenure ended on 28 June when Truman nominated him as Ambassador to Ireland and named Under Secretary of the Navy Dan Able Kimball to be his successor. The customary sighting for inventory purposes of the classified documents in his office on 1 July portended his exodus. On 15 July Sherman left Washington to visit various European countries, including Spain, where he reputedly got Generalissimo Francisco Franco to agree in principle to the building of American bases in his country. Among Matthews's last acts was his sending of condolences to Sherman's widow following his death from a heart attack on the twenty-second while visiting Naples.

Speculation on Matthews's successor had centered upon Ambassador Robert Butler and Kimball. Kimball, it may be recalled, entered the Army in 1917 as an air cadet and won his wings. Mustered out in 1920, he joined the sales force of the General Tire Company—and remained with the company for the next twenty-nine years. His good work with the Aerojet Engineering Corporation, of Azuza, California, a subsidiary of General Tire that developed JATO (jet assisted take-off) and high altitude research rockets, led to his promotion to vice president and director of the company. Secretary of the Navy John L. Sullivan had then brought him into his office as Assistant Secretary for Air, in February 1949. His part in the "revolt of the admirals" has already been described. Dissuaded by Louis Johnson from resigning when Sullivan did over the scrapping of the supercarrier *United States*, Kimball moved up to Under Secretary when Matthews replaced Sullivan. Kimball had a knack of getting along with everyone. This fact, together with his having been on the scene for twenty-eight months and would provide continuity in the Navy Department, may have influenced Truman to choose him rather than Butler. Senate confirmation was routine, and at noon on 31 July 1951 he relieved Matthews—at the very moment the administration verged upon enlarging and revitalizing what naval forces had escaped Johnson's meat-ax.

One of Kimball's first tasks was to find a successor to Sherman. Truman and Matthews had already discussed the matter but deferred to Kimball, who would work most closely with him. Admirals Robert W. Carney, William M. Fechteler, and Arthur W. Radford, all strong and able men, were considered. Radford took himself out of contention "for the good of the service"—because his role in the B-36 and unification controversies might reopen old wounds. Fechteler, well known to and highly respected by Kimball, was also a favorite of Vinson and had had no part in the admirals' revolt. Confirmed on 9 August, he was sworn in on the sixteenth. Kimball's old post of Under Secretary went for purely political reasons to a lawyer named Francis P. Whitehair. Overbearing in attitude and preoccupied with political maneuvering in his home state of Florida, Whitehair soon alienated most of the naval officer corps.[9] Upon the protests of Secretary of Defense Lovett, one of the special assistants Whitehair hired was quickly removed from office. On the other hand, Kimball was pleased when his good friend and management expert Herbert D. Askins agreed to serve as Assistant Secretary starting 3 October, and when General Lemuel C. Shepherd succeeded General Clifton B. Cates as Commandant of the Marine Corps at the end of the year. The continuation of John F. Floberg in the post of Assistant Secretary for Air also helped provide continuity in Kimball's office.

Kimball energetically worked to keep the Navy prepared for combat in Korea and ready if necessary to deter communist aggression elsewhere, overcome manpower and industrial delays that postponed the receipt of end items, and to expand the industrial base to permit adequate mobilization for any contingency. To this end he had independent management studies made of methods of improving defense production and adopted their recommendations with good results.[10] The demothballing of ships and aircraft and use of reserve personnel enabled him to fight in Korea and also to maintain a general readiness level. Because of new weapons he issued a revised policy for fleet air defense. By using 456 ships per month in the Military Sea Transport Service he was able to provide the men, dry cargo, and petroleum requirements for his widely disparate forces, and a new Master Shore Development Plan assured an orderly and economical expansion of needed facilities. He ordered a battleship, two cruisers, and two submarines converted to missile-firing ships. While the contract for the building of CVB-59, the *Forrestal*, had been awarded on 12 July 1951 while he was still the Under Secretary, he was the Secretary when the contract was awarded on 21 August for the first atomic-powered submarine, the *Nautilus*. Although jet fighters like the F2H and F9F were an important part of naval aviation, he knew of the value of such propeller-driven planes as the F4U and AD, which were "paying off" in Korea, and he also approved the widespread use of helicopters in Korea for antisubmarine warfare work and for other purposes as well. Above all he stressed the need of sea power and especially of modern aircraft carriers, saying in his semiannual report for 30 June 1952, dated 22 September.

Control of the sea today requires control of the air above the sea, but control of the air depends upon planes in the air at the point of contact and not on planes on the ground or enroute. With fixed bases only, other factors being equal, the line of equal air power is the midpoint between the bases. To control the sea therefore, we must have the aircraft carrier move our bases to the enemy's shoreline.

The carrier is one more example of the Navy's continuous effort to adapt the developments of technology to the art of war at sea. As the technology advances, the ships too must change if they are to take advantage of the products of American inventive genius and technical ingenuity. . . .

Most obvious, of course, has been the growth in the size of aircraft.

World War II experiences and lessons from the tests of atomic weapons had been incorporated in the *Forrestal*-class carriers, Kimball continued. While *Essex*-class carriers were being modernized, there was a limit to what could be done with ships designed in 1938. "Based on current world conditions, a minimum of twelve FORRESTAL carriers are required if the Navy is to carry out its primary mission."[11]

In 1946 the Army Air Force had drafted plans to develop an unspecified five-thousand-mile guided missile. In 1947, while the services were trying to adjust to the National Security Act, the Chief of Naval Operations, Chester W. Nimitz, suggested that the bureaus of Aeronautics and of Ordnance not air their differences over the production of naval missiles. During his economy wave of 1948 Truman ordered missile work dropped completely. In 1949, when work resumed, Under Secretary W. John Kenney appealed to the Secretary of the Navy, John L. Sullivan, to force the bureaus of Aeronautics and of Ordnance to cooperate.[12] It was Matthews who revealed to the public that the Navy had engaged in the production of missiles for purposes besides experiments, the latter having been carried on since March 1949 on a converted seaplane tender, the *Norton Sound*.[13] Truman's order to stop work on missiles notwithstanding, the Convair division of the General Dynamics Corporation continued the research involved in the Army Air Force weapon. Meanwhile missile development had so proliferated that Secretary of Defense James V. Forrestal had on 13 December 1949 requested the three service secretaries and the military chiefs to coordinate the program, with the Air Force made responsible for presenting a report to the next meeting of the Armed Forces Policy Council. A board appointed by the service secretaries approved continuing fourteen projects by unanimous vote and ten others by majority vote. It also recommended that further study be made of various other missiles, that three proving grounds be established on a joint-use basis, and that an Interdepartmental Operational Requirements Group be formed to advise the chiefs of each service. Although the Air Force adamantly supported the proposition "No Service should henceforth pursue more than one current guided missile weapons project in any single field of its operational responsibility"—a proposition that would have precluded long-range missile development by the Army and Navy and eliminated ten projects—both Army and Navy demurred.

In consequence of the report, the Joint Chiefs of Staff established a Guided Missile Interdepartmental Requirements Group that would submit quarterly reports on its success in coordinating missile production. In January 1950 the Joint Chiefs approved three guided missile proving grounds and ranges, one for the Army in New Mexico, one for the Navy in California, and one for the Air Force in Florida. By the end of May, with extensive production of missile components and the need for plans to produce complete missiles, the Joint Chiefs provided guidance to the services in the form of lists of types of missiles to be employed offensively and defensively if M-Day occurred in July 1950, July 1952, and July 1955. On 24 October, Secretary of Defense George C. Marshall established in his office a Director of Guided Missiles who would direct and coordinate research and development and production of guided missiles. By mid-October a requirements program had been developed: the Army would have Hermes A-1 and A-3 and *Nike;* the Navy, *Meteor, Regulus, Sparrow,* and *Terrier*, or both air-to-air and submarine-to-surface types; and the Air Force, *Matador* and *Rascal*. By early February 1951, in consequence of the Korean War, the Navy recommended that facilities for producing guided missiles be expanded and that a schedule of production be established after a stockpile was assured. For example, the Army would stockpile a thousand *Nikes* and produce a thousand a month, and the Navy would stockpike a thousand *Terriers* and produce five a month.[14] At about the same time the Air Force awarded to Convair a contract that eventually produced the *Atlas* booster rocket.[15] Meanwhile, on 18 September 1950, Matthews agreed with the other service secretaries and the Joint Chiefs of Staff that the services be furnished additional fissionable material and atomic weapons.[16]

When Matthews, among other top defense officials, was interrogated in mid-August 1950 by the House Appropriations Committee, he was pleasantly astounded when asked not to justify his request for funds but whether he demanded enough. He also noted that Secretary of Defense Johnson stated that military funds would be allocated to the three services "on a concept of over-all defense" instead of an equal percentage basis and that the services could expand their public relations staffs.[17] From the end of World War II until the Korean War got under way, the military budget had been fixed by the Director of the Budget and other economic advisers in the government. The shock of Korea caused the burden of recommending what force levels were needed to fall upon the Joint Chiefs of Staff, who therefore made judgments of the highest foreign policy and economic significance. That it was difficult for them to abandon the "balanced" program they had followed for years would be evident until the middle of 1951, when they finally abandoned the balanced forces method and, in this instance, highly favored the Air Force. In any event, as appropriations and powers tumbled over one another from Congress to the armed services, for the first time in his tenure Matthews could report that morale in the Navy was high.

Between 25 June 1950 and September 1951, Congress appropriated about $8 billion for aircraft procurement alone, with which the Air Force would acquire 4,428 aircraft and the Navy 3,357. In December 1951 Truman recommended a supplemental appropriation of $17 billion, of which $2.3 billion would be for additional aircraft procurement, and stated that "within one year, we will be turning out planes at five times the present rate of production."[18] With carrier-borne, atomic-laden aircraft, the Navy now assumed the offensive air role it had sought to obtain since denied it in the National Security Act as "interpreted" at Key West and at Newport in 1948. Moreover, could he have his way, Kimball would seek alternatives for the heat sources of steam-powered ships, such as atomic energy. In light of the Soviet submarine threat, on the defensive side he approved the use of helicopters and of hunter-killer groups for antisubmarine operations. Shortly after he left office in January 1953, the designator CVS (Antisubmarine Support Aircraft Carrier) was given to five old fleet carriers, with two more to follow in 1954.[19]

While the Chief of Staff of the Air Force, General Hoyt S. Vandenberg, sought 150 air groups and the Army's General Collins sought more men and more tactical air power, Admiral Sherman greatly pleased the Senate Armed Services Committee in the summer of 1951 by saying that the Navy stood ready to meet an all-out war and needed no additional forces to do so. He knew whereof he spoke because he had been a member with the other service chiefs and service secretaries of a General Planning Group that was projecting expenditures through fiscal year 1955, revising NATO's force structure, and hoping that West Germany would be admitted to NATO and contribute to an integrated force in Europe. When the Joint Chiefs deadlocked on the future size of the Air Force, the recently installed Secretary of Defense, Lovett, gave the problem to the civilian secretaries, who had been meeting weekly on an informal basis to discuss common problems and the apportionment of the budget. Lovett accepted their recommendations and forced the chiefs to agree to them. As has been well said, "This marked the end of the domination of purely military considerations in defense policies. It also marked the return of the secretaries to full participation in policy making"[20]

In mid-1951, when the threat of a global war had largely evaporated, the Joint Chiefs of Staff recommended retaining the 1952 force levels through 1954 except for the Air Force, which should be expanded from 95 to 143 wings, thereby increasing the defense budget from $60 billion to $70 billion annually. Although the 1952 budget approximated $56 billion and he faced objections from the Army and Navy, Truman accepted the advice of the National Security Council and granted the Air Force a special position even though he stretched completion of its program by one year, to 1955. The Marine Corps would have the three divisions and three air wings called for by a law he signed on 19 June 1952. The Navy would lose about half the number of combatant ships it used during the Korean War. On the other hand, with $16 billion of the 1952 budget it would have augmented funds for naval aviation and sufficient funds to build 229,000 tons in new construction and also to undertake some conversion work. Among the last would be the replacement of forty-mm antiaircraft batteries by rapid-fire three-inch fifty-caliber guns and the conversion of two heavy cruisers, the *Boston* and *Canberra*, into the fleet's first guided missile cruisers. When for fiscal year 1953 Kimball asked for funds for another *Forrestal*-class carrier, two additional carrier air groups, continued modernization of *Essex*-class carriers, and assurance that the Navy could have one new big carrier each year for ten years, he got only one new carrier on condition that he absorb the costs from lower priority items in the Navy's budget. The Air Force thus won priority over the other services with respect to funds and recognition for air-atomic primacy—a primacy acknowledged by the Eisenhower and many subsequent administrations.[21]

But Kimball was not through fighting. Early in the summer of 1952 the Atomic Energy Commission authorized the development by the Westinghouse Corporation of reactors to provide steam for the engines of a carrier. Kimball substituted steam catapults for hydraulic ones, thus enhancing safety even while using heavier planes than the hydraulic "slingshots" could handle, and adopted a second British development, the angled, or canted, deck for carriers being modernized. On 16 December he witnessed the keel laying of the *Saratoga*. However, his calls for nuclear power for the *Forrestal* and *Saratoga* and for the building of two additional carriers remained unheard even though he specified that they were needed to counter any threats posed by communists anywhere in the world and particularly in light of the approximately three hundred submarines in the Soviet Navy. Even his demand for one more large carrier remained unanswered by the Bureau of the Budget. In the defense budget Lovett prepared for fiscal year 1953, which was subject to modification by the incoming administration, the Navy received $11.4 billion of the $41.5 billion, a cut of $1.75 billion over 1952 but enough to operate 406 combatant ships and also to build a third *Forrestal*-class carrier.

By September 1950 a rearrangement in the top national security decision-making process had occurred. The Korean War had drawn Secretary of State Marshall, the Joint Chiefs of Staff, and the service secretaries into such a close relationship that Johnson had not participated for four months in weekly State-Joint Chiefs meetings, even though the service secretaries were kept fully apprised on the diplomatic front.[22] In late August, for example, Matthews had been apprised of NSC-73/3, United States action if Russia moved militarily in

Europe in light of the Korean situation,[23] and on 11 September he approved NSC-81, the suggestion to authorize MacArthur to move land, sea, and air forces north of the 38th parallel.[24] On the twelfth, the Secretary of State, now Dean Acheson, soon joined by Marshall in his new post of Secretary of Defense, began two weeks of talks with French Foreign Minister Robert Shuman, British Foreign Secretary Aneurin Bevan, and others that resulted in sending additional American troops to Europe and the appointment of a Supreme Commander for all NATO forces even if the creation of a West German army was as yet frowned upon by the French. As already noted, Truman replied to a unanimous request by NATO members and on 18 December appointed Dwight David Eisenhower as the Supreme Commander. Last, the foreign aid program, which had been administered previously in uncoordinated fashion by various government agencies, was regularized in the Mutual Security Act of 1951. Whereas emphasis had been placed upon economic assistance from 1948 to 1951, thereafter reliance would center upon military aid. By 1953 military aid would be more than double the economic, and the direction of the aid would shift from Western Europe toward Latin America, the Far East, and Southeast Asia.[25]

On 14 July 1952, a bit over a year after the fighting ended in Korea, the keel of the *Forrestal*, the Navy's first flush-deck carrier, was laid. In addition to presidential, Department of Defense, Joint Chiefs of Staff, and Navy and Army representatives, the ceremonies were attended by former Secretary of the Navy John L. Sullivan and Representative Mendell Rivers, a member of the House Naval Affairs Committee who was a staunch Navy supporter—but not by a single high-ranking Air Force officer. To explain the last, Floberg, Assistant Secretary of the Navy for Air, opined that the Air Force "didn't like" Forrestal, who as Secretary of Defense had approved the first supercarrier, the *United States*. Rear Admiral Luis de Florez, now retired, pointed up the undercurrent of Air Force-Navy feuding by remarking that he wondered "whether the Air Force will stop this one the way they stopped the *United States*," and Sullivan stated that he still felt that the scrapping of the *United States*, over which he had resigned, was a "big mistake" and that the keel-laying of the *Forrestal* was "three years too late."[26]

Kimball was as much a hawk on communism as Matthews. During a visit to Tokyo and Taipei in the late spring of 1952, he said that if the Chinese Communists tried to invade Formosa "we would clobber the hell out of them." When he stated as his personal opinion that the United States would cheer a Nationalist invasion of the China mainland, however, the Department of State immediately repudiated his statement.[27] He nevertheless had restored purpose and discipline to a naval organization shaken by the revolt of the admirals and Louis Johnson's economy-at-the-expense-of-the-Navy drive, and in businesslike fashion directed the refashioning of the post-Korean War Navy. As Herbert Askins, the Assistant Secretary of the Navy from 3 October 1951 until 20 January 1953, told this writer, "Dan A. Kimball was a great leader with the God-given abilities to inspire loyalty and provide leadership. Outside of the friction of Whitehair he smoothed out all the wrinkles in the Naval Establishment and the Admirals were happy under his direction."[28]

With the outbreak of war in Korea, the Department of Defense greatly increased its use of the academic scientific community on large-scale research and development projects. Studies of tactical air and air defense levels needed to counter Soviet military power especially if it was applied to Western Europe in 1952, were also initiated in 1951 by all the military services. Project Vista was undertaken by the California Institute of Technology, Project Charles by the new Lincoln Laboratory of the Massachusetts Institute of Technology built near Bedford, Mass., which also had a Summer Study Group look into air defense problems that might be encountered in the decade of the 1960s. Out of the report of the last grew the in-depth, distant early-warning line or "electronic fence" of radars located as far north as the 70th parallel. In 1952 Project East River, sponsored by the Air Force and National Security Resources Board, outlined the requirements of a civil defense program.

Vista recommended the augmentation of ground and tactical air forces and of tactical nuclear weapons in Western Europe. It also stated that while Air Force doctrine could be followed in the establishment of joint operations centers at tactical Air Force-field army levels and serve as an allocating agency, detailed control functions should be exercised by tactical air direction centers at the corps levels, thus supporting Army and Navy doctrine. Moreover, Supreme Headquarters Allied Powers Europe should be authorized to coordinate Strategic Air Command and naval air operations in the NATO theater. The Summer Study Group concluded that defense required three to six hours of early warning of approaching jet aircraft; Captain Lloyd V. Berkner, USNR, who headed Project East River, thought that at least one hour of early warning was needed to put a civil defense program into effect. The reports of all the study groups challenged to a degree a national strategy that depended heavily upon the Strategic Air Command. Reliance solely upon that command, said Vista, might weaken rather than strengthen the political and psychological position of the nations of Western Europe because an attack on Russia might provoke a retaliatory air attack upon their cities and still not stop Russian armies moving westward. If, however, plans called for the use of the strategic and tactical air power of all the American services against the Russian armies, the United States would deservedly win the confidence of the NATO nations and discourage a Russian attack. Although the Strategic Air Command was not central to the work of any of the study groups, Captain Berkner dealt it a mightly blow, saying in essence what Admiral Radford had told the House Armed Services Committee in October 1949 during the "revolt of the admirals":

The crux of our present danger is in our complete dependence upon the "Strategic Striking Force" as the principal element in our defense. This Maginot-Line type of thinking can be out-maneuvered by an intelligent enemy by any one of a number of ways. Opposed to the Maginot-Line concept of "putting all our eggs in one basket" is the balanced and flexible force. Because a balanced force cannot be achieved at tolerable cost through conventional means, we have ignored both the vital need for such a force and the possibility of achieving it through new and unconventional measures.

Berkner wrote thus even though the test explosion of an H-bomb on 1 November 1952 increased the power of strategic bombing to the point that Bernard Brodie said that knowing whether the conduct of war was an art or science "will come only in finding out what not to hit."[29]

Just before he left office Secretary Finletter underscored the Air Force position. He accepted the counterstrike philosophy but would add the atomic air units of the Tactical Air Command to the Strategic Air Command under a new command called the Strategic-Tactical Air Command, or STAC. Rather than strike an enemy's cities initially, he would use an atomic front-to-rear attack, from the front lines along an enemy's communications and logistics lines back to the seats of industry and government. After tentatively suggesting that the Navy should join its atomic aircraft to STAC, he decided to rely upon the Air Force's STAC alone. He would give priority first to the Strategic Air Command; second to air defense; third to Army, Navy, and Air Force units needed to provide a force-in-being in NATO and in the "Gray Areas," by which he meant a line running from Turkey to the Aleutians; and last to general forces that could be used in a general or limited war. The Navy thus played a very small part in Air Force plans.[30]

As Chief of Staff of the Army from December 1945 to February 1948, Eisenhower had advocated two pet projects—universal military training and the unification of the armed forces. Neither of these had been realized. As he saw it, the unification of the services was "too much form and too little substance"; it provided for "cooperation" instead of "consolidation." He preferred a single civilian secretary in a consolidated Department of Armed Forces, with each of the services commanded by a military officer who would direct purely military operations. Moreover, he thought the National Security Act was a triumph for the Navy and a defeat for the Army.[31] It was partly on his advice that the Truman administration kept the Air Force at forty-eight groups in 1949 and 1950 instead of expanding it to seventy, and it was whispered that he would not be averse to the abolishment of the Marine Corps.

During the "Great Debate" over the Kenneth S. Wherry resolution of 8 January 1950 on whether American troops should be sent to bolster Western Europe, Eisenhower decided to test congressional sentiment toward his presidential candidacy. He spoke at the Pentagon with Senator Robert Taft, the leading conservative contender for the Republican presidential nomination. If Taft would support collective security in Europe on a bipartisan basis, he would direct NATO for the next several years; if Taft would not, he would run for president. Dissatisfied with Taft's refusal to commit himself, he decided to run.[32] On 11 April 1952 Truman approved his relief as commander of NATO, effective 11 June. In Baltimore, on 25 September, Eisenhower pledged "security with solvency" and promised that if elected he would appoint a commission to study Department of Defense operations and also revitalize the National Security Council. Particularly needed, he added, were increased military unification and efficiency. He also said many times that he would seek an honorable end to the Korean War. In the ten weeks between his election and his inauguration he selected the top members of his administration, planned the transfer of government from the Democrats, and arranged a personal trip to Korea.

On 18 November Truman, Dean Acheson of the State Department, John W. Snyder of the Treasury, Robert A. Lovett of Defense, and Averill Harriman, the Mutual Security Administrator, briefed the Eisenhower team on the numerous problems facing the nation, with Lovett predicting less defense spending at home and abroad in fiscal year 1954 than in 1953. If the meeting found Eisenhower surly, it was because Truman charged that his trip to Korea was designed for "partisan political purposes." Thereafter Eisenhower would have nothing to do with Truman.[33]

Although truce talks began in Korea in July 1951, fighting continued while negotiations were stalled primarily over the prisoner-exchange issue. Eisenhower concluded from his visit that "small attacks on small hills would not end this war" but that the stalemate must not blossom into a global war. When MacArthur told a convention of the National Association of Manufacturers that he had "a clear and definite solution to the Korean conflict," Eisenhower had to listen. He flew from Seoul on 5 December to Guam, where he boarded the cruiser *Helena*. Among the many others with whom he took counsel on the way to and back from Korea was Admiral Radford, Commander in Chief Pacific Fleet. Radford had led the Navy's attack on the B-36 and unification in the years 1947-49, and was very highly regarded by naval airmen. He confessed to Eisenhower that he had been wrong. He now believed in a unified command and shared Eisenhower's belief that nuclear war demanded a close coordination of all the services. Eisenhower took Radford's measure as "extremely useful . . . a man of tough conviction who would . . . time and again modify his views." Moreover, Radford agreed with Eisenhower that the prime battleground of the Cold War would be in Asia rather than in Europe, as the Democrats from Roosevelt through Truman believed. Furthermore, he agreed with the prospective Secretaries of State and of Defense, John Foster Dulles, and Charles E. Wilson, that because the United States could not maintain static defenses about the communist perimeter it should deter attack by maintaining in being a strong retaliatory sea and air power capable of striking swiftly at sources of aggression.[34] Eisenhower determined that Radford should succeed Bradley, who was "tainted" as Chairman of the Joint Chief of Staff by his commitment to Truman's foreign policies.[35]

On 17 December Eisenhower and Dulles heard MacArthur tell of his plan for ending the Korean War—either China did America's bidding or the United States would drop atomic bombs on North Korea—a plan Eisenhower rejected, but atomic missiles were soon placed in Okinawa. Then, at a preinaugural conference of his prospective cabinet and staff members, Eisenhower established policy lines—end the Korean War, lift the wage and price controls established by Truman, and balance the budget, with consequent reduction of taxes. He promised to create a bipartisan commission to reform the operations of the Department of Defense, add a number of civilian top policy-makers to the National Security Council, improve the weapons systems evaluation program, and save money and increase efficiency by simplifying weapons designs. He would cut costs, not strength. Since he would not drain America's financial resources, a finite number of dollars must determine defense strategy. The defense budget for fiscal year 1954, completed by Lovett on 23 October 1952, totaled $46 billion, of which $17 billion would go to the Air Force. More important for the subject of this study, after having served as Secretary of Defense for twenty-six months Lovett had been reaching conclusions about changes needed in the National Security Act as amended that were largely to be reflected in Eisenhower's Reorganization Plan No. 6, which would go into effect on 30 June 1953.

In his semiannual report dated 6 December 1952, Lovett noted that since the outbreak of the Korean War the nation's military manpower and strength and industrial base had been greatly strengthened and that the security of allies against communist aggression had been improved. Although military expenditures would remain high for several years—they had been $155.6 billion for fiscal years 1950-53—they should be lower in the near future. Meanwhile, the delivery of end items requiring long lead time—twenty-one months for a fighter plane and thirty to thirty-six months for a big bomber—had begun in the summer of 1952, with much of the payment therefore to come in fiscal years 1953 and 1954. He ended the introduction to his report by saying:

> The organizational pattern of the Department of Defense has been determined by the National Security Act of 1947, as amended in 1949. It gives the Secretary of Defense the power of "direction, authority, and control" over the three military departments, "separately administered." The Act, a compromise between various points of view, was approved in the conviction that unification, rather than merger, would best promote efficiency and economy in the armed forces and, at the same time, increase their military effectiveness. Unification is necessarily a gradual evolutionary process, in which actual operating experience provides the major guide to future action. The amendments passed in August 1949 resolved the main problems apparent at that time. Since that date, unification has brought considerable savings to the taxpayer and increased security to the United States. In order to facilitate the continued evolution of an increasingly efficient defense

establishment and to take advantage of the additional experience gathered during the last 3 years, a further review of the Act appears appropriate in the coming months.[36]

Among his conclusions he noted that the United States faced "a continuing, not a temporary, threat to its security" and that "we cannot have a sound military establishment and adequate national security if the Army, Navy, and Air Force are to be princes today and paupers tomorrow" and alternately suffer "feast or famine." He added:

> Experience gained during the past 2 years in combat, procurement, and industrial mobilization has identified certain areas in which the organization of the Department of Defense, the military department, and the statutory agencies—the Joint Chiefs of Staff, the Munitions Board, and the Research and Development Board—should be improved and their authorities and responsibilities clarified. Certain of the desirable steps would appear to require legislative action to make them fully effective, and clarification of some of the language in the existing statutes seems essential if the smooth functioning of the Department is to be assured under the strains imposed by a higher degree of mobilization, which would inevitably involve magnified problems in connection with the "distribution of shortages"—one of the primary problems that must be solved by any Secretary of Defense.
>
> The problems range from what appears to be excessive rigidity in the language of the National Security Act of 1947, as amended in 1949, to purely administrative and organizational problems. Practically all of them involve the need for greater flexibility in order to meet rapidly changing conditions. Some of them can be resolved by administrative action as experience indicates that traditional procedures are ill adapted to current conditions. Others present entirely new situations where solutions by trial and error constitute the only method of approach. The latter, especially, require that those responsible for the conduct of military affairs are not unnecessarily hampered in their search for effective solutions by rigid prescriptions created for greatly different circumstances.
>
> Many of these problems have been discussed in general terms with various Committees of the Congress, and special attention has been devoted during the past year to those relating to the organization and responsibilities of the Munitions Board. In such an agency we find the composition of the Board rigidly prescribed by the National Security Act, together with an outline on its intended functions. However, the membership of the Board, as prescribed by law, makes extremely difficult, if not impossible, the effective discharge of the assigned functions since each member of the Board, except for the Chairman, is both a claimant and a judge of his own requests. This fault is common to the three statutory agencies and would cause their unsatisfactory operation during a period of serious shortages in manpower, materials, or money.
>
> The general areas of concern have been reported to the President, and such interim corrective measures as were found to be administratively desirable and possible, pending consideration of legislative amendments, have been taken where the action did not inject delay or uncertainty. We feel that enough experience through operations has been accumulated to warrant the active pursuit of corrective measures with the Congress, and it now would

appear appropriate that discussions be undertaken with the parent Committees of the Department of Defense to develop a proper program for the continuation of efforts to make the organization of this Department as modern as the world we live in.[37]

In his last report, dated 19 January 1953, Lovett noted that with the completion of various programs "the United States will achieve . . . the minimum military strength considered essential for national security under present conditions and the capability of rapidly increasing this strength if necessary." In accordance with the 1953 Appropriations Act, he had issued regulations that promised efficiency and economy in the supply management field. Offices of Analysis and Review had been established in each military department to audit and review all military requirements for manpower, materials, and facilities. A revised charter for the Munitions Board gave full power of decision to its chairman, and a separate Defense Supply Management Agency had been established in the Office of the Secretary of Defense. All military construction work had been centralized in one office under a Director of Installations. In addition, he had appointed special civilian committees to help him solve particular problems. Among these were the Citizens Advisory Commission on Manpower Utilization in the Armed Forces and a temporary advisory Committee on the Defense of North America. "An organization of the size of the defense establishment, totalling nearly 5,000,000 people, military and civilian, and responsible for an annual expenditure of 40 to 50 billion dollars, can never be considered to have solved all its organizational difficulties," said Lovett.[38] Moreover,

the period of partial mobilization highlighted some of the administrative and operational problems that are likely to be encountered to an even greater extent in time of full mobilization, and in an informal letter to the President, dated November 18, 1952, areas for further study of the organization of the Department were pointed out.

The purpose of these suggestions was to identify certain controversial areas and specific problems whose effective solution required, based on the experience of the past years, greater administrative freedom for civilian and military officials than had been granted under the present law. Thoroughly considered amendments in these fields should enable the Department to discharge its responsibilities with increased efficiency and economy and facilitate the distribution of the inevitable shortages in tools, materials, and manpower that will develop in time of war. Administrative reforms can assist the progress of unification, but eventual success will depend on unity of purpose and on the confidence and teamwork established among the military departments and between them and the Office of the Secretary of Defense.[39]

Truman authorized Lovett to make public his thirteen-page letter of 18 November 1952 when Lovett discussed its contents with the House Armed Services Committee on 8 January 1953.

Lovett believed that the authority granted the Secretary of Defense would prove inadequate in certain instances in actual war "because one of the principal elements of control lies through the budget process, the dollar being the single common denominator of all requirements." Some better system than mere dollar control should be provided him. Since the National Security Act as amended denied him a military staff, he must use interservice committees to do much of his staff work. In time of crisis, he would be handicapped in "distributing shortages." Lovett thought it better to make reforms in a "few of the most important areas" than to wait and reorganize radically in time of war.

A compromise enactment, the National Security Act as amended, contained various "contradictions and straddles." The relationship of the Secretary of Defense to the President and to the Joint Chiefs of Staff should be clarified so that the Secretary alone would be the chief military adviser to the President. The act provided that the Secretary should have "direction, authority, and control" over the three military services but that the services would be "separately administered." This straddle had caused "certain ardent separatists" to suggest that the Secretary of Defense "play in his own back yard and not trespass on their separately administered preserves." The act should be changed so that the Secretary of Defense clearly had authority to exercise "direction, authority, and control" within the limitations that he must not transfer, reassign, abolish, or consolidate any combatant functions assigned the services.

One of the greatest weaknesses of the act was its description of the responsibilities of the three statutory boards it created: the Joint Chiefs of Staff, the Munitions Board, and the Research and Development Board. Their functions and composition were too rigidly prescribed. Because they were charged with performing inappropriate functions, they operated inefficiently and too slowly. Because they wore two hats, the Joint Chiefs of Staff found it extremely difficult to assume an impartial and nonpartisan position. They could divorce themselves from their service viewpoint only at the cost of having their services feel let down, particularly in times of shortages of men, money, or materials. Too many papers were referred to them. They thus became immersed in day-to-day operations and administrative details instead of devoting themselves to the preparation of strategic and logistic plans and to a review of those plans in light of available men, materials, and weapons. The difficulties were compounded because the Secretary, denied a military staff, must refer to them a vast amount of administrative and policy matters that originated in the military departments, the statutory agencies, other executive agencies, and congressional committees. The fear of a general staff had also rendered it very difficult for the Chiefs to adopt a broad national service point of view, a point highlighted by the fact that the future careers and promotions of those who served on the staff were controlled by their single service superiors. In consequence. some "back scratching" occurred.

What changes did Lovett recommend? His most important recommendations were that either new legislation or a Presidential directive should make clear the authority of the Secretary of Defense over the Joint Chiefs and over the services, particularly with respect to supply, warehousing, and issue. He would correct also the "statutory weaknesses with respect to the Joint Chiefs of Staff, the Munitions Board, and the Research and Development Board."

With respect to the Joint Chiefs, Lovett proposed two alternatives, the second more "radical" than the first: (a) Confine the Chiefs to planning functions and the review of weapons systems and techniques and transfer their remaining functions to the Office of the Secretary of Defense, who must then have an augmented military and civilian staff; (b) Appoint as Chiefs of Staff only men who had served as the heads of their services. Having thus served, they would become members of a combined staff that would deal with strategic planning, logistic planning, military requirements, and overall military policies.

Lovett thought that a reorganization of the technical services was long overdue, saying that he was "always amazed . . . that the system worked at all and the fact that it works rather well is a tribute to the inborn capacity of teamwork in the average American." In addition, he would reduce the number of headquarters both at home and abroad, reduce the number of noncombatant personnel, provide additional protection for official secrets, and fend off those who would add functions to the Department of Defense.[40]

In his semiannual report to the President made public on 2 January 1953, Lovett had noted that the nation faced a continuing, not a temporary, threat to its security and that feast or famine defense budgets must be leveled out in order to provide security for any contingency. The buildup of men, materials, and industrial plant to provide those materials developed during the Korean War should be maintained. He then focused on weaknesses in the statutory boards in his own office that passed on plans of the three services to accomplish a "unified" military program. He especially objected to the fact that memberships of the three agencies were comprised of coequal representatives of the three services who judged their own claims, a situation that lent itself to log-rolling and in the end "could cause their unsatisfactory operation during a period of serious shortages in manpower, materials, and money." One solution could be to disassociate the military leaders of the agencies and make them responsible only to the Secretary of Defense, thereby increasing the control over that department by him.[41]

In a parting message to Congress in mid-January, Lovett asserted that the Department of Defense was not geared for war. Instead of mere "dollar control" over the services through the budget process, the Secretary of Defense should be allowed a military staff responsible only to him. Specifically, the Joint Chiefs of Staff should delegate their command functions to others and operate purely as an advisory body; the Munitions Board should be absorbed by the Office of the Secretary of Defense; and each service should study its organization to determine if it was so organized as to be able to function effectively in time of war. Reform could logically proceed either by providing for greater civilian control in the Department of Defense or by more unification, the latter of which would further curtail the authority of the military services. The Joint Chiefs could be denied authority over their services and made to act as a purely advisory group. Or they could be taken out of the chain of command, with the result that orders would flow to the services not from them but from the civilian secretaries.[42]

How would Lovett's recommendations fare in the Eisenhower administration?

NOTES

1. J. Lawton Collins, *War in Peacetime: The History and Lessons of Korea* (Boston: Houghton Mifflin, 1969), p. 74.
2. Secret. JCS to Louis A. Johnson, 6 July 1950; Secret. F.P. Matthews, Memorandum to the SECDEF, 10 July 1950; Conf. Louis A. Johnson to the Secretary of the Army, Secretary of the Navy, Secretary of the Air Force, Chairman Joint Chiefs of Staff, 14 July 1950, SNP.
3. ANAFJ, 4 August, 8 September, and 27 October 1951; *New York Times*, 13 November 1952.
4. Secret. F.P. Matthews, Memorandum for SECDEF 17 July 1950, SNP.
5. Top Secret. A.S. McDill, Memorandum to Francis P. Matthews, 22 July 1950, SNP.
6. Dean G. Acheson, *The Korean War* (New York: W.W. Norton, 1971), p. 115.
7. Secret. F.P. Matthews, two memoranda to SECDEF, 19 February and 13 April 1951, SNP.
8. Thomas K. Finletter, "A New Look at Air Policy, "*The Atlantic* 192 (September 1953): 27-28.
9. Herbert Askins to the writer, 12 December 1975.
10. The management firms of Arthur D. Little, McKinsey and Co, and Coverdale and Colpitts had looked into armed services procurement practices by 14 August 1952. (Kimball to Lewis L. Strauss, 2 and 28 May and 17 June 1952; idem, Memorandum for the SECDEF, 4 July 1952, SNP.)
11. *Semiannual Report of the Secretary of the Navy, January 1, 1952 to June 30, 1952* (Washington: GPO, 1952), pp. 25, 26, 145-50, 152-53, 155-56, 191-93.
12. W. John Kenney to SECNAV, 17 March 1949, SNP.
13. *New York Times*, 6 March and 13 May 1949; *Christian Science Monitor*, 3 and 4 November 1949.
14. Insight into the interservice battle over guided missiles has been obtained from JCS File 1620/42-1620/43, CNO Papers. See also George C. Marshall, Memorandum for Deputy Secretary of Defense, Secretaries of the Military Departments . . . . , 24 October 1950, CNO Papers. As one could expect him to, Ned Root, "Who Will Guide the Missiles?" AF 32 (October 1949): 15-19, demanded exclusive Air Force control over the largest missiles.
15. *Washington Post*, 7 August 1975.
16. Top Secret. Pace, Matthews, and Finletter to Chairman of the Military Liaison Committee, 18 September 1950, SNP.
17. "'Congress' New Defense Attitude," ANJ 87 (26 August 1950): 1410-11, and "Division of Defense Dollars," ibid., p. 1411.
18. See Donald J. Mrozek, "The Truman Administration and the Enlistment of the Aviation Industry in Postwar Defense," *Business History Review* 48 (Spring 1974):73-94.
19. ANAFJ, 15 September and 8 December 1951; *Navy Times*, 1 August and 29 December 1951 and 5 December 1953.
20. K. Jack Bauer, "Dan Able Kimball," MS Essay, p. 10, courtesy Dr. Bauer.
21. ANAFJ, 19 January, 2 February and 5 April, 1952; *Navy Times*, 20 October 1951, 26 January 1952, 15 and 23 March, 12 and 19 April, 3 May, 14 June, and 5 and 26 July 1953; Donald J. Mrozek, "A New Look at 'Balanced Forces': Defense Continuities from Truman to Eisenhower," MA 38 (December 1974):145-51.

22. Paul Y. Hammond, "Effects of Structure on Policy," *Public Administration Review* 18 (Summer 1958):176.
23. Top Secret. Dan A. Kimball to F.P. Matthews, 24 August 1950, SNP.
24. Top Secret, SECNAV to SECDEF, 11 September 1950, SNP.
25. Harold J. Clem, *Collective Defense and Foreign Assistance* (Washington:ICAF, 1968), pp. 11-15, 36-37.
26. *New York Times*, 15 July 1952.
27. *Ibid.*, 23 March and 10 April 1952; Walter Hermes, *Truce Tent and Fighting Front* (Washington: GPO, 1966), p. 211.
28. Letter to the writer, 12 December 1975.
29. The two preceding paragraphs follow very closely Robert Frank Futrell, *Ideas, Concepts, Doctrine: A History of Basic Thinking in the Unites States Air Force, 1907-1964* (Maxwell Air Force Base, Ala.: Air University, 1971), pp. 167-74. The quotation from Berkner is on p. 169.
30. Thomas K. Finletter, *Power and Policy: United States Foreign Policy and Military Power in the Hydrogen Age* (New York: Harcourt, Brace, 1954), pp. 54-55, 202-11, 242-45.
31. Dwight D. Eisenhower, *The White House Years: Mandate for Change, 1953-1956* (Garden City, N.Y.: Doubleday, 1963), pp. 12-13.
32. Ibid., pp. 13-14, 23.
33. Ibid., p. 85.
34. "Washington Roundup," AW 57 (8 December 1952):12.
35. Eisenhower, *Mandate for Change*, pp. 93-96.
36. *Semiannual Report of the Secretary of Defense . . . July 1, 1952 to December 21, 1952* (Washington: GPO, 1953), pp. 9-10.
37. Ibid., pp. 65-66.
38. Statement of 19 January 1953 included in ibid., p. 2.
39. Ibid., pp. 7-8.
40. R. A. Lovett to the President, 18 November 1952, copy in SNP.
41. *New York Times*, 9 January 1953.
42. "Lovett Says Defense Not Geared to War," AW 58 (19 January 1953):16.

14

The Price of Unification

In his State of the Union address, 2 February 1953, President Dwight D. Eisenhower stated that in accordance with policies laid down by the National Security Council the Secretary of Defense "must take the initiative and assume the responsibility for developing plans to give our Nation maximum safety at minimum cost." While before the House Committee on Appropriations late in February, Secretary of Defense Charles E. Wilson said he had established a committee to recommend within sixty days the best ways of improving the organization of the Department of Defense. He also made it very clear that he interpreted the National Security Act as giving him complete authority to direct his Department even though the act specified that each service would be "separately administered."[1]

Except for Wilfred J. McNeil, who had served as Comptroller of the Department of Defense since the days of James V. Forrestal, for John F. Floberg, Assistant Secretary of the Navy for Air since the days of Francis P. Matthews, for Earl Johnson, Under Secretary of the Army, and for General Lemuel C. Shepherd, Commandant of the Marine Corps, Eisenhower made a clean sweep of the leading civilian and military leaders in the Defense Department. Robert B. Anderson, a Texas industrialist and oil man, the Secretary of the Navy, was utterly new to that service. In the Joint Chiefs of Staff, Admiral Arthur W. Radford succeeded General Omar N. Bradley as Chairman; Admiral Robert B. Carney replaced William N. Fechteler; Matthew B. Ridgway, J. Lawton Collins; and Nathan F. Twining, Hoyt S. Vandenberg. All the new men were given merely two-year appointments. Although he told them they were part of his team, Eisenhower ordered them to abide by administration policies and not to make public any disagreements with them. Dissent was thus not permitted.[2]

Upon reviewing American defense strategy, Eisenhower found that the Truman administration had been trying to prepare the services to conduct various kinds of wars. There being no set policy on the use of atomic weapons, funds were allocated to the Army and Navy for the conduct of nonnuclear war

Even before Reorganization Plan No. 6 was approved by Congress, Secretary of Defense Charles E. Wilson stated that he would administer his department in disregard of the clause in the National Security Act that stated that the military services would be "separately administered." Given nine assistant secretaries by the plan, he could largely bypass the service secretaries, who were thus demoted to middle managers.

while the Air Force was preparing for a nuclear war in response to Soviet aggression. The Air Force demanded that its strategic air arm and the overseas bases on which it depended be maintained and kept strong. The Navy wanted a minimum of twelve *Forrestal*-class carriers and suggested that its aerially refueled attack bombers could perform the missions assigned the more expensive long-range Air Force bombers. The Army gave top priority to "all aspects of atomic warfare." All the services were producing their own aircraft and guided missiles and integrating them into offensive and defensive weapons systems.[3] Each service conducted its own research program, with Eisenhower pointing out that this was a very expensive way of doing things, that the Air Force recently used twenty-one thousand uniformed personnel and nineteen

Except for a few old hands, President Dwight D. Eisenhower made a clean sweep of the leading civilian and military leaders in the Defense Department. The new Joint Chiefs of Staff included, *left to right* General Nathan B. Twining, Air Force Chief of Staff; Admiral Arthur W. Radford, Chairman of the Joint Chiefs of Staff; General **Matthew B. Ridgway, U.S. Army Chief of Staff; General Lemuel C. Sheperd, Jr.,** Commandant of the Marine Corps (on matters pertaining to the Corps); and Admiral Robert B. Carney, Chief of Naval Operations.

OFFICIAL U.S. ARMY PHOTOGRAPH

thousand civilians in fundamental research and that savings could be made by combining all fundamental defense research in one agency.[4]

Air Force spokesman asked why their force was cut from 143 to 120 wings, thus setting its force levels for many years, while the number of Army divisions and that of Navy combat ships were retained. If the main deterrent to aggression was no longer considered to be the atomic-laden, long-range Air Force bomber, why were the second and third supercarriers needed? The Under Secretary of Defense, Roswell Gilpatric, replied that the Secretary of Defense should be granted authority "to stop service competition and aspiration." Charles Wilson stated that overall air power included naval and Marine aircraft as well as Air Force planes, that the entire Western world would rise to crush any Soviet aggression, and that he, not the Joint Chiefs of Staff, had approved the Navy's request for new carriers. Moreover, the Air Force was already "overfinanced."[5]

Eisenhower found that the Truman administration had prepared plans for "short wars, for police actions like the Korean War, for peripheral wars, for infantry wars, for air wars, and for completely destructive atomic attacks." As the Secretary of the Treasury, George M. Humphrey, said after looking at the defense budget that Secretary of Defense Robert A. Lovett had prepared the prior October for fiscal year 1954, the military planners seemed to be following six plans of strategy simultaneously, two for each branch of the services. Determined to obtain greater unity and economy in defense, Eisenhower asked Congress to grant more power and staff facilities to the Secretary of Defense.[6] Reports by Senator Lyndon B. Johnson's Preparedness Investigating Subcommittee had already resulted in Lovett's creating the position of Assistant Secretary of Defense for Properties and Installations and the passage of the Defense Cataloging and Standardization Act.

In anticipation of the power the House of Representatives gave him on 3 February to reorganize the executive branch of government for the next two years, Eisenhower on 29 January had established a President's Advisory Committee on Government Organization, containing Nelson Rockefeller, Arthur I. Flemming, and Milton Eisenhower. The committee would investigate the need for reorganization in "the entire creaking federal establishment." On 19 February Eisenhower added David Sarnoff, Lovett, General Bradley, and Dr. Vannevar Bush to a Defense Committee also containing Rockefeller, Flemming, and Milton Eisenhower. In a covering message to this committee, the President noted the need for "clear and unchallenged civilian responsibility in the defense establishment," for "effectiveness with economy," and for the development of "the best possible military plans." He added that the Secretary of Defense would soon issue a revision of the Key West Agreement of 1948 that would provide that the Secretary of Defense, not the Joint Chiefs of Staff, would upon recommendation of the Joint Chiefs designate the military department that would serve as executive agent for unified commands. The military heads of a department would then issue directives for field operations. However, the Secretary of Defense would "look to the Secretaries of the three military departments as his principal agents for the management and direction of the entire defense enterprise." The Joint Secretaries Committee would thus remain in full force. While decision-making and policy control would rest with the Secretary of Defense, he would decentralize the management of his department by delegating the administration of the military services to their secretaries.[7]

Although Eisenhower's argument carried the weight of authority of one who had been a distinguished professional soldier, he was greatly irked by the charges that he approached defense reorganization with a "military mind" and that his reforms would create a Prussian type of general staff. To some onlookers it seemed that "something like the old Collins plan [was] blossoming again under the guise of Department of Defense reorganization for economy," for no member of the Rockefeller committee had knowledge of the elements of sea power, and the "Bush-Lovett-Bradley Axis" was on record as favoring a more powerful chairman of the Joint Chiefs of Staff and a more powerful Secretary of Defense. Hence the committee was "stacked against the interests of a maritime—and insular—nation.[8] However, the committee had immediately demanded the advice of senior military consultants and with Wilson's approval invited retired General George C. Marshall, Fleet Admiral Chester W. Nimitz, and Air Force General Carl Spaatz to serve. The committee's legal counsels were H. Struve Hensel, who had been Assistant Secretary of the Navy in 1945-46, Roger Kent, General Counsel of the Department of Defense, and Frank X. Brown, Assistant Counsel of the Department. A small staff worked under Don K. Price. Each of the twenty-four witnesses invited—all of whom had been intimately connected with the Department of Defense since passage of the National Security Act of 1947—was given a list of ten key questions to study prior to his appearance.[9] Wilson set 30 April as the deadline for the committee to forward its recommendations.

For two months the Rockefeller Committee heard testimony from leading military men, civilian administrators, consultants, and seventeen military officers—nine Navy, five Army, and three Air Force. Whereas great preparations had been made by both naval "stalwarts" and "radicals" for the B-36 and unification hearings of 1949, and for the hearings on amending the National Security Act in the same year, the files of Navy Secretary Anderson show that the Navy Department merely kept itself informed on the committee's progress and did not in any way try to influence the naval officers, all retired, who were called to testify. The same attitude animated the other service secretaries. On 28 May Leverett Saltonstall, chairman of the Senate Armed Services Committee, questioned Admiral Arthur W. Radford as the nominee for Chairman of the Joint Chiefs of Staff.

> Chairman SALTONSTALL. Do you feel that the reorganization plan, together with the President's message and the report of the Rockefeller Commission, indicate a tendency to bypass or whittle down the Secretaries of the three military departments? . . .

> Admiral RADFORD . . . In connection with the service Secretaries, in the last few days I have been with all three Secretaries, and as I gathered from their conversation, they support this plan which I am sure they would not if they felt that they were going to be bypassed.

Furthermore, the committee won part of the battle even while it listened to testimony, for the Joint Chiefs, criticized for seeking to preserve the status quo and wishing to do "business as usual," tried to stave off extensive curtailment of their authority by agreeing to give up log-rolling procedures and letting the

Secretary of Defense decide disagreements among them after a full presentation of the issues. They would also agree to a strengthening of the administrative staff of the Secretary of Defense in order to preclude his creating
his own independent military staff, as Lovett had proposed. In addition they
agreed that the Munitions Board should be abolished and that its charter
should be given to the Secretary of Defense, and that the National Security
Resources Board should be totally abolished.[10]

The Rockefeller Committee report dealt with five major areas. First, the
Secretary of Defense, subject only to the President and statutory limitations,
was to have effective and complete control over his entire department. The
phrase in the original National Security Act that the three military departments
be *separately administered* had permitted service challenges to the authority of
the Secretary—indeed, had limited it. The committee's legal counsels found
the phrase to have no legal validity in statute or legislative history. Except for
being subject to the President, the authority of the Secretary of Defense was
limited by statute in only the following respects: he could not transfer,
reassign, abolish, or consolidate the combatant functions of the military services without congressional approval; accomplish the purposes listed above by
the assignment of personnel or expenditure of funds; merge the three services
or deprive their secretaries of their legal rights to administer their departments;
establish a single military commander in chief or general military staff; or pro-
hibit a service secretary or Joint Chief from offering recommendations concerning defense to the congressional armed services committees. Second,
rather than a bilineal chain of command, one for military and one for civilian
aspects of the services, there should be "a single channel of command or line
of administrative responsibility within the Department of Defense and each of
the military departments." The service secretary would thus control both
military and civilian elements. Third, the Secretary of Defense, rather than the
Joint Chiefs of Staff, as provided in the Key West Agreement, should have
command authority, that is, authority to assign executive responsibility for
unified commands. Instead of single service representatives, the Joint Chiefs
should be a corporate advisory body, with their chairman responsible for
organizing the structure of the Joint Chiefs and Joint Staff so that it could
heighten the joint planning role. The chiefs should delegate their administrative duties to deputies and, while coordinating with the Secretary of
Defense, also keep the service secretaries fully informed. Fourth, the unwieldy
Munitions Board and the Research and Development Board should be abolished and their duties transferred to Assistant Secretaries of Defense. To
strengthen the administrative staff of the Secretary of Defense, six additional
Assistant Secretaries should be added to the two already provided, with a
General Counsel in addition, for a total of nine assistants. Last, to free
military officers on duty in the Office of the Secretary of Defense from service
influence, civilians instead of military men would write efficiency reports on
subordinates in that office.[11]

Eisenhower adopted most of the recommendations of the report for his

Reorganization Plan No. 6, which he sent to Congress with a covering letter on 30 April.[12] Reduced to those items in the report on which congressional approval was necessary or desirable, the plan was referred in the House to the Committee on Government Operations, chaired by Clare E. Hoffman, rather than to the Armed Services Committee, which might oppose it. In the Senate it went to the Armed Services Committee, chaired by Leverett Saltonstall. The greatest public criticism of it, as voiced particularly by pundits David Lawrence, Hanson Baldwin, and Arthur O. Sulzberger, and by the Navy League, was that it permitted the Chairman of the Joint Chiefs of Staff, who was empowered to manage the Joint Staff and approve all appointments to it, to operate a general staff.[13] Hoffman moved that the offending provisions be deleted and then called for hearings on the plan for four days in June. The complete change of leadership in the Joint Chiefs of Staff between 7 and 9 May had failed to quiet criticism on this point. When Representative Leslie C. Arends, the Republican leader in the House, requested assurance that the Joint Chiefs of Staff provision would not result in the creation of a general staff, Eisenhower reassured him that it would not.[14] The feeling would not down in the House, however, that the administration was attempting an end run with Plan No. 6, that it was an unconstitutional delegation of power from the President to the Secretary of Defense, and that legislation was required in the matter.[15]

While Secretary of Defense Wilson and Deputy Secretary Roger Kyes denied it, almost all the military witnesses—with Bradley an exception—asserted that the plan violated the National Security Act, which emphasized the autonomy of the services, and persistently reiterated that with augmented powers the Chairman of the Joint Chiefs of Staff would operate a Prussian-like general staff that would destroy the liberties of the people.[16] Ferdinand Eberstadt held that the plan would centralize control in the Defense Department without fortifying civilian control or increasing the efficiency of its operations.[17] Thomas K. Finletter, who had served as Secretary of the Air Force from May 1950 until January 1953, was even more critical, for he said that the plan "would lead us 1 step further toward a single monolithic establishment, with one service in one uniform, and toward a diminution of civil control" that would result in a "monstrosity" and a "mess."[18] He reflected the bad feeling in the Air Force because the 143-wing strength set in October 1951 had been stretched out to 1 January 1956, Eisenhower had cut $7 billion from the Defense budget, of which $5 billion came from the $16.7 billion granted the Air Force in the Truman budget for fiscal year 1954, and it appeared that the position of primacy the Air Force had enjoyed during the Korean War would be replaced by the balanced forces concept.[19]

Eberstadt preferred a decentralized defense organization. Finletter would return to the federated structure created in the original National Security Act, which had provided for "coordination" instead of "domination" of the services. Fleet Admiral Ernest J. King, Admiral Richard S. Edwards, and former Secretary of the Navy Dan A. Kimball generally opposed Plan No. 6, which

Major General Merritt Edson, USMC (Ret.) could not stomach at all.[20] Nimitz believed that if the Secretary of Defense would preside over the meetings of the Joint Chiefs of Staff as chairman, he would soon delegate to other agencies in the Defense Department all matters not germane to their primary planning function. Moreover, by transferring certain responsibilities to the various agencies in the department and to the services, he could also greatly decrease the work load in his own office.[21] Admiral Charles E. Cooke not only agreed with Eberstadt and Finletter on the need for additional decentralization, but also would have the service secretaries returned to the President's cabinet.

Hoffman's committee was denied both information on the proposed revision of the Key West Agreement and transcripts of the testimony given the Rockefeller Committee. The House first killed Hoffman's attempt to delete the sections of Plan No. 6 that increased the powers of the Joint Chiefs of Staff, then adopted the plan on 27 June by a vote of 235 to 109. With the Senate agreeable, it went into effect at 12:01 on 30 June.

On 1 October Charles Wilson issued a revision of the Key West Agreement that conformed to the recommendations of the Rockefeller Committee. While no changes were made in the roles and missions of the services, the Secretary of Defense, on the advice of the Joint Chiefs, would appoint a military department, not a Joint Chief, as executive agent for a particular task. Through its civilian secretary, that department would be responsible for the unified command that would perform the task. In order that the civilian secretary not make military decisions, however, he would immediately authorize his Chief of Staff to act for his department. That chief, however, must keep the other Joint Chiefs, his secretary, and the Secretary of Defense fully informed of all decisions and actions he took.[22]

The new reorganization act abolished the Munitions Board, the Research and Development Board, and the Directorate of Installations, and transferred their functions to the Secretary of Defense. It also vested "overall direction and control . . . in the field of research and engineering" in him; gave him broader powers to transfer, reassign, abolish, or consolidate the combatant functions of the services pending congressional approval; authorized him to assign or reassign to one or more services the development and operational use of new weapons or weapons systems; and in addition empowered him to "provide for the carrying out of any supply or service activity common to more than one military department by a single agency or such other organization entities as he deems appropriate."

With nine assistant secretaries, the Secretary of Defense should now be able to give much more detailed direction to his department—a direction that service leaders and such military analysts as Hanson Baldwin immediately characterized as too detailed. The new Chief of Staff of the Air Force, Nathan F. Twining, for example, believed that the new act permitted future military strategy to be "controlled by a civilian *transient* political appointee," for he could decide what "hardware" the services could have or not have and thus "whip a reluctant service into conformity with a predetermined political position."[23] Moreover, although they were not to impose themselves in the line of responsibility and authority between the Secretary of Defense and the service secretaries, it was possible that policy decisions would be made on the assistant secretary level. The assistant secretaries, it was predicted, would be faceless men lacking military experience and unknown to the public, who would serve an average of only two years.[24] Yet they would have assigned to them about a third of the entire number of officers assigned to the Office of Secretary of Defense, officers who would be torn between representing their service or the Secretary of Defense on any particular issue. The assistant secretaries of defense would issue directions or require reports from the services without the knowledge or intervention of the Secretary of Defense and Joint Chiefs of Staff.[25] Such a superstructure between the Secretary of Defense and the services was bound to delay decision-making and to diffuse responsibility. The trend toward centralization was also evident in the Chairman of the Joint Chiefs of Staff, who increasingly became the major contact point between the Joint Chiefs of Staff and the President, the Secretary of Defense, and the National Security Council. As Hanson Baldwin put it:

> Unification has meant triplification in many ways, as far as our bureaucracy and overhead is concerned and as far as numbers of people involved and the multiplication of purely administrative and bureaucratic tasks. . . . Now you have no control over anything, except by a deputy to a deputy to a deputy, and this goes, as you know, to the utmost extremes. . . .
> I think it's absurd that you try to standardize everything by four civilians who essentially don't know anything about the process. They haven't got the background of experience. They're in office for a short time and they really can't say what the mission of this or that school should be. . . . Too often, they get down to the finest details of administration.
> Today's organization would have been far from Forrestal's concepts and far from the concept of anybody who originally participated in unification. It's civilian control gone mad. The "layering" process has endangered, I think, to a high degree, our military effectiveness.[25]

About a year after Plan No. 6 went into effect, Secretary of the Navy Anderson produced a report on its naval implementation that was quickly approved by Secretary of Defense Wilson, who authorized Anderson to effectuate certain parts of it by administrative action while he sought approval for those parts which required legislation.[26] In prior debates over the character of the organization of the Department of Defense, the Navy had vociferously expounded its particular views. It was different in 1953, when no Navy Department official was asked his opinion on reorganization or volunteered one. Instead of argument, Anderson furnished compliance. The deed was done.

NOTES

1. U.S. Congress. *Department of Defense and Related Independent Agencies Appropriations for 1954*. Hearings before the Subcommittee of the Committee on Appropriations, House of Representatives, 83rd Cong., 1st Sess. (Washington: Committee print, 1953), pp. 4-9, 16; "Washington Roundup," AW 58 (2 February 1953):9.
2. The new Under Secretary of the Navy, Charles Thomas, was not really new because he had served as a special assistant to the Assistant Secretary of the Navy for Air, Artemus Gates, and then to Secretary of the Navy James V. Forrestal.
3. "Stage Set for Defense Shakeup," AW 58 (12 January 1953):14; "Washington Roundup." AW 58 (26 January 1953):13, (6 April 1953):12, and (18 May 1953):13.
4. Robert Cutler, Administrative Assistant to the President, to SECDEF, 20 March 1953, SECNAV, copy in NWRC, Suitland, Md., RG 80, Papers of the Secretary of the Navy (hereinafter cited as SNP).
5. *Department of Defense . . . Appropriations, 1954*, pp. 356-57, 390-96, 475-80; Thomas K. Finletter, *Power and Policy: U.S. Foreign Policy and Military Power in the Hydrogen Age* (New York: Harcourt, Brace, 1954), pp. 257-70; "AF Chief Says Reds Ahead in Air Buildup," AW 58 (5 January 1953):13-14; "Defense Fight," AW 58 (18 May 1953):12; "USAF," AW 58 (1 June 1953):13; "Vandenberg Warns Against AF Cutback," AW 58 (8 June 1953):7; "Wilson Hits AF 'Over-Financing,' " AW 58 (29 June 1953): 1546.
6. *Public Papers of the Presidents: Dwight D. Eisenhower*, 7 vols. (Washington: GPO, 1953-61), 1:54, 114, 308; Sherman Adams, *Firsthand Report: The Story of the Eisenhower Administration* (New York: Harper and Bros., 1961), pp. 398-99; Robert J. Donovan, *Eisenhower: The Inside Story* (New York: Harper and Bros., 1956), pp. 53-54; Secretary George M. Humphrey, with James C. Derieux, "It Looks Easier on the Outside," *Collier's* 133 (2 April 1954):31-34.
7. *New York Times*, 1, 10, and 22 December 1952, 4, 14, and 21 January, and 15 and 20 February 1953; "Seven-Man Committee to Study Defense," AW 58 (2 March 1953):38.
8. Davis Merwin to Hon. Dewey Short, Chairman, House Armed Services Committee, 2 and 3 March 1953, copy in SNP.
9. ' "Questions to be included in discussions with witnesses before the Committee—Department of Defense Organization," copy is SNP, File A3/EM, dated 14 March 1953.
10. Timothy W. Stanley, *American Defense and National Security* (Washington: Public Affairs Press, 1956), pp. 103-4. More detail is available in Comments of Staff, Office of SECDEF, on 10 July 1953, JCS Paper, Reorganization Plan, copy in SNP. Radford's testimony is found in *Report of the Rockefeller Committee on Department of Defense Organization, April 11, 1953,* Committee Print, Senate Committee on Armed Services, 83rd Cong., 1st Sess. (Washington, 1953), Appendix, p. 263.
11. *Report of the Rockefeller Committee.*
12. *Public Papers of the President: Eisenhower*, 1:227-30.
13. Baldwin in *New York Times*, 23 April and 3 May 1953; David Lawrence in *Washington Evening Star*, 1, 4, and 8 May 1953, and *U.S. News and World Report*, 8 May 1953; Arthur O. Sulzberger, "Concept for Catastrophe," USNIP 79 (April 1953):399-407; Frank A. Hecht, President, Navy League, to Robert B. Anderson and to Charles S. Thomas, copies of letters to Senator Saltsonstall, 27 May 1953, in SNP.
14. Leslie Arends to the President, 20 May 1953; Eisenhower to Arends, 25 May 1953, in U.S. Congress, Committee on Government Organization. *Reorganization Plan No. 6 of 1953. Hearings before the Committee on Government Operations, House of Representatives, 83rd Cong., 1st Sess., on H.J. Res. 264, 17, 18, 19, and 10 June 1953* (Washington: Committee Print, 1953), pp. 201-2.
15. Donovan, *The Inside Story*, pp. 53-54; Dwight D. Eisenhower, *Mandate for Change: The White House Years, 1956-1961* (London: William Heinemann, 1963), pp. 447-48.
16. Ibid., pp. 20-22, 161, 170-71.
17. Ibid., pp. 67-109.
18. Ibid., pp. 109-24, 189-94.

19. See Finletter, *Power and Policy*, pp. 257-70.
20. Hoffman *Hearings*, pp. 128, 225-29, 248-51.
21. These conclusions are drawn from the DOD copy of his answers to the ten questions asked of witnesses to testify before Hoffman's committee, copy in SNP.
22. Stanley, *American Defense and National Security*, pp. 106-7.
23. GEN Nathan F. Twining, USAF (RET), *Neither Liberty nor Safety: A Hard Look at U.S. Military Policy and Strategy* (New York: Holt, Rinehart and Winston, 1966), pp. 130-31.
24. J. Lawton Collins, *War in Peacetime: The History and Lessons of Korea* (Boston: Houghton Mifflin Co., 1969), pp. 373-74; Stanley, *American Defense and National Security*, p. 130.
25. "The Reminiscences of Hanson Weightman Baldwin," transcript of oral interview by John T. Mason (Annapolis, Md.,: U.S. Naval Institute, 1976, pp. 477-80.
26. R.B. Anderson to SECDEF, 27 April 1954, C.E. Wilson, Memorandum for the SECNAV, 28 April 1954; Committee on Organization for the Department of the Navy, *Summary of Management Studies Concerned with the Organization and Functional Operations of the Department of the Navy, October 1953*, SNP.

15

Conclusion

While authority over the military services has always rested with the President as Commander in Chief, the need to mobilize and allocate ever vaster resources to support national policy has required changes in national security organization. Especially was this true following World War II, when the nation essayed a large role in world affairs, challenged Russia in the Cold War, forcibly resisted communist aggression in Korea, and prepared to contest Russia if she wished to engage in general war by expanding in Europe or attacking the United States. Speedier aircraft, atomic weapons, and guided missiles made it impossible to prepare for war after war began. Fighting a war in Korea and also preparing for general war called for new executive-legislative relations and novel military-foreign policy arrangements, strategies, organization, and processes. What was the best way to institutionalize the achievement of national security?

During World War II, in a working compromise without legislative sanction, the functional equivalence given Army Air Force General H.H. Arnold with the Army Chief of Staff and with the Chief of Naval Operations resulted in unrest and disorder and created the need to reorganize the military establishment by destroying its old structure. But the determination of national security policies and organization involved much more than the advice and counsel of the military services. If the Secretary of Defense provided in the National Security Act was authorized to act second only to the President in defense matters, the civilian and military leaders of the services for many years following "unification" spoke with divergent voices with respect to organization, doctrine, roles and missions, funding, force levels, weapons and weapons systems, institutional patterns, management philosophy, and procurement, contract, and mobilization methods. Customs and traditions were involved, as were the status and prestige of personalities. Cases in point are the debates between 1943 and 1947 on unification; between 1947 and 1949 on the B-36, aircraft carriers, national strategy, roles and missions of the services, and strengthening unification by amending the National Security Act; the defense budget for fiscal year 1950 and NSC-68; the Korean War; and Reorganization Plan No. 6 of 1953. Involved were the personalities, management concepts, and organizational philosophies of Presidents Harry S. Truman and Dwight D. Eisenhower; Secretaries of Defense James V. Forrestal, Louis A. Johnson, Robert A. Lovett, and Charles E. Wilson; Secretaries of the Navy John L. Sullivan and Francis P. Matthews; and Secretaries of the Air Force W. Stuart Symington and Thomas K. Finletter. The services seemed to cooperate only when they sought to keep their authority from being absorbed at the Secretary of Defense level. That the Navy tried to adjust to ever-changing conditions is proved by the nearly fifty studies it made of its organization and major functions between 1945 and 1953. The reorganization of 1953, however, transformed a national security organization founded on controversy and resulting in compromise to one in which the Secretary of Defense was the prime military adviser to the President and was authorized to direct and coordinate the three military departments. While the service secretary still had a vital role as a member of the defense management team, he was reduced in prestige and authority and served mainly as an operational manager, as a support element in the Defense Department.

The Navy consistently opposed unification in a single department of the armed forces and single chief of staff because its own bilinear organization and task force concept of operations would be destroyed and it might lose its aviation and the Marine Corps. The Joint Chiefs of Staff Committee established to study defense reorganization in the summer of 1944 favored the single department/single chief of staff system but would let the Navy retain its organic aviation and the Marine Corps and let the Army keep its specialized aviation. But it produced a split report, with Admiral James O. Richardson dissenting from the majority view, primarily because the resulting organization would be too large to manage successfully, the Air Force would become a separate entity, and the Navy might lose its aviation to the Air Force and its Marine Corps to the Army. Unsaid but very real was the fear that the naval member would always remain in the minority in that closed corporation, the Joint Chiefs of Staff, and be subordinated in the councils of a single defense department. It may very well be that Truman accepted the Joint Chiefs of Staff rather than the single chief system because, as his counsel, Clark Clifford, suggested, the service chiefs would perpetually be in competition and thus would be more amenable to presidential authority than would a single chief.[1]

Forrestal, who became the Secretary of the Navy on 19 May 1944, realized that he must prepare the Navy to shift from a wartime to a peacetime organization and that he must offer an alternative to unification, not merely oppose it. At his request, in November 1945 Artemus S. Gates, his Under Secretary, recommended the organization that would be needed with the return of peace. Forrestal largely followed the Gates Board report and in 1946 and 1947 also reorganized the executive offices of his department. Meanwhile, at his request,

Ferdinand Eberstadt submitted a position paper that called for further study of the subject of unification, opposed an organization in which military men could challenge civilian control, and outlined a federated structure in which three separate but equal military services would be coordinated by a number of statutory interservice agencies headed by a secretary of defense. The most important agency to coordinate domestic, foreign, and military policy would be a National Security Council. In the fall of 1945 Forrestal offered Eberstadt's plan as a counter to a single department of defense, remarking that he was not yet ready to agree to a separate Air Force. Although Truman preferred a single department of defense and single chief of staff, as Army and Army Air Force leaders did, he suggested a compromise plan in which the single chief of staff was deleted and the Navy would keep its aviation and the Marine Corps. The Navy felt that it had suffered a major defeat because there would be a separate Air Force and Air Force personnel would man land-based aircraft used in naval reconnaissance, antisubmarine warfare, and protection of shipping. At Truman's urging, sufficient agreement was reached between Forrestal and the Secretary of War, Robert P. Patterson, to permit the enactment of the National Security Act, which Truman signed on 26 July 1947. Roles and missions were established in ambiguous terms by executive order on the twenty-seventh.

As the first Secretary of Defense, Forrestal had to formulate policy, develop principles of operation, and "supervise and coordinate" a budget for a unique agency lacking traditions. His concept of coordination was reflected in the National Security Act, and he meant to avoid the merger and overcentralization of the agencies it created. Rather than acting as a chief of a general staff and ending interagency conflict by issuing directives, he tried to understand and adjust, to persuade rather than command. Nor would he intrude into the internal administration of subordinate agencies, particularly of the military departments, which by statute were autonomous. Of the two military services that already had long traditions, he knew the Navy better, having been its Under Secretary and Secretary, and he opposed the Army's belief that discipline could be achieved by merely passing a law and drawing an organization chart. The Joint Chiefs of Staff had had five years to operate as a unit, and the Munitions Board had a long history as the Army and Navy Munitions Board created in 1922. But the new Air Force and the other agencies still had to develop their doctrines and procedures. Forrestal's administrative policy was to permit interservice competition up to a point and then adopt agreements resulting from the resolution of conflict. He would thus provide gradual evolutionary improvement in the national security organization. While he did not resist innovation, he would accept no organizational change that would impair the efficiency of the services. His efforts to direct the services were hindered, however, by the denial to him of many of the tools he needed in the restrictions placed upon him by the National Security Act. After informing him, the service secretaries could make recommendations to the President or the Director

of the Budget. The military departments were to be "separately administered": all powers not vested in the Secretary of Defense were reserved
to them. He could not have a military staff and was granted only three civilian
assistants who had no rank in the Defense Department's hierarchy. He had only "general direction, authority, and control" over the national security agencies. The "nerve center of unification," the Joint Chiefs of Staff, was the principal corporate advisory group on military affairs, not only to him but to the
President as well. Hence it had two masters and, in addition, its members were
individually responsible to their departmental secretaries as chiefs of their services. Mutual service distrust was legally sanctioned because the National Security
Act provided that the service secretaries would serve on the National Security
Council, War Council, Munitions Board, and Research and Development
Board. Resulting stalemates could be broken only by log-rolling. As Forrestal
indicated after fifteen months in office, when he made his first annual report,
he still believed in the democratic process, which permitted the free expression
of service opinion, and believed that the function of the Secretary of Defense
was to reconcile any conflicts in ideas and try to have loyalty to service give
way to the higher goal of unification. However, his feeling that good men were
more important than neat organization charts, that removing personal friction
was his main task, that "good will can make any organization work," and that
he must not transgress the integrity of the service departments was suspect,
and his authority to "direct" rather than "coordinate" was simply not enough.
He finally came to believe that there must be an accretion in the authority and staff of the Secretary of Defense. On the last point, even as late
as December 1948, except for the Research and Development Board he had
fewer civilian and military men in his own office than did the Munitions Board
and Joint Chiefs of Staff.

John L. Sullivan, the first Secretary of the Navy in the new national security
organization, was the first in that post not to enjoy a cabinet seat yet to have
membership on the National Security Council. He was also the first to face
problems arising from triservice rivalries in foreign policy formulation;
strategic, logistic, and industrial mobilization planning; weapons acquisition;
roles and missions; obtaining funds from the low budgets set by President
Truman; and vying with the other services for popular support. Schooled in
uniservice affairs, he supported the Navy on issues that divided the services, as
on the need to build a supercarrier that would enable the Navy to proceed with
aircraft and weapons developments, including the delivery of atomic weapons.
He opposed Air Force strategy that relied upon a single weapon and single
delivery system, preferring balanced and flexible forces instead. The inability
of the services to agree on many important issues created the environment in
which the power of ultimate decision would rest with the Secretary of Defense
and his staff. Decisions reached on that level, however, would appear to the
service secretaries as intrusions upon their vested rights.

The low defense budgets established by Truman for fiscal years 1948, 1949,
and 1950 meant that military power would be insufficient to support national

foreign policies and that dollars determined strategy, thus favoring the "ultimate weapon" and the Air Force. Unable to agree on the military budget for the first "unified" budget, that of 1950, the Joint Chiefs of Staff split it three ways. The Army and Air Force would cut the Navy down to a mere escort and antisubmarine force and agreed that weapons determined organization. The Air Force thus should control all aircraft and the Army all troops. The Air Force was unhappy that the Navy was authorized to build a supercarrier whose heavy planes, it said, would intrude upon its strategic air-atomic warfare mission. It held that naval ships could not withstand atomic attack; opposed the functional task force concept, which included the use of sea, land, and air forces; and demanded that its air power be put in balance not with that of the Army and Navy but with that of potential enemies. The Navy opposed a strategy based upon air-atomic power alone when the Air Force lacked a truly intercontinental bomber, when its bombers could be shot down by jet fighters, when the numerous missions assigned the Army and Navy in the National Security Act could not be performed by atomic bombs alone, when increases in the size of the Air Force called for additional costly support for it from the Army and Navy, when the air power of the nation was not that of the Air Force alone but the sum of the air power of all its military forces, and when guided missiles would soon make the manned bomber obsolescent. Moreover, aircraft based on carriers could perform the atomic-bombing mission better than Air Force bombers. National security could be provided better by facts than by panaceas; no service should have a monopoly on the development of weapons. Air Force publicity redolent of petty self-interest and institutional jealousy provoked Sullivan to tell the Secretary of the Air Force, W. Stuart Symington, that his Department revealed an "immature attitude," that it should give "more cool and profound consideration to national security problems," and that its attacks upon the Navy were really attacks on the National Security Act. Forrestal meanwhile could not precisely detail service roles and missions until the administration provided an overall national policy and the Joint Chiefs of Staff drafted strategic and logistic plans to support it. In meetings with the Joint Chiefs at Key West in March 1948 and at Newport in August, however, he obtained new definitions of primary and secondary roles and missions.

Under public and congressional fire for providing "triplification" instead of "unification," Forrestal sought an Under Secretary, an augmented and independent staff, the deletion of the service secretaries from the National Security Council and of the reserved powers of the services; clearer authority to direct the services; a representative other than the military Chief of Staff to the President who would chair the Joint Chiefs of Staff, an increase in the number of men on the Joint Staff, and increased authority over Department of Defense personnel policies. These changes fitted in with his idea of gradual evolutionary development of the National Military Establishment, in which he would exercise central control while operations were decentralized to the service departments. They would not decrease the authority of the service secretaries or stop interservice conflict, but they would give him greater authority to solve interservice differences over weapons, cross-service education, and public relations, and particularly those in the Joint Chiefs of Staff, as illustrated when they tried to agree on strategic plans, define responsibilities and functions (or roles and missions), and when they worked to unify the defense budget. The consolidation of competing service functions is illustrated by his creation of the Military Sea Transport Service and the Military Air Transport Service, one directed by the Navy, the other by the Air Force. Still to be resolved were differences over the use of air power, in which the Air Force and Navy both had responsibilities, differences exacerbated by low budgets and the distrust by each service of the other's weapons systems. Similar problems marked the Munitions Board and the Research and Development Board, in which representatives of the services tended to work for their services rather than for the good of the higher whole.

Sullivan thought that the powers already granted the Secretary of Defense were sufficient. Forrestal's asking for more power made it appear that he was unable to administer the National Military Establishment, and he held that it would be a "grave mistake" for him to delegate any of his authority to a chairman of the Joint Chiefs of Staff. He also opposed increasing the powers of the Director of the Joint Staff lest they conflict with those of the Secretary of Defense and end in a general staff that would supplant the Joint Chiefs of Staff. His suggestion was that Forrestal use a secretariat to be provided the War Council. This staff would be comprised of flag officers who would be responsible to him alone and help him to coordinate the agencies established by the National Security Act without detracting from the authority and responsibilities of the service secretaries. The only other modification he wished made was to change the National Security Resources Board from a statutory to an advisory agency. He thus stood quite pat on the National Security Act even though Forrestal and the other service secretaries would alter it. Naval spokesmen before the Eberstadt Committee of the Hoover Commission blasted the Air Force's single air-atomic strategy and insisted that the Navy could place more bombs on Russian targets than the Air Force and that the absorption of naval air by the Air Force would be an act of division rather than of integration because air power was the heart of the Navy. The Air Force countered that the Navy was intruding upon one of its primary missions and demanded that the authority of the Secretary of Defense be increased so that he could direct the Navy to conform. Eberstadt's committee nevertheless agreed that "strategic bombing covered such a broad area that it required the operation of carriers as well as the Air Force, that the two elements should be coordinated, not duplicated." With respect to the services, it found that "the instances of a surviving disunity are outweighed by the substantial . . . progress that has been achieved . . . toward a generally unified system." The Secretary of Defense, it added, should have power to exercise "direction, authority, and control" over all national security agencies and budget, and the reserved powers of the services should be deleted, as should also be their right to appeal over the head of the Secretary of Defense to the President and the Director of the Budget. The Secretary of Defense should be provided an Under Secretary and three additional civilian assistants and be represented on the Joint Chiefs of Staff by a nonvoting chairman. He alone, and not the service secretaries, should be a member of the National Security Council, and a weapons evaluation board should be established.

Even though the Air Force was favored by the general acceptance of its air-atomic strategy, it hoped that Forrestal would be replaced by a more air-minded Secretary of Defense. Sullivan, faced with the prospects of the grant of additional authority to the Secretary of Defense in the National Security Act Amendments of 1949, and having only limited funds for operations and for building a supercarrier, paid no attention when the Air Force rang the changes on the importance of air power. He was incensed with continuing anti-Navy propaganda issued by the Air Force and its persistent demands for an increase to seventy groups that must be paid for from funds taken from the other services, and with the concerted Army-Air Force attack on its carriers. Sullivan was therefore demanding "a complete reexamination of the entire [defense] structure" just at the time when Forrestal resigned and was succeeded by Louis A. Johnson.

An old Army man, Johnson supported air power and additional unification, which meant that the Navy would lose the somewhat favored position it enjoyed while Forrestal was Secretary of Defense and possibly lose its aviation to the Air Force and its Marine Corps to the Army. Furthermore, Johnson made coordinated foreign and military policy impossible by divorcing the Defense Department from the State Department except for contacts between their secretaries. A tremendously ambitious man, he would be aided in directing his department if the increased powers for the Secretary of Defense, suggested by the Eberstadt Committee and the Hoover Commission and recommended to Congress by President Truman, became law. Even without the additional power, however, he made his weight felt. Perhaps to economize, perhaps to show who was boss, perhaps because he favored the Air Force, on 23 April 1949 he directed Sullivan to discontinue construction on the supercarrier, named the *United States*, whose keel had been laid just five days earlier. Funds thus released could buy additional B-36 bombers. In his prompt and angry letter of resignation, Sullivan criticized Johnson's arbitrary prohibition of the development of a powerful weapons system and stated that he feared that the next step would be the transfer of naval air to the Air Force and of the Marine Corps to the Army. Thus unification would become consolidation and concentration. The difficulty of the Navy's position was further compounded when Sullivan's successor, Francis P. Matthews, supported Johnson rather than his own service on unification.

The Navy struck back in congressional hearings held on the procurement arrangements for the B-36 and its capability as an intercontinental bomber, on unification itself, and on the Tydings bill to amend the National Security Act in keeping with the recommendations of the Hoover Commission. The unification hearings also inquired whether Johnson's cutting of its funds left the Navy anything more than a mere defensive antisubmarine force, whether a supercarrier should be built, and whether old carriers should be modernized so that the Navy could carry out its assigned offensive as well as defensive missions. In addition they inquired whether Johnson's economizing in his department—mostly at the expense of naval air and the Marine Corps—would not badly obstruct the provision of military forces needed to support national policy in the "permanent crisis" situation represented by the Cold War. Furthermore, if additional defense was required, would it be obtained by following the Army and Navy suggestion of heavy spending to keep up manpower and industrial mobilization strength or by adopting the Air Force plan of providing a great "force in being" capable of deterring war or of inflicting great damage upon an aggressor? Johnson preferred the Air Force way, which meant that the Navy could not contribute much to national defense. By "distributing shortages" as he did, he substituted financial control for adequate review of military requirements; the dollar, therefore, not national security, dictated strategy. But such was his penchant for economy that he reduced the Air Force to forty-eight groups even though he knew that Russia had acquired the atomic bomb. Rabid exercise of power over the defense budget had reduced the effectiveness of the services. Yet Johnson would be the first Secretary of Defense to enjoy the additional powers vested in him by the National Security Act Amendments of 1949.

These amendments stipulated that the Secretary of Defense would be the principal adviser to the President on defense matters and granted him an Under Secretary. He was given specific power to "direct" a Department of Defense rather than a National Military Establishment. The services would be military rather than executive departments, and their reserved powers were deleted. The Army and Air Force had demanded a single chief of staff. The Navy had opposed and won its point with a nonvoting chairman who would represent the Secretary of Defense in the Joint Chiefs of Staff but could not exercise command over the services. The Secretary of Defense, moreover, could not establish a single chief of staff or general staff, or reassign, transfer, abolish, or consolidate service functions without congressional approval. While a service secretary could no longer appeal to the President and Director of the Budget over the head of the Secretary of Defense, he could appeal to Congress, a point that illustrated the distrust Congress felt in increasing the power of the Secretary of Defense, as did the requirement that he would report semiannually rather than annually. Whereas the restrictions on the Secretary of Defense were not so great as to seriously limit his activities, a service secretary who ran to Congress with a grievance would make his position in the Defense Department untenable. Because the service secretaries were removed from the National Security Council and remained secretaries rather than becoming Under Secretaries to the Secretary of Defense, they headed subsidiary parts of the Department of Defense as middle managers of sorts. They still had sufficient authority and responsibility to warrant the seeking of their advice by a Secretary of Defense. Even if their departments were still to be administered separately, there were instances in which they could be told what to do by the Secretary of Defense in matters in which the services had not been provided with equal representation. Of especial importance were the facts that the Secretary of Defense could make a decision when the Chairman of the Joint Chiefs of Staff reported inability to agree on some matter, and that he alone represented the Defense Department in the National Security Council. The chairmen of the Munitions Board and of the Research and Development Board could make decisions despite the equal military representation on the boards, but his was the last word on departmental budget and fiscal matters. As long as a Secretary of Defense followed the principle that the operating effectiveness of the services came before changes in organization and administration, as Forrestal had, the service secretaries would not feel a heavy hand. Johnson's way, however, was to "crack heads" and force the service secretaries to cooperate. He saved a good deal of money by abolishing a large number of interservice committees and by cutting funds for the services. But by imposing additional unification before as well as after passage of the National Security Act Amendments of 1949, he reduced the effectiveness of the services to the point where they could not support national policy and provoked the revolt of the admirals.

Secretary of the Navy Matthews established a court of inquiry into how certain classified information was made public. Unable to testify, Captain John W. Crommelin violated *Navy Regulations* and publicly criticized the "potential dictatorship" in the Department of Defense, and asserted that "the Navy is being nibbled to death in the Pentagon." He held that the Navy could not obtain needed support as long as there were three men "who may have a landlocked concept of national defense" to outvote the Chief of Naval Operations on the Joint Chiefs of Staff. Rear Admiral Daniel V. Gallery barely missed a court-martial by making similar comments, and reports on morale in the Navy forwarded at his request told Matthews unmistakably that it was very, very low. Naval unrest was fully documented at the Carl Vinson hearings on unification. Before him naval spokesmen loosed their anomosity against increased powers for the Secretary of Defense and asserted that the Air Force's best bombers could easily be shot down by fighters and that naval aircraft could bomb targets much better than could high altitude bombers. Matthews almost completely divorced himself from the Navy's presentation, which was prepared mostly by Arleigh Burke and his staff in OP-23 and Vice Admiral Arthur W. Radford, Commander in Chief Pacific Fleet. Radford, the main speaker for the Navy "radicals," criticized the B-36 as a "symbol of . . . a cheap and easy victory" and as a "billion dollar blunder" that the Air Force had added to its inventory without obtaining clearances from the Secretary of Defense and the other Joint Chiefs of Staff. Torn between supporting Secretary Matthews or the radicals, Louis E. Denfeld, Chief of Naval Operations, eventually leaned toward the latter. He supported unification, but the price for the Navy to pay was too high. The Navy was not being accepted as a full partner in the Department of Defense. The cancellation of the supercarrier was merely one example of the improper operation of unification. To Matthews he thus was "disloyal." Despite Vinson's saying that no reprisals would be permitted, Denfeld had insured his dismissal by Matthews. Civilian authority in military matters must be upheld! But in dismissing Denfeld and in subsequently violating law by trying to block the promotion to rear admiral of Arleigh Burke, Matthews lost the confidence of his service and of many congressmen as well.

While naval aviators were happy with one of their own kind, Forrest Sherman, as Denfeld's successor, the Marine Corps feared that he would absorb the Corps into the Navy if not turn it over to the Army. To his credit, Matthews told Sherman that the Secretary of the Navy, not the Chief of Naval Operations, controlled the Corps. Yet Sherman applied the gag to naval officers who would criticize other officers or the Department of Defense—and there were many of these—while the Air Force propaganda campaign against the Navy continued unabated and was a positive hindrance to attempts to achieve better unification. Matthews, however, held that naval morale was splendid," lauded Johnson, and stated that unification would "ultimately be universally regarded as one of the most constructive developments in the evolution of our system of government."

The $13.5 billion alloted by Truman to defense in the fiscal year 1951 budget increased Army funds slightly but cut into those of the Air Force and of the Navy, with the result that the Air Force would remain at forty-eight groups and the Navy had to curtail operations, forgo new construction and conversion work, and use aircraft 63.5 percent of which on 30 June 1950 would average five years in age. Yet Johnson said the budget provided "sufficiency of defense for the hour." Matthews and Sherman decided to go along with reduced minimum readiness, but Symington, unable to stomach Johnson, left the Air Force—and continued his crusade for seventy groups from his new position as chairman of the National Security Resources Board.

Vinson's report on his unification and strategy hearings, issued 1 March 1950, suggested that the National Security Council provide statements on national policy upon which the agencies of the National Military Establishment could base strategic plans. It also noted shortfalls in strategic air-atomic bombing and called for conventional naval forces that were mobile, flexible, and tailored to perform specific tasks. Moreover, the Air Force was unbalanced in favor of strategic air power, and Johnson had erred in canceling the construction of the *United States* without first conferring with Secretary Sullivan and gaining approval from the congressional military committees. The chiefs of staff of the Army and of the Air Force were not qualified to determine for the Navy the best weapons needed to control the seas, and a supercarrier should be built when the budget permitted. Deeming the ouster of Denfeld to have been a "reprisal," the report noted the great difficulty such a procedure placed in congressional attempts to obtain unbiased testimony on which to base legislation. Furthermore, the report called for adding the Commandant of the

Marine Corps to membership on the Joint Chiefs of Staff, rotating the chairman of the Joint Chiefs every two years, and requiring the Secretary of Defense within certain limits to confer with congressional appropriations committees before withholding by administrative act the expenditure of appropriated funds. It was Vinson who introduced the legislation that would put these improvements into effect. The hearings had at least cleared the air. Despite the eleven percent cut Johnson made in the Navy's funds for 1951, morale and good order were gradually restored in the Navy by the new Chief of Naval Operations, Forrest Sherman.

If Matthews was happy with the Navy's reduced budget, men like Bradley and Eisenhower saw that Johnson's economizing had not transformed fat into muscle but had cut into muscle, and they demanded increased defense appropriations. Congress responded in part by funding the construction of 173 new ships and the conversion of 291 others and a number of fighter and antisubmarine aircraft. By 1950 it was rumored that the Navy had two air squadrons capable of carrying atomic bombs off carriers. These and even larger aircraft would in time be able to operate off the supercarrier Vinson provided in his "atomic age" naval bill. Vinson also called for an atomic-powered submarine. Although authority was granted for a seventy-group Air Force and the growth of the Army to 837,000 men, funding had not been provided before the Korean War began. Therefore the services had to enter that war with what little they had. The war would show that Matthews was incorrect in thinking that the "critical period" of unification had passed. Although Johnson did not change the basic organization of the Department of Defense, he lost the respect of his department. With the same organization, his successor, George Marshall, would be able to win back and keep that respect. The Korean War would also test the philosophy of relying upon a single weapon and single delivery system and show the correctness of those who demanded balanced and flexible forces.

In the spring of 1950, NSC-68 had suggested increased defense spending so that American military forces would achieve the strength they needed to support national policy in the cold war. Truman had just asked for the costing of the programs it recommended when the attack upon South Korea by North Korea caught every agency created by the National Security Act unawares and unprepared. To reverse the deterioration of military strength caused by Johnson's economizing, Congress had to pass mountainous appropriations and expand the industrial mobilization program. The fiscal year 1950 budget had been $13.3 billion; that for 1951 was $48.3 billion; that for 1952, $57.2 billion. Moreover, wartime budgets were determined on the basis of military requirements rather than on the principle of balanced forces or that of paring expenses. Although the budget favored the Air Force, the viability of naval air was recognized in the funding of three supercarriers. With carrier-borne, atomic-laden aircraft, the Navy obtained the offensive air role it had tried to win since denied it as a primary function in the National Security Act as "interpreted" at Key West and Newport. In addition, in 1951 Secretary of the Navy Dan A. Kimball and the Chief of Naval Operations joined the other service secretaries and members of the Joint Chiefs of Staff in projecting defense expenditures through fiscal year 1955, thus in effect carrying out the recommendations of NSC-68. When the Joint Chiefs could not agree on the future size of the Air Force, Secretary of Defense Robert A. Lovett gave the problem to the civilian secretaries to decide, indicating that the secretaries had been returned to full participation in defense policy-making.

Although Matthews administered the Navy Department more effectively in 1951 than in 1949-50, new leadership by Kimball greatly heightened naval morale. Morale also greatly improved in the Marine Corps when legislation Truman signed on 6 June 1952 set corps strength at three divisions and three air wings. The Navy in turn was greatly pleased when Supreme Headquarters Allied Powers Europe was directed to coordinate Strategic Air Command and naval air operations in NATO. Both the Army and the Navy were happy when new thinking stressed reliance upon balanced and flexible forces instead of primary reliance upon the Strategic Air Command, and when new doctrine provided for the augmentation of tactical rather than strategic air forces and provided that although Joint Operating Centers could be established at Army-Air Force headquarters levels, tactical air direction centers would be operated at corps level.

The Korean War proved that reliance upon a single military doctrine had not deterred war and that unification had not prepared the nation to fight a limited war. American military strength and that of her allies in NATO was rebuilt during the war, which on its own part revealed that unification remained a problem not only in Washington but in the field as well, even after Truman fired both Johnson and General Douglas MacArthur and sent Matthews to be his ambassador in Ireland.

Eisenhower's campaign promise to seek "security with solvency" and to reform the operations of the Department of Defense was made rather easy for him to keep because his reforms were foreshadowed by recommendations made by Secretary of Defense Lovett late in 1952. During the three years since the National Security Act was amended in 1949, said Lovett, unification had reduced military costs yet increased the security of the nation. Further improvement, particularly in light of the Korean War experience, was indicated. The military forces should be funded on a continuing rather than "feast or famine" basis, and by some method better than using merely the dollar to measure military requirements. This was a major recommendation that President Eisenhower rejected, for despite the anguished cries from the Air Force, whose wings he clipped when he reduced the Truman defense budget for fiscal year 1954, his "New Look" or "floating M-day" concept restored the dollar as the controlling element in defense planning. Lovett would maintain the mobilization base as expanded during the Korean War. He also sought clarification of the authority and responsibilities of the agencies within the Department of Defense, saying that some changes could be made by administrative directives while others required legislation. He had already established Offices of Analysis and Review in each military department to audit and review all military requirements for manpower, materials, and facilities. A revised charter had given full power of decision to the Chairman of the Munitions Board, a separate Defense Supply Management Agency had been created in the Office of the Secretary of Defense, and all military construction work had been centralized in one office under a Director of Installations. Lovett had also established civilian advisory committees to look into military manpower problems and the defense of North America.

Various "contradictions and straddles" in the National Security Act should be obviated in time of peace rather than in time of war, Lovett continued. The Secretary of Defense alone, not the Joint Chiefs of Staff, should be the chief military adviser to the President. Within the prohibitions upon his authority to transfer, reassign, abolish, or consolidate combatant functions without congressional approval, he should have "direction, authority, and control" over the services. The overburdened Joint Chiefs should be relieved of operational and administrative details concerning their services so that they could concentrate upon planning. To further relieve them from reviewing the many papers sent them by the Secretary of Defense, the Secretary of Defense should be provided an augmented staff of assistant secretaries and their military advisers. The latter group would be insulated against service influence by having their fitness reports prepared by their civilian superiors. An alternative and "more radical" reformation of the Joint Chiefs of Staff would be to replace them with a Combined Staff comprised of men who had already served as service chiefs and who would undertake planning functions only.

Lovett's ideas meshed with those of Eisenhower: more clear-cut lines of authority in the Defense Department, more service unification, more civilian control, strengthening of the planning role of the Joint Chiefs of Staff, less defense spending. Strangely, no witness at the hearings held on defense reorganization by the House Committee on Government Operations or the Rockefeller Committee on Defense Reorganization mentioned the advantages or disadvantages of unification either in Washington or in the field during the Korean War, the failure of the Air Force to provide a doctrinal manual until 1953, or the impossibility of achieving improved unification by means of the studies undertaken since 1951 by a large number of interservice boards on levels below that of the Joint Chiefs of Staff. In any event, Defense Reorganization Plan No. 6, which went into effect on 30 June 1953, firmly established civilian control. A single line of authority ran from the President to the Secretary of Defense and downward, with the Secretary acting through service secretaries viewed as "operating managers" and his "principal advisers."

"Maximum effectiveness at minimum cost" was to be obtained by abolishing several statutory boards and transferring their functions to the Office of Secretary of Defense, wherein nine assistant secretaries would serve the Secretary in a staff capacity, help him develop policies and standards, and provide information on which he could reach decisions. "The best possible military plans" were to be obtained by removing the Joint Chiefs of Staff from the chain of command, thereby freeing them for planning and advisory roles, and vesting in their chairman the responsibilities of choosing the members of and managing the Joint Staff and of revising service roles and missions.

As Secretary of the Air Force Thomas K. Finletter put it, unification had proceeded from multiplication to quadruplication. Two services could cooperate, but when a third was added a fourth was required to manage the three. But the character of the management authority had changed greatly between 1947 and 1953. The Secretary of Defense was no longer a coordinator of three autonomous military departments; he was the prime decision maker. Furthermore, he was armed with a staff of assistants who would see that his decisions were carried out. The new system discouraged rather than encouraged interservice conflict; to reach the Secretary of Defense, the service secretaries had to go through his assistant secretaries. Forrestal had envisaged a horizontally organized, federated structure in which a Secretary of Defense managed three autonomous military departments enjoying equal representation in the agencies of the Department of Defense. According to Reorganization Plan No. 6, the service secretaries had no legal right to demand a share in defense policy making. Indeed, the Secretary of Defense could seek advice from any group he found useful to him. Thus the horizontal-federal structure of 1947 had given way to the vertical-unitary structure of 1953. The "passive" philosophy of Forrestal, in which the Secretary of Defense would lead by resolving interservice conflicts, had given way to the "active" philosophy, in which a Secretary of Defense would establish policies the service must support. Plan No. 6 did not eradicate the bases of further debate over unification. Proper defense organization, strategic concepts, weapons systems, and budget allocations, among many other matters, still provided grist for argument. However, the plan established that the decisions of the Secretary of Defense, while they must be within the limits imposed upon him by statute, could be challenged only by the President.[2]

The service secretaries remained important as managers of their departments. Even if the services were submerged, they were still to be administered separately. The service secretary was still the final advocate of the professional viewpoint in the decision-making process on the Office of Secretary of Defense level, as the spokesman for his service to the people and to Congress, as the interpreter of policies established by the Secretary of Defense, and as the translator of policy into operational reality. He still competed with the other service secretaries in developing new ideas or weapons for executing military functions. Such intangibles as tradition, esprit de corps, and pride in service remained, as did single-service expertise and specialization, for no fundamental change had been made in the organization of the services themselves after 1947. Nor had the Joint Chiefs of Staff been divorced from their single-service connections. The fact that the service secretary was made responsible to the Secretary of Defense, however, meant that the price of unification between 1947 and 1953 was the loss of integrity by the military service departments.

NOTES

1. Donald J. Mrozek, "The Transformation of the United States Military Establishment, 1940-1972," MS, Courtesy Dr. Mrozek.
2. See the argument between Eugene S. Duffield, "Organizing for Defense," *Harvard Business Review* 31 (September-October 1953):29-42, and H. Struve Hensel, "Changes Inside the Pentagon," *Harvard Business Review* 32 (January-February 1954):98-108.

Essay on Sources

OFFICIAL DOCUMENTS

The best sources of information on the civil and military leaders involved with unification are their official and personal papers. The most fruitful proved to be the Papers of the Secretary of Defense, Washington: National Archives and Records Service, RG330; the Papers of the Secretary of the Army, RG335; the Papers of the Secretary of the Air Force, RG340; and the Papers of the Secretaries of the Navy, Washington National Records Center, Suitland, Md., RG80. The Papers of the Chief of Naval Operations, which throw much light on the operations of the Joint Chiefs of Staff, are in Washington, Naval History Division, Operational Archives. Some of the papers of James V. Forrestal are in NARG38, others in the Firestone Library, Princeton University. The Harry S. Truman Library, Independence, Missouri, contains the papers of Dean G. Acheson, Clark M. Clifford, Admiral Robert L. Dennison, USN, Thomas K. Finletter, John F. Floberg, Clayton Fritchie, Roswell L. Gilpatric, W. John Kenney, John T. Koehler, Frederick James Lawton, Francis P. Matthews, Frank Pace, Jr., Harry S. Truman, Harry H. Vaughan, and James K. Webb. The Lyndon B. Johnson Library contains transcripts of oral interviews of Arleigh A. Burke, Edward L. Beach, Joseph M. Dodge, Thomas Gates, Jr., James M. Gavin, Henry L. Miller, William W. Outerbridge, Walter Bedell Smith, and Carl Vinson, and of Nelson Rockefeller when he last served as the chairman of the Special Committee on Government Organization. Also useful are such subseries in the presidential files as Bureau of the Budget and Cabinet. The Stephen T. Early and Henry A. Wallace papers are at the Franklin D. Roosevelt Library, the Gordon Gray papers at the Dwight D. Eisenhower Library. Microfilm versions of transcripts of oral interviews of Secretaries of the Air Force Thomas K. Finletter and Eugene M. Zuckert and of Air Force Generals Carl A. Spaatz, James H. Doolittle, Otto P. Weyland, and Curtis E. LeMay; an historical document written by General George C. Kenney, USAC; and a paper entitled "Development of AAF Bombing" were obtained from the Albert F. Simpson Historical Research Center, USAF, Maxwell AFB, Alabama.

Documentation of theoretical and political developments in aeronautics is found in Records of the National Advisory Committee on Aeronautics, 1915-18, at the National Archives. Also available at the Archives are certain records of the Armed Services, Foreign Relations, and Government Operations committees of Congress. Most relevant for this study are the records of the hearings conducted jointly by the Senate Armed Services and Foreign Relations committees into the "firing" of General Douglas MacArthur.

The papers of Ernest J. King, Dudley W. Knox, William D. Leahy, and Hoyt S. Vandenberg were used in the Manuscript Division, Library of Congress. Navy Department "Flag Files, 1911-1962," which document administrative, organizational, and operational activities of the fleet, and some of the papers from the files of the Office of the Secretary of the Navy while James V. Forrestal, John L. Sullivan, and Francis P. Matthews filled the post are in the National Archives.

Documentation of presidential efforts to reorganize the Department of Defense is found in *The Public Papers of the Presidents: Harry S. Truman,* 8 vols. (Washington: GPO, 1961-1966); *The Public Papers of the Presidents of the United States: Dwight D. Eisenhower,* 8 vols. (Washington: GPO, 1953-61), and Robert L. Branyan and Lawrence H. Larsen, *The Eisenhower Administration, 1953-1961: A Documentary History* (New York: Random House, 1971). First under the imprint of the National Military Establishment, 1947-49, and since 1949 under that of the Department of Defense, are the annual and, after 1949, semiannual *Report of the Secretary of Defense,* which contain the reports of the service secretaries also. These are published by GPO. Most pertinent among the publications of the Navy Department are: *The United States Navy: A Description of Its Functional Organization,* Navexos 435, rev. 1952 (Washington: GPO, 1952) and the revision dated May 1962, and the *Navy Department Bulletin,* which I have used from 1947 through its last issue in mid-1952. Salient Air Force productions include: Top Secret. NAFI 168.15-5. *Comparison of Strategic Bombing Systems, 25 October 1949* (Maxwell Air Force Base, Ala.: Albert F. Simpson Historical Research Center); Headquarters, USAF, Office of the Deputy Chief of Staff, Operations. *The United States Air Force Policy on Doctrine and Procedures for the Air Defense of the United States* (Washington: Department of the Air Force, 30 June 1949); *Report of General Carl Spaatz, the Chief of Staff, U.S. Air Force, to the Secretary of the Air Force, 30 June 1948* (Washington: GPO, 1949); and *United States Air Force Operations in the Korean Conflict,* 3 vols. (Maxwell Air Force Base, Ala.: Historical Division, 1952-56); and Confidential. C. L. Grant, *The Development of Continental Air Defense to 1 September 1954* (Maxwell Air Force Base, Ala.: Air University, Research Studies Institute. Historical Studies No. 126, 1957). Helpful also are: Secret. *Emergency Air Defense Forces, 1946-1954* (Colorado Springs, Col.: Directorate of Historical Services Headquarters, Air Defense Command. Historical Study No. 5, 30 June 1954); Secret. Thomas A. Sturm, *Organization and Responsibility for Air Defense, March 1946-September 1955* (Colorado Springs, Col.: Continental Air Defense Command. Air Defense Command. Historical Study No. 9,

1955); and *The Progressive Development of the Strategic Air Command, 1947-1970* (Offut Air Force Base, Neb.: Strategic Air Command, Office of the Historian, 1970 [courtesy Dr. John Bohn]. Relative also are *Major Changes in the Organization of the Joint Chiefs of Staff, 1942-1969* (Washington: U.S. Joint Chiefs of Staff, Historical Division), and *U.S. Marine Corps Operations in Korea, 1950-1953*, 5 vols. (Washington: Headquarters, USMC, Historical Branch, G-3, 1954-72). An Army study of unification is Lieutenant Colonel Lawrence J. Legere, Jr., Infantry, USA, *Unification of the Armed Forces* (Washington: Chief of Military History, 1959).

Congressional hearings on appropriations, nominations, and special subjects cast illuminating light on the funding, personnel, and organizational problems associated with defense unification. The most rewarding of these have been: U.S. Congress. Senate. Subcommittee on Appropriations, *Military Establishment*, Hearings before Subcommittee, 80th Congress, 1st Session, June 24-28, 1947 (Washington: GPO, 1947): U.S. Congress. House, Subcommittee Hearings before Subcommittee, 80th Congress, 2nd Session, 16 March-22 May 1948 (Washington, GPO, 1948); U.S. Congress. House, Committee on Appropriations, *Military Functions, National Military Establishment Appropriations Bill*, Hearings before the Subcommittee of the Committee on Appropriations, 3 parts (Washington: GPO, 1948); U.S. Congress. House. Subcommittee on Military Affairs, *Military Establishment*, Hearings before Subcommittee, 81st Congress, 1st Session, 25 January-24 March 1949 (Washington: GPO, 1949); U.S. Congress. House. Committee on Armed Services, *Composition of the Army and Air Force*, Hearings before Committee, 81st Congress, 1st Session, 27 January-9 February 1949 (Washington: GPO, 1949); U.S. Congress. Senate. Subcommittee on Appropriations, *National Military Establishment*, Hearings before Subcommittee, 81st Congress, 1st Session, 16-24 June 1949 (Washington: GPO, 1949); U.S. Congress. Senate. Subcommittee on Armed Services, *Army-Air Composition*, Hearings before Subcommittee, 81st Congress, 1st Session, 21 March-1 April 1949 (Washington: GPO, 1949); U.S. Congress. House. Committee on Armed Services, *National Defense Program*, Hearings before Committee, 81st Congress, 1st Session, 6-21 October 1949 (Washington: GPO, 1949); U.S. Congress. House, Committee on Appropriations, *Hearings on National Military Establishment Appropriations Bill for 1950*, 81st Congress, 1st Session (Washington: GPO, 1950); U.S. Congress Senate Subcommittee on Appropriations, *Department of Defense*, Hearings before Subcommittee, 81st Congress, 2nd Session, 13 March-15 May 1950 (Washington: GPO, 1950); U.S. Congress. House. *Department of Defense Appropriations for 1951*, 81st Congress, 2nd Session (Washington: GPO, 1951); U.S. Congress. House. Committee on Appropriations, *Department of Defense and Related Independent Agencies, Appropriations for 1954*, Hearings before Subcommittee, 83rd Congress, 1st Session (Washington: GPO, 1953).

After hearings held by the 80th Congress, 1st Session, in December 1947, there appeared U.S. President's Air Policy Commission, *Survival in the Air Age: A Report* (Washington: GPO, 1948), and Report of the Congressional Aviation Policy Board, *National Aviation Policy* (Senate Report 949, 80th Congress, 2nd Session).

The year 1949 saw a rash of congressional hearings and reports on defense unification: U.S. Congress. House. Committee on Armed Services, *B-36 Bomber*, Hearings before Committee, 81st Congress, 1st Session, 9-22 August 1949 (Washington: GPO, 1949); U.S. Congress. House. Committee on Armed Services. *Investigation of the B-36 Bomber Program*, 81st Congress, 1st Session, 2 parts, (Washington: GPO, 1949); U.S. Congress. House. Committee on Armed Services, *National Defense Program: Unification and Strategy*, Hearings before the Committee, 81st Congress, 1st Session (Washington: GPO, 1949); U.S. Congress. House. Committee on Armed Services, *The National Security Organization* (Report of the Commission on the Executive Branch of Government) 81st Congress, 1st Session (Washington: GPO, 1949); U.S. Commission of the Executive Branch of the Government, *National Security Organization Appendix G* (The Eberstadt Report) (Washington: GPO, 1949); U.S. Congress. House. Committee on Armed Services, Hearings, *to Convert the National Military Establishment into an Executive Department of the Government to be Known as the Department of Defense*, 81st Congress, 1st Session (Washington: GPO, 1949); U.S. Congress. Senate. Committee on Armed Services, *National Security Act Amendments of 1949, Hearings on S. 1269 and S. 1843 before the Committee, 81st Congress, 1st Session, and Hearings on S. 1843 before the House Committee on Armed Services*, 81st Congress, 1st Session (Washington: GPO, 1949); U.S. Congress. House. Committee on Armed Services, *Unification and Strategy: A Report of Investigation* (Washington: GPO, 1950).

The outstanding hearings of 1951 were: U.S. Congress. Senate. Committee on Foreign Relations and Senate Committee on Armed Services. Hearings, *Assignment of Ground Forces of the United States to Duty in the European Area, on S. Con. Res. 8*, 82nd Congress, 1st Session (Washington: GPO, 1951); U.S. Congress. Senate. Committee on Foreign Relations and Senate Committee on Armed Services, *Hearings on The Military Situation in the Far East*, 5 parts, 82nd Congress, 1st Session (Washington: GPO, 1951). Also pertinent are House Report No. 666, 82nd Congress, 1st Session, *Hearings on Douglas-Mansfield Marine Corps Bill, April-May 1951* (Washington: GPO, 1951), and U.S. Congress. Senate. Committee on Armed Services, *Hearings on Douglas-Mansfield Marine Corps Bill, S. 677*, 82nd Congress, 1st Session (Washington: GPO, 1951).

Department of Defense reorganization in 1953 was considered in U.S. Congress. Committee on Government Operations, *Reorganization Plan No. 6 of 1953, Department of Defense, Hearings* before the Committee . . . on H.J. Res. 264. 17, 18, 19, and 20 June 1953, 83rd Congress, 1st Session (Washington: GPO, 1953), and U.S. Congress. Senate. Armed Services Committee. *Report of the Rockefeller Committee on Department of Defense*

Organization, 83rd Congress, 1st Session (Washington: GPO, 1953).

Laws approved may be found in the latest edition of the *Statutes of the United States*, executive orders establishing service roles and missions and myriads of other matters in the *Federal Register*.

NEWSPAPERS AND JOURNALS

Good reports on defense unification and editorial comment thereon are found especially in the *New York Times, New York Herald-Tribune, Baltimore Sun, Christian Science Monitor*, and *Washington Post*. The first contains the remarks of military commentator Hanson Baldwin, the second those of Walter Millis, and the third those of Mark Watson. Other syndicated columnists who dealt with defense matters as well as other things are Marquis Childs, David Lawrence, and Drew Pearson.

Articles dealing with unification have been followed in various learned, popular, military, and scientific journals. Among these are *Aerospace Historian, Air Force, Airpower Historian, Air University Quarterly Review, Army and Navy Journal* (known after 1950 as *Army, Navy, Air Force Journal* and by other names), *Armed Forces Management, Aviation, Aviation Weekly, American Political Science Review, Collier's, Congressional Quarterly Almanac, Foreign Affairs, Journal of American History, Life, Marine Corps Gazette, Military Affairs, Military Review, Naval Aviation News, Navy Times, Newsweek, Pacific Historical Review, Readers Digest, Saturday Evening Post, Scientific American, Time, United States Air Services, U.S. Naval War College Review*, U.S. Naval Institute *Proceedings, U.S. News and World Report, Yale Review*.

Particularly important among the unsigned articles in these and other journals are: "Revolt of the Admirals," *Air Force 32* (December 1949):22-27; "Seversky, Says General Eaker, Is the Mahan of Air Power," *U.S. Air Services* 35 (January 1951):7-9; "The Air-Ground Operation in Korea," *Air Force* 34 (March 1951):19-58; An Air Force Magazine Staff Study, "There Is No Easy Way Out—a Second Look at Mainbrace," *Air Force* 36 (January 1953):21-23; and Air Force Magazine Staff Study, "The Truth About Our Air Defense," *Air Force* 36 (May 1953):25-29, 34, 36; "The Air Defense Command," *Air Force* 36 (April 1953):37-38, 42; "The Strategic Air Command—A Special Report," *Air Force* 39 (April 1956):39-138; U.S. Department of the Air Force, Far Eastern Air Force Bomber Command, "Heavyweights over Korea: B-29 Employment in the Korean War," *Air University Quarterly Review* 7 (Spring 1954):99-115; Editorial, "The Navy and Security," *Life*, October 24, 1949, p. 44; "Admiral Nimitz Sees Navy with Air as First Line," *Army and Navy Journal* 85 (January 10, 1948):473, 495; "Texts and Documents in Naval Discussion," *Army and Navy Journal* 86 (October 8, 1949):139, 158, 164, "Unification Anniversary," *Army and Navy*

Journal 88 (September 12, 1950):3; "Unification Assessed after 5 Years with Four Secretaries," *Army and Navy Journal* 90 (September 13, 1952):36; "Unification, Coordination, Concentration, Consolidation," *Reserve Officer* 27 (June 1950):6-8; *The Reorganization of the Department of Defense: Philosophy and Counter Philosophy*, (Annapolis, Md.: U.S. Naval Institute, 1961); "B-36: Superplane or Sitting Duck?" *U.S. News and World Report* 27 (July 1, 1949):30.

A selected list of the most useful signed articles includes: Dillon Anderson, "The President and the National Security," *Atlantic Monthly* 197 (January 1956):42-46; James A. Bell, "Defense Secretary Louis Johnson," *American Mercury* 70 (June 1950):643-63; Bernard L. Boyland, "Army Reorganization: The Legislative Story," *Mid-America* 49 (April 1967):115-28; Philip B. Brannen, "A Single Service: Perennial Issue in National Defense," U.S. Naval Institute *Proceedings* 83 (December 1957):1280-87; Bernard Brodie, "The Atomb Bomb as Policy Maker," *Foreign Affairs* 27 (October 1948):17-33; Rear Armiral Charles R. Brown, USN, "American National Strategy," U.S. Naval Institute *Proceedings* 76 (April 1950):355-63; Admiral Arleigh Albert Burke, USN, "How Military Planning Looks to a Member of the Joint Chiefs of Staff," *U.S. News and World Report* 43 (August 1957):101-2, and "The Role of Naval Forces," *Naval War College Review* 22 (July 1970):5-11; Commander Malcolm W. Cagle, USN, "A Philosophy for Naval Atomic Warfare," U.S. Naval Institute *Proceedings* 83 (March 1957):249-58; Colonel Wallis G. Carter, USAF, "Strategic Bombardment and National Objectives," *Air University Quarterly Review* 4 (Spring 1951):5-14; General Mark W. Clark, "The Truth About Korea," *Collier's* 133 (February 5, 1954):34-38, (February 19, 1954):88-93; Robert H. Connery, "Unification of the Armed Forces—the First Year," *American Political Science Review* 43 (February 1949):38-52; Lieutenant Colonel Robert L. Cushman, USMC, "Amphibious Warfare: Naval Weapon of the Future," U.S. Naval Institute *Proceedings* 74 (March 1948):301-7; Admiral Louis E. Denfeld, "Reprisal: Why I Was Fired," *Collier's* 125 (March 18, 1950):13-15, 62, 64; Eugene Duffield, "Organizing for Defense," *Harvard Business Review* 31 (September-October 1953):29-42; Ferdinand Eberstadt, "The Historical Evolution of Our National Defense Organization," *Naval War College Review* 6 (January 1954):1-17; Stanley A. Falk, "The National Security Council Under Truman, Eisenhower, and Kennedy," *Political Science Quarterly* 79 (September 1964):403-34; Thomas K. Finletter, "New Thinking Needed," *Air Force* 35 (October 1952):33-34, and "New Look at Air Policy," *Atlantic Monthly* 192 (September 1953):25-30; Colonel Angus M. Fraser, "The Marine Corps as a Separate Service," U.S. Naval Institute *Proceedings* 101 (November 1975):19-25; Rear Admiral Daniel V. Gallery, USN, "If This Be Treason," *Collier's* 125 (January 21, 1950):15-17, 45; Lieutenant Commander Carl L. Henn, Jr. (SC) USN, "Sustaining an Air-Atomic Navy," U.S. Naval Institute *Proceedings* 83 (May 1957):471-78; H. Struve Hensel, "Changes Inside the Pentagon," *Harvard Business Review* 33 (January-February 1954):98-108;

Lieutenant Colonel James D. Hittle, USMC, "Sea Power and a National General Staff," U.S. Naval Institute *Proceedings* 75 (October 1949): 1091-1103, "Korea—Back to the Facts of Life," U.S. Naval Institute *Proceedings* 76 (December 1950):1289-97, and "Military Planning at the Seat of Government," U.S. Naval Institute *Proceedings* 83 (July 1957):713-22; Lieutenant Colonel William R. Kintner, USA, "Political Limitations of Air Power," U.S. Naval Institute *Proceedings* 76 (March 1950):249-55; Charlotte Knight, "Air War in Korea," *Air Force* 58 (June 1975):59-63; Eric Larrabee, "Korea: The Military Lesson," *Harper's* 201 (November 1950):51-57; John F. Loosbrock, "Carriers to the Rescue," *Air Force* 35 (December 1952):25-30; Brigadier General S. L. A. Marshall, USA (Ret.), "Our Mistakes in Korea," *Atlantic* 192 (September 1953):46-49; Commander George H. Miller, USN, "Strategy of the Future—A Second Look," U.S. Naval Institute *Proceedings* 76 (May 1950):473-83; Walter Millis, "Our Defense Program: Master Plan or Makeshift?" *Yale Review* 39 (March 1950):386-401; Paul H. Nitze, "Atoms, Strategy, and Politics," *Foreign Affairs* 34 (January 1956):187-98; Rear Admiral W.S. Parsons, USN, "Problems, and Prospects in Atomic Energy," *Information for Service Officers* 1 (December 1948):1-18, and "Capabilities of the Atom Bomb, Including Naval Thinking on its Employment," *Information for Service Officers* 2 (April 1950):23-30; John R. Probert, "Pentagon Reorganization: Phase Three," U.S. Naval Institute *Proceedings* 81 (January 1955):51-62; George C. Reinhardt and William R. Kintner, "The Need for a National Staff," U.S. Naval Institute *Proceedings* 78 (July 1952):720-27; Clark G. Reynolds, "American Strategic History and Doctrines: A Reconsideration," *Military Affairs* 39 (December 1975):181-90; John C. Ries, "Congressman Vinson and the 'Deputy' to the Joint Chiefs of Staff Chairman," *Military Affairs* 30 (Spring 1966):16-24; Colonel S.R. Shaw, USMC, "A General Staff for the Navy," U.S. Naval Institute *Proceedings* 77 (August 1951):821-27; Brigadier General Dale O. Smith, USAF, "The Role of Air Power in Recent History," *Military Affairs* 19 (Summer 1955):71-76; Peter Marsh Stanford, "Limited War: A Problem in Maritime Defense," U.S. Naval Institute *Proceedings* 77 (December 1951):1311-17; Samuel S. Stratton, "Korea: Acid Test of Containment," U.S. Naval Institute *Proceedings* 63 (March 1952);23-49; Robert Strausz-Hupé and Stefan T. Possony, eds., "Air Power and National Security," *Annals of the American Academy of Political and Social Science* 229 (May 1955):1-140; Admiral John S. Thach, USN (Ret.), " 'Right on the Button': Marine Close Air Support in Korea," U.S. Naval Institute *Proceedings* 101 (November 1975):54-56; Captain James P. Totten, USA, "A Study of Generalship," *Armor* (November-December 1976), pp. 33-88; General O.P. Weyland, USAF, "The Air Campaign in Korea," *Air University Quarterly Review* 6 (Fall 1953):3-41; Gerald E. Wheeler, "Naval Aviation in the Korean War," U.S. Naval Institute *Proceedings* 83 (July 1957):762-77; Lieutenant (junior grade) Donald G. White, "Admiral Richard L. Conolly: A Perspective on His Notions of Strategy," *Naval War College Review* 24 (November 1971):73-79; John Edward Wiltz,

"The MacArthur Hearings of 1951: The Secret Testimony," *Military Affairs* 39 (December 1975):167-81; Colonel Richard C. Wolfinbarger, USMC, "Tactical Air Operations," *Information Service for Officers* 3 (February 1951):1-24; Herbert F. York, "The Debate over the Hydrogen Bomb," *Scientific American* 233 (October 1975):106-13; Eugene M. Zuckert, "The Service Secretary: Has He a Useful Role?" *Foreign Affairs* 44 (April 1966):458-79. Perceptive comment is also found in Dr. Frank N. Trager, "The National Security Act of 1947: Its Thirtieth Anniversary," *Air University Review* 29 (November-December 1977):2-15.

Three papers read at a session on defense unification at the American Historical Association's annual convention held at San Francisco in December 1973 have been published: Paolo E. Coletta, "The Defense Unification Battle: 1947-1950: The Navy," *Prologue: The Journal of the National Archives* 6 (Spring 1975):6-17; Herman S. Wolk, "The Defense Unification Battle, 1947-1950: The Air Force," *Prologue* 6 (Spring 1975):18-26; and Richard F. Haynes, "The Defense Unification Battle: 1947-1950: The Army," *Prologue* 6 (Spring 1973):27-31.

PERSONAL HISTORIES AND PUBLISHED CORRESPONDENCE

The relations of Presidents Truman and Eisenhower with political and defense leaders are discussed in various autobiographies, biographies, statements and speeches, personal recollections, and published letters and diaries. Caustic comments about Truman and especially about top defense and naval leaders are found in Tyler Abell, ed., *Drew Pearson Diaries, 1949-1959* (New York: Holt, Rinehart and Winston, 1974), while Richard A. Aliano, *American Defense Policy from Eisenhower to Kennedy: The Politics of Changing Military Requirements 1957-1961* (Columbus: Ohio University Press, 1975), likes Eisenhower and dislikes Kennedy. Particular diplomatic-military views are detailed in Charles Eustis Bohlen, *Witness to History, 1929-1969* (New York: W.W. Norton, 1973); Admiral Joseph J. Clark, USN (Ret.), with Clark Reynolds, *Carrier Admiral* (New York: David McKay, 1967); General Mark W. Clark, *From the Danube to the Yalu* (New York: Harper and Bros., 1954); Robert H. Ferrell, *George C. Marshall* (New York: Cooper Square Publishers, 1966); Daniel V. Gallery, Rear Admiral, USN, (Ret.), *Eight Bells and All's Well* (New York: W.W. Norton, 1965); George Kennan, *Memoirs 1925-1950* (Boston: Little, Brown, 1967); Curtis LeMay, with MacKinlay Cantor, *Mission with LeMay: My Story* (Garden City, N.Y.: Doubleday, 1965); General Matthew B. Ridgway, USA (Ret.), as told to Harold H. Martin, *Soldier: The Memoirs of Matthew B. Ridgway* (New York: Harper and Bros., 1956). Truman set forth his views in *Memoirs by Harry S. Truman*, 2 vols. (Garden City, N.Y.: Doubleday, 1955-56); Dwight D.

Eisenhower in *The White House Years: Mandate for Change, 1953-1956* (Garden City, N.Y.: Doubleday, 1963).

Studies of varying value of the presidency of Truman include Robert J. Donavan, *Conflict and Crisis: The Presidency of Harry S. Truman, 1941-1948* (New York: W.W. Norton, 1977): Louis W. Koenig, ed., *The Truman Administration: Its Principles and Practice* (New York: New York University Press, 1956); Merle Miller, *Plain Speaking: An Oral Biography of Harry S. Truman* (Published by Berkley Publishing Corp., distributed by G.P. Putnam's Sons, New York, 1973); and Alfred Steinberg, *The Man from Missouri: The Life and Times of Harry S. Truman* (New York: G.P. Putnam's Sons, 1962). Similar studies of Eisenhower include Sherman Adams, *First Hand Report: The Story of the Eisenhower Administration* (New York: Harper and Bros., 1961); Robert J. Donovan, *The Inside Story* (New York: Harper and Bros., 1956); and the superbly written Peter Lyon, *Eisenhower: Portrait of the Hero* (Boston: Little, Brown, 1974). Of special value is Richard Kirkendall, ed., *The Truman Period as a Research Field* (Columbia: University of Missouri Press, 1967).

The only biography of Arleigh Burke to date is the popularly written Ken Jones and Hubert Kelley, Jr., *Admiral Arleigh (31-Knot) Burke: The Story of a Fighting Sailor* (New York: Chilton Books, 1962). The same quality permeates Paul I. Wellman, *Stuart Symington: Portrait of a Man with a Mission* (Garden City, N.Y.: Doubleday, 1960). Quite idolatrous are Major General Charles A. Willoughby and John Chamberlain, *MacArthur 1941-1951* (New York: McGraw-Hill, 1954), and Courtney Whitney, *MacArthur: His Rendezvous with History* (New York: Knopf, 1956), with self-idolatry also evident in Douglas MacArthur, *Reminiscences* (New York: McGraw-Hill, 1964). A popular account is Clark Lee and Richard Henschel, *Douglas MacArthur* (New York: Henry Holt, 1952). Much better balanced are Richard H. Rovere and Arthur M. Schlesinger, Jr., *The General and the President and the Future of American Foreign Policy* (New York: Farrar, Strauss and Young, 1951), and John W. Spanier, *The Truman-MacArthur Controversy and the Korean War* (New York: W.W. Norton, 1965). James V. Forrestal is well delineated in Robert G. Albion and Robert Howe Connery, *Forrestal and the Navy* (New York and London: Columbia University Press, 1962), and is psychoanalyzed in Arnold A. Rogow, *James Forrestal: A Study of Personality, Politics, and Policy* (New York: Macmillan, 1963). Pertinent selections from his diaries are in Walter Millis, ed., with Eugene S. Duffield, *The Forrestal Diaries* (New York: Viking, 1951). Special insights are found in Dean G. Acheson, *Present at the Creation: My Years in the State Department* (New York: W.W. Norton, 1969); Marquis Childs, *Witness to Power* (New York: McGraw-Hill, 1975); Flint O. Dupré, *Hap Arnold: Architect of American Air Power* (New York: Macmillan, 1972); Ernest J. King and Walter Muir Whitehill, *Fleet Admiral King: A Naval Record* (New York: W.W. Norton, 1952), and A.A. Vandegrift and Robert B. Asprey, *Once a Marine: The Memoirs of General A.A. Vandegrift, USMC* (New York: W.W. Norton, 1964). Chester W. Nimitz's relations with unification are detailed in the biography of him by Elmer B. Potter published by the Naval Institute Press in 1976. Marshall's services as both Secretary of State and Secretary of Defense can be expected in Forrest Pogue's ongoing biography of the splendid soldier (1963-   ), and a superior picture of MacArthur is appearing in the ongoing biography by D. Clayton James (1975-). Quirks in the personality of Louis A. Johnson appear in Keith D. McFarland, *Harry H. Woodring: A Political Biography of FDR's Controversial Secretary of War* (Lawrence: University Press of Kansas, 1975). A first-hand account of the trauma of the first three months of the Korean War was completed in 1952 by the first Secretary of the American embassy in Seoul, Harold Joyce Noble. It is available, with amplifying data, in Harold Joyce Noble, *Embassy at War: Harold Joyce Noble*. Frank Baldwin, ed., (Seattle: University of Washington Press, 1975).

SELECTED SECONDARY WORKS

The relations of the professional soldier to his government, his service, the other services, and society in general are treated in Bengt Abrahamsson, *Military Professionalization and Political Power* (Beverly Hills and London: Sage Publications, 1972); Stephen Ambrose, ed., *The Military and American Society* (Riverside, N.J.: Free Press, 1972); Donald Bletz, *The Role of the Military Professional in United States Foreign Policy* (New York: Praeger, 1972); James Clotfelter, *The Military in American Politics* (New York: Harper and Row, 1973); Harry L. Coles, ed., *Total War and Cold War: Problems in Civilian Control of the Military* (Columbus: Ohio State University Press, 1962); Trumbull Higgins, *Korea and the Fall of MacArthur: A Précis in Limited War* (New York: Oxford University Press, 1960); Samuel P. Huntington, *The Common Defense: Strategic Programs in National Politics* (New York: Columbia University Press, 1961), and *The Soldier and the State: The Theory and Politics of Civil-Military Relations* (Cambridge, Mass.: The Belknap Press of Harvard University Press, 1967); Morris Janowitz, *The Professional Soldier: A Social and Political Portrait* (Glencoe, Ill.: Free Press, 1960); Arthur D. Larson, *Civil-Military Relations and Militarism* (Manhattan: Kansas State University, 1971); Walter Millis, *Arms and Men: A Study of American Military History* (New York: G.P. Putnam's Sons, 1956), Walter Millis, ed., *American Military Thought* (New York: Bobbs-Merrill, 1966), and Walter Millis with Harvey C. Mansfield, Harold Stein, *Arms and the State: Civil-Military Elements in National Policy* (New York: The Twentieth Century Fund, 1958); and Harold Stein, ed., *American Civil-Military Decisions: A Book of Case Studies* (Birmingham: University of Alabama Press, 1963); and Gerke Tietler, *The Genesis of the Professional Officer's Corps* (Beverly Hills, Calif.: Sage Publications, 1977).

Of special value in providing background for the defense unification struggle from 1943 to 1947 are Ferdinand Eberstadt, *Unification of the War and Navy Departments and Postwar Organization for National Security. Report to Hon. James Forrestal, Secretary of the Navy, on Unification of the War and Navy Departments and Postwar Organization for National Security, October 22, 1945* (Washington: GPO, 1945); Demetrious Caraley, *The Politics of Military Unification: A Study of Conflict and the Policy Process* (New York and London: Columbia University Press, 1966); Michael S. Sherry, *Preparing for the Next War: American Plans for Postwar Defense, 1941-1945* (New Haven: Yale University Press, 1977); and Perry McCoy Smith, *The Air Force Plans for Peace, 1943-1945* (Baltimore and London: Johns Hopkins University Press, 1970). On the subject of military staffs, see James D. Hittle, *The Military Staff*, 3d ed. (Harrisburg, Pa.: Stackpole Co., 1961); Lawrence J. Korb, *The Joint Chiefs of Staff: The First Twenty-five Years* (Bloomington: Indiana University Press, 1976); Major General Otto L. Nelson, Jr., *National Security and the General Staff* (Washington: Infantry Journal Press, 1946); and Arthur O. Sulzberger, *The Joint Chiefs of Staff, 1941-1954* (Washington: U.S. Marine Corps Institute, 1954).

Works dealing with national defense and foreign policy are: Dean G. Acheson, *The Korean War* (New York: W.W. Norton, 1971); Barton J. Bernstein, ed., *The Atomic Bomb: The Critical Issues* (Boston, Toronto: Little, Brown, 1976); Carl W. Borklund, *Men of the Pentagon: From Forrestal to McNamara* (New York: Praeger, 1966), and *The Department of Defense* (New York: Praeger, 1968); J. Lawton Collins, *War in Peacetime: The History and Lessons of Korea* (Boston: Houghton Mifflin, 1969); Vincent Davis, *Postwar Defense Policy and the U.S. Navy, 1943-1946* (Chapel Hill: University of North Carolina Press, 1962), and *The Admirals Lobby* (Chapel Hill: University of North Carolina Press, 1967); Seymour J. Deitchman, *Limited War and American Defense Policy* (Cambridge, Mass.: MIT Press, 1964); Eugene E. Emme., ed., *The Impact of Air Power; National Security and World Politics* (Princeton, N.J.: D. Van Nostrand, 1959); Thomas K. Finletter, *Power and Policy: U.S. Foreign Policy and Military Power in the Hydrogen Age* (New York: Harcourt, Brace, 1954); Morton Halperin, *Limited War in the Nuclear Age* (New York: John Wiley and Sons, 1963), and *Contemporary Military Strategy* (Boston: Little, Brown, 1967); Paul Y. Hammond, *Organizing for Defense: The American Military Establishment in the Twentieth Century* (Princeton, N.J.: Princeton University Press, 1961); Richard F. Haynes, *The Awesome Power: Harry S. Truman as Commander in Chief* (Baton Rouge: Louisiana State University Press, 1973); I.B. Holley, Jr., *An Enduring Challenge: The Problem of Air Force Doctrine* (Colorado Springs, Colo.: U.S. Air Force Academy, 1974); Wynfred Joshua, *Nuclear Weapons and the Atlantic Alliance* (New York: National Strategic Information Center, 1976); R. Earl McClendon, *The Question of Autonomy for the United States Air Arm, 1907-1945* (Maxwell Air Force Base, Ala.: Air University, Documentary Research Study, 1948), *Unification of the Armed Forces: Administrative and Legislative Developments, 1945-1949* (Maxwell Air Force Base, Ala.: Air

University Documentary Research Study, 1952), *Army Aviation, 1947-1953* (Maxwell Air Force Base, Ala.: Air University Documentary Research Study, 1954), and *Autonomy of the Air Arm* (Maxwell Air Force Base, Ala.: Air University Documentary Research Study, 1954); Robert Endicott Osgood, *Limited War: The Challenge to American Strategy* (Chicago: University of Chicago Press, 1957); Glenn D. Paige, *The Korean Decision, June 24-30, 1950* (New York: Free Press, 1968); Jack Raymond, *Power at the Pentagon* (New York, Evanston, and London: Harper and Row, 1964): David Rees, *Korea: The Limited War* (New York: St. Martin's Press, 1964); the excellent John C. Ries, *The Management of Defense: Organization and Control of the U.S. Armed Forces* (Baltimore, Md.: Johns Hopkins University Press, 1964); the also excellent Martin J. Sherwin, *A World Destroyed: The Atomic Bomb and the Grand Alliance* (New York: Knopf, 1975); Timothy W. Stanley, *American Defense and National Security* (Washington: Public Affairs Press, 1956); Maxwell Taylor, *The Uncertain Trumpet* (New York: Harper and Bros., 1959); Frank N. Trager, compiler, edited by Frank N. Traeger and Philip S. Kronenberg, *National Security and American Society: Theory, Process, and Policy* (Lawrence: University of Kansas Press, 1973); Gordon B. Turner and Richard D. Challener, eds., *National Security in the Nuclear Age* (New York: Praeger, 1960); General Nathan F. Twining, USAF, (Ret.), *Neither Liberty nor Safety: A Hard Look at U.S. Military Policy and Strategy* (New York: Holt, Rinehart and Winston, 1966); Russell Frank Weigley, *History of the United States Army* (New York: Macmillan, 1967); and *The American Way of War: A History of U.S. Military Strategy and Policy* (New York: Macmillan, 1973); and Allen S. Whiting, *China Crosses the Yalu: The Decision to Enter the Korean War* (New York: Macmillan, 1960). The "missile gap" of the late 1950s and early 1960s is traced by Edmund Beard, *Developing the ICBM: A Study in Bureaucratic Politics* (New York: Columbia University Press, 1976), who stresses the reluctance of the Air Force to give up the manned bomber.

Emphasis on the impact of science and technology on foreign and military policy is found in: Bernard Brodie, *Strategy in the Missile Age* (Princeton, N.J.: Princeton University Press, 1959); A. Hunter Dupree, *Science in the Federal Government* (Cambridge, Mass.: Harvard University Press, 1957); Jerome C. Hunsaker, *Forty Years of Aeronautical Research*, Pub. No. 4237 (Washington: Smithsonian Institution, 1956); Don K. Price, *Government and Science* (New York: New York University Press, 1954); Alice Kimball Smith, *A Peril and a Hope: The Scientists Movement in America* (Chicago: University of Chicago Press, 1965); Sir Charles Percy Snow, *Science and Government* (Cambridge, Mass.: Harvard University Press, 1961). A demand for the optimization of technology is made in Stefan E. Possony and J.E. Pournelle, *The Strategy of Technology: Winning the Decisive War* (New York: Dunellen, 1970).

Books dealing with strategy, tactics, field organization, and operations in Korea have come largely from writers for the military services. These and others include Roy E. Appleman, *South to the Naktong, North to the Yalu,*

June-November 1950 (Washington: Chief of Military History, 1960); Commander Malcolm W. Cagle, USN, and Commander Frank A. Manson, USN, *The Sea War in Korea* (Annapolis, Md.: U.S. Naval Institute, 1957); James A. Field, Jr., *History of United States Naval Operations: Korea* (Washington: Department of the Navy, 1962); Robert Frank Futrell, Lawson S. Moseley, and Albert F. Simpson, *The United States Air Force in Korea, 1950-1953* (New York: Duell, Sloan and Pearce, 1961); Allen Guttman, *Korea and the Theory of Limited War* (Boston: D.C. Heath, 1967); Colonel Robert D. Heinl, Jr., USMC, *Victory at High Tide: The Inchon-Seoul Campaign* (Philadelphia and New York: J.B. Lippincott, 1968); Walter G. Hermes, *Truce Tent and Fighting Front* (Washington: Chief of Military History, 1966); Captain Walter Karig, USNR, Commander Malcolm W. Cagle, USN, and Lieutenant Commander Frank A. Manson, USN, *Battle Report: The War in Korea* (New York: Rinehart, 1952); Robert Leckie, *Conflict: The History of the Korean War* (New York: G.P. Putnam's Sons, 1962); James F. Schnabel, *Policy and Decision: The First Year, United States Army in the Korean War* (Washington: Chief of Military History, 1972); Colonel James T. Stewart, USAF, ed., *Airpower: The Decisive Factor in Korea* (Princeton, N.J.: D. Van Nostrand, 1957).

Works concentrating on the development of weapons and weapons systems and their impact upon military organization include: John T. Bohn, *The Development of Strategic Air Command: 1946-1973* (Offut Air Force Base, Neb.: Strategic Air Command, 1974); Clay Blair, Jr., *The Atomic Submarine and Admiral Rickover* (New York: Henry Holt, 1954); Heather M. David, *Admiral Rickover and the Nuclear Navy* (New York: G.P. Putnam's Sons, 1970); the excellent Robert Frank Futrell, *Ideas, Concepts, Doctrine: A History of Basic Thinking in the United States Air Force, 1906-1964* (Maxwell Air Force Base, Ala.: Air University, Aerospace Studies Institute, 1971); Alfred Goldberg, ed., *A History of the United States Air Force, 1907-1957* (Princeton, N.J.: Van Nostrand Reinhold, 1957); Colonel Robert Debs Heinl, Jr., USMC (Ret.) *Soldiers of the Sea: The United States Marine Corps, 1775-1962* (Annapolis, Md.: U.S. Naval Institute, 1962); Richard G. Hewlett and Francis Duncan, *Nuclear Navy, 1949-1962* (Chicago: University of Chicago Press, 1974); U.S. Navy Department, Naval History Division, *Aviation in the United States Navy*, 3d ed. (Washington: GPO, 1968); Richard S. Lewis and James Wilson, eds., *Alamogordo Plus Twenty-Five Years: The Impact of Atomic Energy on Science, Technology, and World Politics* (New York: Viking Press, 1972); Donald John Mrozek, *Peace Through Strength: Strategic Air Power and the Mobilization of the United States for the Pursuit of Foreign Policy, 1945-1955* (New Brunswick, N.J.: Rutgers University Press, 1972); Clark Van Vleet, Lee M. Pearson, and Adrian O. Van Wyen, *United States Naval Aviation. 1919-1970* (Washington: GPO, 1972).

Most useful among the many books dealing with defense economics have been: Harold J. Clem, *Collective Defense and Foreign Assistance* (Washington: ICAF, 1968); Richard F. Fenno, *The Power of the Purse: Ap-*

propriations Politics in Congress (Boston: Little, Brown, 1966); Elias Huzar, *The Purse and the Sword: Control of the Army Through Military Appropriations, 1933-1950* (Ithaca, N.Y.: Cornell University Press, 1950); Warner R. Schilling, Paul Y. Hammond, and Glenn H. Snyder, *Strategy, Politics, and Defense Budgets* (New York and London: Columbia University Press, 1962); J.A. Stockfisch, *Plowshares into Swords: Managing the American Defense Establishment* (New York: Mason and Lipscomb, 1973); Harry B. Yoshpe, ed., *Emergency Economic Stabilization* (Washington: ICAF, 1964), and Yoshpe, et al., *Defense Organization and Management* (Washington: ICAF, 1967).

Public opinion on defense questions was obtained in part in George H. Gallup, *The Gallup Poll: Public Opinion, 1935-1971*, 3 vols. (New York: Random House, 1972). Unprejudiced in assessment is Armin Rappaport, *The Navy League of the United States* (Detroit, Mich.: Wayne State University Press, 1962). Marshall Andrews, *Disaster Through Air Power* (New York: Rinehart, 1950); Tristam Coffin, *The Passion of the Hawk: Militarism in Modern America* (New York: Macmillan, 1964); William Bradford Huie, *The Fight for Air Power* (New York: L.B. Fischer, 1942) and *The Case Against the Admirals: Why We Must Have a Unified Command* (New York: Dutton, 1946); and John M. Swomly, *The Military Establishment* (Boston: Beacon Press, 1964) and *Press Agents of the Pentagon: A Study of Publicity Methods of the Department of Defense* (Washington: National Council Against Conscription, 1953), are examples of uniservice propagandists, of leftist blatherings against military conscription, and diatribes on the theme that the military have gained control over civilians. Clark R. Mollenhoff, *The Pentagon: Politics, Profits, and Plunder* (New York: G.P. Putnam's Sons, 1967), gives pejorative interpretations of military actions and seeks sensationalism in Pentagon investigations. The animus of K. Bruce Galloway and Robert Bowie Johnson, Jr., *West Point: America's Power Fraternity* (New York: Simon and Schuster, 1973), is evident from the title. In contrast, C. Robert Kemble, *The Image of the Army Officer in America: Background for Current Views* (Westport, Conn.: Greenwood Press, 1973), is well balanced.

The lack of understanding of the theory and practice of military deterrence in foreign policy matters, particularly by the Air Force, is detailed in Bernard Brodie, *Escalation and the Nuclear Option* (Princeton, N.J.:Princeton University Press, 1966); Alexander L. George and Richard Smoke, *Deterrence in American Foreign Policy: Theory and Practice* (New York and London: Columbia University Press, 1974); Henry A. Kissinger, *Nuclear Weapons and Foreign Policy* (New York: Harper and Bros., 1957); William W. Kauffmann, *Military Policy and National Security* (Princeton, N.J.: Princeton University Press, 1956); George Quester, *Nuclear Diplomacy* (New York: Dunellen, 1970); and Glenn Snyder, *Deterrence and Defense: Toward a Theory of National Security* (Princeton, N.J.: Princeton University Press, 1961).

Important studies of problems encountered in reforming defense organization and administration are William A. Lucas and Raymond H. Dawson, *The*

Organizational Politics of Defense. Occasional Paper No. 2 (Pittsburgh, Pa.: International Studies Association, 1974); *Naval Strategy in a Period of Change: Interservice Rivalry, Strategic Interaction, and the Development of a Nuclear Attack Capability, 1945-1951.* Part I of a *Supporting Study, U.S. Aircraft Carriers in a Strategic Role*, itself part of a larger study entitled *History of Strategic Arms Competition, 1945-1972* (Falls Church, Va.: Lulejian and Associates, October 1975); James E. Hewes, Jr., *From Root to McNamara: Army Organization and Administration, 1900-1963* (Washington: Center of Military History, 1975); and U.S. Department of the Air Force, Air University, Aerospace Studies Institute. *Development of Organization for National Defense, 1898-1960* (Maxwell Air Force Base, Ala., 1963).

Works that analyze the job description and functions of the service secretary are John A. Ballard, comp., *The Job-Concept of the Civilian Secretary* (Cambridge, Mass.: Harvard University Defense Policy Seminar, 1956-1957, Serial No. 93, 8 November 1956); W. Barton Leach, *The Job of a Service Secretary* (Cambridge, Mass.: Harvard University Press, December 27, 1956); and Lieutenant Colonel William F. Schless, USA, "The Service Secretaries—An Analysis." Student Research Report M-65-152, Washington, Industrial College of the Armed Forces, 31 March 1965 (courtesy Colonel Schless).

UNPUBLISHED SOURCES

The diary of Fleet Admiral Chester W. Nimitz, USN, from December 15, 1947, through September 30, 1949, contains several comments on unification matters. Use has been made by permission of five manuscript essays written for *The American Secretaries of the Navy*, published by the U.S. Naval Institute Press in 1980: "James V. Forrestal," by Joseph Zikmund; "Dan Able Kimball" and "Robert B. Anderson," by K. Jack Bauer, and my own "John L. Sullivan" and "Francis P. Matthews." The Lyndon B. Johnson preparedness subcommittee is analyzed in Commander Edward B. Gibson, USN, "The Role of Congress in Naval Affairs," A Research Paper Submitted to the Faculty of the Air University War College, Maxwell Air Force Base, March 1973. Professor J. Samuel Walker, University of Maryland, kindly sent me a copy of his paper "Henry A. Wallace and the Cold War," as did also Donald J. Mrozek, "The Transformation of the United States Military Establishment, 1940-1972," and John Probert, "Executive Branch Organization and Execution of National Security Policy."

Pertinent doctoral dissertations are: Frances Elizabeth Biadasz, "Defense Reorganization during the Eisenhower Administration," Georgetown University, 1961; Sherman Floyd Carter, "An Analysis of the Influence of the Evolution of the Department of Defense on the Role of the Secretary of the Army: A Case Study in Organization and Management," American University, 1968; Kenneth J. Comfort, "Nuclear Security Policy and the Development of Tactical Nuclear Forces, 1948-1958," Columbia University, 1970; Robert C. Dart, "Flexible Response: A Case Study of the Policy Process for National Security," University of Virginia, 1973; Martin I. Elzy, "The Origins of American Military Policy, 1945-1950," Miami University, Oxford, Ohio, 1975; Calvin William Enders, "The Vinson Navy," Michigan State University, 1970; Thomas A. French, "Unification and the American Military Establishment, 1945-1950," State University of New York, Buffalo, 1972; Paul Y. Hammond, "The Secretaryships of War and Navy: A Study of Civilian Control of the Military," Harvard University, 1953; Edward Kolodziej, "The Influence of Congress on Military Policy Through the Determination of Force Levels and Weapons Systems, 1946 to the Present," Chicago University, 1964; Laurence J. Korb, "Budget Strategics of the Joint Chiefs of Staff, Fiscal Years, 1948-1968," State University of New York, Albany, 1970; Nathan Yu-jen Lai, "United States Policy of Limited War in Korea, 1950-1951," University of Massachusetts, 1974; Robert J. McGeehan, "American Diplomacy and the German Rearmament Question, 1950-1953," Columbia University, 1969; David McIsaac, "The United States Strategic Bombing Survey, 1944-1947," Duke University, 1970; Naiven Francis Mathews, "The Public View of Military Policy: 1945-1950," University of Missouri, 1964; Carroll French Miles, "The Office of the Secretary of Defense, 1947-1953: A Study in Administrative Theory," Harvard University, 1956; Harland B. Moulton, "American Strategic Power: Two Decades of Nuclear Strategy and Weapons Systems, 1945-1965," University of Minnesota, 1969; Donald John Mrozek, "Peace Through Strength: Strategic Air Power and the Mobilization of the United States for the Pursuit of Foreign Policy, 1945-1955," Rutgers University, 1972; Peter E. Picillo, "The Role of the Budget Bureau in Truman's Domestic Legislative Program: An Examination of Atomic Energy Control, Military Unification, Housing, and Civil Rights," State University of New York, Binghamton, 1974; John R. Probert, "Staff Arrangements in the Organization for National Security," University of Pennsylvania, 1956; James R. Riggs, "Congress and the Conduct of the Korean War," Purdue University, 1972; Mark B. Schneider, "Nuclear Weapons and American Strategy," University of Southern California, 1974; Paul Richard Schratz, "The U.S. Defense Establishment: Trends in Organizational Structures, Functions, and Interrelationships, 1958-1970," Ohio State University, 1972; Robert L. Smith, "The Influence of U.S.A.F. Chief of Staff General Hoyt S. Vandenberg on United States National Security Policy," American University, 1965; Curtis W. Tarr, "Unification of America's Armed Forces: A Century and a Half of Conflict, 1789-1947," Stanford University, 1962; and James Devers Weaver, "The Commander in Chief, Civilian Supremacy, Command and Control: Civil-Military Relations in the Eisenhower Presidency," New York University, 1972.

Useful also were two masters's theses: Major Gordon Wyman Keiser, USMC, "The U.S. Marine Corps and Unification: 1944-1947," Tufts University, **1971, and Kenneth L. Moll, "Nuclear Strategy, 1945–1949: America's**

First Four Years," University of Nebraska at Omaha, 1965.

The transcripts of oral interviews of a number of men shed light on defense unification in Washington and in the field. The most revealing of these are: "The Reminiscences of Rear Admiral Walter C.W. Ansel, USN (Ret.)," by John T. Mason, U.S. Naval Institute, 1972; "The Reminscences of Vice Admiral Bernard L. Austin, USN (Ret.)," by Commander Paul L. Hooper, USNR (Ret.), U.S. Naval Institute, 1971; "The Reminscences of Hanson Weightman Baldwin, USN (Ret.)," by John T. Mason, 2 vols., U.S. Naval Institute, 1976; Transcript of oral interview by Commander Etta-Belle Kitchen, USN (Ret.), with Vice Admiral Gerald F. Bogan, USN (Ret.), U.S. Naval Institute, 1969; "The Reminiscences of Vice Admiral John Barr Colwell, USN (Ret.)," by John T. Mason, U.S. Naval Institute, 1974; "The Reminscences of Admiral Richard L. Conolly, USN (Ret.)," Columbia University Oral History Research Office, 1960; Transcript of oral interview by Jerry N. Hess of Admiral Robert Lee Dennison, USN (Ret.), Independence, Mo., Harry S. Truman Library, 1972; "The Reminscences of Vice Admiral George Dyer, USN (Ret.)," by John T. Mason, U.S. Naval Institute, 1971; "The Reminscences of Admiral Harry D. Felt, USN (Ret.)," by John T. Mason, U.S. Naval Institute, 1974; Transcript of oral interview with Thomas K. Finletter, Independence, Mo., Harry S. Truman Library, 1972; "The Reminscences of Rear Admiral Daniel V. Gallery, USN (Ret.)," by John T. Mason, U.S. Naval Institute, 1976; Transcript of oral interview with Roswell Gilpatric, Independence, Mo., Harry S. Truman Library, 1972; "The Reminscences of Admiral Charles Donald Griffin, USN (Ret.)," by John T. Mason, 2 vols., U.S. Naval Institute, 1973; "The Reminscences of Vice Admiral Felix L. Johnson, USN (Ret.)," by John T. Mason, U.S. Naval Institute, 1972; "The Reminscences of Admiral Thomas Cassin Kinkaid, USN (Ret.)," Columbia University Oral History Research Office, 1961; "The Reminscences of Vice Admiral Fitzhugh Lee, USN (Ret.)," by Commander Etta-Belle Kitchen, USN (Ret.), U.S. Naval Institute, 1970; "The Reminscences of Vice Admiral Herbert D. Riley, USN (Ret.)," by John T. Mason, U.S. Naval Institute, 1972; "The Reminscences of Vice Admiral Lorenzo S. Sabin, USN (Ret.)," by Commander Etta-Belle Kitchen, USN (Ret.), 2 vols., to date, U.S. Naval Institute, 1970; "The Reminscences of Vice Admiral Paul D. Stroop, USN (Ret.)," by Commander Etta-Belle Kitchen, USN (Ret.), U.S. Naval Institute, 1970; "The Reminscences of Admiral John S. Thach, USN (Ret.)," by Commander Etta-Belle Kitchen, USN (Ret.), 2 vols. to date, U.S. Naval Institute, 1970; "The Reminscences of Vice Admiral Charles Wellborn, Jr., USN (Ret.)," by John T. Mason, U.S. Naval Institute, 1972; and "The Reminscences of Rear Admiral Joseph Muse Worthington, USN (Ret.)," by John T. Mason, U.S. Naval Institute, 1972.

Made available by the Washington Headquarters, U.S. Marine Corps, History and Museums Division, U.S. Marine Corps Oral History Program, courtesy Dr. Benis M. Frank, was the transcript of an oral interview with Major General Omar T. Pfeiffer, USMC (Ret), by Major L.E. Tatem, USMC,

1968, and the following transcripts of oral interviews, all undertaken by Dr. Frank: with General Clifton B. Cates, USMC (Ret.), 1967; with Lieutenant General Victor H. Krulak, USMC (Ret.), 1973); with General Vernon Megee, USMC (Ret.), 1967; with Lieutenant General Merwin H. Silverthorn, USMC (Ret.), 1969); and with General Oliver P. Smith, USMC (Ret.), 1969.

ADDENDUM

Since the manuscript went to press, various sources have appeared or have been discovered that provide additional depth to the text. The most important of these are: *The History of the Joint Chiefs of Staff: The Joint Chiefs of Staff and National Policy*, 3 vols. (Washington: JCS, Joint Secretariat, Historical Division, 1979). Vol. 1, by James F. Schnable, covers 1945–47; vol. 2, by Kenneth W. Condit, covers 1947–49; vol. 3 deals with the Korean War. The last is in two parts, both written by James F. Schnable and Robert J. Watson. All volumes are available from Wilmington, Delaware; Michael Glazier, 1979. Among signed articles is the excellent David Alan Rosenberg, "American Atomic Strategy and the Hydrogen Bomb Decision," *Journal of American History 66* (June 1979): 62-87. Among books are Ralph N. Clough. *Deterrence and Defense in Korea: The Role of U. S. Forces* (Washington, D.C.: Brookings Institution, 1976); Francis H. Heller, ed. *The Korean War: A 25-Year Perspective* (Lawrence: Regents Press of Kansas, 1977); Harold J. Noble. *Embassy at War* (Seattle: University of Washington Press, 1975); Michael S. Sherry. *Preparing for the Next War: American Plans for Postwar Defense, 1941-1945* (New Haven: Yale University Press, 1977); and Herbert F. York. *The Advisors: Oppenheimer, Teller, and the Superbomb* (San Francisco: W. H. Freeman, 1976.)

Index